Legislating Against Liberties

CONSTITUTIONAL THINKING

Sanford Levinson
Jeffrey K. Tulis
Emily Zackin
Mariah Zeisberg
Editors

Legislating Against Liberties

How Congress Suppresses Constitutional Rights After Wars

Harry Blain

UNIVERSITY PRESS OF KANSAS

Published by the University Press of Kansas (Lawrence, Kansas 66045), which was organized by the Kansas Board of Regents and is operated and funded by Emporia State University, Fort Hays State University, Kansas State University, Pittsburg State University, the University of Kansas, and Wichita State University.

Library of Congress Cataloging-in-Publication Data

LCCN: 2025032274
ISBN: 9780700641055 (cloth)
ISBN: 9780700641062 (e-book)

British Library Cataloguing-in-Publication Data is available.
EU Authorised Representative Details: Easy Access System Europe
Mustamäe tee 50, 10621 Tallinn, Estonia | gpsr.requests@easproject.com

Jacket design by Karl Janssen
Cover photograph: Fotosearch

This book will be made open access within three years of publication thanks to Path to Open, a program developed in partnership between JSTOR, the American Council of Learned Societies (ACLS), University of Michigan Press, and the University of North Carolina Press to bring about equitable access and impact for the entire scholarly community, including authors, researchers, libraries, and university presses around the world. Learn more at https://about.jstor.org/path-to-open/.

CONTENTS

SERIES FOREWORD

My happy task, as one of the editors for the University Press of Kansas's Constitutional Thinking series, is to introduce Harry Blain's important study *Legislating Against Liberties: How Congress Suppresses Constitutional Rights After Wars.* One important way to engage in such thinking is to challenge assumptions that might be deeply rooted, even (or especially) in the minds of professional academics.

This book is being published at an especially freighted moment. It is no secret that, for most constitutional analysts, Donald Trump's presidencies have served as evidence of presidential overreach and the dangers of what Arthur Schlesinger labeled the "imperial presidency" more than half a century ago. The reference to Schlesinger underscores that it is a mistake to assume Trump emerged out of a void, even if one agrees that the extent of his overreach, both realized and proposed, has gone well beyond that of his predecessors. Still, as Harvard Law Professor Jack Goldsmith argued in an important May 2025 essay in the *New York Times*, even George Washington was plausibly accused of overreaching, and that claim has been a constant feature of American politics. We often build memorials to presidents on the basis of their audacity, not their cautious commitment to constitutional niceties. A standard part of this narrative is the necessity of presidential action against what is often described as a torpid Congress unwilling or unable to meet the great challenges facing the polity. However, there are inherent dangers in any facile acceptance of strong presidents and presidencies.

So it is not surprising that much contemporary constitutional discourse focuses on presidential overreach and its threat to constitutional democracy. To the extent Congress features in such discussions, it often takes the form of pleas for members of Congress to step up to their assigned role as checkers and balancers against rampaging presidents. The danger, it is believed, comes from the executive branch, and the cure can be found in the legislative.

Blain offers a profound challenge to this particular narrative. He is like Paul Revere, warning us that it is naïve, perhaps dangerously so, to place our faith in Congress as the guarantor of American liberties. He focuses on one particular phenomenon: the aftermath of war and the consequent decisions about what needs to be done to prevent future conflicts. As he notes on the first page of his introduction, "The aftermath of war is a crucial test for a democracy." What lessons have been learned, and do they necessarily strengthen what we think of as American democracy? In particular, can Congress be trusted to make wiser decisions than those emanating from the executive branch? The answer for Blain is no.

He looks in particular at the aftermath of five wars. First, the American Civil War, which was followed by a self-conscious effort at "reconstruction"—an ambiguous term at best. He then turns to the two world wars—the first, defended as making the world "safe for democracy," and the second part of the worldwide conflict between "democracies and dictatorships" (putting aside the status of the USSR, which was instrumental in winning the war against Germany). Finally, there are the "undeclared" wars, including Vietnam and the War on Terror. In all these cases, Congress scarcely comes out covered in glory compared with the executive.

Blain emphasizes, for example, the extent to which the first great campaign against immigrants, immediately after World War I, was led by Congress, and its effects were significantly limited by a courageous undersecretary in the Department of Labor, Louis Post. This illustrates, as many political scientists are quick to point out (more so than many lawyers), that the executive is a "they," not an "it"—a point originally made with regard to Congress itself. Institutions do not speak with one voice. They inevitably feature contending forces and personalities vying for power over public policies.

In any event, one cannot understand the aftermath of World War I without acknowledging the importance of congressional coalitions determined to clamp down on so-called dangerous immigrants, who were almost always defined as those coming from places other than northern Europe and were often non-Christian. This was especially important during what Blain calls the first Red Scare following the 1918 victory in Europe. Similar events occurred during the second Red Scare after World War II. Harry Truman and Dwight Eisenhower were scarcely devotees of Senator Joseph McCarthy or the onerous "loyalty" programs being pushed by many members of Congress. Although Truman acquiesced, Blain persuasively argues that he resisted as much as he could and was fearful that obstinacy might result in even worse congressionally mandated legislation (such as the postwar regulation of labor unions passed over Truman's vetoes).

Blain presents an interestingly revisionist account of Congress's response to the excesses of US agencies such as the FBI and CIA following the Vietnam War. Although respectful of the so-called Church Committee and its attempts to curb the basically unfettered powers of the CIA in particular, Blain emphasizes the crucial role of the press and of direct action, some of it illegal, by Americans who were properly worried about such powers. Moreover, he argues that, whatever the intentions at the time, congressional "reforms," including the creation of explicit intelligence committees to monitor the intelligence agencies, created a small group of legislators who act primarily as protectors rather than critics of such agencies.

For most readers, the most challenging parts of Blain's arguments will involve the aftermath of the Civil War. Did Reconstruction mean returning as quickly as possible to the "good old" Constitution, minus its support for slavery? Or did it require what, in the aftermath of American involvement in the Middle East, we now call regime change? If the latter, how was it to be achieved? How many eggs must be broken to make a palatable omelet? For example, how should those who vociferously oppose regime change be treated in terms of their own civil liberties, whether they are simply articulating opposition to proposed changes or running for public office and using the power of those offices to impede such changes? More ominous, of course, was the armed resistance (following the Iraq example, what we might call the insurgency) led by members of the Ku Klux Klan and others who scarcely accepted Appomattox as a genuine defeat of white supremacy. And who should assess an individual's liability for punishment? Should it be military commissions, which would be inclined to enforce the national policy? Or should it be local, politically representative juries, where even one holdout would be enough to prevent conviction?

Blain readily demonstrates that Reconstruction posed many challenges to purported verities of American constitutionalism. The civil liberties of Confederate sympathizers were stifled. Southern governments, recognized as legitimate by US President Andrew Johnson, were reorganized through the imposition of military Reconstruction at the behest of those usually described as radicals in Congress. Johnson was impeached—but not convicted—because of his adamant attempts to block serious regime change.

Blain throws down the gauntlet and asks his readers: what do "we" (I use scare quotes here because there is unlikely to be a unified "we" who will necessarily agree) think of these vigorous acts of Congress, including impeachment? They can all be described as "legislating against liberties" to provide the conditions for what Lincoln termed the "new birth of freedom" for millions of formerly enslaved persons who would, as a result of the Fourteenth Amendment, be welcomed into the Union as full citizens (and would receive, if they were male, the right to vote under the Fifteenth Amendment). But the provenance of the Fourteenth Amendment, let alone its subsequent interpretation, is hardly unproblematic; it is, in fact, a standard topic of semester-long courses at most law schools. The defeated entities of the Confederacy (to call them "states" begs an important constitutional question) had been excluded from participation in Congress during the all-important session in which the Fourteenth Amendment was drafted and then proposed by what some have called a rump Congress. And Congress made it clear that the price of readmission to the Union, with full representation in Congress, was ratification of the Fourteenth Amendment. This scarcely fits the standard notion of Article V of the Constitution, which presumably relies on the states' truly voluntary consent to proposed amendments. No episode in American history more significantly forces one to assess the relationship between admirable constitutional ends—such as "establishing justice"—and the means by which those ends are achieved.

Most of us, I dare say, support the Fourteenth Amendment, and many of us may wish that Reconstruction had been directed at a more thoroughgoing regime change, with whatever limitation on civil liberties was necessary during the period of change. Frederick Douglass, for example, gave a remarkable speech in 1867 setting out the terms for a far more radical reconstruction than was thought to be politically feasible by those in power in Congress, let alone the unabashed white supremacists in the Johnson administration. For them, ending slavery as a formal legal institution and suppressing secession counted as total achievement of the war's aims and justification for the killing of 750,000 Americans between 1861 and 1865.

The central point is that Blain's argument cannot be reduced to a simple battle between "good guys" committed to liberties and their opponents. Constitutional arguments and the hard thinking necessary to make sense of them require attention to context and nuance. Inevitably, such attention may provoke discomfort and challenge one's own certainties. Justice Holmes argued long ago that "general principles do not decide concrete cases." This, of course, complements his well-known aphorism about the "life of the law" being "experience" and not "logic." Harry Blain delves into important aspects of our national political experience and challenges us to test them against our general principles. That is, after all, what constitutional thinking entails. On behalf of my coeditors, I am happy to present this book not as the last word on the subject but as a set of essential first words to which, in Arthur Miller's famous phrase, "attention must be paid."

Sanford Levinson

ACKNOWLEDGMENTS

This book began as a doctoral dissertation in 2020 and was completed in that form in 2022. The chair of my doctoral committee, Professor Susan Woodward, was a constant source of support and guidance during this period and beyond. I also thank committee members Professors Zachary Shirkey and Andrew Polsky, who provided me with excellent feedback on my initial dissertation proposal and were always available to respond to my questions, comments, and drafts. Special thanks are also reserved for my fellow graduate students who patiently read numerous early and rough drafts of chapters during a dissertation-writing workshop at the City University of New York Graduate Center: Sarah Shah, Thuy Anh Tran, Dean Schafer, Philip Johnson, Kyong Mazzaro, Osha Smith-Gittelman, and Merrill Sovner. Finally, I thank Professors Mark Graber, Mariah Zeisberg, and Sanford Levinson for their valuable criticisms of the manuscript that became this book. They improved it immensely and played a vital role in guiding it along the difficult path from doctoral dissertation to publication.

Introduction
The Most Dangerous Branch

No one is surprised or shocked when democratic governments curtail civil liberties during wartime. Fighting a war—let alone winning one—is a collective struggle in which blind devotion to the rights of the individual can be a recipe for self-destruction. But the cure is not supposed to outlive the disease. When tools of war seep into times of peace, the fearful prospect of a permanent crisis government—and permanently curbed freedoms—looms. The aftermath of war is a crucial test for a democracy—a fraught moment when liberties should be revived but could be damaged beyond repair. These postwar moments, as experienced in the United States of America, are the subject of this book.

Scholars have generally done a better job of explaining violations of civil liberties that occur during wars rather than after them. Throughout American history, we have at least known that wartime can provoke repressive impulses in the government and the broader population, that these impulses are often unleashed on foreign-born people or ethnic minorities, that the Supreme Court rarely confronts a wartime government, and that, in some wars, civil rights and liberties seem to paradoxically expand, as the power of entrenched political elites is weakened. But the question of why or under what conditions wartime restrictions on civil liberties outlive their original purposes is not particularly well understood.

This book began as an effort to answer that question. It ends, like most do, by answering only part of it. As I read the relatively sparse scholarly arguments about postwar moments in the United States, along with the documentary record of primary sources and historiography, I got the impression that the record was at odds with the arguments on one key issue: the role of Congress. Whereas the record was rich with evidence of resurgent postwar Congresses curtailing civil liberties through a wide variety of tools, scholars and commentators seemed to be preoccupied with the alleged menace of executive power, if they were concerned with postwar moments at all.

The logic behind this preoccupation was and is understandable. During war, lawmakers require "decision, activity, secrecy, and dispatch,"[1] so they tend to enable executive leadership. Executives may promise to wield extraordinary powers temporarily, only to entrench them indefinitely and to tar critics with accusations of disloyalty. Perhaps checking and balancing institutions will lack the strength and the unity to restore normal constitutional arrangements once a crisis passes; perhaps new emergencies will consistently—and conveniently—justify permanent changes to the constitutional landscape. Either way, the expansion of executive power during wartime can pose a threat to civil liberties even after the war is over.

In recent years, many scholars concerned with the apparently endless War on Terror have made arguments along these lines.[2] Yet, across US history—including parts of the War on Terror—there is scant evidence for such claims. Presidents do not tend to emerge from war in anything resembling an "imperial" position, while legislators tend to reassert themselves. Andrew Johnson could barely obstruct, let alone bully, a Congress determined to impose martial law on the former Confederacy after the Civil War; Woodrow Wilson probably had more influence over foreign leaders than he did over the Senate after the First World War; Harry Truman was beaten and bruised by McCarthyism after the Second World War; Gerald Ford was at the mercy of congressional investigators after the Vietnam War; and Barack Obama—as commander in chief of the armed and naval forces—could not even close down a military detention facility leased from a foreign country because members of Congress refused to allow it.

In these postwar moments of weakened executives and resurgent Congresses, legislators have been decisive in initiating, sustaining, and expanding postwar restrictions on civil liberties. They have done more than pass punitive legislation aimed at dissidents or rebels. They have deployed a range of powers over their own institution, the executive branch, the judiciary, and the states in ways that have tested and strained the nation's constitutional commitment to the principles of freedom of speech, due process of law, and a fair trial. This historical record underpins the core argument of this book: Congress, in the aftermath of war, is more powerful—and dangerous—than we have been led to believe.

I develop this argument by examining five different categories of congressional powers, each of which is discussed in a separate chapter. The first category is what I call repressive legislation: that is, laws that curtail civil liberties. Examples include the Military Reconstruction Acts, which imposed martial law on the American South in the aftermath of the Civil War; the 1918 Immigration Act, which authorized the mass deportation of "radicals"; the 1950 McCarran Act, which forced so-called subversive organizations to register with the attorney general and permitted mass internment in the event of a national emergency; and the 2001 PATRIOT Act, which gave the federal government various new surveillance powers and broadened the statutory definition of "material support for terrorism" in a way that endangered freedom of association.

These laws (among others) are examined in chapter 1. Two key findings emerge from this comparative legislative history. First, unilateral executive repression has been extremely rare in the aftermath of war. Indeed, some of the most infamous cases of alleged executive abuse—such as the 1919–20 Palmer Raids—have been legislatively sanctioned. Second, although Congress has frequently delegated powers to the executive that appear menacing on paper, executive branch officials have not always exercised such powers with enthusiasm. Indeed, in multiple instances, both high- and low-ranking executive officials—with both high and low motives ranging from raw partisan calculation to genuine moral concern—have refused to exercise such powers at all or have outright obstructed the implementation of repressive legislation.

Here, the reader might detect a possible tension in my argument. On the one hand, I am emphasizing the crucial role of Congress in driving postwar restrictions on civil liberties. On the other, I am documenting several cases of punitive legislation passed by Congress that was half-heartedly or clumsily enforced by the executive. One could reasonably conclude from this picture that Congress's capacity to curtail civil liberties is only as good as the executive branch's will and capacity to "take care that the laws be faithfully executed."[3]

However, as other scholars have amply demonstrated in other contexts, the power to legislate is far from the only constitutional tool at Congress's disposal.[4] Chapter 2 discusses how legislators have damaged civil liberties in the aftermath of war by using their own independent powers, which do not require the usual hurdles of legislation and often resemble executive and judicial powers. These independent powers include the right of each chamber of Congress to make its own rules, determine the qualifications of its members, and, with a two-thirds vote, expel members.[5] These powers allowed congressional Republicans to exclude ex-Confederates from both chambers after the Civil War, propose a constitutional amendment in their absence, and then condition their readmission to Congress on the ratification of this amendment—all while the former Confederates were subjected to martial law. The House of Representatives also utilized the exclusion power in 1919 and 1920 to prevent the seating of Wisconsin Socialist Party Representative Victor L. Berger, arguing that his opposition to US involvement in the First World War amounted to insurrection or rebellion, thus requiring his disqualification from public office under section 3 of the Fourteenth Amendment. Despite the US Supreme Court's recent invalidation of state efforts to exclude presidential candidates from the ballot under section 3, Congress retains the power to exclude its own members under that section and, as a result, can effectively disenfranchise voters who choose allegedly subversive candidates.[6]

Chapter 2 also devotes significant attention to the power of the House and Senate to compel testimony before their committees or to hold noncooperative witnesses in contempt of Congress. Although the Constitution does not explicitly grant this authority, legislative investigative powers—especially the contempt power—have deep roots in the Anglo-American legal and parliamentary tradition and have been acknowledged by all branches of government (perhaps most importantly by the Supreme Court) as necessary for informed legislating.[7] These powers, which can be exercised—at least in the first instance—by a single committee or chamber of Congress, have created serious problems for civil liberties. Congressional investigations, in particular, have proved especially valuable to legislators who wish to expose, discredit, or humiliate their political enemies without having to go through the trouble of a judicial process. The period from 1946 to 1956 was probably the worst time in American history for this type of "McCarthyite" legislative activity, but the first Red Scare, after the First World War, was characterized by similar, if more primitive, tactics in the Senate.

Such tactics seemingly receded in the 1960s, but they never completely disappeared and have arguably reemerged in recent years. For example, in late 2023 members of Congress scolded the presidents of Harvard, the University of Pennsylvania, and the Massachusetts Institute of Technology for tepidly defending the First Amendment rights of groups such as Students for Justice in Palestine and, with the aid of donor pressure, forced the presidents of Harvard and UPenn to resign.[8]

In early 2024 Senator Tom Cotton (R-AR) provoked more direct comparisons with Senator Joseph McCarthy when he repeatedly asked Shou Zi Chew, the CEO of TikTok, whether he was or ever had been a member of the Chinese Communist Party, to which Chew repeatedly responded: "No Senator, I am Singaporean."[9] This cross-examination was part of a wider effort by legislators to ban the widely used social media platform on dubious national security grounds.[10] These recent examples of members of Congress using their investigative powers to bully and intimidate have been motivated by the Israel-Hamas war and by what increasingly resembles a "new cold war" with China. Chapter 2 concludes by warning that if this new cold war accelerates—or if the United States becomes more directly involved in a war of its own—full-blown McCarthyism could well return to Congress, if it has not already done so.

Chapters 3 through 5 document how Congress has curtailed civil liberties through its powers over and relations with other branches of government and the states. Chapter 3 examines how, in the aftermath of war, legislators have confronted the executive by deploying or threatening to deploy various constitutional powers such as impeachment, the power to create quasi-independent executive agencies, control of the federal purse strings, and the power to confirm or deny executive branch nominees. Almost all these tools were used by congressional Republicans during Reconstruction to ensure the continuation of martial law in the former Confederacy despite the objections of the president. A congressional threat to create an "independent" loyalty commission insulated from presidential control after the Second World War prompted President Truman to reluctantly implement an executive loyalty program for federal government employees. Congress prevented President Obama from closing the Guantanamo Bay detention facility by refusing to fund the transfer or release of detainees.

Chapter 3 also documents how legislators' informal relationships with executive officials have enabled violations of civil liberties. The most striking example is the relationship between congressional McCarthyites and Federal Bureau of Investigation (FBI) Director J. Edgar Hoover after the Second World War. Although President Truman opposed McCarthyism and repeatedly likened Hoover's FBI to an "American gestapo," Hoover covertly provided legislators with classified information about alleged subversives within the United States.[11] Legislators, in turn, advanced Hoover's objectives by exposing these "subversives," which saved the FBI from having to disclose its files and investigative methods to the accused—something that would have been required in court. Chapter 3 argues that this informal relationship between legislators and the FBI was formalized after the Vietnam War when the House and Senate created permanent intelligence committees. These committees are supposedly designed to conduct oversight of not only the FBI but also the entire national security state; however, they have much stronger incentives to act as "guardians" or "cheerleaders" for the intelligence agencies that provide them with exclusive access to classified information.[12]

In a larger sense, the evidence presented in chapter 3—especially when viewed alongside chapter 1—strongly suggests that, in the aftermath of war, the executive branch is not as unitary as it seems. To borrow Kenneth Shepsle's comment about Congress: the executive is a "they," rather than an "it."[13] After the Civil War, President Johnson could not control the US military, despite being its commander in chief. After the First World War, the attorney general advocated mass deportations while the assistant labor secretary resisted them. After the Second World War, President Truman could not control the FBI. Since the Vietnam War, the intelligence community can rely on consistent support and funding from congressional intelligence committees, hampering the president's ability to control the "national security state."

While chapter 3 focuses on legislative-executive relations, chapter 4 is concerned with legislative-judicial relations. The Constitution tilts this balance of power firmly in favor of the legislative branch. Although federal judges serve for life and Congress is prohibited from diminishing their salaries, Congress can obstruct the appointment of or impeach federal judges, alter the appellate jurisdiction of the US Supreme Court, and create tribunals inferior to the Supreme Court (where most federal cases are heard). During various postwar political struggles, Congress has either used or threatened to use these powers to deter the judiciary from protecting civil liberties. After the Civil War, congressional Republicans removed Supreme Court jurisdiction over habeas corpus petitions to prevent judicial review of military Reconstruction. After the Second World War, legislators came close to curbing the Supreme Court's jurisdiction again—this time over cases involving the civil liberties of alleged communists and their "fellow travelers." The court narrowly survived this campaign, but it got the message, reversing its fairly modest efforts at defending free speech and due process rights against the tactics of McCarthyism. A similar event occurred prior to the end of the Vietnam War, but with consequences that long outlasted the war, when Congress statutorily overruled several of the Warren Court's criminal procedure decisions in 1968 and the Senate filibustered the nomination of Abe Fortas for chief justice, thereby terminating the Warren Court's so-called criminal procedure revolution. After 9/11, Congress restricted the Supreme Court's jurisdiction over habeas corpus petitions from Guantanamo Bay detainees.[14]

Chapter 5 documents how legislators have contributed to attacks on civil liberties at the state and local levels. During the first and second Red Scares (after the First and Second World Wars), national legislators inspired their state-level counterparts to create investigating committees modeled on congressional examples. During the second Red Scare, in particular, members of the House Un-American Activities Committee (HUAC) offered strategic advice to state-level "little HUACs" that pursued targets and summoned "friendly" or expert witnesses identified or exposed by the "big" HUAC. These little HUACs were not merely tools of the more experienced and sophisticated anticommunists on Capitol Hill; they had their own local origins and concerns. However, at a minimum, they followed a road map drawn up in Washington.

Chapter 5 also demonstrates how national legislators can influence state and local behavior through financial incentives, such as by subsidizing the militarization of local police forces in response to the domestic civil disturbances that accompanied the Vietnam War. Although these financial incentives have not always resulted in local-level attacks on civil liberties, they have increased the repressive capacity of local actors across the United States.

Chapter 6 addresses the historical period that poses the clearest challenge to my argument: the aftermath of the Vietnam War. During this time, Congress investigated a wide range of executive abuses of civil liberties, reformed the national intelligence community, and created permanent intelligence committees in both chambers. Despite these achievements, to the extent that civil liberties were restored after the Vietnam War, this was accomplished mostly by executive branch officials. The much-celebrated Senate Select Committee to Study Governmental Operations with Respect to Intelligence Activities (better known as the Church Committee) primarily investigated legally dubious surveillance practices that had already been terminated by executive officials for various reasons, including judicial pressure, the view that the programs were no longer useful, or in response to dramatic acts of civil disobedience. Furthermore, notwithstanding significant conflict over "covert action" abroad, the Church Committee conducted its investigations in cooperation, rather than in conflict, with the executive. The result was a joint commitment to bring legislators—as well as the judiciary—back to the table of national security decision making. Ultimately, chapter 6 concludes that the post-Vietnam Congress did more for the stature and prestige of the legislative branch than it did for civil liberties.

The concluding chapter provides provisional responses to four major questions raised but not answered by the body of the book. First, why does Congress seem to regularly curtail civil liberties in the aftermath of war? Second, when, if at all, are postwar restrictions on civil liberties justified? Third, why are there different outcomes for civil liberties in different postwar moments? Fourth, are my findings useful to policymakers or to advocates of civil liberties, and if so, how? My firmest response is to the second question: that is, the imposition of martial law on the former Confederacy in the aftermath of the Civil War—while undoubtedly curtailing the civil liberties of many Southerners—was justified by the need to pursue what W. E. B. Du Bois called "full democracy."[15] If anything, this martial law was imposed too temporarily, unevenly, and cautiously. The other questions I answer tentatively at best, primarily in an attempt to stimulate further research and scholarship.

The Theoretical Framework

Overall, the following chapters paint a picture of resurgent postwar Congresses that are neither afraid to restrict civil liberties nor incapable of doing so. The goal is not to claim that Congress is solely responsible for postwar political repression in the United States. There is far too much serious scholarship on the vast subject of political repression—revealing the roles of state and private actors, federal and local institutions, and mass and elite opinion—suggesting otherwise.[16] I am not, in other words, trying to develop anything like a total causal theory of why and under what conditions civil liberties are violated in the aftermath of war. I am, above all, seeking to foreground an institution that has been largely—and in my view, incorrectly—left in the background.

Although I often refer to Congress as a singular "it" rather than a plural, disunited "they," I do so only for the sake of brevity. I know that Congress is a large, complex institution with many different interests, motivations, members, committees, and factions.[17] My argument does not depend on the fiction of unified congressional intent. On the contrary, it is concerned with how the institutional powers of Congress as a whole, as well as the formal and informal powers of individual chambers and legislators, can be used in the service of political repression.

Chapters 1–5 each focus on one category of congressional power: chapter 1 on repressive legislation, chapter 2 on Congress's independent powers, chapter 3 on relations with the executive, chapter 4 on relations with the judiciary, and chapter 5 on relations with the states. Like any effort at categorization, this is a simplification, with the goal of conveying the diversity of the repressive tools at Congress's disposal. The categories overlap in various ways, do not always involve the formal constitutional powers of Congress, and do not always involve Congress exercising power *over* but rather members of Congress exercising power *with* other institutional actors.

By structuring my argument in this way, I draw on Josh Chafetz's theoretical framework in *Congress's Constitution*.[18] Broadly, Chafetz argues that scholars have paid insufficient attention to powers that individual members or chambers of Congress can exercise outside the regular legislative process. Each of his chapters focuses on one of these extralegislative powers, which he divides into "hard" and "soft" powers. The hard or coercive powers include the ability to withhold funding from the federal government ("the power of the purse"); to confirm, oversee, or impeach executive officials ("the personnel power"); and to hold uncooperative witnesses in contempt of Congress ("the contempt power"). The soft powers are those that help Congress "compete for the affections of the public," including legal immunity for statements made during official legislative proceedings ("the freedom of speech or debate"), the authority of each chamber to punish or discipline its members ("internal discipline"), and the authority of each chamber to make its own rules ("cameral rules").

I discuss several of these powers in the context of civil liberties. However, I depart from Chafetz in five major respects, other than the obvious fact that my study has a narrower scope than his. First, I do not adopt his "hard" and "soft" distinction, in part because I think any of these powers can be coercive or persuasive, depending on how many members of Congress use them and on the historical context in which they are used. Second, while Chafetz primarily focuses on legislative-executive relations, I also focus—much more than Chafetz does—on legislative-judicial and legislative-state relations. Third, when analyzing legislative relations with other institutional actors, I examine both formal constitutional powers and informal political connections, whereas Chafetz is largely concerned with the former. Fourth, while I build on Chafetz's crucial insights about "Congress's Constitution" beyond the legislative process itself, I nevertheless examine the legislative process in significant depth, especially in chapter 1. Fifth, although Chafetz acknowledges that Congress's diverse set of tools can be misused or abused, his main aim is to explain the historical origins of these tools and their creative and constructive potential. Mine, in contrast, is to illuminate the misuses and abuses.

Beyond Chafetz, scholars of the US Congress have generally had little to say about civil liberties, at least compared to how much they have said about congressional influence over policy areas such as foreign relations and control over the federal bureaucracy.[19] Conversely, scholars of civil liberties have not said much about Congress or legislatures in general, apart from scolding them for failing to check executive power.

In studies of the institutional drivers of wartime political repression, executive power appears to be the overriding concern. This concern can be traced at least as far back as Machiavelli's *Discourses* on the Roman Republic.[20] The *Discourses* inspired Clinton Rossiter's 1948 comparative study of "Crisis Government in the Modern Democracies," which applied Machiavelli's concept of "constitutional dictatorship" to the twentieth century.[21] Rossiter argued that national crises tend to increase executive power in two ways: executives can act unilaterally and dare legislatures to defy them, as Abraham Lincoln did in the early weeks of the Civil War; or legislatures can delegate emergency powers to the executive. Often, there will be a combination of unilateralism and delegation. Whatever the precise process, Rossiter agreed with James Madison's conclusion in *The Pacificus-Helvidius Debates of 1793–1794* that "war . . . is the true nurse of executive aggrandizement."[22] For Rossiter, the only institution capable of checking this aggrandizement and averting long-term constitutional degeneration under cover of crisis was a robust and alert legislature.

Rossiter was optimistic that "strong government can be democratic government" and that "dictatorship can be constitutional."[23] Yet in the second half of the twentieth century, Rossiter's optimism was challenged by scholars focused on the rise of "terrorism." In the United Kingdom, Paddy Hillyard and Clive Walker recounted how the British government responded to the "Troubles" in Northern Ireland by adopting various tools of emergency rule, including military intervention in 1969, the Falls Curfew in 1970, internment without trial in 1971, and the dissolution of the Northern Irish Parliament in 1972. Over the long term, Hillyard and Walker argued, the most substantial threat to the idea of time-bound "constitutional dictatorship" in Britain was the 1974 Prevention of Terrorism (Temporary Provisions) Act, which granted the home secretary unprecedented powers of arrest, detention, and proscription of "terrorist" organizations. Despite its ostensibly temporary character, Parliament habitually renewed the Prevention of Terrorism Act every year, until it was replaced in 2000 by the permanent Terrorism Act.[24] Other scholars documented similar conflicts between civil liberties and counterterrorism across European democracies, including Kurt Groenewald's study of the West German government's campaign against the Red Army Faction from 1970 to 1990 and Peter Chalk's comparative study of the Spanish government's "dirty war" against separatists in the Basque country from 1983 to 1987 and the Italian government's covert battle against the Red Brigades from 1969 to 1974.[25]

Collectively, these scholars observed how emergency delegations to the executive that are sold as "temporary" can permanently curtail civil liberties. Since September 11, 2001, scholars of civil liberties in democracies have had no difficulty finding additional evidence to support this argument, highlighting the continual renewal of counterterrorism statutes and the normalization of restrictions on civil liberties as evidence of flaws in the theory of temporary emergency powers.[26] A notable but empirically vague assessment comes from Giorgio Agamben's *State of Exception*, which frames the War on Terror as only the most recent example of a persistent fact: once legislatures hand over power to presidents or prime ministers, they do not get it back.[27] With greater specificity, Kim Lane Scheppele highlights how a variety of governments have enacted a common "emergency script," beginning with "executive centralization," followed by restrictions on free speech and due process, excessive state secrecy, state-sponsored violence, and, eventually, the normalization of emergency government.[28] While Scheppele suggests that "the other branches of government [often] collude in their own marginalization," Sanford Levinson and Jack Balkin raise the specter of "presidential Ponzi schemes," when presidents seek "to convert the felt sense of crisis into a durable advantage," continually finding "new ways of stoking the public's sense of urgency to maintain their [emergency] mandate."[29]

Presidential Ponzi schemes seemed more than a speculative concern after Donald Trump's election to the US presidency in 2016. In their popular 2018 book *How to Save a Constitutional Democracy*, Tom Ginsburg and Aziz Huq bemoaned that "liberals and conservatives alike have been captivated by the prospect of a decisive president capable of slicing through the Gordian knot of partisan disagreement to achieve great things for the people." While agreeing that "deadlock is undesirable," Ginsburg and Huq emphasized the need for greater "bureaucratic autonomy" within the executive branch to counteract Trump-like personal crusades against FBI directors, attorneys general, and special counsels.[30] Similar proposals emerged in Bob Bauer and Jack Goldsmith's *After Trump*, and each of the teams of scholars who participated in the National Constitution Center's post-Trump constitution drafting project—libertarian, progressive, and conservative—all called for additional constraints on the executive branch.[31]

Many of these scholars, particularly Ginsburg and Huq, see Trump's alleged flirtation with authoritarianism as the predictable product of an "unchecked and unbalanced" executive that has fattened itself on crisis government.[32] Indeed, scholars of American politics have long feared the impact of endless (undeclared) war on the separation of powers and civil liberties. According to Michael Glennon, the dominant executive branch that has emerged and become permanent since the Second World War "threaten[s] civil liberties and personal freedom in ways never seen before in the United States."[33] Louis Fisher observes that "presidents have pushed the limits of executive power under the theory that an activist agenda inevitably promotes the nation's interest," but this "concentration of power in the Executive always puts at risk the Constitution and individual rights and liberties."[34] Laura Donohue writes, "the drive to increase [executive] power" during wartime "is a function of the office, not of the political affiliation of those in power." After more than half a century of this "drive," "expanded executive authority"—especially in the realm of surveillance—has become a menace to "popular dissent" and a mechanism of "social control."[35]

To be sure, several scholars have critiqued these arguments. Scholars of the US presidency have cast doubt on the idea that war expands executive power in the first place.[36] William Howell, who extensively cataloged and evaluated "the politics of direct presidential action" in his 2003 study *Power Without Persuasion*, argues that Congress and the courts may initially defer to the executive during wartime, but these checking and balancing institutions often become more assertive as wars drag on.[37] Andrew Polsky and Eric Schickler have found evidence of this legislative assertiveness during the era of ostensibly imperial presidents, particularly in the twilight and aftermath of the Vietnam War, when Congress enacted the 1973 War Powers Resolution and other checks on the executive.[38] By 2009, Benjamin Wittes saw evidence of "the waning over time of society's willingness to tolerate unrestrained executive leadership" during the War on Terror, which enabled "the imposition of legal rules" by "the courts and Congress."[39]

Other scholars see no reason to believe that a strong executive inherently threatens civil liberties, let alone democracy itself. Eric Posner and Adrian Vermeule argue that a presidency "unbound" from the other branches of government will still be "constrained by the shifting tides of mass opinion."[40] An energetic executive may well be the surest protector of rights and liberties, they suggest, because it is led by the only politician with a national constituency who can be held personally accountable for the actions of his subordinates. This is the central tenet of the "unitary executive" theory, which sees executive centralization under presidential leadership as a central pillar of American democracy.[41]

Comparative scholars have also debated the extent to which executive power threatens civil liberties. Comparative studies of "democratic backsliding" have warned about the dangers posed by "executive aggrandizement" under cover of crisis. This aggrandizement involves the incremental marginalization of courts and legislatures, often with popular or plebiscitary approval. Aggrandizement is distinguished from blunt power grabs, when executives simply dissolve legislatures or ignore courts and decide to rule by decree. On its face, the slow pace of aggrandizement might allow democratic institutions to regroup and resist their marginalization. However, aggrandizement might also be hard to detect—even in supposedly stable democracies—enabling what Tarunabh Khaitan calls "the killing of a Constitution by a thousand cuts."[42] Arguments such as these draw heavily on Juan Linz and Alfred Stepan's long-standing warnings about the tendency of "presidential democracies" to fall prey to "a single leader" who "enjoys, or thinks he or she enjoys, a 'democratic' legitimacy that allows him or her to ignore, dismiss, or alter other institutions."[43]

The focus of these comparative studies is democracy, whereas mine is civil liberties. The two are not the same. Nevertheless, scholars of democracy and democratic backsliding recognize that any meaningful conception of democracy must involve civil liberties—which is why almost every comparative study of democracy includes civil liberties as indicators of democratic inclusion, as components of a definition of democracy, or even as primary goals of democracy.[44] An erosion of civil liberties may be an early warning sign of democratic backsliding—or, perhaps, an early symptom of it. At a minimum, an erosion of civil liberties can undermine core promises of democracy: that members of the polity will be able to speak and associate freely, organize politically without state repression, and defend themselves vigorously if they are accused of violating the law. If executive aggrandizement is a danger to democracy, it is surely a danger to civil liberties as well.

Other comparativists are not convinced by this logic. José Antonio Cheibub has argued that the supposed dangers of "presidential democracies" are exaggerated by selection effects because presidential systems have been disproportionately concentrated in countries and regions where the prospects for democratic consolidation were already bleak.[45] Steven Levitsky and Daniel Ziblatt argue that while "would-be autocrats often use economic crises, natural disasters, and especially security threats—wars, armed insurgencies, or terrorist attacks—to justify antidemocratic measures . . . legislatures may also overindulge their constitutional prerogatives." Levitsky and Ziblatt go on to describe cynical impeachment processes in Latin America that have triggered spiraling attacks on the democratic "guardrails" of "mutual toleration and institutional forbearance."[46]

Legislative "overindulgence" was also a primary fear of the framers of the US Constitution, who repeatedly stressed the dangers of "legislative tyranny" to their new republican regime and created an independent executive to counter this. As Gouverneur Morris put it, "One great object of the Executive is, to controul the Legislature." Morris worried that "the Legislature will continually seek to aggrandize and perpetuate themselves; and will seize those critical moments produced by war, invasion, or convulsion, for that purpose." As a result, "the Executive magistrate should be the guardian of the people, even of the lower classes, against legislative tyranny; against the great and the wealthy, who, in the course of things will necessarily compose the legislative body."[47] James Madison also wanted the executive to check the legislature, though his fears of "legislative tyranny" did not carry Morris's populist overtones.[48]

While the Constitution undoubtedly constrained executive power—for example, by dividing historically "executive" war powers between Congress and the executive—it created an executive that was stronger, more independent, and more unitary than most executives that were created under postrevolutionary state constitutions.[49] Moreover, during debates over the ratification of the Constitution, critics overwhelmingly focused on the powers of Congress and, to a lesser degree, the Supreme Court, not those of the national executive.[50] In short, and at the risk of oversimplification, a strong body of evidence suggests that Congress was "the most dangerous branch" in the eyes of the framers.[51] After all, Congress made laws, while the executive and the judiciary were confined to law execution and interpretation.

Scholars familiar with the career of Senator Joseph McCarthy would not find legislative tyranny to be a far-fetched concept. A recent biography by Larry Tye describes how McCarthy's combination of luck, ruthlessness, opportunism, and rough charm made the heavy-drinking Wisconsinite one of the greatest demagogues in the history of the United States. During his anticommunist crusade that began in February 1950, McCarthy hounded more than one person to suicide and subjected many more to severe trauma, unemployment, and ostracism. Tye hesitates to settle on a number for the McCarthy "body count," but it was surely high in terms of both personal costs and costs to the institutions McCarthy attacked, especially the State Department.[52] Other historians have addressed the wider phenomenon of McCarthyism, exploring the politics of red-baiting in the United States both before and after the career of the Wisconsin senator.[53]

Aside from recounting historical examples such as the life and legacy of Senator McCarthy, scholars have generally identified three ways that legislatures can damage civil liberties. The first is excessive delegation of emergency power to the executive branch. As described above, this is common during wartime because legislators recognize the need for "decision, activity, secrecy, and dispatch"—attributes the executive has in greater abundance. Especially since the Second World War, however, Congress has permanently given the executive what Bruce Ackerman calls "disorganized, but massive grants of substantive authority to declare emergencies" on issues ranging from workplace health and safety and environmental regulation to economic sanctions on foreign nations and border security.[54] Not all these emergency powers threaten civil liberties, but the potential for abuse is obvious. Indeed, as the liberal Ackerman and several more conservative legal scholars have underlined, many of the most infamous abuses of civil liberties have been authorized either prospectively or retroactively by legislative delegation.[55] From this perspective, the executive can be blamed for abusing emergency authority, but Congress can be blamed for creating that authority and failing to monitor it.

The second, and related, way that scholars have identified legislative complicity in restricting civil liberties is through inadequate oversight of executive agencies. Michael Glennon makes this point most forcefully in the US context, arguing that Congress has been so inept at oversight of the national security bureaucracy that it has inadvertently created a system of "double government" in which the presidency, Congress, and the judiciary pretend to govern, while the real rulers are unaccountable spy chiefs and generals.[56] In a similar vein, Loch Johnson and Amy Zegart document legislators' reluctance to conduct meaningful oversight of the nation's intelligence agencies because it only brings minimal or negligible electoral payoffs.[57] Poor oversight, like excessive delegation, does not inevitably threaten civil liberties. But agencies that are allowed to operate in the dark have a long track record of intrusive surveillance practices, infiltration of social movements, and overpolicing of dissent.[58] By turning a blind eye to these practices, Congress bears responsibility for them.

Finally, scholars have identified legislative gridlock as a possible threat to civil liberties. Gridlock, they argue, paralyzes the political system, and this empowers authoritarian populists who promise to "drain the swamp" of feckless, corrupt, and inefficient lawmakers. While some legislators resist populist challenges to their authority, others embrace these challenges. Partisan polarization exacerbates these problems, as legislators value their partisan identity over their institutional responsibilities. Hence the dynamic described by Kim Lane Scheppele, in which legislators "collude in their own marginalization."[59] Scholars of democratic backsliding have increasingly argued that such legislative degeneration is afflicting constitutional democracies, including the United States, laying the foundation for future attacks on civil liberties and on democracy itself.[60]

In these accounts, the legislative threat to civil liberties is indirect and a consequence of inaction or abdication. In my account, the threat is more direct. Damage is done not just through excessive delegation to the executive branch, inadequate oversight, or gridlock but also through repressive legislation, independent congressional or cameral powers, Congress's relations with other branches, and Congress's relations with the states. With these tools at its disposal, Congress has been a valuable institutional vehicle for legislators who are eager to exploit and sustain wartime restrictions on civil liberties.

Concepts, Definitions, and Sources

Before proceeding further, it is important to explain what I mean by concepts such as "civil liberties," "repression," and "postwar." "Civil liberties" are widely understood to encompass "negative" protections for individual conduct against governmental intrusion.[61] In the United States, when we are asked to give examples of civil liberties, we are likely to start with the First Amendment's guarantees of freedom of religion, speech, press, assembly, and petition, as well as the various criminal procedure protections in the Fourth, Fifth, Sixth, and Eighth Amendments against unreasonable searches and seizures, unfair trials, and arbitrary, cruel, or unusual punishments. Only recently has the US Supreme Court tried to put the Second Amendment right to keep and bear arms on an equal footing with these other sections of the Bill of Rights.[62] The right to vote is often regarded as a "civil right" (that is, a "protection against discriminatory treatment") rather than a civil liberty ("freedom from oppressive government authority") in the United States. Moreover, the question of "unenumerated" rights and liberties remains controversial within and outside the judicial system.[63]

Because I am evaluating postwar restrictions on civil liberties—which are usually at least somewhat related to wartime—I am dealing primarily with restrictions on freedom of expression and on rights of criminal procedure. These, after all, tend to be the liberties that suffer most during and after war. A sightly thornier issue surrounds whether and to what extent these liberties are enjoyed by noncitizens. I say that they are, and the US Supreme Court has said so too, at least in its interpretations of the due process and equal protection clauses of the Fourteenth Amendment.[64] Courts have debated what this means in practice. I do not contest the widely accepted conclusion that the US government does not violate civil liberties by deporting noncitizens or by erecting barriers to entry.[65] On the other hand, freedom of speech is clearly implicated if deportation is retaliation for political dissent, and en masse deportations may not provide elementary due process. Similarly, although it is not necessarily a violation of civil liberties to subject a noncitizen to military detention, when such detention is potentially indefinite and takes place on US soil—as in the case of Guantanamo Bay, which is de facto if not de jure US territory—civil liberties are implicated.[66] Arguably, the same principle should apply to other US military bases and Central Intelligence Agency (CIA) sites across the world, however prevailing definitions of civil liberties concern how governments treat people within their own territory. I would thus describe the global US detention regime as implicating human rights rather than civil liberties.

Drawing on the work of Conor Gearty, I also include in my conception of civil liberties an implicit and qualified right to self-government. Civil liberties can exist without democracy, but if a society that has enjoyed the right to elect its own representatives has this right curtailed by the state, even a narrow idea of "negative liberty"—freedom from undue governmental constraints—is violated.[67] Thus, I consider either direct disenfranchisement of citizens or disenfranchisement through the exclusion of candidates for office tantamount to restrictions on civil liberties.

For better or worse, I use the term "repression" or "political repression" as shorthand for "restrictions on civil liberties." This is primarily a stylistic choice, aimed at avoiding excessive repetition of a somewhat clunky turn of phrase. The concepts are also similar. The downside is that, while the concepts are similar, they are not really interchangeable: on an intuitive level, "repression" sounds worse than "restrictions on civil liberties." Readers might be particularly disturbed by my references to the "repression" of former slaveholders by the US government during Reconstruction, detecting an air of Lost Cause mythology or Dunning School historiography. But the fact is that the ex-Confederate states of America were subjected to martial law, or what W. E. B. Du Bois—as far from the Dunning School as one can get—called "temporary dictatorship" after the Civil War.[68] I prefer the directness and candor of Du Bois to euphemism or obfuscation.

I admit that of all my concepts, the concept of "postwar"—which also, of course, includes "war"—is probably most problematic. Mary Dudziak, among others, has underlined the difficulty of distinguishing between war and peace in the United States since the Second World War, when a permanent national security state emerged and became entrenched. Congress no longer formally declares war, in line with global trends, but the US government is constantly involved in global military entanglements. The War on Terror—in the United States and abroad—resembles a condition of war in which there is death, destruction, and chaos, but nothing approaching the mass social and economic mobilizations demanded by the so-called conventional wars of the past.[69]

What, then, is "war"? Or "postwar"? I do not think the answer has ever been clear-cut. For example, in some sense, the core dispute between advocates and opponents of military Reconstruction after the US Civil War was about whether a state of war still existed after the surrender of the Confederate armies. As chapter 2 demonstrates, the congressional Joint Committee on Reconstruction said that a state of war existed until the "rebel states" were readmitted to representation in Congress. Throughout the nineteenth century, the United States conducted declared wars with Britain, Mexico, and Spain, as well as undeclared wars with itself and with the original inhabitants of the North American continent. I am concerned with a slightly narrower category of wars: military conflicts that generated some kind of threat to American civil liberties. These conflicts include the 1798 quasi-war with France, the Civil War, the First World War, the Second World War, the Korean War, the Vietnam War, and the wars in Iraq and Afghanistan, the last of which could be placed under the general banner of the War on Terror.[70] The Revolutionary War—which was prolonged and deadly and raises its own interesting set of questions about republican institutions fumbling around for tools of self-preservation—does not make the cut because it was not fought under the modern Philadelphia Constitution.[71]

At times, the domestic consequences of these conflicts overlapped with one another, particularly the Second World War and the Korean War, which were both drivers of what we could call an early Cold War Red Scare. More frequently, the aftermath of these wars either brought about or coincided with another type of crisis such as a strike, an economic recession, or general political unrest. In these contexts, it has not been uncommon—or, indeed, implausible—for legislators to argue that the war is not really over and that wartime restrictions on civil liberties should be retained.

The bottom line is that I cannot—and therefore will not—always draw a sharp line between "wartime" and "postwar" or between wars and other types of crises. Undoubtedly, this leaves me open to accusations of concept stretching, mission creep, or some other crime against good methodological standards. However, I see no better way to deal with the inevitable ambiguity and confusion of "wartime" and "postwar" moments.

Another potential complication for my theoretical and conceptual framework is that war can expand rights and liberties as the demands of mobilization force rulers to offer concessions to the ruled, or as public backlash against wartime repression generates fresh protections for civil liberties.[72] In the pages that follow, I tend to pay more attention to the latter because I am focusing on the specific theme of war and civil liberties rather than wider themes like war and citizenship, war and democratization, or war and nation building. In particular, the idea of a postwar restoration or expansion of civil liberties is central to my discussion of the Vietnam War in chapter 6. I have more trouble—as, I believe, any study of civil liberties should—discussing Reconstruction in the aftermath of the Civil War, which involved significant restrictions on the long-held liberties of former Confederates in order to make emancipation mean something more than a reformed serfdom. My primary response to this trouble is to accept a potentially uncomfortable fact about Reconstruction: at times, democracy can benefit from some degree of wartime repression, even after war ends.

The historical events discussed throughout this book have been extensively documented in their own right. I cannot claim to be using any new or hitherto undiscovered sources. Nevertheless, as much as possible—and even when I engage in the potentially fraught practice of regularly citing secondary sources[73]—I try to build my claims on an evidentiary foundation of primary sources such as the *Congressional Record*, transcripts from congressional hearings, opinions from the Supreme Court and federal appellate courts, FBI records, the archives of the American Civil Liberties Union (ACLU), and the personal and official papers of US presidents. The chapter that probably covers the least well-trodden documentary ground is chapter 5, on the relationship between Congress and the states. There, I consult various primary sources, especially documents from state "un-American activities" committees that have not been widely studied, and certainly not as windows into the "networked repression" of the McCarthy era.[74]

Although this book is, above all, a historical study, each chapter includes reflections on more recent debates about civil liberties in the United States. These reflections are advanced with caution—a caution that may leave many readers unsatisfied. However, a larger commentary on civil liberties and the separation of powers in the twenty-first century is far beyond the scope of this book and would naturally be based on a significant amount of speculation about the future and the fairly recent past for which the documentary record remains thin. As a result, the pages that follow focus on history first and current events second—beginning with a historical overview of repressive legislation that has enabled restrictions on civil liberties in the aftermath of war.

1

Repressive Legislation

In 1804 President Thomas Jefferson explained to Abigail Adams, "I discharged every person under punishment or prosecution under the sedition law, because I considered, and now consider, that law to be a nullity, as absolute and as palpable as if Congress had ordered us to fall down and worship a golden image." Jefferson was referring to the Sedition Act of 1798, which criminalized the printing, publishing, or uttering of "any false, scandalous, and malicious" statements against the Congress or the president of the United States, as well as statements that brought the US government "into contempt or disrepute." While Jefferson conceded that his actions could be seen as an attempt to "protect, encourage and reward slander," he argued that he acted under "the obligations of an oath to protect the constitution," which had been "violated by an unauthorised act of Congress." He would ultimately submit judgment of his motives "to the nation at large" and "to posterity."[1] A century and a half later, an unequivocal judgment came from the United States Supreme Court: "Although the Sedition Act was never tested in this Court," Justice William Brennan wrote in *New York Times v. Sullivan*, "the attack upon its validity has carried the day in the court of history."[2]

The reasons for the Sedition Act's infamy are straightforward. Only ten people were convicted under the law, but they were prominent opponents of the Adams administration and the Federalist Party—and they were prosecuted solely because of dissent.[3] Moreover, despite the fact that the act was conceived during a "quasi" rather than a declared war between the United States and France, it was a clear-cut case of Congress and the executive curtailing civil liberties under cover of crisis—less than a decade after the ratification of the Bill of Rights.[4]

The Sedition Act is not, however, infamous for its longevity: it expired in 1801, and the US Congress would not pass another sedition law for more than a century. Yet, as this chapter demonstrates, even though Congress has since passed legislation curtailing civil liberties that executive branch officials have requested, written, and then gladly enforced, President Jefferson's defiance of the Sedition Act was not the last time repressive legislation was stymied by the executive branch. During the Red Scare that followed the First World War, Assistant Labor Secretary Louis F. Post canceled nearly thirteen hundred deportation warrants issued against alleged radicals under the 1918 Immigration Act. During another Red Scare that followed the Second World War and the Korean War, similarly punitive deportation legislation was obstructed by the internal rules and procedures of the executive branch, while a 1950 law authorizing the establishment of concentration camps under conditions of national emergency was never enforced by any president. President Truman vetoed three of the four laws that curtailed civil liberties after the Second World War: the 1947 Taft-Hartley Act, the 1950 McCarran Internal Security Act, and the 1952 McCarran-Walter Immigration Act. All three vetoes were overturned by congressional supermajorities.

No repressive legislation was passed by Congress in the aftermath of the Vietnam War, but broad criminalization of "material support for terrorism"—supported by majorities in Congress and by the executive branch—threatened and may still threaten freedom of association in the era of the War on Terror. Stronger party discipline, the frequency of divided government, narrow margins of control in Congress, and, perhaps, a stronger presidency may make major confrontations between Congress and the executive over legislation affecting civil liberties less likely in the twenty-first century than they were during Reconstruction or the second Red Scare. Nevertheless, the evidence presented in this chapter strongly undercuts the view that legislative restrictions on civil liberties have stemmed exclusively or even primarily from excessive deference to the executive.

In short, this chapter paints a varied picture of the history of repressive legislation in the aftermath of war. Such legislation has sometimes been enforced enthusiastically; at other times, it has been enforced tepidly, if at all. Sometimes the initiative for such legislation has come from the executive; at other times, it has come from members of Congress with minimal executive input or executive opposition. One fact that stands out from this discussion of legislative process and enforcement is that legislation has been passed in the first place—meaning that unilateral executive abuses of civil liberties in the aftermath of war have been rare in the extreme. Even supposedly stark examples of executive unilateralism, such as the Palmer Raids that followed the First World War, were authorized and, to a large extent, encouraged by Congress.

The Reconstruction Acts

After the quasi-war with France, the next war that generated significant restrictions on civil liberties within the United States was the Civil War.[5] Scholars have extensively debated these restrictions, which included President Lincoln's unilateral decision to suspend the writ of habeas corpus, the imprisonment of American citizens without the right to challenge their detention, the imposition of martial law, and the suppression of certain newspapers.[6] Reviewing this history, scholars of civil liberties have asked several questions: Were Lincoln's actions justified by necessity?[7] How do Lincoln's actions compare with more recent cases, such as the War on Terror?[8] How many people had their civil liberties curtailed by the Lincoln administration?[9]

Although these questions have been hotly debated, even Lincoln's harshest critics grant him this: his radical constitutional cures did not outlast the life-threatening diseases of war and secession. As one of these critics, James G. Randall, puts it, "The Constitution, while stretched, was not subverted. The measures taken were recognized by the people as exceptional; and they were no more exceptional than the emergency for which they were used. . . . If Lincoln was a dictator, it must be admitted that he was a benevolent dictator."[10] Friendlier scholars have gone so far as to promote "Lincoln's Example" as a model of crisis management. It is better, they argue, for a president to temporarily push the limits of his authority than to seek legal sanction and entrench a state of exception.[11]

The reality, however, is that several wartime restrictions on civil liberties outlasted the Civil War. After the surrender of the Confederate armies, Northerners could no longer expect censorship, summary detention, or martial law, but Southerners were subjected to continued—and in some ways expanded—curtailments of their long-held liberties. Among other affronts, their elected leaders were removed by officers of the US military, their civilian justice system was undercut by a system of military commissions, and their representatives were excluded from Congress.

Perhaps out of understandable revulsion toward Lost Cause or Dunning School historiography—which portrayed Reconstruction as a corrupt tyranny that turned the naïve and obsequious Southern black population against their gentle former masters—scholarly discussion of civil liberties during Reconstruction is not nearly as widespread or vibrant as discussion of civil liberties during the Civil War.[12] But the federal government unquestionably did restrict the civil liberties of Southerners during Reconstruction, especially through the various Reconstruction or military Reconstruction acts passed by the Thirty-Ninth Congress.[13]

"If one means by 'constitutional' something provided for in that instrument or foreseen by its authors or reasonably implicit in its words, then the Reconstruction Acts were undoubtedly unconstitutional," W. E. B. Du Bois wrote in *Black Reconstruction*. Yet he hastened to add that the Civil War itself was also "unconstitutional." "In fact, the main measures of government during 1861–1870 were 'unconstitutional.' . . . And why not? No more idiotic program could be laid down than to require a people to follow a written rule of government 90 years old, if that rule had been definitely broken in order to preserve the unity of the government and to destroy an economic anachronism." He continued, "In such a crisis, legalists may insist that consistency with precedent is more important than firm and farsighted rebuilding. . . . Rule-following, legal precedence, and political consistency are not more important than right, justice and plain common sense." During Reconstruction, Du Bois wrote, legislators such as Thaddeus Stevens (R-PA) had to cut "through the cobwebs of such political subtlety" and demand that "military rule must continue in the South until order was restored, democracy established, and the political power built on slavery smashed."[14]

What were the Reconstruction Acts, and in what sense were they "unconstitutional"—or at least unusual and unprecedented? The most sweeping was the First Reconstruction Act, enacted over the veto of President Andrew Johnson on March 2, 1867. This act divided the "rebel States" of Virginia, North Carolina, South Carolina, Georgia, Mississippi, Alabama, Louisiana, Florida, Arkansas, and Texas into five military districts that would be overseen by a commanding general with the authority to "protect all persons in their rights of person and property, to suppress insurrection, disorder, and violence, and to punish, or cause to be punished, all disturbers of the public peace and criminals" through either civil courts or military commissions.

This form of government would continue in each of the rebel states until two key conditions were met. First, a state had to ratify and present to Congress a new constitution "in conformity with the Constitution of the United States in all respects, framed by a convention of delegates elected by the male citizens of said State, twenty-one years old and upward, of whatever race, color, or previous condition, who have been resident in said State for one year previous to the day of such election."

Second, a state had to ratify the Fourteenth Amendment to the US Constitution, which Congress had proposed the previous year. Section 1 of the amendment made "all persons born or naturalized in the United States, and subject to the jurisdiction thereof . . . citizens of the United States and of the state wherein they reside," and it prohibited any state from abridging "the privileges or immunities of citizens of the United States," depriving "any person of life, liberty, or property, without due process of law," or denying "to any person within its jurisdiction the equal protection of the laws." Section 2 promised to proportionally reduce the congressional representatives of any state that denied the right to vote to males over the age of twenty-one, and section 3 prohibited federal or state officeholding for anyone "who, having previously taken an oath, as a member of Congress, or as an officer of the United States, or as a member of any state legislature, or as an executive or judicial officer of any state, to support the Constitution of the United States, shall have engaged in insurrection or rebellion against the same, or given aid or comfort to the enemies thereof." Section 4 did not allow the "validity of the public debt of the United States" to be "questioned" and declared "any debt or obligation incurred in aid of insurrection or rebellion against the United States, or any claim for the loss or emancipation of any slave" to be "illegal and void." Section 5 gave Congress the power to enforce the amendment.

The First Reconstruction Act also connected these two conditions—a new, more democratic state constitution and ratification of the Fourteenth Amendment—by excluding anyone disqualified under section 3 of the Fourteenth Amendment from being "eligible to election as a member of the convention to frame a constitution for any of said rebel States" or from voting "for members of such convention."[15]

The Second, Third, and Fourth Reconstruction Acts, which were also enacted over presidential vetoes on March 23, 1867, July 19, 1867, and March 11, 1868, elaborated on key elements of the first act: requiring that "rebel State" elections be overseen by military-appointed registration boards[16] and clarifying that these boards could make judgments about voter eligibility,[17] that district commanders could remove or suspend from their duties any "rebel State" official "whenever in the opinion of such commander the proper administration of [the First Reconstruction Act] shall require it,"[18] and that new state constitutions could be ratified by a majority of those who voted rather than those who were registered to vote.[19]

In short, the Reconstruction Acts subjected all the former Confederate States of America (except Tennessee) to a form of martial law until Congress was satisfied that they had been "reconstructed." The Reconstruction that Congress demanded was based on democratic principles. Indeed, members of Congress argued that they were simply fulfilling the promise of Article IV of the federal Constitution: that "the United States shall guarantee to every State in this Union a Republican Form of Government."[20] Congress probably would not have passed the Reconstruction Acts at all if President Johnson had not so stubbornly resisted its attempts, throughout 1866, to pass civil rights legislation and legislation extending the life and mandate of the Bureau of Refugees, Freedmen, and Abandoned Lands; if he had not so hastily tried to restore the former Confederate states to the Union under his own authority in 1865; and if he had not so virulently campaigned against Congress during the 1866 election campaign.[21] Certainly, Southern cries of "tyranny" against the Reconstruction Acts do not tend to resonate with modern readers and scholars, who are now acutely aware of the daily tyranny and terror against freedmen—and "loyal" men more broadly—that the Reconstruction Acts tried to stop.[22]

All the same, it cannot be denied that the Reconstruction Acts curtailed civil liberties. Military commanders were authorized to prosecute civilians in military courts. These courts were required, under section 4 of the First Reconstruction Act, to provide trials "without unnecessary delay." They could not impose "cruel or unusual punishment," and they could not impose a death sentence "without the approval of the President."[23] However, they deprived defendants of the "esteemed" and "inestimable" protection of a jury comprising members of the community,[24] and their track record throughout the Civil War called into question the strength of their procedural protections.

Five prominent wartime examples were particularly controversial from the standpoint of the rights of the accused. First, former Congressman Clement Vallandigham (D-OH) was arrested in May 1863 for "publicly expressing, in violation of General Orders No. 38, from Head-quarters Department of the Ohio, sympathy for those in arms against the Government of the United States" and for "declaring disloyal sentiments and opinions, with the object and purpose of weakening the power of the Government in its efforts to suppress an unlawful rebellion."[25] After his conviction before a military commission, Vallandigham's application for a writ of habeas corpus was denied by a federal district court judge in Ohio. "Those who live under the protection and enjoy the blessings of our benignant government, must learn that they can not stab its vitals with impunity," the judge concluded.[26] When the case eventually came before the Supreme Court, it held that it had no jurisdiction over military commissions.[27] The army thus tried and convicted a prominent politician for antiwar speech.

Second, Lambdin P. Milligan was arrested pursuant to a military order in Indiana in October 1864. He was accused of creating and leading a secret society opposed to the war and working on behalf of the Confederacy. After his habeas appeal was denied, a military commission found him guilty and sentenced him to death by hanging. In contrast to the case of Vallandigham, the Supreme Court denounced the military proceedings after the war, ordering Milligan's release and underlining the importance of limiting military commissions to areas and times in which civilian courts cannot function.[28]

Third, Henry Wirz was executed in November 1865 after being convicted of conspiracy and murder by a military commission. Wirz was not a civilian—he was the commandant of Camp Sumter, an enormous prisoner-of-war facility near Andersonville, Georgia. Although the filthy and overcrowded conditions at Camp Sumter were unquestionably horrendous—causing the deaths of many thousands of Union soldiers—Wirz's personal responsibility for these conditions was far from fully proved. His trial by military commission was accompanied by furious press coverage in the North. Witnesses struggled to pin specific abuses on Wirz, and his main defense—that he lacked the necessary support from the Confederate government to maintain the facility—was swiftly dismissed. No one responsible for conditions similar to Andersonville in the North—particularly at the notorious Camp Douglas facility in Chicago—faced justice. In short, Wirz may well have been a scapegoat.[29]

Fourth, much earlier in the war—in September 1862—a military commission was convened to try 392 Dakota Indian men for their participation in an uprising against white settlers in Minnesota. These proceedings were so farcical and rushed that President Lincoln commuted most of the death sentences, reducing their number from 303 to 38. In explaining his actions, Lincoln told the Senate that he was "anxious to not act with so much clemency as to encourage another outbreak on the one hand, nor with so much severity as to be real cruelty on the other." Therefore, he culled the numbers through "a classification of all who were proven to have participated in *massacres*"—and rape—"as distinguished from participation in *battles*."[30]

Fifth, war crimes charges were leveled against the alleged assassins of Abraham Lincoln. In the case of Wirz, the War Department had accused him of "wholly disregarding the usages of civilized warfare"—a charge that was at least rooted in existing understandings of the laws of war.[31] It was more tenuous to charge the alleged assassins with war crimes because Robert E. Lee had already surrendered to Ulysses S. Grant, essentially ending the war.[32] Yet the alleged assassins were accused of "maliciously, unlawfully, and traitorously" devising a conspiracy "in aid of the existing armed rebellion against the United States of America."[33] As Detlev Vagts notes, "the conduct of the trial has been subject to severe criticism, including charges that the prosecution had presented perjured testimony and that the court's recommendation of leniency for some of those convicted was concealed from President Johnson."[34]

Mark E. Neely estimates that "during the Civil War, the army conducted at least 4,271 trials by military commission," with more than half taking place in "the strife-torn border states of Missouri, Kentucky, and Maryland."[35] The concentration of military trials in the border states should caution us against seeing the Vallandigham and Milligan cases as typical. Suspected guerrillas and smugglers accounted for almost all the border state cases. Neely tallies the total number of cases during Reconstruction (1865–70) at approximately fourteen hundred, but Vagts suggests that most of these "had little to do with Reconstruction and resistance" and more to do with "maintaining military discipline—punishing civilians who sold liquor to soldiers or purchased military gear from them." Vagts estimates the "real" number—of what we might call political cases brought under Reconstruction laws—at around five hundred.[36] Based on this statistical evidence—along with the specifics of the five cases discussed above and the impossibility of any appeal to a jury of one's peers—we can reasonably conclude that military tribunals did diminish the long-held criminal procedure rights enjoyed by white Southerners.

Clearly, however, military commissions were not invented by the Reconstruction Acts. Even President Johnson was initially willing to tolerate their existence—and substantial military control over governance and daily life—in the former Confederacy, despite the cessation of hostilities.[37] Yet the Reconstruction Acts greatly expanded the scope of military power over civilian affairs, explicitly authorizing district commanders to employ military commissions for the broad purpose of protecting "all persons in their rights of person and property," suppressing "insurrection, disorder, and violence," and punishing "all disturbers of the public peace and criminals."[38] The nation's highest and most-respected general, Ulysses S. Grant, privately recognized this reality, despite his public reticence. "Reconstruction measures have passed both houses of Congress over one of the most ridiculous Veto messages that ever emanated from any President," he wrote to Elihu Washburne on March 4, 1867. "There is nothing clearer to my mind than that Congress intended to give district Commanders entire control over the Civil government," he told General Philip Sheridan, commander of the Fifth District (Louisiana and Texas). "Enforce your own construction of the Military Bill until ordered to do otherwise," he instructed General John Pope, commander of the Third District (Alabama, Georgia, and Florida). "The law," he emphasized to Edward Ord, commander of the Fourth District (Arkansas and Mississippi), "makes District Commanders their own interpreters of their power and duty."[39]

Daniel Sickles, commander of the Second District (the Carolinas), believed that Congress had authorized "the removal of nearly every Civil officer in the South from Governors down." Sheridan argued that he could remove the mayor of New Orleans, the Louisiana attorney general, and "Judge E. Abell of the Criminal Court of New Orleans" without "giv[ing] any reason." Pope believed he could prohibit "newspapers or speakers in their discussions about the policy of Reconstruction under the late acts of Congress, from abusing or denouncing the Govt or any of its Departments or using personal epithets or misrepresentation personally of any officer of the US Government for any acts done in performance of his duty."[40] In addition, Grant and his district commanders agreed, prior to passage of the Third Reconstruction Act, that they could instruct local voter registration boards to cross-examine new registrants to determine whether they should be disenfranchised due to past affiliations with the Confederacy. This contradicted the US attorney general's opinion that voters only had to sign a loyalty oath.[41]

District commanders and their subordinates exercised their powers with varying degrees of enthusiasm. In the Fourth District, Major General Alvin Gillem arrested and detained William McCardle, editor of the *Vicksburg Times*, and charged him with "disturbing the peace, inciting to insurrection and disorder, libel, and impeding reconstruction, solely on the basis of several vituperative, anti-reconstructionist editorials he had authored and published."[42] General Sheridan did not hesitate to remove the city and state officials he blamed for the New Orleans race riots—perhaps better labeled pogroms—of July 1866. From his point of view, this tool was a priceless deterrent. "The moment that the office holders here find out I have not the power to remove them," he wrote to Grant, "[at] that moment they become defiant and I lose nearly all my strength." Sheridan ended up removing not only the officials implicated in the New Orleans riots but also the governors of Louisiana and Texas. He also ordered the desegregation of New Orleans streetcars. Sickles removed twelve local and state officials in the Carolinas within three months of the First Reconstruction Act.[43] Pope, in contrast, feared that such dismissals would bring charges of "military despotism." In Georgia, he believed that "nearly all the State officers are rebels and opposed to the execution of these Acts of Congress, but I had rather keep them where they *are (silenced)* than by displacing them, make martyrs of them."[44]

Pope also feared that "many worthy and now loyal men who could be safely trusted, are disfranchised by these clauses of the Military Bills."[45] Grant tried but struggled to collect reliable data on the extent of disenfranchisement. Very rough estimates from his generals suggested that the number of whites disenfranchised under the Reconstruction Acts was around 16,000 in Virginia, 11,700 in North Carolina, 8,200 in South Carolina, 10,500 in Georgia, and 350 in Florida. Generals in other states did not even venture to guess.[46] Other, even rougher, estimates from scholars trying to pin down an overall number for all ten "rebel States" go as high as 200,000.[47] As Forrest G. Wood has noted, these high-end estimates seem fanciful because "the five states with recorded disfranchisements accounted for 53 per cent of the total southern white population, including the three largest states." Therefore, "if one merely doubled the known disfranchisements to account for the other five states, the total is considerably less than 100,000. A computation based on the state with the most known disfranchisements would result in an overall estimate of 97,000. Or one based on the state with the highest percentage of known disfranchisements would be about 108,000."[48]

Whatever the precise number was, Congress authorized and the military implemented—unevenly and often reluctantly—disenfranchisement, removal of state officials, military commissions for civilians, and restrictions on freedom of the press. Georgia-born lawyer George W. Paschal—who had supported the Union during the Civil War—spoke for many white Southerners when he told President Grant in 1870 that he could not celebrate the Fourth of July "while there lingers in a loathsome dungeon a single American citizen with no constitutional warrant for his imprisonment."[49] Nevertheless, when we consider the obstinacy and violence of its enemies, we could say that Congress legislated against the liberties of former Confederates—and, it bears repeating, *for* the liberties of the formerly enslaved—with a significant degree of caution and restraint. Congress never claimed the right to sustain military Reconstruction indefinitely or without limits. All the former rebel states had ratified the Fourteenth Amendment and thus restored civilian governments by February 1871. Thereafter, unreconstructed Southerners dug in for a long-term—and ultimately successful—strategy of terror and intimidation against the new Southern governments and their supporters.[50]

To be sure, Republicans in Congress did not simply surrender to Southern "Redeemers." In 1871 Congress passed the Ku Klux Klan Act, which was aimed at "unlawful combinations" plotting "to either overthrow or set at defiance the constituted authorities" of the state and federal governments. If these "combinations" could not be prosecuted by the "constituted authorities," then "it shall be lawful for the President of the United States, when in his judgment the public safety shall require it, to suspend the privileges of the writ of *habeas corpus*, to the end that such rebellion may be overthrown."[51] Grant, who succeeded Johnson as president in 1869, used this power on one occasion. On October 17, 1871, the writ was suspended in nine Klan-ravaged South Carolina counties. Federal marshals and troops arrested six hundred men in these areas before the end of the year. Prosecutors managed to get only five convictions in federal court, but they obtained forty-nine guilty pleas. The suspension of the writ and the mass arrests certainly spooked Klan members in South Carolina, who fled and snitched in far greater numbers than those who ended up in court. Ultimately, however, this brief and limited war on white terror was nowhere near enough to prevent "Redemption" in South Carolina, let alone the rest of the former Confederacy.[52]

The fate of the Reconstruction Acts, the Ku Klux Klan Act, and Reconstruction itself may lead us to conclude that, even if Congress did pass repressive legislation after the Civil War, it was not repressive enough. The consequences were obvious to the prescient Philip Sheridan, who told General Grant in 1867, "We can never have peace or quiet until the States which were in rebellion surrender their attempts at political power as absolutely as Lee surrendered the Military strength of the rebellion at Appomattox Court House."[53] This political surrender never happened, and the federal government never did enough to make it happen.

Nevertheless, warlike constitutional powers were central to the Reconstruction project. The military enfranchised black Southerners; indicted, tried, and punished hundreds of defiant white Southerners; facilitated the election of black officeholders for the first time in American history; and, in some places, desegregated public accommodations.[54] Later in the nineteenth century—especially during the 1890s—the Jim Crow system would reverse these gains.[55] But even Jim Crow could not extinguish the Fourteenth Amendment, emancipation, historically black colleges and universities (HBCUs), or the powerful and inspiring memory of Reconstruction.[56] Black activism and courage were undoubtedly the foundation of these achievements, but martial law was a necessary enabler. In a narrower sense, the Reconstruction Acts achieved exactly what they set out to achieve: reintegrating the former Confederate states, under military tutelage, on terms acceptable to Congress—namely, ratification of the Fourteenth Amendment. In this sense, legislative restrictions on the civil liberties of former Confederates were integral to Reconstruction.

The First World War and the First Red Scare

In contrast to Reconstruction, the aftermath of the First World War did not bring anything resembling martial law in the United States. During the war, however, Congress passed two laws that have since been widely criticized for their impact on freedom of speech and freedom of the press: the 1917 Espionage Act and the 1918 Immigration Act.

The 1917 Espionage Act strictly punished the leaking or publication of state secrets and made "every letter, writing, circular, postal card, picture, print, engraving, photograph, newspaper, pamphlet, book, or other publication, matter or thing, of any kind, containing any matter advocating or urging treason, insurrection, or forcible resistance to any law of the United States . . . nonmailable."[57] Within twelve months, Postmaster General Albert Sidney Burleson had compiled a list of forty-four "publications whose second-class mail privilege has been revoked after a hearing on account of violation of the Espionage Law."[58] Nevertheless, the Espionage Act was not a blank check. Its initial drafter, Assistant Attorney General Charles Warren, envisaged that it would have an explicit "prior restraint" censorship provision akin to that contained in Britain's wartime Defense of the Realm Act. In his "War Notes," Warren recounted how early versions of the espionage bill "had become the subject of violent newspaper attacks because of the censorship feature." He added, "in both the House and Senate, a furious fight was waged over the section of the Espionage Chapter under which a censorship of the press was made possible." Eventually, "after nine weeks of grueling debate," Congress rejected the press censorship provision, and Warren later claimed (perhaps dubiously) that the censorship proposal was "nothing we were particularly insistent on."[59] In contrast, when Congress passed a sedition amendment to the Espionage Act in May 1918—reviving the sweeping language of the 1798 Sedition Act—the Justice Department thought Congress had gone too far. "Can a Democratic Administration afford, even by silence, to give consent to so repressive a statute?" Warren asked Attorney General Thomas Gregory. Gregory shared Warren's concerns but did not air them publicly.[60]

Walter Nelles, chief legal counsel of the National Civil Liberties Bureau, tallied 1,181 prosecutions brought under the original Espionage Act. In his famous study *Freedom of Speech in Wartime*, Harvard Law Professor Zachariah Chafee included the "sedition" cases and put the figure closer to 2,000 for the entire war.[61] The most famous defendants were those whose appeals were eventually heard—and rejected—by the US Supreme Court: Charles Schenck, general secretary of the Socialist Party in Philadelphia, who had published and distributed pamphlets condemning conscription; Eugene Debs, Socialist Party of America leader, who had published and advocated an "Anti-War Proclamation and Program"; and a group of New York–based activists who had distributed pamphlets opposing American troops being sent to Russia in the aftermath of the Bolshevik Revolution.[62]

Even though the Supreme Court heard these appeals after the war, neither the Espionage Act nor the sedition amendment were used to suppress civil liberties in the aftermath of the First World War. The newly established American Civil Liberties Union (ACLU) launched a vigorous postwar campaign to repeal the Espionage Act and pardon those convicted under it.[63] In 1920 the ACLU succeeded in its efforts to repeal the sedition amendment, but its primary ally in the Senate, Joseph France (R-MD), could not get his proposed repeal of the Espionage Act out of the Senate Judiciary Committee, whose members claimed that it would aid the enforcement of liquor prohibition.[64] Ultimately, the Espionage Act's main future function, over the long term, was to build up a "secrecy regime" in the US government, which would include accelerated prosecutions of leakers of classified information under the Obama administration and the first Trump administration.[65]

The legislation with the most severe impact on civil liberties in the aftermath of the First World War was the lesser-known 1918 Immigration Act. Congress had twice passed restrictive immigration bills with provisions for the deportation of "anarchists" during the war, and President Wilson had twice issued a veto. The earlier Immigration Act of 1917 became law only through a veto override. Wilson's objections to this law were rooted in its introduction of a literacy test and a measure that he said would "all but close entirely the gates of asylum."[66] However, pressure for additional legislation to facilitate the mass deportation of alleged "radicals" accelerated toward the end of the war as congressional Democrats and Republicans reacted particularly vociferously to the 1917 Bolshevik Revolution, fearing that foreign-born or foreign-influenced workers in the United States would attempt to emulate the Bolsheviks' revolutionary methods. The 1918 Immigration Act authorized the deportation of:

> aliens who are anarchists; aliens who believe in or advocate the overthrow by force or violence of the Government of the United States or of all forms of law; aliens who disbelieve in or are opposed to all organized government; aliens who advocate or teach the assassination of public officials; aliens who advocate or teach the unlawful destruction of property; aliens who are members of or affiliated with any organization that entertains a belief in, teaches, or advocates the overthrow by force or violence of the Government of the United States or of forms of law, or that entertains or teaches disbelief in or opposition to all organized government, or that advocates the duty, necessity, or propriety of the unlawful assaulting or killing of any officer or officers, either of specific individuals or of officers generally of the Government of the United States or of any other organized government, because of his or their official character, or that advocates or teaches the unlawful destruction of property.[67]

The primary author of the act, Representative John Burnett (D-AL), told the House that "the purpose of the bill" was to provide "a summary means of getting rid of" foreign-born anarchists and radicals "without the long delays of the court." In fact, as Burnett acknowledged, "it has been the law for years and years to deport without any trial," but his bill streamlined the existing process in two ways. First, it removed procedural protections for "anarchists who have been here for more than five years." Second, it was aimed not only at "anarchists" but also "at all who are conniving and scheming for the destruction of this Government."[68] Although the House debates on the Immigration Act suggested some wartime fear of the "pro-German" immigrant, the most dishonorable mentions were reserved for the "bolsheviki," the "anarchist," the "socialist," and the "I.W.W." (International Workers of the World)—targets of what would become a postwar Red Scare.[69] Only New York Socialist Congressman Meyer London spoke out against the bill.[70] In the end, the bill comfortably passed both houses, and Woodrow Wilson signed it into law on October 16, 1918, less than a month before the armistice.[71]

The Immigration Act was the legal basis for what became known as the Palmer Raids, named after Attorney General A. Mitchell Palmer, whose Justice Department ordered the arrest of around three thousand alleged radicals and anarchists in late 1919 and early 1920.[72] The raids were not models of due process or fairness, as a group of outraged, nationally recognized lawyers later pointed out in their scathing and detailed *Report upon the Illegal Practices of the Department of Justice.*[73] By April 1920, 263 victims of the Palmer Raids had been deported—most of them (249) in a single boatload aboard the USAT *Buford*, nicknamed the "Soviet Ark." "It was 4:20 a.m. on the day of our Lord, December 21, 1919," the ark's most famous passenger, Emma Goldman, recalled. "I felt dizzy, visioning a transport of politicals doomed to Siberia, the étape of former Russian days. Russia of the past rose before me and I saw the revolutionary martyrs being driven into exile. But no, it was New York, it was America, the land of liberty!"[74]

Future Soviet Arks were prevented by a relatively obscure executive branch official: Assistant Labor Secretary Louis F. Post. Post's boss, Labor Secretary William B. Wilson, had the authority to issue deportation warrants because the Bureau of Immigration was a Labor Department agency until 1940. However, after authorizing the Soviet Ark deportations, Wilson stepped back from his cabinet duties because of illness. "I had often administered the immigration duties of the Department," Assistant Secretary Post later recalled. "But now I was plunged into responsibility for the aftermath of this crusade to the full."[75] In February and March 1920 Post reviewed 3,000 outstanding deportation warrants requested by the Department of Justice and canceled 1,293 of them. In April 1920 the Republican chairman of the House Committee on Immigration and Naturalization, Albert Johnson of Washington, raged at the realization that only 263 "radicals" arrested during the Palmer Raids had been deported. Johnson held a special hearing to consider impeachment charges against Post. "When Congress writes laws that anarchists shall be deported, Congress means that very thing," Johnson told his colleagues on the Rules Committee. "In my opinion the public is not seeing red without a reason. It is seeing its laws violated by public officials in behalf of aliens who have contempt for this Government . . . if necessary, Congress should clean out any executive department that encourages these aliens or indorses their ideas."[76]

The author of the resolution to consider impeachment, Kansas Republican Homer Hoch, argued that "Assistant Secretary of Labor Post, by his attitude toward the law and by his action in specific cases, has virtually nullified the law against alien reds and anarchists." Fellow Kansas Republican Jasper Tincher agreed that "Mr. Post has violated the law, acted without authority and acted against the interests of the Government of the United States." Johnson alleged that Post was "boring within" the Labor Department—an expression alluding to dual loyalties.[77]

Post was confident that he had acted lawfully. "The entire function of deportation is vested in the Secretary of Labor," he told the Rules Committee. "He decides whether a warrant shall issue or shall not issue and controls the examination from the beginning, except in one respect that it must be conducted by an inspector under the immigration bureau at a station."[78] Because Secretary Wilson had delegated this authority to Post, Post could exercise prosecutorial discretion. "To permit aliens to violate the hospitality of this country by conspiring against it is something which no American can contemplate with patience," Post conceded. "Equally impatient, however, must any patriotic American be with drastic proceedings on flimsy proof to deport aliens who are not conspiring against our laws and do not intend to."[79] Post later recounted events more bluntly, describing how foreign-born radicals were held "*incommunicado*, old Spanish fashion, for days at a stretch," while immigration inspectors "lawlessly intercept[ed] their letters in the mail, depriving them of the help of friends and the services of lawyers, [and] placing them beyond the reach of writs of *habeas corpus*."[80]

Post won the fight. The House never held an impeachment vote, and Congress could do little to reverse what Post had done. He created facts on the ground and dared Congress to defy him; he leveraged the fragmented chain of command for deportations within the executive branch to protect the victims of the Red Scare. In theory, Congress could have removed him from office and rewritten the law to give all power to Palmer and the Justice Department. In practice, this would have involved large, time-consuming, and complex legislative challenges—challenges that Congress had already experienced when pondering passage of a postwar replacement for the Sedition Act.[81] In any event, a new law still might not have reversed Post's decisions. Another administrative procedure would have to be established, and it would have to provide some discretion to some executive officer somewhere down the line. Louis Post thus succeeded in using his prosecutorial discretion to impede Congress's appetite for mass deportations.

The Second World War and the Second Red Scare

In the aftermath of the Second World War—which soon bled into the Korean War and the more nebulous Cold War—four laws played a key role in a second Red Scare that saw at least ten thousand Americans excluded or expelled from public and private employment between 1946 and 1956 because of their alleged disloyalty. Many more were traumatized by far-reaching public inquisitions into their personal affairs, and several hundred were subjected to deportation or criminal proceedings.[82] These laws were the 1940 Smith Act, the 1947 Taft-Hartley Act, the 1950 McCarran Act, and the 1952 McCarran-Walter Act.

The 1940 Smith Act, as Richard W. Steele writes, was "rushed" through Congress "with little public or official debate," passing the House by a 382–4 vote on June 22, 1940—"the same day that the French officially ended their resistance to the Germans."[83] Title I of the Smith Act prohibited the advocacy of violent revolution, and Title II required the compulsory registration of aliens residing in the United States.[84] Zachariah Chafee wrote to Attorney General Robert Jackson and advised that Title I "will not do much harm if you yourself keep it as a revolver in your bureau drawer to use when burglars are ever in the house. On the other hand, if you let your district attorneys over the country take it out to play with it, I am afraid that some of them may enjoy using it to snipe at soapbox orators outside the front fence." Chafee recommended "a circular directing United States district attorneys to send no more cases to grand juries . . . without first submitting a statement of facts to the Attorney General and receiving by wire his opinion as to whether or not the facts constituted an offence under the act." "I mention this," Chafee concluded, "before this statute leads to a repetition of the consequences of the Espionage Act of 1918 [*sic*]." Jackson promptly responded, "I agree with you pretty fully about Title I. . . . My purpose in creating the Neutrality Unit of this Department was to supervise the activities of United States Attorneys in matters of this kind and to profit by the lesson of the World War."[85] In the end, the Justice Department barely enforced the Smith Act during the war. As the ACLU reflected in 1945, "In sharp contrast with World War I, the federal government has brought comparatively few prosecutions for utterances or publications alleged to obstruct the conduct of the war."[86]

President Truman's attorney general, Tom Clark, initially seemed to take the same position as his predecessors, telling Congress in February 1948 that the Smith Act could not be used against the Communist Party of the USA (CPUSA) because it applied only to individuals, not to organizations. Congressmen J. Parnell Thomas (R-NJ) and Richard Nixon (R-CA) responded by threatening to outlaw the party.[87] Rather than face this prospect, Clark had the US attorney for the Southern District of New York, John McGohey, prepare a Smith Act case against the CPUSA's national leaders in April 1948. They were indicted by a grand jury on July 20.[88] According to Ellen Schrecker, "there is no evidence that the President was ever consulted about the pending action."[89]

In its case against the CPUSA, the government provided no evidence of a concrete or realistic conspiracy to carry out a communist revolution in the United States. The case rested instead on the general doctrines of the US Communist Party, which, the government argued, amounted to the illegal advocacy of violent revolution. In June 1951, in *Dennis v. United States*, the Supreme Court ruled 6–2 in the government's favor, agreeing that the Communist Party leaders "intended to overthrow the Government of the United States as speedily as the circumstances would permit." "No matter how it is worded," Justice Hugo Black fumed in dissent, "this is a virulent form of prior censorship of speech and press, which I believe the First Amendment forbids." "On this record," Justice William O. Douglas added, "no one can say that petitioners and their converts are in such a strategic position as to have even the slightest chance of achieving their aims."[90]

Overall, the Smith Act could probably be described as fairly typical of the legislation feared by advocates of civil liberties. It was passed during what was technically peacetime for the United States but a terrifying and expanding wartime in Europe, which drove Congress to grant vast powers to the executive branch. Although the Roosevelt administration did not abuse these powers, the Truman administration did, albeit under external pressure, including the threat of even more repressive legislation from Congress.

Truman, however, actively tried to resist another law that curtailed civil liberties in the aftermath of the Second World War: the 1947 National Labor Management Act, better known as the Taft-Hartley Act after its sponsors, Senator Robert Taft (R-OH) and Representative Fred A. Hartley Jr. (R-NJ). The Taft-Hartley Act broadly sought to reduce the power of labor unions and increase the power of employers in American workplaces. The legislative debates on Taft-Hartley were dominated by concerns about an unprecedented wave of strikes in 1946 in which "a total of 4.6 million workers were directly involved in stoppages" in the coal, steel, meatpacking, and railroad industries—"a figure larger than in any previous year on record."[91] "I don't think this Nation could stand too many coal strikes like the last one," Representative Howard Smith

(D-VA) warned during the House committee hearings on the Taft-Hartley bill.[92] When reviewing the constitutionality of the Taft-Hartley Act in May 1950, the Supreme Court noted that "the incident most fully developed" in the House hearings "was a strike at the Milwaukee plant of the Allis-Chalmers Manufacturing Company in 1941, when that plant was producing vital materials for the national defense program." Crucially, the court added, "a full hearing was given" in Congress "not only to company officials, but also to leaders of the international and local unions involved. Congress heard testimony that the strike had been called solely in obedience to [Communist] Party orders for the purpose of starting the 'snowballing of strikes' in defense plants."[93]

To combat the alleged domination of labor unions by the Communist Party, the Taft-Hartley Act prohibited any union officer from receiving any collective bargaining protections from the National Labor Relations Board unless that officer signed an affidavit (under penalty of perjury) pledging that "he is not a member of the Communist Party or affiliated with such party, and that he does not believe in, and is not a member of or supports any organization that believes in or teaches, the overthrow of the United States Government by force or by any illegal or unconstitutional methods."[94]

When the Taft-Hartley bill was placed on President Truman's desk in June 1947, he vetoed it. "I share with the Congress the conviction that legislation dealing with the relations between management and labor is necessary," he stated. However, "the bill taken as a whole would reverse the basic direction of our national labor policy, inject the Government into private economic affairs on an unprecedented scale, and conflict with important principles of our democratic society." Among his lengthy list of complaints against the bill, Truman protested that "the mere refusal by a single individual to sign the required affidavit would prevent an entire national labor union from being certified for purposes of collective bargaining. Such a union would have to win all its objectives by strike, rather than by orderly procedure under the law." This would result in "the union and the affected industry" being "disrupted for perhaps a long period of time while violent electioneering, charges and counter-charges split open the union ranks. The only result of this provision would be confusion and disorder, which is exactly the result the Communists desire." The affidavit, Truman concluded, was "an attempt to solve difficult problems of industrial democracy by recourse to oversimplified legal devices. I consider that this provision would increase, rather than decrease, disruptive effects of Communists in our labor movement."[95]

Truman's veto was overturned by Congress three days later. When the Taft-Hartley Act reached the Supreme Court in 1950, Justice Hugo Black likened the "anti-Communist" affidavit to the "test oaths" used throughout history "for inflicting penalties and disabilities on obnoxious minorities" such as "the Huguenots in France" and "'heretics' during the Spanish Inquisition."[96] However, Black was the lone dissenter on a court that deferred to Congress's assurances about the necessity of the affidavit to protect the free flow of interstate commerce. Of all the provisions of the Taft-Hartley Act that reduced the power of American labor unions, it is perhaps hardest to measure the impact of the anticommunist affidavit. Yet, as Justice Black suggested, the affidavit did contribute to a dynamic of suspicion, denunciation, and division within the labor movement that resembled the consequences of test oaths imposed on religious and ideological minorities in earlier historical periods.[97] In this sense, the affidavit amounted to a clear restriction on the rights of free expression and association.

After the Taft-Hartley Act, Congress continued its efforts to purge the country of communist influences. The House of Representatives passed the Subversive Activities Control Act by a margin of 319 to 58 on May 19, 1948. As the Senate considered this bill, known as the Mundt-Nixon bill—which would effectively destroy the Communist Party and its "fronts" through compulsory registration with the attorney general—Vice President and Progressive Party presidential nominee Henry Wallace organized a march on Congress that was attended by up to five thousand people who denounced the bill as "fascism."[98] Although President Truman claimed, "I never make comments on bills that are pending until they come before me," he clearly signaled his intent to veto this one. "As to outlawing political parties in the United States," he told a reporter, "I think that is entirely contrary to our principles. I don't think the splinter parties do any harm, and if there is conspiracy to overthrow the Government of the United States, we have laws to cover that."[99] The Mundt-Nixon bill stalled in the Senate until the end of the legislative session.[100]

When a revised version of the Mundt-Nixon bill eventually reached his desk in September 1950—this time under the sponsorship of Senator Pat McCarran (D-NV)—Truman vetoed it with fury. The McCarran

Act gave a five-member Subversive Activities Control Board the power to compel members of the Communist Party and "front organizations" to register with the attorney general. It also permitted summary internment of "each person as to whom there is a reasonable ground to believe that such person probably will engage in, or probably will conspire with others to engage in, acts of espionage or sabotage" during a national emergency.[101] This legislation "would put the Government of the United States in the thought control business," Truman argued. Worse, "it would give Government officials vast powers to harass all of our citizens in the exercise of their right of free speech . . . no considerations of expediency can justify the enactment of such a bill as this, a bill which would so greatly weaken our liberties and give aid and comfort to those who would destroy us."[102] Truman's veto was overturned by a coalition of Republicans and Southern Democrats, along with some liberals who, shaken by the 1949 Soviet atomic bomb test and the outbreak of the Korean War, also turned on the president.[103]

In the end, the McCarran Act was blunted not by a veto but by nonenforcement. Truman never invoked the internment provision, nor did any of his successors.[104] The compulsory registration provision, which had the potential to cripple so-called subversive organizations through the manifold legal consequences associated with an official designation as "subversive," was barely enforced either.[105] "After five years of operation," writes Francis Thompson, "not one organization had registered under the Act, nor had any received [a] final order to register."[106] Moreover, as Tom Clark correctly predicted when the registration provision was first floated in the 1948 Mundt-Nixon bill, the whole process was vulnerable to litigation because it offended the Fifth Amendment's privilege against self-incrimination. The "subversive" designation came from the Justice Department, which had openly pursued Smith Act prosecutions against so-called subversive organizations, most notably the CPUSA. Registration forced potential defendants to cooperate with their potential prosecutors. At best, such a requirement was constitutionally questionable, allowing the Communist Party to fight its "subversive" designation in court until the Supreme Court eventually accepted the party's Fifth Amendment defense in 1965.[107]

In the final year of the Truman administration, Congress attempted to orchestrate another "deportations delirium," to use Louis Post's term. Pat McCarran was again the architect. As chair of the Senate Judiciary

Committee, McCarran convinced his colleagues to authorize a "complete investigation" of the nation's immigration laws in 1947. Part of the motivation was anticommunist sentiment, and part of it was a practical effort to clean up and clarify what was becoming an unwieldy web of immigration statutes. In April 1950 the committee produced its findings in Senate Report 1515, which became the basis for the McCarran-Walter Immigration and Nationality Act of 1952.[108]

The McCarran-Walter Act was the product of a Senate bill sponsored by McCarran and a House bill sponsored by Francis E. Walter (D-PA). McCarran said in joint hearings before the House and Senate Judiciary Committees that his bill was designed to address "many inequities, weaknesses, loopholes, and inconsistencies in our present hodgepodge immigration and naturalization system." The matter was urgent because the immigration and naturalization system was "the conduit through which a stream of humanity flows into the fabric of our society. If that stream is healthy the impact on our society is salutary, but if that stream is polluted our institutions and our way of life become infected." Part of the task was "eliminat[ing] the deadwood from our present immigration and naturalization laws" and "making numerous technical and minor changes," but McCarran also underlined the bill's strengthening of "exclusion and deportation procedures" and "naturalization and denaturalization procedures," which would serve to "weed out subversives and other undesirables." According to Walter, his bill was "not very much different" from McCarran's.[109]

The final version of the McCarran-Walter Act affirmed and greatly expanded the 1918 Immigration Act's provision for the deportation of "aliens who are anarchists" and "aliens who advocate or teach, or who are members of or affiliated with any organization that advocates or teaches, opposition to all organized government."[110] President Truman was disgusted. "These provisions are worse than the infamous Alien Act of 1798," he wrote in his veto message. In "empower[ing] the Attorney General to deport any alien who has engaged or has had a purpose to engage in activities 'prejudicial to the public interest' or 'subversive to the national security,'" the act provided "no standards or definitions . . . to guide discretion in the exercise of powers so sweeping. To punish undefined 'activities' departs from traditional American insistence on established standards of guilt. To punish an undefined 'purpose' is thought control."[111]

Again, Truman's veto was overturned.[112] However, as in 1919 and

1920, any actual deportations of "subversives" were held up in the bureaucracy of the executive branch. As Ellen Schrecker notes, "Most of the men and women slated for expulsion because of their communist ties never left the United States. Between 1946 and 1966 only 253 aliens were officially deported as political subversives."[113] This time, there was no one like Louis F. Post to keep the numbers down. Attorney General Tom Clark, whose Department of Justice now oversaw the Immigration and Naturalization Service (INS), had told Congress back in 1948 that he wanted "deportation, through established procedure, of all aliens adhering to subversive principles."[114] His subordinates, FBI Director J. Edgar Hoover and INS Commissioner Watson Miller, shared this view.[115] Truman did not (as his veto indicated), but he would soon be leaving office. The judiciary, for its part, took the same basic stance it had taken during the first Red Scare: essentially, the federal government could deport anyone for whatever reason, so long as the deportation was authorized by legislation and adhered to minimal standards of due process.[116]

In the end, the dampener on deportations came not from a thoughtful executive official or a high-minded judge but, as Schrecker recounts, from "an INS regulation that did not allow it to send undesirable aliens back to their home countries if these countries refused to accept them." Many of these "undesirables" were "Jews from Eastern Europe; and neither the Soviet Union nor the other Eastern Bloc countries would agree to take them back." Thus, "most of the people actually deported were natives of countries friendly to the United States, like Great Britain and Canada."[117]

In short, the deportation provisions of the 1952 McCarran-Walter Act suffered much the same fate as those of the 1918 Immigration Act. Both laws were supported by the attorney general and promised the mass removal of alleged subversives, but neither fully delivered on this promise once they encountered the rules and procedures of the executive branch. The 1950 McCarran Act was similarly toothless in practice. In the early Cold War period, the Smith Act and the Taft-Hartley Act ultimately curtailed civil liberties to the greatest extent.

Vietnam and the War on Terror

Repressive legislation of the early Cold War era was not resurrected in any recognizable form during or after the Vietnam War. One reason for this, as chapter 6 examines in greater depth, is that during the Vietnam War, restrictions on civil liberties were carried out by a variety of executive branch agencies in relative secrecy. Another possible reason is that the American public and their elected representatives no longer tolerated legislation that criminalized sedition, expelled radicals, or compelled allegedly subversive organizations to register with the government. The US Supreme Court also played an important though belated role in this shift. In 1965 it unanimously invalidated the compulsory registration provision of the 1950 McCarran Act as a violation of the Fifth Amendment's privilege against self-incrimination.[118] In 1957 the Supreme Court appeared to back away from its *Dennis* decision when it held that "the Smith Act does not prohibit advocacy and teaching of forcible overthrow of the Government as an abstract principle, divorced from any effort to instigate action to that end."[119] However, in 1961 it upheld the Smith Act conviction of Junius Irving Scales for membership in the CPUSA.[120] In truth, the Smith Act was not decisively laid to rest until 1969, when the Supreme Court ruled that the First Amendment protected all advocacy of illegal or revolutionary conduct that did not amount to an imminent and likely plan of action.[121] The court more cautiously held in 1957 that mere membership in the Communist Party was not sufficient cause for deportation; the government could deport only those having a "meaningful relationship" with the party.[122]

Although neither sedition nor internal security legislation returned to the United States during the Vietnam era, Congress has more recently defined a wide range of nonviolent activities as "material support" for terrorism, thereby effectively criminalizing forms of free association.[123] After the 2001 PATRIOT Act, section 2339b of the federal code defined "material support" as "any property, tangible or intangible, or service, including currency or monetary instruments or financial securities, financial services, lodging, training, expert advice or assistance, safehouses, false documentation or identification, communications equipment, facilities, weapons, lethal substances, explosives, personnel . . . and transportation, except medicine or religious materials."[124] The words "expert advice or assistance" were the key contributions of the US PATRIOT Act, along with heavier legal penalties.[125] The remainder of the definition had been created in 1996 through the Anti-Terrorism and Effective Death Penalty Act (AEDPA), which Congress passed a year to the day after the Oklahoma City bombing. The Humanitarian Law Project

(HLP), a US-based nonprofit organization, sought to enjoin the statute in 1998, suing the Justice Department on the grounds that "material support" was defined so broadly that it threatened nonviolent advocacy, including the legal advice HLP provided to the Liberation Tigers of Tamil Eelam and the Kurdistan Workers Party ("terrorist organizations," according to the State Department's designation). After a "complicated 12-year history," the HLP litigation reached the Supreme Court in 2010, and in *Holder v. Humanitarian Law Project*, the court upheld the material support statute by a 6–3 margin.[126]

The court's opinion, written by Chief Justice John Roberts, argued that the material support statute rationally concluded that almost every association with a "terrorist" group—including something as apparently mundane as providing legal advice—was "fungible": that is, without the need to pay lawyers, the proscribed group could redirect its resources to terrorism. The most alarming potential consequence of this reasoning was that the government could imprison someone under a counterterrorism statute even if they never came anywhere near to committing or plotting an actual act of terrorism.[127]

As of 2023, 54 percent of the 972 people charged with terrorism offenses by the Department of Justice since 9/11 were accused of providing material support.[128] We cannot assume that every material support case involves the type of scenario feared by the HLP. However, cases such as the 2008 material support conviction of the founders and fund-raisers of the Holy Land Foundation (HLF)—the largest Muslim charity in the United States—are cause for concern. The government never provided any evidence that HLF was linked with Hamas (a designated terrorist organization); instead, it argued that HLF's "zakat committees," which provided humanitarian assistance to the Occupied Palestinian Territories, were Hamas "front organizations." "Although these entities performed some legitimate charitable functions," the Fifth Circuit Court of Appeals concluded in 2011, "they were actually Hamas social institutions. By supporting such entities, the defendants facilitated Hamas's activity by furthering its popularity among Palestinians and by providing a funding resource. This, in turn, allowed Hamas to concentrate its efforts on violent activity."[129] The Fifth Circuit upheld the criminal convictions of the "Holy Land Five" and their sentences of between fifteen and sixty-five years in federal prison, and HLF ceased to function.[130] Under *Holder v. Humanitarian Law Project*, this was the correct outcome. Under a precedent giving more weight to the value of free association—which, in other contexts, the Supreme Court has ruled includes donations to charitable or political organizations—the outcome might have been different.[131]

Although advocates of civil liberties during the War on Terror have focused much of their criticism on the 2001 PATRIOT Act, this omnibus law (other components of which are discussed in subsequent chapters) just expanded what was already a material support statute with considerable breadth and reach. The idea that almost everything supplied to a designated "terrorist organization" or "front group" is "fungible" and thus potentially criminal was incorporated into US law by the AEDPA. In any event, both laws are open to the charge that their capacious definitions of "material support" revived the principle of guilt by association that underpinned the sedition and internal security legislation of previous eras. Both are also open to the charge that they were rushed responses to terrorist attacks—with bipartisan and cross-branch support—that did not adequately consider the long-term implications for civil liberties.

The War on Terror also involved several unilateral executive actions that were later ratified by Congress, including the indefinite detention of enemy combatants at the Guantanamo Bay Naval Base and the expansion of government surveillance programs. These actions and the congressional responses to them are discussed in more depth in later chapters. Yet the historical picture developed in this chapter suggests that executive unilateralism in the aftermath of war is unusual and that the legislative foundation for postwar restrictions on civil liberties—particularly during the Andrew Johnson and Harry Truman administrations—can be and has been created despite presidential resistance. Moreover, several laws with ostensibly repressive content have not always been vigorously implemented by the executive branch. Postwar moments do not, in general, seem to be characterized by an "unbound" executive.

2

Independent Tools

Legislation is not a tool that allows Congress to independently exercise power. Even if congressional supermajorities—which are increasingly difficult to find in an era of greater party discipline—can override presidential vetoes, Congress still cannot enforce its own legislation. Hence, as chapter 1 demonstrated, legislation that appears repressive on paper may not be vigorously implemented in practice, as executive officials like Louis F. Post can exercise prosecutorial discretion, or the internal rules and procedures of the executive branch can frustrate the will of Congress.

Yet Congress does possess several tools that it can exercise without executive or, for the most part, judicial involvement. Chief among these is the power to compel testimony before congressional committees. Josh Chafetz calls this the "contempt power," and he demonstrates how it can be wielded—at least in the first instance—by a congressional committee rather than by Congress as a whole. As this chapter argues, the power to hold uncooperative witnesses in contempt is underpinned by various other features of congressional investigations: the potential publicity surrounding them, the absence of a neutral judge that witnesses can appeal to about an objectionable line of questioning, and the fact that members of Congress are constitutionally insulated from any libel lawsuits for accusations they make during congressional speech or debate.

Congress's investigatory powers are limited in two key and related ways. First—in the modern contempt-of-Congress criminal process—although a chamber can issue a contempt citation against an uncooperative witness on the recommendation of a committee, subsequent criminal prosecution (with a potential penalty of one to twelve months in jail or a fine of $100 to $100,000) must be initiated and carried out by the US attorney for the District of Columbia. Second, the US attorney is appointed by the president and works for the Department of Justice. As a result, as Chafetz puts it, "the president is unlikely to authorize one of his subordinates (the United States Attorney) to file charges against another of his subordinates who was acting according to his orders," so "it is safe to assume that the executive branch will generally decline to prosecute an executive branch official for criminal contempt of Congress."[1]

Because of these constraints, a private citizen is much more likely to be successfully prosecuted for contempt of Congress than an executive branch official. Furthermore, as this chapter demonstrates, sometimes a contempt citation alone—or even the unfavorable publicity created by a congressional investigation—can do grave damage to a private citizen. The gravity of this damage depends on the willingness of the wider society to ostracize or render unemployable private citizens who have been accused or harangued by members of Congress. This method of repression was not used by Congress in the nineteenth century but was unleashed in the twentieth. American society was especially willing to ostracize individuals investigated by Congress during the second Red Scare, from approximately 1946 to 1956, when thousands of Americans lost their jobs and livelihoods because of their past or present political affiliations. This period naturally occupies a large portion of this chapter.

The first Red Scare prefigured these methods, albeit to a much lesser degree. In 1919 a special subcommittee of the Senate Judiciary Committee, chaired by Lee Overman (D-NC), investigated "Bolshevik propaganda" in the United States, and its star witness, Archibald E. Stevenson, publicly named a long list of alleged members of the "Bolsheviki movement." It is difficult to measure the impact of this subcommittee on civil liberties. Compared to that of the permanent, well-staffed investigating committees of the post–World War II period, the impact must have been slight. Nevertheless, during the first Red Scare, Congress exercised other independent powers that served to disenfranchise Socialist Party voters and to build public pressure for the mass deportation of "radicals." It disenfranchised Socialist Party voters by twice refusing to seat their elected representative for Wisconsin's Fifth Congressional District, Victor L. Berger, in 1919 and 1920, claiming that his opposition to US involvement in the First World War rendered him ineligible for office under section 3 of the Fourteenth Amendment to the Constitution.

Congress also built public pressure for mass deportations through the Poindexter Resolution of October 1919, which condemned the Department of Justice for not acting fast enough to remove foreign-born "radicals" from American soil. All these powers—to conduct investigations, create committees, pass resolutions expressing the will of the chamber, and determine the qualifications of members—can, according to either the letter or the spirit of the Constitution, be exercised independently by a single chamber of Congress.

The power to refuse to seat—or, with two-thirds of a chamber, to expel—members was essential to the imposition of martial law on the former Confederacy during Reconstruction. Both chambers of Congress exercised this power in December 1865 to deny seats to the former Confederate states that had been initially reconstructed by President Andrew Johnson. Reconstruction would not have been possible with these representatives and senators in Congress. Throughout 1866—and certainly into 1867 and 1868—President Johnson increasingly questioned the legitimacy of acts passed by this "rump" Congress. Yet he could not force Congress to readmit the ex-Confederate delegations.

I conclude the chapter by discussing whether and to what extent Congress can still use its independent powers to curtail civil liberties. Some independent congressional powers have seemingly receded into historical memory. The War on Terror, for instance, has not led to the creation of another House Un-American Activities Committee or to the exclusion or expulsion of members who criticized the conduct of the wars in Iraq and Afghanistan.

However, it would be naïve to assume that apparently dead practices cannot or will not be resurrected. When I wrote my doctoral dissertation in 2022, I described section 3 of the Fourteenth Amendment—which was used to deny Victor L. Berger his seat in the House of Representatives—as "long-neglected." Yet in 2024 it was used by a state court and a state secretary of state to remove a presidential candidate from the ballot. These attempts, which were ultimately nullified by the US Supreme Court,[2] may have been justified by the text, history, and structure of section 3 and by Donald Trump's conduct before, during, and after January 6, 2021.[3] But the fact that these attempts were made at all suggests that something like the exclusion of an elected candidate from Congress or the presidency under section 3—justified or unjustified—is not inconceivable in the future.

The same can be said for congressional McCarthyism. Although the War on Terror did not revive public investigations of "un-American activities," Israel's war against Gaza, begun in response to the terrorist attacks of October 7, 2023, generated something of a McCarthyite atmosphere in Congress. The House of Representatives censured its only Palestinian American member, Rashida Tlaib (D-MI), on November 7 for "promoting false narratives" about the October 7 attacks and "calling for the destruction of the state of Israel"—accusations based on distortions of Tlaib's actual statements.[4] In December the House Committee on Education and the Workforce—especially Elise Stefanik (R-NY)—grilled the presidents of Harvard, the Massachusetts Institute of Technology (MIT), and the University of Pennsylvania on their alleged failure to combat anti-Semitism on their campuses. After all three rather reluctantly pointed out that even genocidal rhetoric is protected under the First Amendment unless it is part of an actual plan of illegal activity or harassment of individuals, Stefanik called for their resignations and got two out of three, with the aid of significant pressure from university alumni and donors.[5] This process of congressional taint followed by private sanction closely resembles the legislative McCarthyism of the early Cold War era.

In other words, the historical examples in this chapter are just that: historical examples. They are not necessarily a good guide to the present or the future. Nonetheless, they demonstrate how Congress's independent powers have been used to constrain civil liberties in the aftermath of war. Even though the US Supreme Court has curbed some of these powers, they remain part of the congressional tool kit as potentially potent weapons of disenfranchisement, censorship, and intimidation.

Exclusions, Expulsions, and Reconstruction

This much seems clear: without the power to exclude and expel its own members, in December 1865 Congress would have been burdened with a cadre of Southerners who—at best—were willing to formally abolish slavery and forswear secession but largely continue the slave-based social and economic system in a slightly modified form. In fact, Congress would have been burdened with twenty-seven more Southerners than it had prior to the Civil War. Under the Constitution, slave states were allowed to count three out of every five slaves toward their House and

Electoral College apportionments, but with slavery abolished, every single freedman could be counted, no matter how awfully the former slave was treated.[6]

Between May 29 and July 13, 1865, when Congress was not in session, President Andrew Johnson had appointed provisional governors to the former Confederate states. These governors were tasked with overseeing constitutional conventions and fresh elections to the state legislatures on the condition that the states repudiated secession and Confederate debt, abolished slavery, and pledged their loyalty to the Union. The military was tasked with "aid[ing] and assist[ing] the said provisional governor" in this effort and was "enjoined to abstain from, in any way, hindering, impeding, or discouraging the loyal people from the organization of a State government."[7] By December, the president was satisfied that this job was complete.

Congress, however, was receiving sobering reports from the South. Although General Ulysses S. Grant painted a generally optimistic picture of the former Confederacy during a brief tour of the South at the end of 1865, he believed that "four years of War, during which law was executed only at the point of the bayonet, throughout the states in rebellion, has left the people possibly in a condition not to yield that ready obedience to civil authority the American people have generally been in the habit of yielding." Because of this obedience deficit, "small garrisons throughout the states" would be "necessary until such time as labor returns to its proper channel and civil authority is fully established." "I did not meet any one," he added, "either those holding place under the Government or citizens of the Southern States who think it practicable to withdraw the Military force from the South at present. The white and black mutually require the protection of the General Government."[8] "A great number of murders are committed in almost every portion of the State where there are negroes," Major General Peter J. Osterhaus wrote from Vicksburg, Mississippi. There was "hardly an instance in which the offender was arrested by the civil authorities. It is altogether a very mysterious affair."[9] Former General Carl Schurz bluntly concluded after his tour of the South that "the people are not yet in a fit condition to legislate."[10]

Although President Johnson believed Southerners were ready to return to Congress and to civil government, evidence of continual lawlessness in the South, along with the obvious practical problem of additional

Southern representatives, given the death of the three-fifths clause, convinced an overwhelming majority of sitting representatives and senators otherwise. Consequently, they decided to exclude the Southerners with the assistance of the clerk of the House of Representatives, Edward McPherson, on December 4, 1865—the first day of the first full session of the Thirty-Ninth Congress. When McPherson simply called the roll without acknowledging the representatives from the former Confederate states, Congressman James Brooks (D-NY) objected, particularly to the clerk's refusal to recognize "the honorable gentleman from Tennessee." He reasoned, "if Tennessee is not in the Union, and is not a loyal state, and the people of Tennessee are aliens and foreigners to this Union, by what right does the President of the United States usurp his place in the White House and in the capital of the country when an alien, as he must be, a foreigner, and not from a State in the Union?" Brooks went on to ask, "by what right has the Virginia delegation been excluded by the Clerk of the House?"[11] Elliptically, the clerk replied, "if it be the desire of the House to have my reasons, I will give them; but I have not felt justified or called upon to give any reasons; I have acted in accordance with my views of duty, and I am willing to let the record stand." "It is not necessary," Thaddeus Stevens replied. "We know all."[12]

Stevens then introduced a resolution to establish a Joint Committee on Reconstruction to determine on what terms the Southern delegations would be allowed to return to both the House and the Senate.[13] In its final form, this joint committee was composed of fifteen members: nine representatives and six senators, of whom twelve were Republicans and three were Democrats. The chairman was Senator William Pitt Fessenden (R-ME), who was generally regarded as a conservative figure—much more conservative, for sure, than Stevens, who was also a member of the joint committee. Its official charge was "to inquire into the condition of the States which formed the so-called Confederate States of America, and report whether they or any of them are entitled to be represented in either house of Congress."[14]

As Mark Graber clarifies, the Joint Committee on Reconstruction did not explicitly invoke Article I, Section 5, of the Constitution when deciding to exclude the ex-Confederate states from Congress because congressional Republicans believed this section allowed them only to determine the qualifications of individual members. The ex-Confederate states were excluded, instead, because Congress had the authority, largely derived from the republican guarantee clause of Article IV, to govern the ex-Confederate states directly until they established a satisfactory "Republican form of government."[15] In June 1866, after documenting the dire condition of the ex-Confederate states, the committee emphatically declared that those states had "voluntarily deprived themselves of representation in Congress for the criminal purpose of destroying the federal Union." As a result, "the burden now rests upon them, before claiming to be reinstated in their former condition, to show that they are qualified to resume federal relations."[16] The committee stated that it welcomed President Johnson's views on Reconstruction, but "it was not for him to decide upon the nature or effect of any system of government which the people of these States might see fit to adopt." Rather, "this power is lodged by the Constitution in the Congress of the United States, that branch of the government in which is vested the authority to fix the political relations of the States to the Union, whose duty it is to guarantee to each State a republican form of government."[17]

This theory of exclusion quoted directly from the Constitution's republican guarantee clause.[18] Other theories had been floating around the Republican Party, including the idea that Congress could treat the ex-Confederate states as if they were territorial possessions. Territorialization was too extreme for conservative Republicans like Fessenden because this would give Congress total and indefinite control over the affairs of the former Confederacy.[19] Nevertheless, the conservatives on the joint committee did accept what seemed at first like an even more extreme proposition: that the "conquered rebels" should be "at the mercy of the conquerors."[20] Under this theory, Congress could hold the South in what Republican lawyer Richard Henry Dana called "the grasp of war" until the federal government "secured whatever it has a right to acquire."[21]

This maneuver may have been unconstitutional, as the Supreme Court would suggest more than a century later. In 1969, in *Powell v. McCormack*, Chief Justice Earl Warren wrote for an 8–1 Supreme Court that Congress cannot exclude duly elected members for reasons other than enumerated constitutional disqualifications because the principle of representative government is "undermined as much by limiting whom the people can select as by limiting the franchise itself."[22] Under this standard, the exclusion of ex-Confederates based on the republican guarantee clause or the "grasp of war" theory was arguably unconstitutional, at least until section 3 of the Fourteenth Amendment was ratified in 1868.[23] Warren argued in *Powell* that legislative expulsions and exclusions—for any reason not predefined in the Constitution—are potentially repressive acts for the simple reason that they can effectively allow Congress to dissolve the people—at least in one district—and elect a new one. The right of electors to choose their representatives was one of the "ancient liberties" cherished by the framers of the US Constitution, who were outraged and galvanized by the many expulsions and exclusions of John Wilkes from the British Parliament between 1768 and 1782. More pointedly, as Justice William O. Douglas asked in his *Powell* concurrence: if "the electors choose a person who is repulsive to the Establishment in Congress, by what constitutional authority can that group of electors be disenfranchised?"[24]

Warren and Douglas were applying these arguments to the case of Harlem Congressman Adam Clayton Powell, who had been excluded from the House because of allegations that he "had misappropriated public funds and abused the process of the New York courts."[25] Readers might be more inclined to sympathize with Powell than with representatives and senators from former Confederate states who stood unapologetically for the principle of a white man's government. Yet, for readers so inclined, the honest conclusion would be not to deny that some elementary principles of representative government were curtailed in December 1865 but rather that they were curtailed for noble reasons.

The expulsion power was also used by Congress on one notable occasion during Reconstruction. When the white members of the Georgia state legislature expelled their black colleagues just two months after the state's restoration to Congress in 1868, federal legislators promptly reexpelled Georgia's congressional delegation and, following escalating reports of Ku Klux Klan violence in the state, reimposed martial law. Commander Alfred H. Terry reinstated the state's black lawmakers but then, continuing the expulsion frenzy, threw six ex-Confederate senators out of the state legislature. Georgia was re-reconstructed (or, if we count the first attempt by Andrew Johnson in 1865, re-re-reconstructed) in February 1871. After all that, Democrats regained control of the state legislature and the governorship—with the aid of violence and intimidation—in 1871. By 1872, Georgia was "redeemed."[26]

No other state had Georgia's back-and-forth experience. The Constitution does allow "each House" to "determine the Rules of its

Proceedings," "punish its Members for disorderly Behaviour," and determine the qualifications of its members, but expulsion requires "the Concurrence of two thirds."[27] By 1870, such a process was procedurally and politically difficult, especially as Republican lawmakers became increasingly exhausted by the financial commitments of Reconstruction and increasingly uncomfortable with the continual exclusion of Southern representatives from Congress five years after Appomattox.[28]

The Exclusion of Victor Berger and the Poindexter-Palmer Raids

The next time Congress used the exclusion power in the aftermath of war was in 1919. Victor L. Berger, who cofounded the Socialist Party of America with Eugene Debs and was elected as the first Socialist Party member of Congress, representing Wisconsin's Fifth District, in 1910, was not in good company in 1919. After losing the 1912, 1914, and 1916 elections, he won again in 1918, despite (or perhaps because of) being under indictment for violating the Espionage Act. In January 1919 Berger was convicted and sentenced to twenty years in prison—basically for the same reason other prominent socialists such as Debs, Rose Pastor Stokes, and Charles Schenck were persecuted: for opposing American involvement in the First World War. Released on bail while his appeal was heard in higher federal courts, Berger "presented himself before the speaker's desk on May 9, 1919, to be sworn in," but "Representative Frederick W. Dallinger of Massachusetts challenged his right to a seat, whereupon a resolution was offered and passed without dissent, suspending Berger from all rights as a member of the House until final action was taken."[29]

This "final action" was to be decided by a special committee that held hearings, with Berger present, between June 11 and September 16. In October eight of the nine members of the committee concluded that Berger "obstruct[ed], hinder[ed], and embarrass[ed] the Government of the United States in the prosecution of the war and did give aid and comfort to the enemy." Therefore—and because he had previously taken an oath of office under the United States—he was rendered ineligible for office under section 3 of the Fourteenth Amendment. The only dissenting member of the committee wanted to delay judgment until Berger's Espionage Act appeal was complete. The full House of Representatives debated and voted on the special committee's recommendations on

November 10. Dallinger recounted Berger's wartime activities with the Socialist Party and told the House:

> The men who framed our Constitution in 1787 never had the faintest idea that any constituency in this country would deliberately and intentionally choose as a Representative in the Congress of the United States a man who, when the country was at war, fighting for its existence—because counsel for Mr. Berger admitted before our committee that he believed that if England and France had been annihilated our turn would have come next—say, if they had had any idea that any constituency would choose a man who had done everything he could do to destroy the Government, they would have undoubtedly placed an express provision in the Constitution making such a thing impossible. But there is an unbroken line of precedents in this House. This House has excluded men for various reasons and has always insisted upon its right to exclude.[30]

Berger, in a lengthy response, warned the House that "it may depend upon your decision in this case to a great extent whether the common people are to lose all faith in political election and representative government—whether they are to turn to 'direct action' and 'soviets.'" "Remember, gentlemen," he concluded, "you may exclude me once. You may exclude me twice. But the fifth district of Wisconsin can not permit you to dictate what kind of a man is to represent it. If representative government shall survive, you will see me or a man of my kind—let us hope many men of my kind—in the Nation's Legislature. Therefore, whatever decision you may make, I will just say 'Au revoir.'"[31]

Berger was, in the end, excluded twice. After the House overwhelmingly voted for his initial exclusion, he won the special election for his vacant seat and was excluded again when he returned to the House on January 10, 1920. On this occasion, Dallinger was somewhat defensive. "No objection is raised to Victor L. Berger now because he is a member of the Socialist Party or because of his political or economic views," he argued. "Objection has been made and is now being made because in 1911 he took a solemn oath as a Member of Congress to support the Constitution of the United States and to defend it against all enemies, foreign and domestic, and then when war was declared he deliberately gave aid and comfort to the enemies of his country." Although "it is said that the people of the fifth district of the State of Wisconsin have a right to choose anyone they see fit as a Member of Congress and to have him seated . . . if they persist in electing a man whom the House has found is ineligible under [the] Constitution, they can not expect to have him seated." Just "because he has constituents un-American enough that they approve his infamy," Congressman Joe Eagle (D-TX) added, the House should not have to "allow to sit in your company one who, at the time the Nation's destiny was at stake, struck in the interest of the Central Empires treacherously against the flag that protected him." Berger's second exclusion vote went slightly better for him than the first, with six votes in his favor instead of only one.[32]

Berger was finally seated in December 1921 after winning election to the Fifth District and after the US Supreme Court invalidated his original Espionage Act conviction—not on free speech grounds but on the grounds that the trial judge, having shown evidence of personal bias against the defendant, should have recused himself from the case.[33] In the 1969 *Powell v. McCormack* case, which so emphatically compared exclusion from Congress to disenfranchisement, the case of Victor Berger earned only a footnote, which read: "[The House of Representatives] twice excluded Victor L. Berger, an avowed Socialist, for giving aid 'and comfort to the enemy.' Significantly, the House committee investigating Berger concluded that he was ineligible under the express provision of §3 of the Fourteenth Amendment."[34] The implication of this is clear: whereas Adam Clayton Powell's exclusion lacked a textual foundation and was therefore unconstitutional, Victor Berger's had at least some basis in the text of the Constitution. At any rate, Berger's exclusion was certainly not condemned by the Supreme Court. Therefore, even though Berger eventually won his fight, there is no legal or constitutional barrier to a house of Congress using section 3 of the Fourteenth Amendment to make another Victor Berger in the future.

In addition to Berger's exclusions from the House, the Senate fomented the first Red Scare through two independent powers. First, it created a special subcommittee of the Senate Judiciary Committee—chaired by Lee Overman (D-NC)—to investigate "Bolshevik propaganda" in February and March 1919. Created under a Senate resolution passed near the end of the war, the Overman Subcommittee was initially charged with publicizing the links between "brewing and liquor interests and German propaganda" and published a 2,975-page report on this subject.[35] Senate Resolution 439, passed on February 4, 1919, authorized Overman to expand his remit to "any efforts being made to propagate in this country the principles of any party exercising or claiming to exercise authority in Russia," particularly if those principles involved "any effort to incite the overthrow of the Government of this country."[36]

For its new assignment, Overman's subcommittee heard from twenty-five witnesses.[37] Arguably, the most important was a witness who had testified in the earlier hearings related to the brewing industry. Archibald E. Stevenson called himself "a special agent in the Department of Justice, Bureau of Investigation," and claimed that "the Bolsheviki movement is a branch of the revolutionary socialism of Germany." He proceeded to name organizations and individuals in the United States that allegedly sympathized with that movement. These included Roger Baldwin and Albert de Silver of the National Civil Liberties Bureau, Morris Hillquit and Victor L. Berger of the Socialist Party, and various editors of foreign-language newspapers.[38] With the exception of Berger, Congress did not take any direct action against the individuals named by Stevenson, partly because the Overman Subcommittee held hearings for only a short period and partly because several of the individuals were already in prison for violating the Espionage Act. More generally, the subcommittee was preoccupied with the subject of the Bolshevik Revolution itself, Bolshevik literature in the United States, and the nature of the new revolutionary government in Russia.[39]

A likely more impactful action by the Senate was the 1919 Poindexter Resolution. This resolution, authored by presidential aspirant Senator Miles Poindexter (R-WA), publicly denounced A. Mitchell Palmer's Justice Department in October 1919 for its hesitancy in implementing the Immigration Act of 1918.[40] The Poindexter Resolution demanded that Palmer "advise and inform the Senate [of] the reason for the failure of the Department of Justice to take legal proceedings for the arrest and punishment of the various persons within the United States who . . . have attempted to bring about the forcible overthrow of the Government of the United States." In particular, "the Attorney General is requested to advise and inform the Senate why the Department of Justice has failed to take legal proceedings for the arrest and deportation of aliens who, it is alleged, have . . . committed the acts aforesaid."[41] Although some of Palmer's Democratic allies feared that the Poindexter Resolution "conveys the idea that there has been a neglect of duty or a failure to perform duty on the part of the Attorney General," the Senate passed it on October 17.[42]

Palmer, who had assumed the office of attorney general in March, finally acted in November, conducting the first multicity raid on the Union of Russian Workers. "I was being shouted at from every editorial sanction in America," he later reflected. "I was preached upon from every pulpit; I was urged—I could feel it dinned in my ears—throughout the country to do something and do it now, and do it quick, and do it in a way that would bring results to stop this sort of thing in the United States."[43] His tone was different in the immediate aftermath of the November raids. He reveled in the opportunity to write a formal reply to the Poindexter Resolution on November 14, in which he described his raids and blamed Congress for not giving him the funds to carry them out sooner.[44]

Which Palmer should we believe? The retrospective Palmer was aware of the bad press the raids received in the 1920s, so he was eager to downplay his role in them. The Palmer of November 1919 was biting back against senators who had publicly embarrassed him, so he was eager to blame them for delays and claim as much personal credit as possible. We can be sure that Poindexter did not give Palmer the idea for the raids. J. Edgar Hoover, head of the Department of Justice's General Intelligence Division (colloquially called the Radical Division), had been planning for a possible roundup of radicals since he assumed office in August 1919.[45] Still, in her recent biography of Hoover, Beverly Gage gives the impression that both Hoover and Palmer acted under pressure from Poindexter. "Despite Hoover's memo writing and file processing, despite Palmer's grandiose promises, by October 1919 there were no deportations," Gage writes. Only after Poindexter condemned the Justice Department did Hoover and Palmer act.[46]

Palmer was likely to be susceptible to pressure from Poindexter. Like Poindexter, Palmer was planning to seek his party's nomination for the 1920 presidential contest.[47] Palmer did not want to concede the antiradical mantle to his potential rival for the highest office in the country, especially after antiradicalism—or at least antisocialism—seemed to play so well for Republicans during the 1918 election campaign, when Henry Cabot Lodge, the preeminent Senate Republican from Massachusetts, accused President Wilson of surrounding himself with "socialists and Bolsheviks"; Will Hays, the national Republican Party chairman, called for "just restriction of the present socialistic tendency in our government"; and former President Theodore Roosevelt and Senator Poindexter piled on with criticisms of the government's willingness to accept something short of unconditional surrender from Germany.[48]

The political fight between Palmer and Poindexter continued after the November raids. Poindexter and other Republicans claimed that they had forced Palmer into action; Palmer repeated his claim that he would have acted earlier if not for a stingy Congress. More raids followed in January 1920.[49] This political context has great bearing on the extent to which we agree with the view—expressed by several scholars of civil liberties in the United States—that the Palmer Raids were an abuse of executive power.[50] The Palmer Raids were legally sanctioned by Congress, and Senate Republicans, especially Poindexter, were goading Palmer to act. The raids may or may not have happened without the legislative clamor for them. But the fact that there *was* legislative clamor, especially in the Senate, should at least cause us to see the raids as something larger than the personal project of A. Mitchell Palmer. Perhaps we might go so far as to rename them the Poindexter-Palmer Raids.

The Second Red Scare

During the second Red Scare, the independent authority of each house of Congress to create committees and grant them far-reaching investigatory powers did significant damage to civil liberties. The clearest example of this was the "extraordinary career" of the House Un-American Activities Committee (HUAC).[51]

HUAC, in its original, temporary form, was created on May 26, 1938, when Texas Democrat Martin Dies presented a House resolution proposing "a special committee to be composed of seven members for the purpose of conducting an investigation of (1) the extent, character, and objects of un-American propaganda activities in the United States, (2) the diffusion within the United States of subversive and un-American propaganda that is instigated from foreign countries or of a domestic origin and attacks the principle of the form of government as guaranteed by our Constitution, and (3) all other questions in relation thereto that would aid Congress in any necessary remedial legislation." This "special committee, or any subcommittee thereof," would also be "authorized to sit and act" anywhere in the United States and at any time "to hold such hearings, to require the attendance of such witnesses and the production of such books, papers, and documents, by subpoena or otherwise, and to take such testimony as it deems necessary." These subpoenas "shall be issued under the signature of the chairman and shall be served by any person designated by him." If a subpoena was not complied with, the chairman could refer the matter to the House for a contempt-of-Congress citation, which in turn would be referred to the US attorney in the District of Columbia for criminal prosecution.[52]

"I have absolutely no patience with any effort in this country to abridge the rights of speech," Congressman Dies told his colleagues. But "I have a mass of information that has been supplied to me that is shocking, information which shows the extent of the Nazi and Communist movements in the United States." He added, "I regard Communism and Nazism and Fascism as having one underlying principle," and that principle is "dictatorship—the theory that government should have the right to control the lives, the fortunes, the happiness, the beliefs, and every detail of the life of the human being, and that man is a pawn of the government, rather than the American conception that government is created for the benefit of mankind."[53]

The emphasis on both Nazism and communism was crucial to winning the support of liberals in Congress, who feared that Dies was setting up "a smelling expedition aimed at liberal organizations in the United States." More bluntly, Rules Committee Chairman John J. O'Connor (D-NY) concluded the May 26 HUAC debate with a call to "save this country . . . from this horde of radicals, this horde of Communists, before the hour becomes too late." The Dies Resolution passed by a vote of 191 to 41.[54]

Martin Dies became the chairman of HUAC, and HUAC became known as the Dies Committee. Dies initially showed some interest in domestic Nazis, "issuing a subpoena to the pro-German propagandist, George Sylvester Viereck" in August 1938 "upon learning that Viereck was about to pay a call to Adolf Hitler."[55] Dies then aired the claims of John P. Frey, chair of the Metal Trades Department of the American Federation of Labor, who alleged that the Congress of Industrial Organizations had been infiltrated by communists. Similar claims were made about the Federal Theatre and Writers Project within the Works Progress Administration. Dies accused Labor Secretary Frances Perkins of shielding the Australian-born president of the International Longshoremen and Warehousemen's Union, Harry Bridges, from deportation for his open communist affiliations.[56]

The Dies Committee's focus on the Left, rather than the Right, was accelerated by the Molotov-Ribbentrop Pact in August 1939. Dies, who had justified the committee's creation on the theory that communism and fascism were two sides of the same coin, claimed vindication when he saw Hitler and Stalin collaborating in the dismemberment of Poland. His cause was helped by the "disarray" the Molotov-Ribbentrop Pact sowed within the American communist movement, as Stalinists toed the party line and anti-Stalinists abhorred any accommodation with Nazism.[57]

For the remainder of the war, the Dies Committee mainly punched left. In February 1941 the ACLU accused Dies of "indiscriminately attack[ing] liberal and labor movements"; "conceiv[ing] un-American activities primarily in terms of the Communist movement" rather than "Nazis and Fascists"; "hear[ing] an array of accusers with little or no opportunity for the accused to reply"; "smearing" Eleanor Roosevelt, Vice President Henry Wallace, Attorney General Robert Jackson, and Interior Secretary Harold Ickes as communist sympathizers; and intervening "in the election campaigns in Michigan, Minnesota and California in a manner calculated to defeat New Deal candidates."[58]

It was not inevitable that HUAC would outlast the Second World War. Unlike standing committees, which were permanent, the Dies Committee had to be reauthorized every year. By 1945, its entire existence was in doubt. Dies himself—who was exhausted and unwell after fourteen years in the House—had not run for reelection in 1944, and that year's elections brought more liberal Democrats into both houses of Congress. The end of the war was in sight. The end of HUAC—a product of the war—seemed possible.[59]

Yet on the first day of the Seventy-Ninth Congress in January 1945, Mississippi Democrat John Rankin—who had sat on the Dies Committee in the previous Congress—maneuvered to save and entrench HUAC. The first order of business for each house is usually adopting the rules of the previous Congress, subject to minor amendments. However, when Congressman Adolph Sabath (D-IL) moved "that the rules of the seventy-eighth Congress be adopted . . . as the rules of the seventy-ninth," Rankin proposed an amendment to "extend the life of the Committee on Un-American Activities . . . and to make it one of the standing committees of the House." This would allow HUAC to "report legislation in order that its recommendations may be brought to the floor of the House for consideration in the regular way." HUAC had done "marvelous work" throughout the war, Rankin added. "It is no time to relax our vigilance."[60]

Sabath objected, saying that a matter of such substance should be considered by the Rules Committee before coming to the floor. "I do not know when in the history of our country the National House of Representatives has ever provided by rule for a permanent investigating committee," Massachusetts Democrat John William McCormack protested. But Rankin pressed for a roll-call vote, and the amendment succeeded by a margin of 208 to 186.[61] Voting aye were "137 Republicans and 70 Democrats, 63 of them from the South."[62] The entrenchment of HUAC met more opposition than its creation (186 no votes in 1945, 41 in 1938), but the bottom line was that Rankin's parliamentary maneuver not only saved HUAC from extinction but also made it permanent.

HUAC was further bolstered by the 1946 Legislative Reorganization Act (LRA), which Truman signed into law on August 2. The LRA was, in Roger Davidson's words, "the most ambitious, comprehensive, and publicized reorganization effort in the history of Congress." Reformers both inside and outside Congress had long bemoaned the messy committee system, which was beset by overlapping and confused jurisdictions, unclear responsibilities, and ill-defined powers. The LRA grappled with these problems by reducing the number of standing committees in both houses and increasing their staffing. The LRA was not intended to strengthen HUAC specifically, but because HUAC was now a standing committee, it stood to benefit from the broader strengthening of standing committees under the LRA.[63] "Rankin's coup" in making HUAC permanent was thus ratified.[64]

As a permanent standing committee, HUAC's first chairman was New Jersey Democrat Edward J. Hart, but he was soon replaced by John S. Wood of Georgia. The other members were Rankin, Herbert C. Bonner (D-NC), John R. Murdock (D-AZ), J. Hardin Peterson (D-FL), J. W. Robinson (D-UT), Gerald W. Landis (R-IN), Karl E. Mundt (R-SD), and J. Parnell Thomas (R-NJ). Mundt, Thomas, and Rankin soon emerged as the most enthusiastic proponents of a postwar Red Scare. In 1946 they set their sights particularly firmly on the Joint Anti-Fascist Refugee Committee (JAFRC), which was founded by Dr. Edward K. Barsky to provide humanitarian aid to refugees of the Spanish Civil War and became a consistent voice of opposition to the Franco dictatorship thereafter. There was never any evidence that the JAFRC participated in Soviet espionage, but there were certainly communists in the anti-Franco movement. This was enough to earn the JAFRC a charge of un-Americanism and to earn each of its sixteen executive board members and its secretary subpoenas from HUAC in late March. These subpoenas summoned the board members to testify before HUAC and "to bring with you all books, ledgers, records, and papers relating to the receipt and disbursement of any money by or on account of the [JAFRC] . . . together with all correspondence and memoranda of communications by any means whatsoever with persons in foreign countries."[65]

The JAFRC leaders appeared before HUAC on April 4, 1946. Helen R. Bryan, JAFRC secretary and custodian of the documents requested by the committee, bluntly told Rankin that "the subpoena was not valid" because it was so broad as to constitute a fishing expedition. In response, Mundt moved "that we cite all witnesses who have appeared before us today as being in contempt of Congress." The motion carried, and the House of Representatives referred the matter for criminal prosecution.[66]

This was the beginning of JAFRC's slow and painful death. As Phillip Deery recounts:

> The JAFRC was the first to be subpoenaed by HUAC [in its permanent form], the first to challenge its legitimacy, and the first to set the pattern for Cold War inquisitions. In 1950, after three years of unsuccessful legal appeals, the Committee's entire Executive Board was jailed. Barsky received the most severe sentence. It was the biggest single incarceration of political prisoners in America during the early Cold War. Upon release, Barsky lost his right to practice medicine. By early 1955, the JAFRC had dissolved: like Barsky's career, it had been crippled by McCarthyism.[67]

By my count, based on HUAC's annual reports, HUAC cited 147 people for contempt between 1946 and 1964.[68] Many had similar stories to Dr. Barsky and the JAFRC. In 1947 HUAC famously investigated the communist infiltration of Hollywood and held ten noncooperative witnesses in contempt: the "Hollywood Ten."[69] Apart from their criminal prosecution for contempt of Congress, the case of the Hollywood Ten inspired the November 1947 Waldorf Statement, in which Hollywood's leading film executives announced that they "deplore the action of the 10 Hollywood men who have been cited for contempt by the House of Representatives. We do not desire to prejudge their legal rights, but their actions have been a disservice to their employers and have impaired their usefulness to the industry." The executives then pledged to either fire or refuse to hire the Hollywood Ten or any other communist. This may have been the birth of the "official" Hollywood blacklist, but as Arthur Eckstein puts it, "the blacklist also occurred unofficially through instruments such as the irresponsible red-baiting newsletter *Red Channels*, which named whole swathes of people as subversives; this led, for example, to the ruin of the career of the left-wing but non-Communist actress Marsha Hunt." Moreover, "the blacklist often functioned in secret: jobs just dried up."[70]

The Hollywood blacklist was an example of how a contempt-of-Congress citation could prompt private sanctions and thus chill and suppress free political association without the need to put anyone on trial or throw anyone in prison. After the "fall of China" and the first Soviet nuclear test in 1949, as well as the outbreak of the Korean War in 1950, Senator Joseph McCarthy further illustrated the severe professional consequences that could result from an accusation by an individual member of Congress. Owen Lattimore was denied tenure at Johns Hopkins University and ostracized from American public life after McCarthy accused him—first in 1950—of doing "incalculable and irreparable harm" to the United States by advising the State Department to adopt a pro-communist policy during the Chinese Civil War and in East Asian affairs more broadly.[71] "I submit," McCarthy stated, "that the background of Mr. Lattimore, his close collaboration and affiliation with numerous Communist organizations; his friendship and close cooperation with pro-Communist individuals, leaves absolutely no doubt that he is an extremely bad security risk."[72] McCarthy and Senator Pat McCarran (D-NV) leveled similar accusations at the Institute of Pacific Relations (IPR) in 1951. IPR then "lost most of its financial support from corporations and foundations after 1952, lost (and several years later regained) its tax-exempt status as an educational body, and dissolved itself (along with its American Council) at the end of 1960."[73]

Overall, it is hard to measure how many people were either fired or rendered unemployable during the "age of McCarthyism"—something of a misnomer, given the obvious fact that this age both predated and outlasted the career of McCarthy. Given the breadth and depth of testimony in industries ranging from Hollywood to higher education and from individual schoolteachers to dockworkers, the number must be several thousand at least.[74] Regardless of the total number, there is no doubt that employers across the United States considered a congressional allegation of disloyalty—either a contempt citation or an accusation by a prominent member of Congress—solid grounds for dismissal or refusal to hire. And as chapter 5 illustrates, state legislative investigating committees saw these allegations as a valuable guidepost for their own localized McCarthyism.

Congressional McCarthyism After HUAC

HUAC was not formally abolished until 1975. Well before then, however, congressional accusations of disloyalty stopped generating anything like the harsh private sanctions and career consequences they caused in 1946–56. Another HUAC was not created in the aftermath of the Vietnam War, the 9/11 terror attacks, or the invasions of Iraq and Afghanistan. It is possible that the political and legal culture of the United States has evolved, rendering the methods of HUAC and Senator McCarthy unacceptable at either the mass or the elite level.[75]

It is also possible that the Supreme Court's belated efforts to curtail McCarthyism played a role in its long-term interment. Chief among these efforts was *Watkins v. United States*, a 1957 case in which Chief Justice Earl Warren (writing for a 6–1 court) forcefully described the impact of McCarthyite congressional investigations on civil liberties:

> Abuses of the investigative process may imperceptibly lead to abridgment of protected freedoms. The mere summoning of a witness and compelling him to testify, against his will, about his beliefs, expressions or associations is a measure of governmental interference. And when those forced revelations concern matters that are unorthodox, unpopular, or even hateful to the general public, the reaction in the life of the witness may be disastrous. This effect is even more harsh when it is past beliefs, expressions or associations that are disclosed and judged by current standards rather than those contemporary with the matters exposed. Nor does the witness alone suffer the consequences. Those who are identified by witnesses and thereby placed in the same glare of publicity are equally subject to public stigma, scorn and obloquy. Beyond that, there is the more subtle and immeasurable effect upon those who tend to adhere to the most orthodox and uncontroversial views and associations in order to avoid a similar fate at some future time. That this impact is partly the

result of non-governmental activity by private persons cannot relieve the investigators of their responsibility for initiating the reaction.

"We have no doubt," Warren wrote, "that there is no congressional power to expose for the sake of exposure."[76]

Yet these lofty words obscured the narrowness of the court's actual ruling in the *Watkins* case. Watkins's conviction for contempt of Congress was not overturned because his rights of free political association were violated or his career or reputation ruined. Instead, Watkins won because he had been insufficiently informed of which questions were pertinent to the committee's inquiry; therefore, he was "not accorded a fair opportunity to determine whether he was within his rights in refusing to answer, and his conviction is necessarily invalid under the Due Process Clause of the Fifth Amendment."[77] Indeed, under *Watkins*, the Supreme Court explicitly rejected a free association defense against a HUAC contempt citation and prosecution in 1959. This led Justice Hugo Black to furiously dissent that "legislative committees" should not "be allowed to punish if they grant the accused some rules of courtesy or allow him counsel. For the Constitution proscribes all bills of attainder by State or Nation, not merely those which lack counsel or courtesy."[78]

Black's view has never been adopted by the Supreme Court. It is easy to understand why: such a view would invite significant judicial intrusion into the internal processes and powers of Congress. Today, the primary constraints on congressional investigations of private individuals are self-restraint by Congress itself, executive noncooperation, and public opinion. In general, some combination of these constraints has seemingly worked against the reemergence of the kind of congressional McCarthyism that existed in the 1940s and 1950s.

However, particularly under the first Trump administration and the Biden administration, Democrats and Republicans have shown a willingness to use the investigatory powers of Congress to "expose for the sake of exposure." "It's not like we're going to go drunk-crazy with subpoenas," Representative Gerald Connolly (D-VA) said when the Democratic Party took control of the House of Representatives in 2018. "But it may seem that way because we are coming off a two-year drought of no subpoenas."[79] The most legally controversial subpoenas were issued in 2019 when, as the Supreme Court later recounted, "three committees of the U.S. House of Representatives issued four subpoenas" in five days, "seeking information about the finances of President Donald J. Trump, his children, and affiliated businesses . . . encompassing a decade's worth of transactions by the President and his family."[80] The House Committee on Financial Services argued that it needed such information for a legislative effort "to close loopholes that allow corruption, terrorism, and money laundering to infiltrate our country's financial system." The House Intelligence Committee needed the information because it "was examining alleged attempts by Russia to influence the 2016 election; potential links between Russia and the President's campaign; and whether the President and his associates had been compromised by foreign actors or interests." The House Oversight and Reform Committee needed it to study whether President Trump "may have engaged in illegal conduct before and during his tenure in office," whether he had "undisclosed conflicts of interest that may impair his ability to make impartial policy decisions," and whether he was "complying with the Emoluments Clauses of the Constitution" and had "accurately reported his finances to the Office of Government Ethics and other federal entities."[81]

The subpoenas were directed at a sitting president and his finances, rather than the political associations of an activist or a dissident. From this perspective, they should not necessarily be seen as a threat to civil liberties. Still, as the Supreme Court has repeatedly underlined, congressional investigations must be tied to a "valid legislative purpose" to prevent them from turning into unhinged fishing expeditions.[82] Although the subpoenas against Trump could conceivably be linked to a valid legislative purpose, they were initially framed by congressional Democrats as an effort to expose Trump's misconduct, and their link to legislative activity was tenuous. It seems obvious, for example, that the House Committee on Financial Services could have pursued legislation "to close loopholes that allow corruption, terrorism, and money laundering to infiltrate our country's financial system" without examining Trump's financial records. The claim that Trump was merely a useful case study in this legislative process—who just happened to be the president and the leader of the opposing political party—is dubious at best. In other words, the House of Representatives was "exposing for the sake of exposure."

The special congressional investigation into the January 6, 2021, Capitol attacks involved more searching inquiries into the communications of private citizens. As Elizabeth Goitein, codirector of the Brennan

Center's Project on Security and Liberty, wrote in September 2021, the January 6 committee "sent 35 letters to telecommunications and social media companies—including Google, Microsoft, and all major cell phone carriers—requesting that they preserve certain records that the committee might need for its work." Those letters requested the records of "individuals who were listed on permit applications or were otherwise involved in organizing, funding, or speaking at the January 5, 2021, or January 6, 2021, rallies in the District of Columbia relating to objecting to the certification of the electoral college votes." As Goitein points out, this request went far beyond individuals who either planned or participated in the attack on the Capitol. While Goitein sympathized with the goals of the January 6 committee, she warned about the precedent such requests could set regarding the right to protest: "it is not difficult to envision a future congressional committee subpoenaing the communications and location information of Black Lives Matter activists as part of a supposed investigation into Antifa."[83]

On the other side of the aisle, when the Republican Party took control of the House of Representatives after the 2022 midterm elections, its leaders promised to weaponize their investigatory powers against President Biden and his family, as well as various other targets.[84] In March 2023, for example, the chair of the House Energy and Commerce Committee, Cathy McMorris Rodgers (R-WA), began a five-hour cross-examination of the CEO of the social media company TikTok by saying, "To the American people watching today, hear this: TikTok is a weapon by the Chinese Communist Party to spy on you and manipulate what you see and exploit for future generations." Senator Tom Cotton (R-AR) quoted almost directly from Joseph McCarthy when he repeatedly asked the CEO of TikTok (a citizen of Singapore) whether he was or ever had been a member of the Chinese Communist Party. A spokesperson for the company later asked why the committee did not discuss "the livelihoods of the 5 million businesses on TikTok or the First Amendment implications of banning a platform loved by 150 million Americans."[85] In April 2024 Congress passed legislation "effectively banning" TikTok in the United States unless the Chinese company ByteDance divested from the social media platform within twelve months.[86]

The McCarthyite maneuver of public accusation followed by private sanction was swiftly executed in December 2023 and January 2024 against the presidents of Harvard and the University of Pennsylvania.

These college presidents, as well as the president of MIT, were summoned to testify before the House Committee on Education and the Workforce about anti-Semitism on college campuses, about which members of Congress displayed heightened concern in the aftermath of the October 7, 2023, terror attacks against Israel. Representative Elise Stefanik (R-NY) asked each president whether genocidal statements against Jews would be allowed on campus. Stefanik apparently believed that common expressions of Palestinian solidarity, such as "from the river to the sea, Palestine will be free" and "intifada," fell into this category. Each president responded, essentially referring to extant First Amendment standards, that such statements would be allowed as long as they were not part of a pattern of individual harassment or a plan of imminent lawless action. Stefanik subsequently demanded their resignations, forcing Liz Magill, president of the University of Pennsylvania, to resign on December 9 with the aid of significant donor and alumni pressure.[87]

Harvard President Claudine Gay held on until January 2, 2024. The Harvard Corporation initially "affirmed our confidence that President Gay is the right leader to help our community heal and to address the very serious societal issues we are facing," but after billionaire hedge fund investor Bill Ackman—a Harvard alum who called for Gay's immediate resignation after her congressional testimony—circulated accusations that Gay was unqualified for the presidency of Harvard (a "diversity hire") or guilty of plagiarism in her scholarship (a claim supported by an investigation by the conservative *Washington Free Beacon* publication), Gay eventually resigned.[88] While the road to Gay's resignation was somewhat more complicated and lengthy than Magill's, there is no doubt that it began with her testimony before Congress.

We should not use the term "McCarthyism" lightly, but the parallels between the Stefanik hearings and McCarthy's or HUAC's are striking. Congressional investigators and their state-level copycats were obsessed with universities during the 1940s and 1950s, scrutinizing students and professors for traces of disloyalty and demanding punitive actions by university administrations.[89] Stefanik and several of her Republican colleagues on the House Education and Workforce Committee demanded that universities censor or suppress allegedly "genocidal" slogans, discipline students who endorsed such slogans or allegedly "pro-Hamas" messages, rescind offers of admission to such students, and discipline or fire allegedly pro-Hamas professors such as Joseph Massad, Mohamed Abdou, and Katherine Franke at Columbia University.[90]

The testimony of Columbia University President Nemat "Minouche" Shafik before the committee on April 17, 2024, suggested that she was anxious to avoid the fate of Gay and Magill. "We have already suspended 15 students from Columbia," Shafik said. "We have six on disciplinary probation" for alleged violations of Columbia's antidiscrimination policies. Professor Abdou, who said he was "with Hamas" in an October 11, 2023, social media post, "will never work at Columbia again," Shafik told Stefanik. "He has been terminated. And not just terminated, but his files will show that he will never work at Columbia again." Professor Massad, who described Hamas's October 7 attacks as "innovative Palestinian resistance," was also "under investigation," Shafik added.[91] In the aftermath of Shafik's testimony, hundreds of nonviolent student protests and encampments at Columbia University and across the country led to mass arrests and clear-outs that the US government would not have hesitated to condemn as heavy-handed acts of political repression if they had occurred in a foreign "authoritarian" country.[92]

The congressional investigations of universities claimed several high-profile scalps in a relatively short time and set off a nationwide wave of repression. These investigations were reactions to a war the United States was not directly fighting but was diplomatically, economically, and militarily supporting. The investigations of TikTok were part of what could be called a new cold war with China. The investigations of January 6 were prompted by an attack on the Capitol itself. None of these investigations occurred during or in the aftermath of a war in which US troops were directly involved. In other words, Congress has appeared willing, in recent years, to weaponize its investigatory and independent powers for various threats short of war, with dangerous consequences for civil liberties—especially freedom of expression and association.

This does not inspire confidence in the proposition that McCarthyism is dead. Instead, it suggests that another "boots on the ground" American war in the future, an escalation of the Israel-Palestine conflict, or even a prolonged great-power confrontation with China could again generate something similar to—or worse than—the wholescale violations of civil liberties carried out by congressional committees in the 1940s and 1950s.

3

Congress and the Executive

Congress, as various scholars have demonstrated, suffers from collective action problems. Its 535 members with different constituencies and interests do not always succeed in finding a unified plan of action, and they often struggle to compete with the more hierarchical executive branch.[1] The executive branch is hierarchical at least to the extent that the president is the head of it. This gives the executive more "speed, energy, and dispatch" than Congress and, in the eyes of many scholars, makes the executive a potential menace to civil liberties.

This chapter argues that the executive branch is not as unitary as it seems. A taste of this argument was provided in chapter 1, where I demonstrated how executive officials have not always faithfully implemented repressive legislation: during the first Red Scare, for example, A. Mitchell Palmer was agitating for mass deportations from the Justice Department while Louis Post was resisting them from the Labor Department. This chapter further shows how members of Congress have developed relationships with executive branch officials in the aftermath of war that have enabled restrictions on civil liberties without presidential involvement and, at times, despite presidential resistance. During Reconstruction, congressional Republicans empowered the military and encouraged its autonomy in order to implement martial law in the former Confederacy. During the first Red Scare, congressional conservatives began to build links with the Justice Department's Bureau of Investigation; these links were deepened during the second Red Scare, when FBI Director J. Edgar Hoover aided McCarthyism in various covert and overt ways. After the Vietnam War, the relationship between Congress and the intelligence community was formalized through the creation of permanent intelligence committees in both houses, but these committees have functioned mainly as advocates for rather than watchdogs over the agencies they are tasked with overseeing.

To be sure, these legislative-executive relationships are a two-way street. One could easily make the case that someone like J. Edgar Hoover was using Congress more than Congress was using him. Certainly, most scholars and biographers of Hoover give this impression.[2] Nevertheless, the fact remains that legislators did use him, and they have used numerous other executive officials in their efforts to curtail civil liberties in the aftermath of war.

This chapter also discusses how Congress has used its formal constitutional powers over the executive to influence executive behavior. Josh Chafetz discusses the history and creative potential of many of these powers in *Congress's Constitution*, especially the power of the purse and what he calls the "personnel power"—primarily the Senate's power to confirm or deny executive appointments.[3] I demonstrate how these powers have been used to hamper executive efforts to protect or restore civil liberties, such as when Congress wielded the power of the purse to stop President Obama from closing the Guantanamo Bay detention facility. I also show how a credible threat to use such powers can provoke repressive executive actions, such as when the House Un-American Activities Committee (HUAC) threatened to establish an "independent" loyalty commission in 1947, prompting President Truman to develop an executive loyalty program aimed at "taking the ball away" from Congress.

Overall, this chapter paints a fairly consistent postwar picture of an executive branch that is neither "imperial" nor unitary. Congress is not particularly unitary itself; however, it has repeatedly demonstrated some collective will and the capacity to undermine executive efforts to protect or restore civil liberties in the aftermath of war. Congress's powers over the executive have provided valuable leverage for legislators who want to engage in political repression, while the persistent postwar disunity of the executive branch has offered such legislators an effective and convenient route around the president.

Reconstruction

Congress formulated a program of military Reconstruction in 1867 that restricted the civil liberties of white Southerners in order to guarantee the freedoms of newly emancipated people. Military Reconstruction did not end until February 1871, when Georgia's delegation was readmitted to Congress and Ulysses S. Grant was president; the majority of the former Confederate states had been readmitted in the summer of 1868, while Andrew Johnson was president. In other words, prior to Grant's 1868 election victory, Congress was satisfied that eight former Confederate states had been successfully reconstructed.[4] How did Congress ensure the enforcement of military Reconstruction when the head of the executive branch, President Johnson, was so hostile to even the mildest reforms proposed for the South, such as the Civil Rights Act of 1866?

The short answer is that congressional Republicans had allies in the US military, even though, constitutionally, President Johnson was its commander in chief. In public, the military did not take sides; in private, however, the most senior man in the military, General Grant, displayed increasing displeasure with the president and sympathy for Congress as "presidential Reconstruction" proceeded in 1865 and 1866. This was evident as early as April 1866, when President Johnson issued his proclamation on the end of the Confederate insurrection, which declared:

> Standing armies, military occupation, martial law, military tribunals, and the suspension of the privilege of the writ of habeas corpus are in time of peace dangerous to public liberty, incompatible with the individual rights of the citizen, contrary to the genius and spirit of our free institutions, and exhaustive of the national resources, and ought not, therefore, to be sanctioned or allowed except in cases of actual necessity for repelling invasion or suppressing insurrection or rebellion.[5]

"The newspapers Contain the intelligence that the President has issued a proclamation declaring the insurrection ended," Major General Alfred Terry wrote to General Grant from Richmond, Virginia, on April 3, 1866. "I suppose this relieves all military Commissions. I have a very important case on trial before one, of a white man for the murder of a negro. I respectfully ask instructions whether this case should be completed or abandoned at once."[6] Brevet Major General John W. Turner, who was also in Richmond, wondered "whether Martial law has been removed in this Department, and the writ of Habeas Corpus restored," while General George Thomas, from Nashville, Tennessee, asked Grant, "Does the President's peace proclamation abrogate martial law, and restore the writ of habeas corpus?"[7] Grant's responses did not show much deference to the president's words. "I do not understand Martial Law to be removed in VA, or the writ of Habeas Corpus to be restored. Obey no writ for taking out of custody any military prisoner without direct instructions to do so," he ordered Turner. "The President's proclamation as I understand it, does not abrogate martial law and restore the writ of Habeas Corpus," he told Thomas. "Complete the case referred to in your telegram of to day, unless you receive other orders. The Judge Advocate General can determine the validity of the proceedings," he wrote to Terry.[8]

In 1867 Congress sought to legally limit Johnson's control over the military. The 1867 Act Regulating the Tenure of Certain Civil Offices (the Tenure of Office Act), which was passed along with the First Reconstruction Act, protected Secretary of War Edwin Stanton from removal by the president without Senate consent.[9] The 1867 Army Appropriations Act also contained a provision requiring that "all orders and instructions relating to military operations, issued by the President or Secretary of War, shall be issued through the General of the Army [Grant]," who "shall not be removed, suspended, or relieved from command, or assigned to duty elsewhere . . . except at his own request, without the previous approval of the Senate." It also had a provision disbanding the state militias in the ex-Confederate states. Johnson protested that this appropriations law "deprives the President of his constitutional functions as Commander-in-Chief of the Army," but he did not want to "defeat . . . necessary appropriations" with a veto.[10]

These two measures flowed from two powers over the executive branch granted to Congress by the Constitution. The power to create—and, by implication, set legal limits on—federal offices is derived from Congress's authority "to make all Laws which shall be necessary and proper for carrying into Execution" its enumerated powers.[11] Although the scope of this power is contested, and the Supreme Court explicitly stated in 1926 that the Tenure of Office Act was an unconstitutional application of the "necessary and proper" clause because it violated the president's constitutional authority to remove executive officers, in 1867 Congress bluntly asserted its right to restrict the president in order to protect military Reconstruction.[12] Similarly, the Army Appropriations Act may have gone too far in its restrictions on the president's removal power, but it was at least rooted in Congress's "power of the purse," derived from Article I, Section 9's injunction that "No Money shall be drawn from the Treasury, but in Consequence of Appropriations made by Law."[13]

Despite the constraints imposed by the Tenure of Office and Army Appropriations Acts, President Johnson attempted to assert his control over the military. The Tenure of Office Act allowed the president to suspend Secretary Stanton while Congress was out of session, and Johnson did so in the summer of 1867, replacing him with General Grant, who reluctantly accepted his recess appointment as secretary of war ad interim. This cleared the path for the dismissal of General Philip Sheridan, commander of the Fifth Military District (Louisiana and Texas), whom Johnson accused of "render[ing] himself exceedingly obnoxious by the manner in which he has exercised even the powers conferred by Congress, and still more so by a resort to authority not granted by law, or necessary to its faithful and efficient execution." Johnson accused Sheridan of creating an "absolute tyranny, without reference to the principles of our government or the nature of our free institutions."[14] General Daniel Sickles was then relieved of his command in the Carolinas on August 26.[15]

General Grant privately protested these dismissals.[16] Congressional Republicans began to contemplate impeachment of the president. In November 1867 the House of Representatives requested "any and all correspondence" from the executive branch relating to the suspension of Stanton and the removal of Sheridan and Sickles.[17] Four days later, in a letter sent to his entire cabinet, Johnson claimed that "certain evil disposed persons have formed a conspiracy to depose the President of the United States." That conspiracy might take the form of "articles of impeachment" or an outright "revolution changing the whole organic system of our Government."[18]

After the Senate—back in session—formally disapproved of Stanton's suspension, Johnson fired him, and the House impeached Johnson for violating the Tenure of Office Act. Privately, Grant had also impeached Johnson for using him as a pawn against Stanton. "Now, Mr. President," he wrote on February 3, 1868 (three weeks before the House impeachment vote), "where my honor as a soldier and my integrity as a man have been so violently assailed, pardon me for saying that I can but regard this whole matter, from the beginning to the end, as an attempt to involve me in the resistance of the law."[19]

Johnson's narrow acquittal by the Senate in May 1868 has led some historians and legal scholars to conclude that the Republicans' campaign against him failed. He was on the ropes, but the Republicans could not unite around his removal, and he survived.[20] However, Johnson's failure to gain his party's nomination for reelection later in the year suggests that his political reputation suffered from the confrontation with Congress. In the more fundamental struggle over Reconstruction, there is more than a grain of evidence to support the idea that, in Harold Hyman's words, "impeachment swerved [Johnson's] course." As Hyman observes:

> While the [impeachment] trial was on, Johnson made clear his intention to name a moderate general to be Secretary of War; forwarded to the Senate the Reconstruction constitutions of Arkansas and South Carolina created by terms of Congress's Reconstruction laws which he said were unconstitutional, including ratification of the detested Fourteenth Amendment and provisions for blacks' voting; and ceased obstructing the progress of congressional Reconstruction in provisional states by devious interpretations of the laws or other overt means.[21]

At the beginning of 1867, Congress faced the enormous task of implementing martial law with a resistant commander in chief. Yet the commander in chief was circumvented by the military's insulation from presidential control. When President Johnson fought back against this wedge driven into the executive branch, legislators called his bluff by impeaching him. Although they did not succeed in removing him from office, they did succeed in neutralizing his opposition, ending his political career, and, most importantly, completing military Reconstruction in most of the ex-Confederate states.

The Reconstruction Acts were the legislative bedrock of congressional Reconstruction after the Civil War, which involved significant restrictions on the civil liberties of white citizens to protect the rights of newly emancipated people. However, the Tenure of Office Act, the Army Appropriations Act, and the threat of impeachment were essential tools for ensuring the enforcement of military Reconstruction. Congress's constitutional powers to create federal offices, fund the federal government, and impeach and remove executive officers were essential complements to its power to legislate. These constitutional powers were further bolstered by the more informal alliance between congressional Republicans and the US military that developed after the Civil War.

The Red Scares

In the aftermath of US wars in the twentieth century, Congress never again deployed the full variety of constitutional powers it used during Reconstruction. As described in chapter 1, there was the halfhearted and ineffective House Rules Committee's impeachment inquiry against Assistant Labor Secretary Louis F. Post in 1920 in response to his obstruction of what he called the "deportations delirium."[22] During and after the Second World War, Congress—or, more accurately, the House of Representatives—tried to use the power of the purse to prevent the federal government from paying the salaries of three allegedly subversive employees. Although the House succeeded in prohibiting the payment of these employees under the Urgent Deficiency Appropriation Act of 1943—to which both the Senate and the president reluctantly acquiesced, fearing that rejection would result in a government funding crisis—the Supreme Court decided in 1946 that this weaponization of the power of the purse was tantamount to a bill of attainder, which is explicitly prohibited by Article I, Section 9, of the Constitution.[23]

A more effective use of congressional power over the executive was the 1947 threat by HUAC Chairman J. Parnell Thomas to establish an "independent commission with authority to investigate and to order the discharge of any employee or official of the Federal Government whose loyalty to the United States is found to be in doubt."[24] From President Truman's perspective, this was a dangerous and credible threat. Republicans controlled both houses of Congress in 1947 and had made the "loyalty question" a central—and successful—part of their 1946 election campaign.[25] Moreover, even though the Supreme Court had, by this time, invalidated laws that required Senate consent for the president's removal of an executive officer (including the Tenure of Office Act), the court had unequivocally accepted Congress's authority to create "independent commissions" whose officers could be removed by the president only for cause such as "inefficiency, neglect of duty, or malfeasance in office."[26]

Recognizing these realities, Truman concluded, "I've got to take the ball away from Parnell Thomas," as he put it to Federal Communications Commission Chair Clifford Durr, because if Thomas "has his way and gets legislation through, we will have the damndest Gestapo any country ever had." Charges of disloyalty, Truman added, were "a bunch of crap. Government employees are as loyal a bunch of people as there ever was." It was better, Truman reasoned, to "protect these people" by preempting Congress and creating a loyalty program within the executive branch, which he did by executive order in March 1947.[27]

On some level, this logic made sense: by creating an executive loyalty program, Truman could protect government employees and get Congress off his back. However, he ended up with the worst of both worlds. With two million careers potentially at stake, his "loyalty order" provoked fierce criticism from elements of his own political base. The ACLU was internally divided.[28] Philip Murray, president of the Congress of Industrial Organizations, bluntly told Truman that "the Executive Order should be repealed outright" because it threatened to bring about "thought police and denial of due process." Abram Flaxer of the United Public Workers of America warned, "we cannot have a Civil Rights Program and a Loyalty Order at the same time." Walter White of the National Association for the Advancement of Colored People expressed similar concerns.[29]

In response, Truman emphasized the program's safeguards. An employee had to be informed in writing of any disloyalty charges and reserved the right to an administrative hearing and to counsel. However, the civil libertarian indictment of Truman focused on the use of confidential informants in loyalty investigations, as well as the wider structure the loyalty program created. Central to this structure was the attorney general's List of Subversive Organizations, which was disseminated across the federal government to assist in implementing the loyalty order. It initially included forty-seven organizations, ranging from the Ku Klux Klan and the Veterans of the Abraham Lincoln Brigade to the Macedonian-American People's League and the Tom Paine School of Social Science. Another thirty-two were added by Attorney General Tom Clark in May 1948, including the Negro Labor Victory Committee, the Peace Movement of Ethiopia, the People's Institute of Applied Religion, and the United Harlem Tenants and Consumers Organization. The list continued to grow under Truman's next two attorneys general, and President Eisenhower's first, Herbert Brownell, "relisted" all 192 previously designated groups in April 1953 and proposed 62 additions.[30]

From 1947 to 1956, five million federal employees were investigated, twenty-seven hundred were dismissed, and twelve thousand resigned.[31] We do not know how many other employers used the attorney general's list to sift out "radicals." In any event, the existence of an "American blacklist" seemed to violate the core principles of free political association.[32] The ACLU's Clifford Forster, who was sympathetic to the loyalty program because of its procedural safeguards and its oversight by a neutral Loyalty Review Board, described the list as an "injustice" and "an application of the unconstitutional doctrine of guilt by association."[33] Supreme Court Justice Hugo Black likened the list to the "tyrannical" and "odious" bills of attainder prohibited by the Constitution.[34]

Meanwhile, Republicans in Congress remained unsatisfied. Just a month after the loyalty order was issued, Thomas told the president, "It will be sheer folly to spend $50,000,000 to purge the Government of communists, or $400,000,000 to stop the communists in Greece, if our Department of Justice is not going to face this issue squarely at home." The loyalty program was a positive step, but "now is the time for you to step in and take a hand in this matter and direct your Attorney General to throw the full weight of his Department behind an effort to bring these criminals and conspirators before the bar of justice."[35] Truman's attempt to outmaneuver HUAC with his own loyalty program only seemed to increase the congressional appetite for red-hunting.

Truman might have been correct that an independent loyalty commission created by this kind of Congress would have violated civil liberties to a greater extent than his executive order. Nevertheless, he must take responsibility for the damage his actions caused and, perhaps, additional responsibility for indirectly encouraging the Red Scare through a foreign policy that identified a global communist threat requiring a global US military presence.[36] If, however, our priority is historical accuracy rather than apportionment of blame, we can only fairly conclude that the loyalty program was forged in response to a credible threat of congressional action.

More informally—and sometimes secretly—one aspect of Reconstruction was revived during the second Red Scare: a close relationship between members of Congress and allies in the executive branch who were against the president. During Reconstruction, this relationship was between Congress and the military, whereas during the second Red Scare, it was between Congress and the FBI. It is also possible that members of Congress and the Bureau of Investigation collaborated in the aftermath of the First World War, when South Carolina Congressman James Byrnes—"the voice of the white South" in the House[37]—spoke publicly and menacingly about the threat of a revolutionary black communist movement in the United States and the Bureau of Investigation conducted far-reaching investigations of the prominent black political leaders Byrnes singled out as agitators.[38] Newly installed Attorney General Harlan Fiske Stone formally prohibited such "political and propaganda activities" by the Bureau in 1924, fired Director William J. Burns, and dissolved its General Intelligence Division.[39] Stone had established a reputation as one of the nation's most prominent civil libertarians; he was an ally of the ACLU and the National Popular Government League, which had fiercely criticized the Palmer Raids. Stone had consistently defended academic freedom during his tenure as dean of Columbia Law School. He was appalled by the "political activities" of the Bureau of Investigation and, in consultation with the ACLU, appointed J. Edgar Hoover as its new director.[40] Hoover distanced himself from the Palmer Raids and sold himself as a reformer. Despite keeping a close eye on communists throughout the 1920s, Hoover largely obeyed Stone's edict against "political activities." Only in the 1930s, under the Roosevelt administration, would Hoover revive and expand the surveillance methods the Bureau had pioneered from 1919 to 1924.[41] After the Second World War, he would do so in close collaboration with and with the encouragement of key members of Congress.

Truman neither liked nor trusted Hoover. When Truman told Durr that HUAC was trying to create "the damndest Gestapo any country ever had," he added, "I don't want J. Edgar Hoover running this country." Privately, Truman frequently associated Hoover with the Gestapo. According to various accounts of conversations that took place as the executive branch deliberated Hoover's plan to create and lead a "World-Wide Intelligence Service," Truman insisted "with considerable vigor that he was 'very much against building up a gestapo'" and "expressed concern regarding the possibility that a World Wide Intelligence organization would gain the reputation of a 'Gestapo.'" Truman later wrote to his wife, Bess, "Hoover's organization would make a good start toward a citizen spy system," and he vowed, "If I can prevent [it] there'll be no NKVD or Gestapo in this country." Another presidential confidant, Clark Clifford, reflected that Truman was "very strongly anti-FBI" because he was deeply "afraid of a 'Gestapo.'"[42]

Truman and Hoover did, however, agree on the need to conceal executive loyalty files from Congress. Truman wanted to keep loyalty investigations within the executive branch, and he underlined this position in March 1948 when he issued a directive declaring that "the efficient and just administration of the Employee Loyalty Program . . . requires that reports, records, and files relative to the program be preserved in strict confidence." Therefore, "any subpoena or demand or request for information, reports, or files of the nature described, received from sources other than those persons in the executive branch of the Government who are entitled thereto by reason of their official duties, shall be respectfully declined."[43] On August 4, 1948, Truman's cabinet elaborated on how this directive would operate. "All unclassified, routine papers" were fair game, but "no information of any sort relating to the employee's loyalty . . . shall be included in the material submitted to a congressional committee." The directive "should be regarded as covering the records of former Federal employees, as well as present employees and applicants for employment."[44]

The Truman administration went on to reject information requests from all the congressional committees seeking to expose and smear government employees, as well as individual requests from Senator Joseph McCarthy, who claimed in February 1950 that the State Department was harboring 205 disloyal employees. McCarthy complained to Truman that the administration was improperly guarding "the files of the individuals whom I have listed as bad security risks" and was hypocritically using the files only to "clear innocent people," rather than expose the guilty.[45] Thomas had earlier fumed that Truman's "administration has failed to keep the people informed about this dangerous situation," and Homer Ferguson (R-MI) of the Senate Investigations Subcommittee was told that he could not expect the administration to provide "any information relating to the loyalty of an employee or any investigative data relating to such employee."[46]

Loyalty files would have been red meat to these legislators. The files contained raw, unfiltered intelligence—gossip, rumor, innuendo, and whatever other tidbits Hoover had dug up. In the hands of Joseph McCarthy, Homer Ferguson, or J. Parnell Thomas, this information would have been put on stark public display, with predictably terrible consequences for federal employees. Truman pushed back because he believed in "fair play" and saw McCarthy as "insolent" and a "pathological liar"—the embodiment of a Congress comprising "more morons than patriots."[47] Truman was also protecting his turf. Few self-respecting presidents would allow their political enemies to rummage freely through sensitive executive branch documents. Regardless of whether his primary motive was the protection of civil liberties, Truman's obstructive actions ultimately saved an untold number of individuals from invasive and damaging inquisitions into their past political associations.

Unlike Truman, Hoover had an amicable relationship with Senator McCarthy, calling him—mostly in private—a "stalwart American citizen," a "fine friend" of the FBI, and "a very earnest man." He even gave McCarthy advice on which "completely American" and "non-denominational" college the daughter of McCarthy's friend should attend.[48] Loyalty files, however, were a different matter. Politely but firmly, Hoover insisted that "the confidential character of our files must be inviolate." In internal Bureau conversations, Hoover intimated that he was willing to risk contempt proceedings for "hold[ing] tight" to this position—not that this was ever a real possibility from Senator McCarthy, who felt that "the American people" should be congratulated "for their good fortune in having J. Edgar Hoover as the head of the Federal Bureau of Investigation." Unfortunately for McCarthy, the feeling was not completely mutual. "Extend usual courtesies," Hoover advised a subordinate in a 1953 memo preparing for a meeting with McCarthy, "but use caution and avoid any disclosure of confidential files."[49]

This stance suited Hoover on several levels. First, it avoided open defiance of Truman's March 1948 directive to withhold loyalty files from Congress. Second, the extension of "courtesies" kept McCarthy in Hoover's camp, at least for what he was worth: gushing public praise of the FBI, occasional tips and gossip, and continuation of a Red Scare that Hoover supported.[50] Third, the red-baiters were not the only members of Congress seeking loyalty files. McCarthy's main adversary, Senator Millard Tydings (D-MD), hoped the files would allow fair scrutiny of McCarthy's numerous public accusations. Hoover did not want Tydings looking through FBI files, especially because these files included information about the FBI's "investigative sources and methods," many of which were of dubious legality.[51]

Hoover instead assisted the Red Scare in other ways. Quietly and through Assistant Director Lou Nichols, he authorized the production of summary memoranda describing the contents of Bureau files to HUAC—notably, in its Hollywood Ten investigation. Nichols assisted McCarthy's Senate committee by running name checks on persons of interest for the senator and his lead counsel Roy Cohn.[52] FBI informants also testified dramatically in several high-profile HUAC investigations. Matthew Cvetic was an especially valuable asset, infiltrating Midwest labor unions throughout the 1940s and then naming and shaming their allegedly communist members before HUAC in 1950. Cvetic's activities became the inspiration for Warner Brothers' popular 1951 film *I Was a Communist for the FBI*.[53] Beginning with Louis Russell in 1946, HUAC also regularly hired former FBI agents to serve on its investigative staff.[54]

Then there were outright leaks. In 1947 the Bureau gave "certain key men in the House and Senate" derogatory information about former State Department employee Alger Hiss, whom HUAC had accused of dual loyalties.[55] Truman's Attorney General Tom Clark later alleged that FBI documents were regularly furnished to Republican Homer Ferguson of the Senate Investigations Committee. "He had a direct pipeline to the F.B.I.," Clark suspected. "No question in my mind about that." Indeed, "he was getting reports before I got them; before they were announced."[56] At a minimum, Ferguson relied on FBI intelligence in his July 1948 cross-examination of former Commerce Department employee William Remington.[57]

An exchange between J. Parnell Thomas and Richard Nixon in 1948 hinted at both the depth and the secrecy of FBI collaboration with HUAC. After Nixon suggested that testimony from ex-communists against their former comrades might need to be corroborated by the FBI, Thomas replied that "the closest relationship exists between this committee and the FBI. . . . It is something, however, that we cannot talk too much about. I am quite certain that if they felt they could give us anything, without endangering their own position, or in any way endangering their sources of information, they would be glad to cooperate."[58] Privately, Thomas made a similarly oblique yet revealing comment to members of Illinois's Broyles Commission on subversive activities:

> We read in the paper that the committee is not getting certain files. If we could get these files, it would be much easier, but this committee is getting excellent cooperation from certain individuals in certain agencies of the Government. We have friends in certain agencies of the Government who are aiding us all the time. It is very evident that when we put on a hearing, that we must be getting some help. We have an organization of

only forty—the FBI has four thousand agents, so it is evident that we are getting some assistance and cooperation.[59]

The Bureau aided HUAC and McCarthy in two other ways. First, Hoover investigated critics of congressional investigators. The National Lawyers Guild was a notable target in 1950.[60] Frank Wilkinson, who campaigned to abolish HUAC and was executive director of the National Committee Against Repressive Legislation, earned himself a 132,000-page FBI file.[61] Second, these campaigns against critics were supplemented by Hoover's "extracurricular ventures," which included "speaking on the anti-communist circuit; appearing before HUAC in March 1947 . . . and writing hundreds of magazine articles on the red menace." In total, according to Kenneth O'Reilly, "from 1940 until his death in 1972, Hoover published some 400 major items—263 articles, 66 speeches, interviews in nationally syndicated magazines, reports, pamphlets—and many lesser items in obscure dailies and periodicals in the American heartland."[62]

Although it is hard to measure their impact on the Red Scare, these ventures were surely valuable to the public image of Capitol Hill's inquisitors. Hoover and the FBI commanded respect across the political spectrum. Even Tydings, McCarthy's leading critic, trusted the FBI to honestly report on communist infiltration. Tydings called Hoover to testify as an expert before his Subcommittee on the Loyalty of State Department Employees, and he considered asking the FBI to assign agents who could directly aid the subcommittee's work.[63] Bipartisan appreciation of Hoover extended beyond Congress. In February 1950, for instance, George Gallup's Public Opinion News Service published a poll indicating that 79 percent of voters thought Hoover had "done a good job" as head of the FBI. Only 2 percent thought he had "done a poor job." The numbers varied little among Republicans, Democrats, and independents, with approval ratings of 83 percent, 77 percent, and 78 percent, respectively, and disapproval ratings of only 2 percent, 2 percent, and 3 percent in each respective category.[64]

Finally, Hoover was an essential link between Congress and the executive in initiating the loyalty program and the Smith Act prosecution of Communist Party leaders described in chapter 1. As early as November 1945, Hoover was warning the Truman administration of "a number of persons employed by the Government" allegedly "furnishing data and information to persons outside the Federal Government who are in turn transmitting this information to espionage agents of the Soviet Government."[65] The President's Temporary Commission on Employee Loyalty then cited "information received from the reports of the Federal Bureau of Investigation" in support of its conclusion that "the employment of disloyal or subversive persons presents more than a speculative threat to our system of government."[66] HUAC was pushing the executive branch from the outside; Hoover was doing so from the inside.

Hoover was also central to the Justice Department's Smith Act case that culminated in *Dennis v. United States.* He was initially leery about pursuing the case because a full criminal process could lead to the opening of FBI files. But Hoover had planted an informant in the Communist Party USA back in 1944, and her reports helped him write a 1,350-page document describing the party's goals and internal workings. When Clark's attorneys pursued an indictment of the CPUSA, Hoover's document was the perfect brief for the grand jury. Hoover's informant then became the perfect witness.[67] In short, even though Truman loathed HUAC, Hoover advanced HUAC's objectives within the executive branch, while HUAC advanced Hoover's objectives in Congress.

Congressional Intelligences Committees: Formalizing a Symbiotic Relationship

The informal connections between legislators and the FBI during the age of McCarthyism were formalized and cemented after the Vietnam War when both houses of Congress created permanent intelligence committees.[68] On their face, these intelligence committees were designed to improve congressional oversight of not only the FBI but also the entire national security state. In reality, the members of these committees have very weak incentives—if any at all—to scrutinize the conduct of the intelligence community. Indeed, they have strong incentives to act either as "guardians" of or "cheerleaders" for the agencies they are supposed to be monitoring.[69]

To be sure, we can point to scattered examples of conflict between the intelligence community and the congressional intelligence committees. A notable example was the Senate Intelligence Committee's condemnation of the CIA's "enhanced interrogation" programs in its 2014 "torture report," which also involved allegations of CIA interference in the committee's investigation.[70] Yet the production and release of that report involved significant interbranch cooperation: at the request of the Obama administration, the Senate Intelligence Committee released only a heavily redacted executive summary of the report; the full version will not be made public until 2028.[71] Other notable revelations of alleged misconduct by the intelligence community—such as the Bush administration's warrantless Terrorist Surveillance Program revealed by the *New York Times* in 2005 and the various surveillance programs of the National Security Agency (NSA) exposed to the public by Edward Snowden in 2013—were known but kept secret by the congressional intelligence committees.[72]

Because of the speech or debate clause of the Constitution, members of the intelligence committees could leak classified information in Congress without facing prosecution under the Espionage Act (unlike Snowden). "Once they have a document, the Speech and Debate clause means there is no way we can prevent its release," as Gerald Ford's White House counsel put it in 1975.[73] However, the intelligence committees do not have strong incentives to bite the hand that feeds them. The committees have special and, in Congress, near-exclusive access to classified information. Although committee members will not go to prison for releasing information they believe the public has a right to know, they can reasonably expect to be denied such information in the future and may find themselves with far less lucrative committee assignments. As a result, even a member concerned about civil liberties may prefer to, at most, cryptically allude to abuses, as Senator Ron Wyden (D-OR) did in 2011 with regard to what later became the Snowden revelations. Wyden warned: "When the American people find out how their government has secretly interpreted the Patriot Act, they will be stunned and they will be angry."[74] After the Snowden revelations, *Rolling Stone* reporter Janet Reitman asked Wyden why he did not blow the whistle on the Senate floor. "If you want to play a watchdog role, you try to work within the rules," Wyden replied. "I can see why plenty of people would criticize me—progressives and others. I can understand why plenty of people who have views similar to mine would say they would have done it differently."[75]

From a professional and career standpoint, the safest option for intelligence committee members—especially committee chairs—is to defend and advocate for the intelligence community. Senate Intelligence Committee Chair Dianne Feinstein (D-CA) was one of the most strident public defenders of the NSA in the aftermath of the Snowden revelations. "The call-records program is not surveillance," Feinstein wrote in October 2013. "It does not collect the content of any communication, nor do the records include names or locations. The NSA only collects the type of information found on a telephone bill: phone numbers of calls placed and received, the time of the calls and duration."[76] In response, *Guardian* journalist Glenn Greenwald, who published numerous articles about the Snowden documents, asked, "Would the senator, each month, publish a full list of people she emailed and called, including the length of time they spoke and their physical locations when the call was made?" Obviously not: "That she would take up the offer was inconceivable precisely because such information is profoundly revealing; making it public would constitute a true breach of one's private realm."[77] Meanwhile, the House Intelligence Committee responded to the Snowden revelations with a hearing titled *How Disclosed NSA Programs Protect Americans, and Why Disclosure Aids Our Adversaries.* The witnesses were NSA Director Keith Alexander, Deputy Attorney General James Cole, Deputy Director of the FBI Sean Joyce, and General Counsel for the Director of the National Intelligence Robert Litt.[78] Feinstein's successor as chair of the Senate Intelligence Committee, Richard Burr (R-NC), was also the leading opponent of reforms to the intelligence community in 2015.[79]

The intelligence committees supported the intelligence community in an even more unified fashion on the question of drone strikes against US citizens abroad, especially the September 2011 assassination of Anwar al-Awlaki—a US citizen born in New Mexico—by a Predator drone in Yemen. Only in May 2013 did Attorney General Eric Holder admit that al-Awlaki had been deliberately targeted, claiming that the cleric "repeatedly made clear his intent to attack U.S. persons and his hope that these attacks would take American lives." Taking out such a target was consistent with "generations-old legal principles and Supreme Court decisions." Holder added that three other US citizens killed by US forces—al-Awlaki's sixteen-year old son 'Abd al-Rahman, Samir Khan, and Jude Kenan Mohammed—"were not specifically targeted by the United States."[80]

In 2014 the Second Circuit Court of Appeals compelled the Obama administration to release a more thorough justification for al-Awlaki's killing. This justification came in the form of an Office of Legal Counsel memorandum that emphasized the US government's right to defend itself against imminent national security threats from citizens and noncitizens alike. It would have been better to capture, prosecute, try, and convict al-Awlaki, but that was not possible due to his persistent elusiveness and the Yemeni government's inability to find him. Contrary to the claims of his harshest critics, the president did not claim the right to kill anyone, anywhere, at any time.[81] But he did claim the right to kill American citizens who posed a threat to the United States when they could not plausibly be detained.[82]

From the perspective of civil liberties, there were two main problems with al-Awlaki's killing. First, the evidence against al-Awlaki was not conclusive. The Christmas Day 2009 "underpants bomber" Umar Farouk Abdulmutallab implicated al-Awlaki in terrorist plots and training. Al-Awlaki also told Muslims in the United States that "*jihad* against America is binding upon myself just as it is binding upon every other able Muslim."[83] However, Abdulmutallab's claims were not subjected to cross-examination in court, and it is not a crime—let alone a capital crime—for an American citizen to advocate violence against the United States.[84] Additional allegations against al-Awlaki—that he was involved in "numerous other plots against U.S. and Western interests"—rested on "information that remains classified to protect sensitive sources and methods."[85] In other words, the rest of the charge sheet was secret and therefore unverifiable.

More troublingly, the Obama administration appeared to embrace a loose definition of "imminent threat." As the Justice Department noted in a 2011 white paper, "the condition that an operational leader present an 'imminent' threat of violent attack against the United States does not require the United States to have clear evidence that a specific attack on U.S. persons and interests will take place in the immediate future." Instead, "imminence must incorporate considerations of the relevant window of opportunity, the possibility of reducing collateral damage, and the likelihood of heading off future disastrous attacks on Americans."[86]

Congress never explicitly approved the killing of US citizens abroad, although the open-ended 2001 Authorization for the Use of Military Force (AUMF) resolution arguably authorizes such killings.[87] Legislators from both parties pressured the Obama administration to release its legal justification for the al-Awlaki killing and threatened to issue subpoenas to obtain these "drone memos."[88] In the Senate, Wyden and Kentucky Republican Rand Paul threatened to obstruct the confirmation of John Brennan as CIA director if Obama continued to conceal the drone memos from Congress. This bipartisan effort bore fruit.[89] Partly in response to congressional pressure, Obama also created a more rigorous interagency review process for drone strikes.[90]

Yet, on the question of substance—could the president kill an American citizen based on a broad definition of "imminent threat"?—legislators were clear. "The decision to use lethal force against Anwar al-Awlaki was a legitimate use of authority granted to the President," Wyden and two other critics of the drone program concluded after reading the memos.[91] By 2015, members and staff of the congressional intelligence committees were regularly traveling to CIA headquarters to watch videos of drone strikes and be apprised of the intelligence behind them. Committee members reportedly criticized the strikes in closed sessions, but only "to express their dismay that the C.I.A. is not being aggressive enough in its killing operations." In 2013, for instance, "senior Republicans on the House and Senate intelligence committees were furious after they heard that the C.I.A. had not yet killed Mohanad Mahmoud Al Farekh, an American citizen who had become a top [al-] Qaeda operations officer and was hiding in Pakistan."[92]

In short, the intelligence committees do not have a robust track record of constraining the activities of the intelligence community. If anything, they aid these activities, regardless of the consequences for civil liberties. They aid them, in the first instance, by simply existing—by reassuring the public that oversight is happening and that the national security state is not operating in the dark or without external checks. They have also aided them by coming to their defense in moments of crisis or scandal.

The relationship between the intelligence committees and the intelligence community is a formalized version of the relationship J. Edgar Hoover cultivated during the second Red Scare. The intelligence community can, in general, count on an exclusive club of legislators for public support and funding; the legislators can count on the intelligence community for classified information. The big difference, of course, is that legislators are not using that information in the same way they used it during the age of McCarthyism. However, as chapter 2 argued, recent

Congresses have shown a growing appetite for McCarthyite tactics, and it would be naïve to believe that if, or perhaps when, such tactics become more widespread and aggressive, classified information will not again be used in congressional smear campaigns.

Guantanamo and the Power of the Purse

During the War on Terror, the enduring capacity of Congress to preserve wartime restrictions on civil liberties was illustrated by President Barack Obama's failure to fulfill his 2008 campaign promise to close the Guantanamo Bay detention facility. Since the Bush administration announced that the facility would hold "enemy combatants" in the aftermath of the 9/11 attacks, 780 people have been detained at Guantanamo. At the time of this writing, thirty people remain there. Nine have died in custody, and the remainder have been either repatriated or transferred to third countries.[93] For civil libertarians, Guantanamo is odious not just because of the number of people who have passed through it but also because of who they are and how they have been treated. A large proportion of the early detainees—the exact number is unknown—were handed over to American forces in Afghanistan by various less-than-reliable allies, including the Northern Alliance. Even before President Obama began to reduce the Guantanamo population, the Bush administration privately conceded that some detainees "had little or no terrorist sponsored or related training" and lacked "the intent to organize, coordinate, participate or support acts against the US, its interests, or allies."[94] This finding was reinforced by President Obama's Guantanamo Review Task Force, which approved 126 of the remaining 240 detainees for transfer to third countries or release, recommended 44 for prosecution in military or civilian courts, and labeled only 48 "too dangerous to transfer but not feasible for prosecution."[95]

The whole notion of "too dangerous to transfer but not feasible for prosecution" posed a problem for civil libertarians because it endorsed indefinite detention—a proposition that seems contrary to the principle of due process of law, which is a constitutional right enjoyed by citizens and noncitizens alike on US soil.[96] Moreover, those who did get the chance to contest their detention were funneled through military commissions that admitted hearsay evidence, were closed to public scrutiny, and admitted confessions obtained under duress.[97] Compounding this dilution of due process, detainees were waterboarded, force-fed, and subjected to other forms of inhuman and degrading treatment.[98]

The Bush administration tried to argue that civil liberties were not at stake because most Guantanamo detainees were not American citizens and because Guantanamo was not technically US territory; it was leased from the Cuban government. Yet, as the US Supreme Court concluded in 2006, Guantanamo was de facto US territory, and this precluded the Bush administration from treating Guantanamo as a law-free zone.[99]

President Obama promised to close Guantanamo when he became president in 2009, but on December 19, 2009, Congress passed the Department of Defense Appropriations Act for Fiscal Year 2010, which contained the following provision:

> None of the funds made available in this or any other Act may be used to release an individual who is detained, as of June 24, 2009, at Naval Station, Guantanamo Bay, Cuba, into the continental United States, Alaska, Hawaii, or the District of Columbia, into any of the United States territories of Guam, American Samoa (AS), the United States Virgin Islands (USVI), the Commonwealth of Puerto Rico and the Commonwealth of the Northern Mariana Islands (CNMI).[100]

The act also prohibited funding for the transfer of Guantanamo inmates into other detention facilities or "for the purposes of prosecuting such individual[s]" in US courts. Transfer to any foreign country would require certification from Congress.[101]

This political problem began for Obama in May 2009, when "conservative Republicans attacked [him] after word leaked that he was planning to release several Guantánamo detainees onto American soil." These detainees were Uyghur Muslims from western China who had been captured in Afghanistan. The government never claimed—let alone demonstrated—that the Uyghurs were affiliated with al-Qaeda, so they seemed like a safe bet for release. But when Republican Congressman Frank Wolf learned that two Uyghurs were set to be released into his northern Virginia district, he publicly told Obama that "the American people cannot afford to simply take your word that these detainees, who were captured training in terrorist camps, are not a threat." Other prominent Republicans, including former House Speaker Newt Gingrich, denounced the planned release. Obama, with one eye on his plan to push health care reform through Congress, backed down and shipped the Uyghurs off to Bermuda. Following this political humiliation, congressional Democrats bluntly told their own president that they would not fund his plan to close Guantanamo.[102]

Congress repeated the same formula contained in the 2009 defense funding bill throughout the Obama administration. Obama still substantially reduced the Guantanamo population and boldly circumvented congressional restrictions in May 2014 when he exchanged five Taliban detainees for US Army Sergeant Bowe Bergdahl.[103] Obama had previously displayed impatience with Congress in his signing statement on the National Defense Authorization Act for 2014, insisting that "the executive branch must have the flexibility, among other things, to act swiftly in conducting negotiations with foreign countries regarding the circumstances of detainee transfers."[104] By pledging not to comply with part of a law he had signed, Obama arguably violated his constitutional obligation to "take care that the laws be faithfully executed." But with congressional obstinacy an unshakable fact since the Republican midterm victories in 2010, Obama had little choice but to stretch his authority to its limits.[105]

Perhaps he could have pushed further. Yet, considering the Constitution's explicit injunction that "no Money shall be drawn from the Treasury, but in Consequence of Appropriations made by Law," it is risky for a president to defy the legislature's power over the national purse strings.[106] It is also risky for legislators to play a game of brinkmanship with funds for the federal government, but the power of the purse is simple, direct, effective, and easier to wield than ordinary legislation.[107] If, for instance, legislators had wanted to enact a "Guantanamo Preservation Act," it would have required passage through both legislative chambers and presidential approval. The power of the purse flips the equation. Because Congress must affirmatively approve new spending, a single chamber—or even a powerful coalition of legislators within one chamber—can threaten to starve the federal government. When an appropriations bill reaches the president's desk, a veto is still possible, but—as Obama well understood—it may not be wise to deny money to an entire department of government because of one objectionable section or subsection.

The War on Terror, many scholars have argued, has been defined by something like a superimperial presidency and a largely quiescent

Congress. But the determination and ability of Congress to sabotage President Obama's attempt to close Guantanamo undermine this narrative. It at least suggests that Congress is still a key player and that the power of the purse is not dead. More importantly, this episode reveals how the prospect of a more assertive Congress as the War on Terror drags on—which some scholars have identified[108]—is not necessarily a positive development for civil liberties.

4

Congress and the Judiciary

There is something approaching a scholarly consensus around the proposition that the US Supreme Court does not usually second-guess the government in wartime.[1] Up to this point, I have not contested this proposition and have even suggested that this judicial deference can extend beyond wartime: for example, when the Supreme Court upheld the Espionage Act prosecutions of prominent political dissidents after the First World War. This chapter, however, documents several instances of the Supreme Court cautiously, belatedly, but meaningfully attempting to challenge the notion that "in war, the law falls silent." During Reconstruction, the court questioned whether martial law could be applied in areas where the civil courts were still functioning, thus threatening to undermine martial law in the former Confederacy; during the second Red Scare, it provided procedural protections for victims of McCarthyism; during the Vietnam War, it expanded the constitutional rights of criminal defendants; during the War on Terror, it questioned the legal regime created for Guantanamo Bay detainees.

Congress retaliated against all these judicial actions. During Reconstruction, it stripped the Supreme Court of jurisdiction over habeas corpus petitions; during the second Red Scare, it came, in the words of the chief justice, "dangerously close" to curbing the court's jurisdiction over loyalty and internal security cases,[2] pressuring it to back away from its relatively cautious defenses of civil liberties; during the Vietnam War, Congress essentially killed the court's criminal procedure "revolution" by attempting to overrule the landmark *Miranda v. Arizona* case and by filibustering the Johnson administration's efforts to replace Chief Justice Earl Warren with Abe Fortas in 1968; in 2006 the Military Commissions

Act (MCA) stripped federal courts of jurisdiction over habeas corpus petitions filed by "enemy combatants" held at the Guantanamo Bay detention facility.

Few, if any, of these congressional efforts were obviously unconstitutional. The Constitution gives Congress significant powers over the Supreme Court and the federal judiciary more generally. Article I gives Congress the power to create tribunals inferior to the Supreme Court, Article II gives the Senate the power to obstruct judicial nominations, and Article III gives Congress the power to alter the appellate jurisdiction of the Supreme Court. Congress can also limit the jurisdiction of the judiciary in a less direct way by retroactively immunizing what was previously criminal conduct, thereby potentially protecting government or private actors who have violated civil liberties.

Just as the previous chapter showed how Congress could influence the executive by credibly threatening to use its formal constitutional powers, this chapter argues that congressional threats have been even more effective in influencing the behavior of the judiciary. The judiciary has been susceptible to such threats because it is, at bottom, the weakest branch of the federal government, and the Supreme Court justices know this, even though they publicly maintain the fiction of "coequal branches."[3]

Reconstruction

The first real instances of Congress bullying the judiciary in the aftermath of war to stop its efforts to restore peacetime constitutional conditions occurred during Reconstruction. As W. E. B. Du Bois notes, this legislative-judicial conflict was somewhat surprising, given that—after the death of Roger B. Taney in 1864—the chief justice of the Supreme Court was President Lincoln's former treasury secretary, Salmon P. Chase. Chase was "a prominent Abolitionist, and after the war, a Radical Republican" who "advocated Negro suffrage, and in May, 1865, made a trip to the South to investigate the position of the Negro. In Charleston, he spoke to the Negroes, and urged them to deserve the suffrage, even if they did not get it." But, Du Bois continues, "Chase did not like the military governments of the South, and favored state rights as against the increased power of the Federal Government. He said once: 'While we freed the Negro, we enslaved ourselves.'"[4]

Whatever the chief justice's motives, the Supreme Court's decisions during the early years of Reconstruction clearly agitated congressional Republicans. In April 1866 Justice David Davis conceded in *Ex parte Milligan* (writing for a unanimous court) that "there are occasions when martial rule can be properly applied"—namely, when "in foreign invasion or civil war, the courts are actually closed, and it is impossible to administer criminal justice according to law." However, "as necessity creates the rule, so it limits its duration, for, if this [martial] government is continued after the courts are reinstated, it is a gross usurpation of power. Martial rule can never exist where the courts are open and in the proper and unobstructed exercise of their jurisdiction."[5] *Milligan* has since become the subject of widespread praise among civil libertarians as a rare example of the Supreme Court's questioning of government violations of civil liberties during wartime.[6]

In 1866, however, *Milligan* appeared to threaten the legality of Reconstruction itself. Although it emerged from a wartime rather than a Reconstruction case—and in Indiana rather than in the former Confederacy—if it was unconstitutional for the federal government to try defendants in military tribunals when the civilian courts were open, then surely the convictions obtained under these tribunals in the Old South after the war were invalid. "That [*Milligan*] decision," Thaddeus Stevens told the House of Representatives, "although in terms perhaps not as infamous as the Dred Scott decision, is yet far more dangerous in its operation upon the lives and liberties of loyal men of this country." The Supreme Court, Stevens argued, had "unsheathed the dagger of the assassin" and "taken away every protection in every one of these Rebel states from every loyal man, black or white, who resides there."[7]

Extension of the *Milligan* principle to the South was prevented by Congress's refusal to acknowledge that the Civil War was legally over. The South was still in the "grasp of war," according to the Joint Committee on Reconstruction, until Congress decided to readmit Southern congressional delegations. Under *Milligan*, military justice could not be applied to civilians outside an active war zone. But the Joint Committee on Reconstruction had determined that, legally, the old Confederacy was still a war zone—and it would remain so until Congress said it was not. The Constitution gives Congress the power to declare war and the president the power to command the armed forces, but it says nothing about which branch of government can terminate a war—let alone an undeclared civil war.[8] Amid such ambiguity, legislators responding to *Milligan* could make a credible and straightforward legal argument: Congress declares war, so Congress gets to decide when to end war. If Congress says the South is still in the "grasp of war," martial law still applies, and *Milligan* is thus (to borrow Mark Neely's word) "irrelevant."[9]

The Reconstruction Acts—which the president of the United States believed were unconstitutional—provoked more direct legal attacks on Reconstruction. Almost immediately after passage of the Second Reconstruction Act in March 1867, the state of Mississippi asked the Supreme Court for an injunction against enforcement of the acts, arguing:

> According to the President's own opinion, as expressed in his veto messages, the Constitution of the United States is, by the Reconstruction Acts, subverted and overthrown, and a military despotism is erected upon its ruins. Ten States are to be expelled from the Union; ten millions of people are to be deprived of all the benefits of the Constitution; deprived of the right of trial by jury. These ten States are cut up into five military districts; people are to be tried outside of their States for offences unknown and undefined, merely at the will of a military officer; deprived of the right of trial by jury; all this in time of profound peace, when Congress itself, speaking, as it has done in several acts, of "States lately in rebellion," admits that there is no rebellion in the land; deprived of their rights and privileges of American citizens. So far as constitutional liberty is concerned, they might as well be living under a Czar or a Sultan, upon the banks of the Bosphorus or the Neva, as in this free country. Life, liberty, and property may be taken from them without due process of law.[10]

A unanimous Supreme Court rejected Mississippi's appeal because of lack of jurisdiction, but another, more serious lawsuit emerged later in the year when the court agreed to hear arguments in *Ex parte McCardle*. William McCardle was a Mississippi newspaper editor who, in one of his more polite columns, called the district commanders governing the ex-Confederacy under the Reconstruction Acts "infamous, cowardly, and abandoned villains who, instead of wearing shoulder straps and ruling millions of people, should have their heads shaved, their ears cropped, their foreheads branded, and their persons lodged in a penitentiary."[11] McCardle was arrested under military authority in 1867 and sought a writ of habeas corpus on the grounds that this authority was unconstitutional.

Without explaining why, Attorney General Henry Stanbery told Ulysses Grant, "I do not propose to appear in the [McCardle] case," leading Grant to ask Republican Senator Lyman Trumbull—an accomplished lawyer—to represent the government and defend the Reconstruction legislation.[12] Stanbery, who was a close ally of President Andrew Johnson, thought military Reconstruction was unconstitutional. By refusing to appear in the McCardle case, he repudiated the executive's "duty to defend" federal statutes in court. The "duty to defend" is a contested doctrine, and presidents and attorneys general have routinely rejected it, usually with negative consequences for the law in question.[13] In rejecting his duty to defend, Stanbery sent a clear signal that he wanted the court to rule for McCardle and invalidate martial law.

By February 1868, General George Meade went so far as to tell Grant that "the fear that reconstruction was, or is to be set aside, has deterred many white voters from taking part in" an Alabama election. "The prevailing opinion," according to Meade, was "that the Supreme Court will pronounce the Reconstruction Laws unconstitutional."[14] These rumors reached Congress. James F. Wilson (R-IA) claimed, "We were told day by day that the majority of the court had practically made up its judgment, not only to pass upon the sufficiency of the return to the writ, which involves the only question properly before them in the McCardle case, but also to do as the court did once before in the Dred Scott case, go outside of the record properly involving the questions really presented for its determination, undertaking to infringe upon the political power of Congress." Wilson claimed a "duty to intervene by a repeal of the jurisdiction and prevent the threatened calamity falling upon the country," so he snuck a provision into an otherwise innocuous amendment of the 1789 Judiciary Act that repealed the Habeas Corpus Act of 1867, which had given the Supreme Court jurisdiction over McCardle's case. President Johnson vetoed the legislation but was overridden by two-thirds of Congress.[15]

"It is quite clear," Chief Justice Chase conceded in his *McCardle* opinion, "that this court cannot proceed to pronounce judgment in this case, for it has no longer jurisdiction of the appeal; and judicial duty is not less fitly performed by declining ungranted jurisdiction than in exercising firmly that which the Constitution and the laws confer." However, Chase carefully emphasized that the court lacked jurisdiction over habeas petitions only under the 1867 legislation; it could still, potentially, hear habeas petitions under the 1789 Judiciary Act.[16] Edward Yerger, who was facing trial by military commission in Mississippi for killing a soldier, tested this proposition when his lawyers claimed that Congress's repeal of the 1867 Habeas Corpus Act applied only to the expanded habeas provisions of that law rather than the narrower provisions of the 1789 Judiciary Act. A unanimous Supreme Court ordered that Yerger receive the writ, and only "isolated congressmen" responded with what Stanley Kutler calls "menacing, yet fruitless, proposals" to retaliate against the court.[17]

Kutler argues that the *Yerger* decision undermines the widespread idea that *McCardle* embodied "judicial impotency." Yet while *McCardle* left the door open to habeas petitions under the 1789 Judiciary Act and *Yerger* provided an impassioned defense of the Supreme Court's habeas jurisdiction under that act, *Yerger* did not invalidate the Reconstruction Acts. Either the Supreme Court never intended to broadly invalidate the legislation or the congressional reaction to *McCardle* spooked the court into an opinion in *Yerger* that would not antagonize Congress. Kutler seems to lean toward the former, claiming, "Although the Republicans lacked direct evidence that the Court intended to void the Reconstruction Acts, they acted" to repeal the 1867 Habeas Corpus Act "because of a climate of opinion that accentuated a determination to protect their southern policy."[18]

Ultimately, this point is moot. As Kutler concedes, the overriding fact remains that Congress gave the Supreme Court expanded jurisdiction over habeas petitions and then took this jurisdiction away when it seemed to pose a potential threat to military Reconstruction. "The congressional action against the Court in 1868 cannot be justified," he concludes. "It can, however, be understood . . . within the context of the [Republican] party's determination to defend its reconstruction program which had been formulated at the cost of great internal strain . . . the Republicans stood ready to maintain their policy at all costs."[19]

The congressional reaction to *McCardle* was not the only indication that the Republicans "stood ready to maintain their policy at all costs." Republicans had been highly suspicious of the Supreme Court ever since the *Dred Scott* decision in 1857. The problem with *Dred Scott* was not only Chief Justice Taney's conclusion that African Americans could never be American citizens but also his declaration that Congress could not regulate the expansion of slavery into US territories.[20] In his first inaugural address, Abraham Lincoln left no doubt about where he stood on the question of the judiciary's role in the separation of powers. "If the policy of the government, upon vital questions, affecting the whole people, is to be irrevocably fixed by decisions of the Supreme Court," he said, referencing *Dred Scott*, "the people will have ceased to be their own rulers."[21]

During the Civil War, the Supreme Court carefully avoided major confrontations with the Lincoln administration, even though Chief Justice Taney, acting alone, tentatively advocated for suspected secessionist John Merryman, who was arrested under military authority in Maryland in 1861.[22] Taney also failed to persuade his colleagues that Lincoln's imposition of a naval blockade on the Confederacy was unconstitutional.[23] After Taney died in October 1864, Lincoln appointed Salmon P. Chase as chief justice. Lincoln ended up appointing five other justices to the court, one of whom was the product of Congress's addition of an extra seat (and circuit) in 1864. Congress later shrank the court back down to seven seats in 1866 to deny Andrew Johnson any judicial appointments.[24]

It would be an exaggeration to claim that the entire Republican Party was hostile toward the Supreme Court or was seeking revenge for the *Dred Scott* decision. Many key Republicans were anxious about attacks on the court or its jurisdiction, as evidenced by the muted congressional response to *Yerger*. Nevertheless, from *Dred Scott* to *McCardle*, congressional Republicans rhetorically denounced the Supreme Court, curbed its appellate jurisdiction, and increased and reduced the number of justices. Surveying this landscape, it is no surprise that the Supreme Court capitulated on the core question presented to it in *Ex parte McCardle*.

In short, military Reconstruction may or may not have been constitutional. However, Republicans in Congress did everything they could to ensure that the Supreme Court did not address this question in 1868 and 1869. Although the court did end up contributing to the demise of Reconstruction in the 1870s, it did so only when Republicans themselves were growing tired of Reconstruction's burdens.[25] By their own standards—that is, above all, achieving ratification of the Fourteenth Amendment—congressional Republicans had realized the objectives of military Reconstruction by 1871 without interference from the judiciary.

The Red Scares

On the question of congressional relations with the judiciary, there is a striking contrast between Reconstruction and the first Red Scare. During Reconstruction, this relationship was hostile, leading Congress to manipulate the size and jurisdiction of the Supreme Court. During the first Red Scare, there were no such disputes. Wartime statutes were uniformly upheld by the court.[26] Meanwhile, the legislation underpinning the Palmer Raids—the 1918 Immigration Act—was never likely to face searching judicial scrutiny. As Representative John Burnett (D-AL) correctly told Congress when proposing the legislation, "it has been the law for years and years to deport without any trial."[27] Judge George W. Anderson, in a Massachusetts district court, condemned the brutality of the Palmer Raids in 1920, but even he acknowledged the almost limitless and long-held authority of Congress to exclude and deport noncitizens.[28] In 1919 and 1920 criminal prosecutions would have required all the messy barriers erected by the Sixth Amendment, including a speedy and public trial, an impartial jury, the right to be informed of the nature and cause of the accusation, and the right to cross-examine witnesses and to have legal representation. A deportation required only a filing by the commissioner general for immigration and approval by the secretary of labor. The relative convenience of the deportation process also helps explain why Congress did not replace the 1918 Sedition Act. The Justice Department's Bureau of Investigation believed (or at least stated) that "fully 90 per cent of the communist and anarchist agitation is traceable to aliens."[29] Remove the "aliens" and remove the "agitation"—no need for a new sedition statute.

The story was different during the second Red Scare. The Supreme Court was initially deferential to Congress and the executive branch, as demonstrated by its decisions to sustain or decline to review contempt-of-Congress convictions between 1945 and 1957 and to uphold the Smith Act prosecution of Communist Party USA leaders in 1951.[30] However, the court began to show signs of discomfort in two decisions handed down on April 30, 1951. *Bailey v. Richardson* was tied 4–4. By then, Tom Clark was an associate justice, and he recused himself from the case because he had been attorney general when Dorothy Bailey was fired from the Department of Labor under the Truman administration's loyalty order. By convention, ties automatically uphold the decision below without a written opinion explaining why. This was no consolation for Bailey—whose dismissal stood—but it did suggest that the justices were becoming more amenable to civil liberties defenses against accusations of disloyalty. More impactfully, the court's decision in *Joint Anti-Fascist Refugee Committee v. McGrath* declared that organizations included on the attorney general's List of Subversive Organizations could sue to have themselves removed from the list, even if it was unclear how favorably the courts would treat subsequent lawsuits against the list.[31]

A turning point for the Supreme Court came after Chief Justice Fred Vinson died in September 1953 and was replaced by former California Governor and Republican vice-presidential candidate Earl Warren. Under Warren's leadership, the court began to question the Red Scare on several fronts. On April 30, 1956, in *Communist Party of the United States v. Subversive Activities Control Board*, the court required the board to reconsider its "subversive" designation of the Communist Party because its original hearings included testimony from perjurious witnesses.[32] The following day, House Democrat George Andrews of Alabama responded by asking, "How much longer will this Congress continue to permit the Supreme Court to usurp the powers of Congress, write the laws of this land, destroy States' rights, and protect the Communist Party?"[33]

The mention of "states' rights" is telling. It certainly referred to the Warren Court's 1954 decision in *Brown v. Board of Education*, which Southern governors and legislators promised to meet with "massive resistance."[34] But "states' rights" were also set aside in *Pennsylvania v. Nelson* (1956) when the court invalidated the state sedition conviction of Steve Nelson, an admitted Communist Party member, on the grounds that Pennsylvania's sedition statute was superseded (or "preempted") by the federal Smith Act. By holding that the Smith Act and state sedition laws could not coexist, the Warren Court also invalidated the forty-one other state sedition laws on the books across the country—a dramatic reversal that Justice Stanley Reed bemoaned in his dissent (in which he was joined by Justices Burton and Minton).[35] Further aggravating congressional red-hunters, the Warren Court ruled—on statutory rather than constitutional grounds—in favor of a Food and Drug Administration employee who had been dismissed because of his alleged association with communists.[36] By the end of the congressional session in July

1956, both the Senate and House Judiciary Committees had reported favorably on bills that would effectively overrule *Nelson* and strip the Supreme Court of its jurisdiction over state sedition laws.[37]

Then, during the Supreme Court's 1956–57 term, it issued eleven decisions defending the civil liberties of accused communists and communist "front" group members. Four such decisions came down on a single "Red Monday" in June 1957. From the perspective of congressional McCarthyites, *Watkins v. United States* was especially galling. John Watkins, an organizer for the Automobile Workers International Union, had been summoned by HUAC in April 1954, and although he agreed to answer questions about current Communist Party members, he refused to discuss people who were no longer affiliated with the party. After HUAC and the House of Representatives held Watkins in contempt, he argued that HUAC lacked the constitutional authority to inquire so widely into his political associations. The Supreme Court heard his plea in 1957 and held that "there is no congressional power to expose for the sake of exposure." The court did not go so far as to invalidate HUAC's existence, but it did hold—by a 6–1 margin—that Watkins had not been properly informed of which questions were and were not pertinent to HUAC's inquiry. He thus had no idea whether he was required to answer and had no fair opportunity to challenge a line of questioning. This violated the due process guaranteed by the Constitution's Fifth Amendment.[38]

Following Red Monday, the chairman of the Senate Internal Security Subcommittee drafted a bill—supported by Judiciary Committee Chairman James Eastland (D-MS)—that would have stripped the Supreme Court of its appellate jurisdiction in all cases involving "contempt of Congress, the federal loyalty-security program, state antisubversive statutes, measures adopted by boards of education to deal with subversion among teachers, and admission to the practice of law in any state."[39] "The objective of my bill," Senator William Jenner (R-IN) stated, "is to check judicial legislation in certain fields where it has been damaging to the internal security of the United States."[40] Jenner's colleague on the committee, John Marshall Butler (R-MD), amended the bill to focus more narrowly on repealing the court's decisions in *Watkins* and *Nelson*, and the Jenner-Butler bill was brought to the floor of the Senate alongside the 1956 bills aiming to insulate state sedition laws from judicial review. By 1958, Senate majority leader Lyndon B. Johnson (D-TX) had "an assortment of court-curbing bills" on his plate that had "moved through the congressional maze."[41]

Senator Johnson opposed all court-curbing efforts, fearing that they would split the Democratic Party, embarrass the Senate, and damage his prospects for a future White House run. President Eisenhower's position was muddled: he was not particularly fond of the Warren Court and regretted his decision to appoint Warren as chief justice, but he said nothing in favor of the court-curbing bills.[42] The president did nothing to oppose the bills either, so this task was left to Johnson, who structured the Senate calendar to delay consideration of the Jenner-Butler bill and H.R. 3 (the final state sedition law bill) for as long as possible. He gave his colleagues the famous "Johnson treatment": gently telling some senators to vote the right way over glasses of whiskey in his office and furiously threatening others of the consequences if they voted the wrong way. In the end, the Jenner-Butler bill was tabled by a close vote of 49–41; H.R. 3 by a vote of 41–40. The Supreme Court narrowly survived.[43]

However, threats from Congress appeared to influence the Supreme Court's behavior. It agreed to hear a steadily declining number of contentious "communist" cases in 1958 and 1959. In the most substantial case it did hear, *Barenblatt v. United States*, it ruled 5–4 in favor of HUAC investigators who were accused of violating the First Amendment rights of university professor Lloyd Barenblatt by compelling him to testify about his political affiliations and convictions.[44] HUAC later praised *Barenblatt* in its 1959 annual report and then set off to Puerto Rico in November 1959, determined to investigate links between the Puerto Rican independence movement and international communism.[45] There, it held thirteen witnesses in contempt after they argued that the committee was not authorized to conduct investigations in US territories—only US states.[46] HUAC later hounded the antinuclear group Women's Strike for Peace, holding its leaders in contempt in 1964.[47]

No Supreme Court justice will ever admit to capitulating in the face of congressional pressure, but Earl Warren came close to such an admission in his memoirs. The court-curbing legislation, he recalled, "came dangerously close to passing" and embodied "the atmosphere of the Cold War hysteria."[48] The events of 1958 are somewhat comparable to those of 1937, when congressional allies of President Roosevelt threatened to pack the Supreme Court in the aftermath of several decisions that endangered the New Deal at both the state and federal levels. Congress did not carry out that threat, but after it was issued, the court backed down and began to uphold almost all the state and federal economic regulations it had previously invalidated.[49] Likewise, after threats to its jurisdiction in 1958, the Supreme Court stepped back from defending the civil liberties of alleged communists and "fellow travelers."

There are differences between 1937 and 1958. In 1937, the court-packing plan was initiated by the president; in 1958, the president was scarcely involved at all. In 1937, the court-curbing bills barely survived the Senate Judiciary Committee and died quickly and quietly before the full Senate; in 1958, two bills made it to the floor of the Senate and were tabled by narrow margins. In 1937, court curbing sought to protect the New Deal; in 1958, it sought to protect the Red Scare. But events in both 1937 and 1958 illustrate how Congress can influence judicial behavior by threatening to exercise its constitutional powers over the Supreme Court. Indeed, these powers reflect the Supreme Court's lowly status in the constitutional structure. Its only constitutional protections are life tenure for justices and small realms of original jurisdiction.[50] Appellate jurisdiction and the structure of federal courts below the Supreme Court are defined by Congress; appointments are reserved to the president with the advice and consent of the Senate. As the weakest branch, the judiciary has always relied on the other branches to see that its decisions and its authority are respected and implemented. In 1958 a powerful coalition in the legislative branch was determined to challenge this authority, and the Supreme Court took notice.

This campaign against the Supreme Court did not cause the second Red Scare, which had already flourished for more than a decade with minimal judicial interference. Yet the legislators' threats against the court's jurisdiction prompted the court to step back from its cautious and tentative defense of civil liberties. This gave HUAC the green light to continue its crusade until as late as 1964. The only consolation for civil liberties was the fact that the Supreme Court never explicitly overruled the decisions that belatedly curtailed the Red Scare. Thus, principles such as "there is no congressional power to expose for the sake of exposure" survived.[51]

How Congress Killed the Warren Court

The next major confrontation between the Supreme Court and Congress over civil liberties occurred during the Vietnam War. This confrontation was not about the war itself but about the Supreme Court's so-called criminal procedure "revolution," which began before the war and continued throughout it.[52] However, the domestic social unrest provoked by the Vietnam War played an important role in driving congressional reaction against the Supreme Court, which culminated on two fronts in 1968: legislation aimed at overruling several landmark criminal procedure decisions, and the successful—and unprecedented—filibuster of President Johnson's nomination of Abe Fortas for chief justice of the Supreme Court.[53]

The most famous—and in many circles, celebrated—decisions of the Supreme Court's criminal procedure "revolution" were probably *Mapp v. Ohio* (1961), *Gideon v. Wainwright* (1963), *Miranda v. Arizona* (1966), *United States v. Wade* (1967), and *Katz v. United States* (1967). *Mapp* made evidence seized through warrantless home searches inadmissible in state courts, *Gideon* required states to provide counsel to indigent defendants, *Miranda* required police officers to inform suspects of their constitutional rights prior to custodial interrogation, *Wade* somewhat ambiguously and tentatively asserted a right to counsel during lineup identifications, and *Katz* extended Fourth Amendment protections to situations in which there is a "reasonable expectation of privacy," including conversations on public telephones.[54]

An earlier and less famous decision, *Mallory v. United States* (1957), prompted congressional backlash in 1966. *Mallory* determined that the arraignment of a convicted rapist in Washington, DC, had not been carried out "without unnecessary delay," and therefore his conviction was inconsistent with the Federal Rules of Criminal Procedure.[55] The Supreme Court promulgates these rules under statutory, rather than constitutional, authority; therefore, Congress can review, alter, or reject the court's proposed rule changes. The 1966 DC crime bill, which passed with comfortable majorities in both chambers (251–131 in the House and 86–7 in the Senate), essentially reversed the *Mallory* ruling. As President Johnson put it in his message vetoing the bill, this meant "that a policeman may pick up a person and question him for 4 hours without making an arrest—6 hours, exclusive of interrogation, after an arrest—perhaps 10 hours of questioning—without taking him before a judicial officer." According to Johnson, this violated the basic principle that "after a person is deprived of his freedom—after he is arrested—the police must take him before a magistrate who will determine whether his arrest is arbitrary or based on probable cause. This must be done without unnecessary delay." Johnson added that, "in the case of a material witness, the bill contains provisions even more extreme than those applicable to suspects themselves," providing that "any citizen at the scene of a crime—including the victim—can be taken into custody as a material witness" and held for six hours without a subpoena or presentment to a magistrate. "In effect, the person can disappear from sight merely on an individual policeman's judgment that he is a material witness, and that there is a reasonable probability that he will not be available to testify at the trial." When they finally were presented to a magistrate, "material witnesses" could be released only "by posting bond or collateral as security"—a procedure harsher than that applicable to criminal suspects.[56]

Attorney General Ramsey Clark believed the 1966 DC crime bill "contained some very repressive and in my judgment several unconstitutional features"—not just its reversal of *Mallory* but also its provision preventing the publication of materials "on the ground that they would be pornographic before they were printed, which is contrary to our constitutional principles."[57] In Clark's view, "the emotional climate in the country about crime had been so great and people had focused so much on the nation's capital in my judgment from racist motivations in part." Indeed,

> it was really a continuation of the old southern belief that the blacks were incapable of self-government. Of course, they never had a chance for self-government or even for government in the District of Columbia. People always liked to focus on the nation's capital as a crime center. The statistics never supported it although there's more crime here than you'd like, as there is in every place in the country. The crime bill that was presented put a heavier burden on us in drafting . . . legislation to satisfy the growing militant interest in harsh measures.[58]

President Johnson also condemned the bill's attempt to "stop the traffic in obscene pictures and literature." Although "no one can have sympathy for those who pander to degraded instincts in man . . . this provision is phrased so broadly that it clearly threatens freedom of the press," authorizing the US attorney in DC to permanently enjoin any publication he deemed obscene. Finally, Johnson described the bill's creation of "mandatory minimum sentences on conviction of certain crimes" as "a step backward in judicial and correction policy," not least because DC already imposed some of the harshest criminal sentences in the country.[59]

Johnson and Clark responded with an alternative approach based on federal aid to local police forces. Publicly, they argued that this was the best way for the federal government to combat crime without compromising federalism and civil liberties.[60] Privately, they perceived political benefits. Local aid, Clark told Johnson during a phone call, would allow the administration to argue that they were the ones who were really "helping the police—giving the police more money," while legislators were only "talking about crime, talking about wiretapping, talking about confessions," and trying to "slap the Supreme Court."[61]

As Yale Kamisar writes, "in February 1967, President Lyndon B. Johnson proposed legislation authorizing massive federal grants to state and local governments for improving law-enforcement facilities and training new and existing police personnel." However, "the Crime Bill that came back to the White House sixteen months later, which the president reluctantly signed on June 19, 1968, was 'a much broader piece of legislation.'"[62] In particular, what became the 1968 Omnibus Crime and Safe Streets Act included "two major provisions about which the president had serious misgivings: Title III, which granted law enforcement officials extensive powers to conduct wiretapping and electronic surveillance, and Title II, which one commentator called 'a grab-bag of anti-Court items.'"[63] "Taken as a whole," the *Congressional Quarterly Almanac* surmised, "passage of the bill was a major defeat for the Johnson Administration and congressional liberals."[64] Johnson pondered a veto but ultimately chose to sign it.

The main anti–Supreme Court item in the Safe Streets Act was an effort to overturn *Miranda*. Section 3501 required that "in any criminal prosecution brought by the United States or by the District of Columbia, a confession . . . shall be admissible in evidence if it is voluntarily given." Trial judges would determine "voluntariness" based on what was essentially a "totality of the circumstances" test: the pre-*Miranda* standard. Thus, as the Supreme Court later acknowledged, the Safe Streets Act aimed to "overrule *Miranda*."[65] The broader spirit of section 3501 was well encapsulated by Senator Sam Ervin (D-NC), who said, "Enough has been done for those who murder and rape and rob! It is time to do something for those who do not wish to be murdered or raped or robbed."[66]

Miranda lost the battle but won the war. In 2000 the Supreme Court invalidated Congress's attempt to overrule *Miranda*. Reagan-appointed

Chief Justice William Rehnquist wrote that "*Miranda* has become embedded in routine police practice to the point where the warnings have become part of our national culture."[67] Yet the Safe Streets Act—earlier versions of which also included threats to the Supreme Court's jurisdiction—sent a strong message to the Supreme Court, as did the 1957–58 court-curbing bills. On June 10, 1968—nine days before President Johnson signed the Safe Streets Act—the Supreme Court, in an 8–1 opinion written by Chief Justice Earl Warren, appeared to put the brakes on its criminal procedure "revolution." In *Terry v. Ohio* the court rejected a Fourth Amendment challenge to a warrantless "stop and frisk" on the streets of Cleveland because the police officer had a "reasonable suspicion" (not "probable cause") that a robbery was being planned.[68] In dissent, Justice Douglas accused his colleagues of caving to political pressure. "There have been powerful hydraulic pressures throughout our history that bear heavily on the Court to water down constitutional guarantees and give the police the upper hand," Douglas wrote. "That hydraulic pressure has probably never been greater than it is today. Yet if the individual is no longer to be sovereign, if the police can pick him up whenever they do not like the cut of his jib, if they can 'seize' and 'search' him in their discretion, we enter a new regime. The decision to enter it should be made only after a full debate by the people of this country."[69]

If *Terry* did not end the Warren Court's "revolution," then Congress did when it undermined Warren's politically calculated effort to be replaced by a Democratic president. Warren resigned as chief justice on June 13, 1968—but on the condition that he would not leave the bench until the Senate confirmed his replacement. With the presidential election only five months away, President Johnson accepted Warren's terms and decided to replace him with sitting Associate Justice Abe Fortas, who would be replaced by Homer Thornberry. As Robert David Johnson recounts, "after the Court-packing fight of 1937, the Senate confirmed twenty-two consecutive Justices, fifteen by a voice vote. It thus was not unreasonable, as most Washington observers thought, to expect little resistance for Warren's replacement." However, "for three reasons . . . Johnson might have anticipated the difficulties any prospective nominee would face." The first was the scattered Senate resistance to Thurgood Marshall's nomination in 1967 (eleven "no" votes). The second was the fact that Johnson's political position was much weaker in 1968 than it had been in 1966, when the DC crime bill came across his desk. Republicans had won net gains of forty-seven House and three Senate seats in the 1966 midterms. The war was going badly both at home and in Southeast Asia—so badly that Johnson declined to seek his party's nomination for a second term. The third reason was that "Warren's resignation coincided with Congress's considering crime and gun control bills—issues that returned attention to the Court's highly unpopular crime-related decisions."[70]

The Senate's opposition to Fortas turned his nomination into an airing of grievances against the Warren Court. Senator Ervin argued that Fortas stood for "tyranny on the bench"; Senator Robert Byrd (D-WV) accused the Warren Court of arrogating "to itself the legislative function."[71] President Johnson, once the "Master of the Senate," fumbled around for a response but could muster nothing much more than calling his opponents anti-Semites who were allergic to the idea of a Jewish chief justice. Fortas's fate was finally sealed on July 19, when the Senate learned that he had received $15,000 to teach a privately funded seminar at American University Law School.[72] After Richard Nixon's triumph in the 1968 presidential election, Earl Warren was replaced in 1969 by Warren Burger, who was committed to rolling back the criminal procedure "revolution."[73]

Although this confrontation between Congress and the court did not involve national security issues, it was heavily shaped by the context of the Vietnam War in at least three ways. First, as the war became increasingly frustrating and self-defeating, the Johnson administration became more politically vulnerable. By 1968—especially after the shock of the Tet Offensive—Johnson and his liberal allies could no longer set the congressional agenda, as they had done so effectively in 1964 and 1965 when constructing the Great Society and the War on Poverty.[74] Conservative legislators capitalized on this weakness when passing the Safe Streets Act. Second, the war threw fuel on the already smoldering fire of protest generated by the civil rights movement. Although most antiwar and civil rights protests were nonviolent, even peaceful protests frequently involved deliberate lawbreaking, and large riots broke out in Harlem in 1964, Watts in 1965, and Detroit in 1967, among other places. For congressional conservatives, violent crime was a natural consequence of this broader lawbreaking culture—a culture that could only be confronted through more aggressive policing unencumbered by judicial restraints.[75] Third, the war exacerbated divisions on the political left, as progressives and liberals fought bitterly over the justice and necessity of US military intervention in Southeast Asia. All this added up to a resurgent conservative movement that was willing and able to "slap the Supreme Court," despite the objections of the Johnson administration. Although this "court slapping" occurred during the Vietnam War, its primary consequence—the death of the Warren Court's criminal procedure "revolution"—ensured that, after the war and into the future, the rights of criminal defendants in the United States would stagnate at best and be rolled back at worst.[76]

The War on Terror

During the War on Terror, Congress once again curbed the jurisdiction of the courts—both directly and indirectly. The Guantanamo detention regime was originally established under the 2001 Authorization for the Use of Military Force (AUMF), given to the Bush administration by Congress. However, in *Hamdan v. Rumsfeld* (2006), the Supreme Court concluded that the AUMF did not provide a sufficiently specific authorization for the detention of "enemy combatants" and their trial by military commissions. In response to Justice Clarence Thomas's claim, in dissent, that the court's decision would "sorely hamper the President's ability to confront and defeat a new and deadly enemy," Justice Stephen Breyer wrote a short opinion—joined by Justices Anthony Kennedy, David Souter, and Ruth Bader Ginsburg—providing reassurance that "the Court's conclusion ultimately rests upon a single ground: Congress has not issued the Executive a 'blank check,'" and "nothing prevents the President from returning to Congress to seek the authority he believes necessary. Where, as here, no emergency prevents consultation with Congress, judicial insistence upon that consultation does not weaken our Nation's ability to deal with danger. To the contrary, that insistence strengthens the Nation's ability to determine—through democratic means—how best to do so. The Constitution places its faith in those democratic means. Our Court today simply does the same."[77]

President Bush took up this invitation to seek additional authority in 2006. At this juncture—with growing public dissatisfaction with the Iraq War—legislators might have curtailed the Bush program. Instead, hours before the end of the 2006 congressional session, with the support of 218 Republicans and 32 Democrats in the House and 53 Republicans and 12 Democrats in the Senate, Congress passed the Military Commissions Act (MCA). The MCA authorized "the use of military commissions to try alien unlawful enemy combatants engaged in hostilities against the United States for violations of the law of war and other offenses triable by military commission," and it broadened the definition of "unlawful enemy combatants" to include indirect "material support" to terrorism. The MCA emphasized that the provisions of the Uniform Code of Military Justice relating to a "speedy trial," "compulsory self-incrimination," and "pretrial investigation" "shall not apply to trial by military commission under this chapter." Furthermore, "no alien unlawful enemy combatant subject to trial by military commission under this chapter may invoke the Geneva Conventions as a source of rights." Finally, "no court, justice, or judge shall have jurisdiction to hear or consider an application for a writ of habeas corpus filed by or on behalf of an alien detained by the United States who has been determined by the United States to have been properly detained as an enemy combatant or is awaiting such determination."[78]

Regarding interrogation, the MCA made an important amendment to the 1996 War Crimes Act. Under that act, any US person responsible for torture could be sued in the United States—including, presumably, US officials who mistreated Guantanamo detainees. The MCA foreclosed this avenue of litigation—prospectively and retroactively.[79] As the White House stated, this "provide[d] legal protections that ensure our military and intelligence personnel will not have to fear lawsuits filed by terrorists simply for doing their jobs."[80]

It is not uncommon for the president to act unilaterally and for Congress to ratify his actions after the fact. This "act first, ask questions later" approach was typical of "Lincoln's Constitution" during the Civil War.[81] Yet the MCA did more than ratify what Bush had already done. It invited the entrenchment and expansion of the Guantanamo legal regime by curbing the jurisdiction of federal courts, immunizing interrogators, and cutting away the due process protections the Supreme Court had tentatively tried to provide Guantanamo detainees.

Most of the MCA's provisions were well grounded in Congress's constitutional powers. Article I grants Congress the authority to "make Rules concerning Captures on Land and Water," to "make Rules for the Government and Regulation of the land and naval Forces," and to "define and punish . . . Offences against the Law of Nations."[82] Article III allows Congress to create "Regulations" and "Exceptions" to the Supreme Court's appellate jurisdiction.[83] Article I, Section 9, prohibits ex post facto laws, but it does not prohibit all retroactive legislating. As the Supreme Court acknowledged back in the founding era, the ex post facto clause applies only to laws that retroactively impose punishments. Congress may immunize or reduce criminal and civil punishments after the fact.[84]

The MCA did eventually run into legal trouble because of its attempts to limit the writ of habeas corpus. In June 2008, in *Boumediene v. Bush*, the Supreme Court found the habeas-stripping provision of the MCA unconstitutional because the Guantanamo Naval Base was de facto if not de jure US territory; therefore, citizens and noncitizens detained there could seek habeas relief in US courts.[85] While the *Boumediene* decision declared that "the laws and Constitution are designed to survive, and remain in force, in extraordinary times," it was careful not to undermine the legal architecture Congress had created for Guantanamo, and it emphasized that "our decision today holds only that petitioners before us are entitled to seek the writ."[86]

Since *Boumediene*, the Supreme Court and the DC Circuit Court of Appeals have largely stepped back from any further questioning of the Guantanamo legal regime. As the Congressional Research Service noted in November 2021, "It has been more than a decade since the Supreme Court has decided a case involving a Guantanamo detainee, and the Court has not squarely addressed whether Guantanamo detainees are entitled to due process under the Fifth Amendment." The DC Circuit has similarly avoided the latter question, not to mention the larger question of how long detainees can be held without having some kind of civilian judicial hearing.[87]

Boumediene bears close similarities to the *Ex parte Yerger* case in 1869. In *Yerger*, the court asserted its right to hear habeas petitions but—in the aftermath of congressional threats to the court's authority during the *Ex parte McCardle* debacle—asserted this right narrowly and in a way that would not threaten the legitimacy of military Reconstruction. In *Boumediene*, the court similarly underscored the judicial branch's authority to hear habeas petitions but—in the aftermath of the MCA—did nothing more.

While the MCA retroactively immunized interrogators, the 2008

Foreign Intelligence Surveillance Act (FISA) Amendments Act retroactively immunized telecommunications companies that participated in legally dubious government surveillance programs, thereby ensuring that no lawsuits or cases involving these companies could proceed. The background for the FISA Amendments Act was a 2005 *New York Times* exposé of the Bush administration's Terrorist Surveillance Program (TSP), the broad aspects of which were outlined by the Sixth Circuit Court of Appeals in 2007: "It has been publicly acknowledged that the TSP includes the interception (i.e., wiretapping), without warrants, of telephone and email communications where one party to the communication is located outside the United States and the NSA has 'a reasonable basis to conclude that one party to the communication is a member of al Qaeda, affiliated with al Qaeda, or a member of an organization affiliated with al Qaeda, or working in support of al Qaeda.'"[88]

After the TSP was exposed, several telecommunications companies were sued by their customers under section 109 of the 1978 FISA, which threatened fines and imprisonment of up to five years for anyone who "engages in electronic surveillance under color of law except as authorized by statute."[89] However, Title II of the 2008 FISA Amendments Act made these lawsuits moot, providing that, upon certification by the attorney general, "notwithstanding any other provision of law, a civil action may not lie or be maintained in a Federal or State court against any person for providing assistance to an element of the intelligence community, and shall be promptly dismissed."[90]

In an abortive attempt to filibuster the FISA Amendments Act, Senator Russ Feingold (D-WI) called Title II a "get out of jail free card," and his colleague Chris Dodd of Connecticut tried to remove the immunity provisions. Missouri Republican Kit Bond retorted that Feingold and Dodd displayed "a lack of understanding about the intelligence community's dependence upon our third-party partners." Without getting "their voluntary cooperation by giving them liability protection," electronic surveillance would become virtually impossible.[91] The chairman of the Senate Intelligence Committee, Senator Jay Rockefeller (D-WV), warned that without the FISA Amendments Act, the intelligence community would miss out on "new opportunities" created by the evolution of digital technology.[92] With bipartisan support, the Senate passed the bill by a filibuster-proof 69–28 margin.[93]

After both the Civil War and the Second World War, legislators were displeased by judicial incursions into weighty questions of civil liberties and national security, and they responded with threats to the Supreme Court's jurisdiction. The Military Commissions Act of 2006, like the repeal of the 1867 Habeas Corpus Act, put this threat into action. During the War on Terror, legislators complemented their power to limit the Supreme Court's jurisdiction with their subtler ability to retroactively legalize possibly illegal conduct. When the FISA Amendments Act immunized telecommunications companies from surveillance-related lawsuits and the MCA immunized torturers from lawsuits brought under the War Crimes Act, judicial interference in the War on Terror was preemptively curbed. No court was formally targeted or stripped of its jurisdiction, but retroactive immunity simply made sure that there would be no cases to adjudicate.[94]

Congress, in short, has a long track record of curbing the judiciary's ability to protect civil liberties—stretching from the Civil War and Reconstruction to the War on Terror. It is possible that this track record is now a thing of the past, as Congress has become more polarized and divided government more common. After the 2020 election, threats from congressional Democrats to reverse Republican packing of the courts ultimately amounted to little more than bluster.[95] The principle of judicial supremacy—the Supreme Court being the final arbiter of constitutional disputes—appears to be widely accepted today.[96]

On the other hand, the fact remains that Congress possesses significant powers over the judiciary and has not historically been afraid to wield or at least credibly threaten to wield these powers. It has done so fairly recently to deter judicial constraints on the War on Terror, and just as in prior legislative-judicial conflicts, the courts have seemingly stepped away from the "political thicket" of War on Terror–related cases after initially stepping into it, albeit cautiously.[97] Ultimately, while this chapter has argued that the "law" does not always "fall silent" during or in the aftermath of war, it has demonstrated how much Congress can and has done to keep the "law" as quiet as possible.

5

Congress and the States

In contrast to its powers over the judiciary, Congress's constitutional powers over the states are sparse. The underlying theory of Article I, Section 8, and the Tenth Amendment of the Constitution is (in James Madison's words) that Congress's powers "are few and defined," while "those which are to remain in the State governments are numerous and indefinite."[1] Nevertheless, as this chapter demonstrates, Congress has managed to encourage state-level violations of civil liberties in the aftermath of war through various informal and indirect mechanisms.

One way, which was particularly pronounced during the Red Scares, was providing state legislatures a model of repression they could copy and adapt to local circumstances. In these postwar periods, federal legislators did far more than set an example: the House Un-American Activities Committee (HUAC), in particular, developed close connections with several "little HUACs" across the country, identifying targets, expert witnesses, methods, and investigative strategies for their partners and imitators at the state level. The results often caused severe damage to civil liberties.

Although this kind of repressive network—with Congress at its core—did not seem to emerge from the Vietnam War or the War on Terror, recent scholarship on American federalism has argued that the seeds of such a network may have taken root in the twenty-first century.[2] Jacob Grumbach's 2022 study *Laboratories Against Democracy* documents how national partisan actors—both elected and unelected—have turned state legislatures into battlegrounds, with the Republican Party in particular using state legislative power to promote "democratic backsliding."[3] I do not enter into this broader conversation about the costs and benefits of American federalism, but I do provide some recent examples of Congress inspiring, guiding, and encouraging repressive actions at the state level, including laws aimed at curbing the boycott, divestment, and sanctions (BDS) movement and—in the aftermath of the October 7, 2023, terrorist attacks against Israel—laws aimed at stifling pro-Palestinian speech on college campuses.

This chapter also discusses another form of congressional influence over the states and other local jurisdictions: congressional control over their federal funds. Generally, the Supreme Court has given Congress wide authority and discretion over the conditions it can attach to state funding, thus allowing Congress to accomplish indirectly—through financial incentives—what it could not do directly through its enumerated constitutional powers.[4] Beginning during the latter years of the Vietnam War, Congress began to financially incentivize what could be called the "militarization" of police forces across the United States. This has not always or necessarily resulted in violations of civil liberties, but it has undoubtedly increased the repressive capacity of local actors.

The First Red Scare

The limits of congressional power over the states were bluntly exposed during Reconstruction. The only way Congress could directly govern the states of the former Confederacy was to hold them in the "grasp of war" and treat them as "conquered rebels" rather than full-fledged states. Once they regained their status as full-fledged states—which all of them did by February 1871—Congress could only try to regulate their conduct through civil rights legislation and, briefly, the Ku Klux Klan Act (discussed in chapter 1). As General Pope put it in a lengthy letter to General Grant in July 1867, once the old Confederate states were readmitted, "the power of Congress over them is reduced practically to the general power which that body has over all States in the Union." In essence, this meant that "Congress and the people disarm themselves—The moment admission into the Union is accomplished the Military power is suspended and with it all restrictions are removed."[5] In general, after the ex-Confederate states were restored to the Union, the civil liberties of ex-Confederates could no longer be restricted by either the state or the federal government. The only rights that could be curtailed were those of freedmen at the hands of the so-called redeemed—that is, white-dominated and white supremacist—Southern governments.

During the first Red Scare, however, congressional legislation and investigations provided a repressive template for the states to follow. The 1917 Espionage Act and the 1918 Sedition Act inspired a cascade of similar legislation at the state level. For example, Ohio's criminal syndicalism law, enacted in 1919, echoed the Espionage and Sedition Acts by prohibiting any advocacy of "the duty, necessity, or propriety of crime, sabotage, violence, or unlawful methods of terrorism as a means of accomplishing industrial or political reform" and association with "any society, group, or assemblage of persons formed to teach or advocate the doctrines of criminal syndicalism." "From 1917 to 1920," the US Supreme Court reflected in 1969, "identical or quite similar laws" to Ohio's "were adopted by 20 States and two territories."[6]

Like the federal laws, the state laws violated civil liberties. Indeed, the state laws punished people for activities the Supreme Court would now regard as firmly protected by the First Amendment. The Supreme Court directly acknowledged this in 1969 when it invalidated the conviction of local Ku Klux Klan leader Clarence Brandenburg under Ohio's criminal syndicalism law.[7] To be sure, local considerations drove the initial passage of these laws, and several of them predated the federal espionage and sedition statutes. Mississippi, for example, did not have a sedition statute based on the federal model in 1919; rather, it had a law assessing "a fine not exceeding 500 dollars or imprisonment not exceeding six months for advocating social equality between the races."[8] New York, meanwhile, had passed a "criminal anarchy" statute in 1902 in the aftermath of the assassination of President William McKinley in September 1901.[9] Congress did not—and, constitutionally, could not—drag the states unwillingly into the passage of sedition or criminal syndicalism legislation, but it gave them a relatively easy model to imitate.

One state, at least, also emulated the investigative methods of the US Senate's Overman Subcommittee on "Bolshevik propaganda." On March 26, 1919, the New York legislature passed a "concurrent resolution authorizing the investigation of seditious activities" in the state. This resolution credited "the sub-committee of the Senate of the United States" with providing "sufficient facts" on the scope and danger of seditious activities, thus "indicat[ing] the necessity of further inquiry and action."[10] Aside from this federal inspiration for the creation of New York's Joint Legislative Committee to Investigate Seditious Activities (known as the Lusk Committee after its chairman, Senator Clayton Lusk), one of the star witnesses of the Overman Subcommittee—Archibald Stevenson—became deeply involved in the work of its New York copycat.

Stevenson was a self-proclaimed expert on radicalism and subversion. During the First World War, he reportedly "volunteered in 1917 to assist the Department of Justice in its investigation of German propaganda, and took upon himself the task of supervising a card-index of the names of those in this country whom he suspected of pro-German leanings, working under the direction of Captain Trevor of the Military Intelligence Department, with offices at 302 Broadway." After Captain Trevor vouched for Stevenson's investigative credentials in a letter to the Overman Subcommittee, Senator Overman described "Archibald Ewing Stevenson of the Propaganda Section, who has studied German propaganda in the United States for over a year and concentrated on the subject," as "probably more familiar with the various interlocking groups of German and radical propaganda in the United States than anyone else in this country." Stevenson's testimony before the Overman Subcommittee was spectacular. "After denouncing various degrees and species of pacifists," a fierce critique recounted, "he finally succeeded [in] reading into the record a list of sixty-two citizens holding, as he asserted, 'dangerous, destructive, and anarchistic sentiments,' including Jane Addams, Bishop Jones, George W. Kirchwey, David Starr Jordan, Frederic C. Howe, Lillian D. Wald, Oswald G. Villard, and a number of ministers and college professors."[11]

Based on these credentials—and the fact that Stevenson's Union League Club in New York City drafted the joint resolution authorizing the creation of the Lusk Committee—Stevenson was hired as counsel for the committee. He was the principal author of its enormous four-volume report *Revolutionary Radicalism: Its History, Purpose and Tactics; with an Exposition and Discussion of the Steps Being Taken and Required to Curb It*. Volumes 1 and 2 of this report cited testimony from the Overman Subcommittee to support the legislative recommendations put forward in volumes 3 and 4, especially loyalty oaths for New

York schoolteachers.[12] These measures—nicknamed the "Lusk Laws"—were eventually adopted by the legislature after initial opposition from Governor Al Smith. They were repealed in 1923 at Governor Smith's urging.[13]

The Lusk Committee, like the successful campaigns for various state sedition and criminal syndicalism laws across the United States, was inspired but not created by the actions of the US Congress. Indeed, the Lusk Committee went much further than the Overman Subcommittee in both the legislation it recommended and produced and its raids against alleged subversives. The offices of the Union of Russian Workers and the socialist Rand School for Social Sciences on East Fifteenth Street in Manhattan were raided in 1919 in collaboration with the New York City Police Department's Bomb Squad, vigilantes from the American Protective League, and federal agents.[14]

New York also followed the federal legislature in excluding five duly elected socialists from the state Assembly. Republican Assembly Speaker Thaddeus Sweet opened the 1920 legislative session with a sermon on "the problems confronting us," which were "many and of grave concern to the future welfare of the State and Nation." He praised "laws that will prohibit the printing and circulation of publications designed to create unrest, discontent, and class distinction; laws to rid our schools of the teaching of socialistic Soviet doctrines." Sweet then "directed the sergeant-at-arms to bring Messrs. Claessens, deWitt, Orr, Solomon, and Waldman before the bar of the House." To these five socialists, Speaker Sweet said: "You are seeking seats in this body—you who have been elected on a platform that is absolutely inimical to the best interests of the State of New York and of the United States." He went on to highlight the Socialist Party's opposition to the late war effort as evidence of its disloyalty. He then presented a motion that resolved to do exactly what Congress had done to Victor L. Berger a year earlier: establish a special investigation into the eligibility of the assemblymen. In the meantime, "they are hereby denied seats in this Assembly." The resolution passed with 140 ayes and 6 nos.[15]

The Assembly, acting on recommendation from the committee, voted to expel the socialists in April 1920. Governor Smith, who condemned the expulsion, convened a special legislative session in September, at which the socialists retook their seats. Three out of five were expelled again at the end of September, and the remaining two resigned in protest.[16] All five ran in the general election in November, and only two—one who had been expelled and one who had resigned—won their seats back. No more expulsions followed.[17]

The New York expulsions were not an exact replica of the federal Berger expulsion, and the resolution that expelled the socialists did not explicitly invoke Congress's example in the same way the Lusk Committee's resolution invoked the work of the Overman Subcommittee. The rationale for Berger's exclusion was section 3 of the Fourteenth Amendment, whereas the New York socialists faced a more general accusation of disloyalty. Berger was convicted under the Espionage Act, whereas the New York socialists were not charged with any crime. However, the overall process in the New York legislature—delegitimizing the socialist legislators, establishing a special investigation, and settling on the effective disenfranchisement of the people who had voted for the socialists—was clearly modeled on the process in Congress. This little Red Scare emulated the tactics and methods of the big one.

The Second Red Scare

During the second Red Scare, a larger number of states emulated HUAC and established closer and more durable connections with federal legislative investigations.

CALIFORNIA

In 1953 the ACLU singled out California's Joint Legislative Fact-Finding Committee on Un-American Activities (CUAC) as the most powerful "little HUAC" of the post–World War II era.[18] CUAC was established as a joint legislative committee in 1941 under the chairmanship of Senator Jack Tenney. Although CUAC had distinctive local origins—emerging from legislative dissatisfaction with the administration of progressive Democratic Governor Culbert Olson—Senator Tenney, who was first elected to the state legislature as a Democrat, regarded his fellow disgruntled Democrat, HUAC founding chairman Martin Dies (D-TX), as an inspirational figure. Tenney wrote that his critics, "capitalizing on what they believed to have been a successful smear of Congressman Martin Dies," labeled CUAC "the Little Dies Committee." However, as "events and disclosures . . . more and more spot-lighted the great courage and ability of the Texan, the opprobrium of 'The Little Dies Committee' became a title of distinction."[19]

Although CUAC (also known as the Tenney Committee) had its own local targets and concerns—including the 1943 Zoot Suit Riots in Los Angeles, the alleged communist subversion of the University of California–Los Angeles (UCLA) Writer's Conference, and the loyalty of Japanese Americans during the Second World War—it regularly based its investigations, reports, and accusations on evidence gathered by HUAC. In its 1943 annual report, the Tenney Committee cited HUAC evidence for the claims that "the *foreign policy*, *need*, and, *ambition* of Soviet Russia itself determines the policies of its Communist branches throughout the countries of the world" and that these branches advocate a combination of "legal and *illegal* tactics"; that Unit 104 of the Professional Section of the Communist Party in California "persuaded the Lubin family to allow them to name" a communist front organization after the well-respected civic leader Simon J. Lubin; that consumer advocate Arthur Kallet was "a professional Communist"; and that the Federation of Architects, Engineers, Chemists, and Technicians was "distinctly a Communist organization."[20] In 1945 Tenney became particularly eager to expose communist front organizations operating in California, especially the Congress of Industrial Organizations (CIO). Again citing evidence from HUAC, Tenney claimed that eighteen of the forty-nine members of the CIO's Political Action Committee "have records of collaboration with the Communist program in the United States."[21]

Beyond labor organizations and other alleged fronts, the Tenney Committee, like HUAC, aimed to expose communist subversion in education. In its 1947 report, the Tenney Committee relied on testimony before HUAC to support various allegations against the staff and leadership of the California Labor School. According to HUAC, the school's director, David Jenkins, had "a long history of activities in organizations and causes initiated by the Communist Party"; teacher Celeste Strack "was a former member of the Debating Team of the University of California and was suspended on October 29, 1934 by the Provost of the University because of her Communist activities"; teacher George Hitchcock was "a member of the Editorial Staff" of the communist paper *People's World*; Al Richmond and Adam Lapin, who taught classes on "America as a World Power Today," were editors and regular contributors to the same paper; Helen Miller, who "is listed among the faculty of this school," was "one of the principal speakers" at an April 1941 rally where she denounced the United States as "an imperialistic nation"; and Donald Thayer, who "teaches a course in advanced economics," was "in charge for the Communist Party of Communist recruits for the Spanish Civil War." The Tenney Committee also cited HUAC when documenting "propaganda in California's grade schools," especially through the textbook *Land of the Soviets*, whose editor, Maxwell S. Stewart, HUAC had labeled an apologist for Soviet crimes.[22] Although the Tenney Committee did not succeed in legally imposing loyalty oaths or textbook bans in California's schools, Tenney did succeed in encouraging the county and city of Los Angeles to impose loyalty oaths on their employees in 1947 and 1948. Moreover, after the committee repeatedly threatened investigations and legislation to counter subversion at the University of California, the university's Board of Regents introduced a loyalty oath in 1949.[23]

Tenney and HUAC also collaborated in their investigations of Hollywood. As Michael Heale recounts, Tenney traveled to Washington, DC, in the spring of 1947, "where he was genially hosted by Congressman [Richard] Nixon and where he warned HUAC of the alarming activities of Charles Chaplin, Frederic March, John Garfield, Edward G. Robinson, and Frank Sinatra."[24] In turn, Tenney credited HUAC for "corroborating the findings of the California Legislative Committee investigating subversive activities" in Hollywood, including the finding that Alvah Bessie was a communist and that the "primary function" of "the Actors' Laboratory Theater" was to "draw ambitious young actors and actresses into the orbit of Communist front organizations."[25] Frontier Films; the Independent Citizens Committee of the Arts, Sciences, and Professions; and the American Committee of Jewish Writers, Artists, and Scientists were also identified by Tenney as front organizations, based on testimonial evidence and citations provided by HUAC.[26] Throughout Tenney's and HUAC's investigations of Hollywood, "national and state red-hunters were egging one another on."[27]

Tenney was ousted as CUAC chairman in 1949 and replaced by Senator Hugh Burns. Like Tenney, Burns focused on distinctly local concerns, such as the alleged communist infiltration of the California Pacific, Gas, and Electric Company. Yet Burns could also draw on both HUAC and the US Senate Subcommittee on Internal Security (SSIS), which was formed in 1951. Burns was particularly captivated by the SSIS testimony of Bella V. Dodd, a former Communist Party member and instructor at Hunter College in New York City, who (in CUAC's words) explained "how one or two Communists in a large [educational] institution could effectively launch broad Communist units and exert an enormous amount of influence out of all proportion to their minority strength." Dodd also claimed that New York's Joint Legislative Committee to Investigate the Educational System of the State of New York, known as the Rapp-Coudert Committee, had effectively diminished communist power within the state's education unions between 1940 and 1942.[28] Claims such as these inspired CUAC, in 1952, to meet with the presidents of the University of California, the University of Southern California, the California Institute of Technology, Claremont College, and other prominent state universities. Following these meetings, CUAC reported that "all present agreed" to "collaborate with the committee in a cooperative, long-range preventive plan to eliminate Communist Party members from the faculties of California institutions of higher learning and to take steps to prevent the infiltration of faculties by Communist Party members, or those whose documentable record of Communist activities were so formidable as to raise a serious question concerning their ability to engage in objective teaching." In the first year of this "long-range preventive plan," CUAC claimed that "more than 100 individuals have been eliminated from various campuses in California."[29]

Under Burns, CUAC began to operate with less publicity and sensationalism than the Tenney Committee. Indeed, its plan for rooting out communism in state universities was justified, in part, because it "virtually eliminates the necessity of the long series of public hearings, which are not only expensive and attended by considerable sensational publicity, but which are inevitably attended, also, by an atmosphere of excitement and tension which makes the work of the committee much more difficult once the smoke of battle has cleared away."[30] Still, CUAC endured as an official state investigating committee until 1970, rivaling HUAC for longevity. Like HUAC, its influence and impact waned throughout the 1950s as the Korean War ended, the US Supreme Court began to constrain the behavior of legislative committees, and prominent legislators such as Joseph McCarthy and Jack Tenney alienated their colleagues with their willingness to throw accusations at a wide range of targets.[31]

WASHINGTON

Also on the West Coast, Washington's state legislature established a Joint Fact-Finding Committee on Un-American Activities in 1947, known as the Canwell Committee after Chairman Albert Canwell. Canwell was elected to the state legislature in 1947 and recalled that, on the campaign trail, "I made only two statements about what I would do. I wouldn't vote for any new taxes and I'd do something about the Communists." Canwell claimed that "a great many families in the state, and particularly . . . in Eastern Washington, were sending their sons and daughters to the University of Washington, an advantage that they themselves had never had." But the young people were "coming back spouting lines that were completely unacceptable to the people who were paying the bill." This "Communist issue" at the University of Washington "kept surfacing," and "there was constant pressure on legislators to get with it and do something." At first, Canwell met with other legislators and "read the copies of legislation that we had acquired from other states pointing out what the national Congress was doing and what the possible solutions to the problem might be." Later, Canwell "came up with House Concurrent Resolution No. 10," authorizing the creation of a legislative un-American activities committee. In drafting the resolution, Canwell recalled, "We worked somewhat from the House Committee on Un-American Activities resolutions and the California [Tenney] committee. They were good, but I felt that they needed a little fine tuning, so I dressed them up a little."[32]

After Canwell's resolution passed on the final day of the 1947 legislative session and the personnel of the committee were confirmed, Canwell's next step was to travel to Washington, DC. There, he "wanted to talk to the people at the House Committee on Un-American Activities. Get whatever advice I might be able to get. And I did." He recalled "talking to Bob Stripling, who was the chief investigator for the Dies Committee and had become quite well identified in the Communist investigation situation." Attempting to provide further information in a 1997 oral history interview, Canwell could not recall specific details of his conversations with Stripling, other than to suggest that Stripling may have introduced him to professional anticommunist investigator J. B. Matthews, who had been research director for HUAC and would later work closely with Joseph McCarthy in the US Senate. Stripling, Canwell recalled, gave him "a cardboard carton full of what became very valuable reports" from HUAC and from New York's Rapp-Coudert Committee. Canwell also recalled meeting FBI Director J. Edgar Hoover, thanks to "doors" being "opened" by Washington Republican Congressman Walt Horan, "who was on the Appropriations Committee for the Justice Department." Although Canwell was impressed by Hoover's professionalism and attention to detail, he did not document any close or enduring relationship between the FBI director and Washington State's little HUAC.[33] Clearly, however, Canwell wanted to do everything he could to model his committee on the big HUAC, as well as California's Tenney Committee.

While Tenney made various claims about communist front organizations in California on the basis of HUAC evidence, Canwell chose to summon "friendly witnesses"—ex-communists who had gained national attention for their dramatic testimony before HUAC. According to Canwell, some of these witnesses, "like Joe Kornfeder, Louis Budenz, had testified before congressional committees, and it was pretty well-known what they could testify to. It was my desire to put this in the record so that it would be obvious to people what the Communist menace was."[34] Although Kornfeder provided only general statements about the goals and ideas of the Communist Party during the Canwell Committee's first hearings in February 1948, Budenz provided both general context about the "Communist menace" and specific information. For instance, he claimed that the Washington Old Age Pension Union, though "formed by non-Communist elements" in 1938, was "largely in accord with the Communist Party position" by 1940. In other words, "the Communists succeeded in infiltrating and in dominating the Old Age Pension Union." Budenz added that William J. Pennock, president of the union in 1947, had been tasked with "carrying out the program of the Communist Party and taking over the Old Age Pension Union." Budenz also described University of Washington psychology professor Ralph Gundlach as not having a history of being an official Communist Party member but nonetheless being "under Party discipline."[35]

In July 1948 Gundlach was one of sixteen witnesses who was subpoenaed by and testified before the Canwell Committee in its second round of public hearings, which focused on an investigation of the University of Washington.[36] J. B. Matthews—proudly identified by the Canwell Committee as "Former Research Director for the Dies Committee"—began the hearings as an "expert witness" and made both general claims about communist efforts to infiltrate higher education and the specific claim that Professor Gundlach had been affiliated with a long list of subversive organizations, including the American Committee for Protection of Foreign Born, the Committee for Democratic Far-Eastern Policy, the Consumers' Union, the National Federation for Constitutional Liberties, and the Citizens' Committee for Harry Bridges.[37] Gundlach, along with Professors Herbert Phillips and Joe Butterworth, refused to answer the committee's questions and were cited for contempt of the legislature. All three were dismissed from the university in 1949. They never worked in academia again. In court, Gundlach was convicted of contempt; he was "fined $250 and spent 30 days in jail." Three other professors were "forced to sign an affidavit that they were not members of the Communist Party and placed on probation for two years."[38]

Reflecting on the University of Washington investigation in 1997, Canwell said, "It was more or less forced on us. The University of Washington and its faculty had become, not only a local, but a national scandal."[39] Indeed, as with the Tenney Committee, the Canwell Committee's agenda was driven by local and external pressures, including from the press. People like Louis Budenz and J. B. Matthews—who had established their reputations as investigators and researchers in Washington, DC—encouraged the committee's focus on higher education and named specific professors in Washington State with a history of allegedly subversive affiliations. As in California, the hunt for un-American activities in the state of Washington was inspired and shaped by the original hunt on Capitol Hill.

ILLINOIS

In 1947 the Illinois state legislature created a Seditious Activities Investigation Commission that included five state senators, five state representatives, and five gubernatorial appointees. It became known as the Broyles Commission after its primary sponsor, Senator Paul Broyles. Like Canwell, Broyles did not just observe the federal legislature and attempt to emulate it; he (and six other commission members) traveled to Capitol Hill to meet and confer with the leaders of the national Red Scare on August 25–27, 1948, when his state investigations were in their early stages. Broyles and his colleagues scheduled a meeting with Congressman Richard Nixon and observation of a HUAC hearing on day 1. They planned conferences with Lou Nichols, assistant FBI director; William Rogers, chief investigator for the Senate Investigations Committee; and

Karl Baarslaag, "research specialist" for the American Legion's Americanism Committee, on day 2 and conferences with HUAC leaders, including Chairman J. Parnell Thomas, on day 3.[40]

According to the Broyles Commission's records, Nichols offered nothing of great value. He insisted, "We [the FBI] try to refrain from injecting ourselves in local affairs" but affirmed that "Americanism has to be taught in the home as well as in the public schools" because "these parlor 'pinks' are generally frustrated individuals who can't make a living in the business world." Rogers, for his part, urged some restraint: "Do not be careless about hurting people," he warned. But he also responded to Broyles's concern that "the real hot spot of the universities is the University of Chicago" with the advice that "if there is anything you can do financially to them, this is what hurts." Rogers also thought Broyles would benefit from warning the president of the university that "there are Communist activities there" that may need to be investigated either internally or externally.[41]

The "primary purpose" of the conference with Baarslag was really to meet Joseph Kornfeder, the ex-communist expert witness who had already testified before HUAC and the Canwell Committee. Broyles Commission members asked Kornfeder various questions about Communist Party goals and methods, as well as his own conversion to anticommunism. Broyles then asked how "a new Commission, such as ours," could "attack" the communist problem in Illinois. Kornfeder, citing his "experience in other cases," emphasized that "your first job is exposure on a local level," such as making "people aware" of "infiltration among the colleges and universities" because this is "something real" to people and "their own youngsters." He referenced the Canwell Committee's ongoing investigations of the University of Washington as a possible example to follow.[42]

The HUAC leaders provided more in-depth and varied guidance. Chairman Thomas told Broyles, "If you are going into the education phase, thoroughly, the University of Chicago would be one of the places we would start. We have more literature on infiltration of Communism in education institutions—but over a period of time, different matters have come into us and just off hand I happen to think of the University of Chicago. We run into it as much as any other university in the States." Richard B. Vail, a HUAC member from Illinois, warned against focusing only on the University of Chicago because "in Chicago you have a close tie between Roosevelt College and Chicago University. You will draw a measure of criticism by selecting the University of Chicago as your main objective. If you include Roosevelt College, you have two elements there that are very vital in the development of the Communist thinking."[43]

With respect to "expert witnesses," Broyles asked Thomas about Kornfeder, and Thomas confirmed that Kornfeder "can be relied upon." Thomas also described J. B. Matthews as a man with "a tremendous amount of experience in the field of un-American activities, particularly Communism." Vail provided additional advice about timing, staffing, and strategy. He counseled against holding any public hearings on the University of Chicago "until you have a qualified staff to take up details." More generally, he advised Broyles, "I would make plans for the next months, but I don't believe I would make an effort to hold hearings to be publicized."[44]

Eventually, the Broyles Commission would incorporate all this advice to some degree. Lacking staff and funds, it did not conduct any public hearings prior to the release of its final report on seditious activities in early 1949. However, after rowdy students from the University of Illinois, the University of Chicago, and Roosevelt College disrupted a state legislative session concerning the recommendations of the Broyles Commission, the commission decided to conduct an emergency investigation of higher education in Illinois. Armed with emergency appropriations from the legislature for this purpose, the commission was able to hire J. B. Matthews as its chief investigator and to finally conduct public hearings in April and May 1949. Matthews was closely assisted by another former communist made famous by his HUAC testimony: Benjamin Gitlow. As Congressman Vail had suggested, the second Broyles Commission investigation focused on the University of Chicago and Roosevelt College.[45]

The public hearings on the Illinois universities lacked the drama of the Canwell Committee investigations. The witnesses included the chancellor and chairman of the Board of Trustees of the University of Chicago, the president of Roosevelt College, six professors, two students, a state representative, and another "expert" witness with HUAC history—naming alleged communists in Hollywood in 1947—Howard Rushmore.[46] However, no one defied the Broyles Commission like the three University of Washington professors defied the Canwell Committee, and no one from either the University of Chicago or Roosevelt College was fired in the aftermath of the hearings. The Broyles Commission could not even issue a unified report on the hearings. Three members, including Senator Broyles, recommended that Illinois universities be punished for employing "subversive" persons. But two other members dissented from this statement, publicly declaring that "at no time did any witness or any Commission member dare assert that any faculty member had engaged in subversive activities," and "the widespread smears of persons who are not Communists or even Communist sympathizers simply divert attention from the real dangers."[47]

Thus, after its work was formally completed in 1949, the Broyles Commission had little to show for its efforts. Yet Broyles persisted in the state legislature, and in 1955 he finally succeeded in sponsoring and passing legislation that required loyalty oaths for all state employees.[48] The salaries of three Chicago schoolteachers—Shirley Lens, Sara Pickus, and Albert Soglin—were withheld after they refused to sign the oath, and the Illinois Supreme Court denied their ACLU-sponsored lawsuit in November 1956.[49]

Generally, it would be accurate to conclude that the Broyles Commission had a less significant impact on civil liberties in Illinois than the Tenney and Canwell Committees had in California and Washington. What all three of these little HUACs shared were close links with the big HUAC. The Tenney Committee—which far exceeded the Washington and Illinois committees in terms of staffing, resources, and longevity—relied primarily on testimony and evidence provided by HUAC to set the broad direction of its own investigations. The Canwell Committee relied on HUAC-proven experts Louis Budenz and J. B. Matthews to educate the legislature about the nature of communism and provide specific details about alleged subversives in the Old Age Pension Union and the University of Washington. The Broyles Commission incorporated various advice from HUAC leaders on experts, targets, and public hearings. The big HUAC did not just inspire the little HUACs; it played a crucial role in their development, strategy, and overall investigative direction.

"Black Struggle, Red Scare"

After the Supreme Court's *Brown v. Board of Education* decision in 1954, the little HUAC model became increasingly popular in the South.[50] Unlike the varied targets of the Washington, California, and

Illinois legislative committees, the little HUACs of the South were squarely focused on exposing links between the civil rights movement and communism. In this effort they were aided by HUAC witnesses and experts. In February 1958, for example, J. B. Matthews told Florida's Legislative Investigation Committee that "the Communists are at work, with their customary fanatical dedication, in stirring up trouble in the field of public school integration in the South." He explained that "the Communists have been at work for some thirty years in the field of agitation among Negroes," and "Communists have established friendly contacts with the Negro leaders of most of the recent integration incidents in the South." Matthews's testimony was subsequently published by the Georgia Commission on Education as a pamphlet titled *Communism and the NAACP*.[51]

The "star witness" before Louisiana's Joint Legislative Committee on Segregation in 1957 was Manning Johnson, a black former communist who had testified before HUAC in 1949 on long-running communist efforts to organize black workers in the South. Joseph Kornfeder also testified before the Louisiana committee. As the FBI paraphrased in an internal report on the committee's work, Kornfeder testified that "the Communist Party had infiltrated the NAACP but did not control it," and he estimated that "about half of the approximately 600 Americans trained for subversion in Moscow in the last thirty years were Negroes."[52] According to Johnson, "Communists in the South favored the churches in the South because they had a cloak of respectability," and "Communists had infiltrated churches all over the black belt." Johnson "criticized Rev Martin Luther King of Montgomery, Alabama, terming him a 'megalomaniac seeking power'" whose "leadership of the Negroes was causing harm to the Negroes and could lead to violence and bloodshed." He claimed "that some of King's explanation of purposes were the same as those of the Communist Party." The FBI quoted the chairman of the Louisiana committee, Senator William Rainach, who concluded that "Communist influence working through such instruments as the NAACP is a prime cause of racial disturbances. Creation of racial uprisings against the existing order is a principal instrument of the Communist Party."[53]

Matthews and Johnson also testified before the Special Education Committee of the Arkansas Legislative Council in December 1958. Matthews "testified that the Southern Conference on Human Welfare was an organization set up by the communists, and was the first major thrust of the communists in the South; this was succeeded by the Southern Conference Educational Fund, of which James A. Dombrowski is the executive director and is noted for his communistic activities." Matthews added that Dombrowski was "quite active" in the Highlander Folk School in Tennessee, which "has been used for communist and communist front purposes for the past 25 years." More broadly, Matthews claimed that "at least 221 individuals associated with the Southern Conference Educational Fund have been cited for their connections with communists or communist activities" and that the fund, in turn, "has penetrated 94 white colleges and universities of the South."[54]

Johnson told the Arkansas committee that "as far as Little Rock is concerned the NAACP is backed by the Communists and set up this situation and they are using Little Rock as a place where they can make a test battle. . . . The Reds are going to do all their devilish work in and through the NAACP." While "there was a time when the NAACP believed in gradualism," according to Johnson, now "the Supreme Court and the NAACP have set the stage for a long period of race bitterness, hate, frustration."[55] Internally, the FBI noted that "while Johnson's testimony is historically accurate, it is noted that he is not in a position to speak authoritatively regarding the present tactics and activities of the CP in the Negro field as he was dropped from the CP in 1939."[56] Despite this fact, the Arkansas committee concluded from Johnson's testimony—along with "credible evidence from the files of the House Un-American Activities Committee, the United States Attorney General's Subversive List, the Senate Internal Security Sub-Committee and others"—that "many of the top officers of the national NAACP have been cited numerous times for aiding and abetting communist or communist front organizations"; that "these top officials have sent individuals of very questionable loyalty to our government to Arkansas as their paid employees"; and that "in turn they met with local officials of the NAACP and planned the events which culminated in the so-called Little Rock incident."[57]

The findings of the Southern little HUACs inspired various legal efforts to impose on local NAACP chapters what the federal government had imposed on the Communist Party: compulsory registration, including the disclosure of members and donors. Although the US Supreme Court obstructed these efforts by defending the free association rights of members and donors in 1958 and 1963,[58] the investigations of and accusations against the NAACP and other civil rights organizations were undoubtedly costly, time-consuming, and draining for the civil rights movement. Anticommunists primed on the national congressional stage—especially J. B. Matthews, Joseph Kornfeder, and Manning Johnson—played a crucial role in driving and legitimizing these local campaigns.

"Laboratories Against Democracy"?

These connections between Congress and state and local legislators will not sound foreign to scholars of American federalism and democracy in the twenty-first century. Jacob Grumbach's *Laboratories Against Democracy*, in particular, illuminates somewhat similar dynamics: national political struggles being pulled into and mixed with state politics, with negative consequences for democracy and civil liberties. For Grumbach, federalism provides opportunities for antidemocratic actors in the United States to subvert democratic norms and values—an argument that pulls him into a much larger conversation among scholars about the costs and benefits of America's decentralized constitutional structure.[59]

Although I cannot enter into that conversation here, I would argue that the problem is not necessarily federalism itself but rather the powerful investigative tools wielded by both the national legislature and the state legislatures in the United States. To be sure, these tools are deeply rooted in American constitutional traditions and are not always menacing to civil liberties. Moreover, state-level McCarthyism did not reemerge after the Vietnam War or during the War on Terror. However, even with gridlock and partisan polarization creating a growing obstacle to legislative action in Washington, DC, members of Congress have shown an enduring ability to guide and inspire repressive legislation and investigations at the state level. One recent example is the spread of so-called anti-BDS (boycott, divestment, and sanctions) legislation. As Human Rights Watch reported in April 2019, "Twenty-seven states have adopted laws or policies that penalize businesses, organizations, or individuals that engage in or call for boycotts against Israel." Although, at the time of this writing, Congress has failed to pass similar legislation at the national level, both houses have repeatedly passed resolutions condemning the BDS movement and applauding state efforts to punish its supporters.[60]

So far, the Supreme Court has declined to rule on the constitutionality of these anti-BDS laws.[61] Although the right to boycott is generally protected by the First Amendment because it is tied to speech and advocacy,[62] the anti-BDS laws pose awkward constitutional questions. Americans undoubtedly have a constitutional right to advocate a boycott of the state of Israel or illegal West Bank settlements, but the states also have a right to essentially boycott BDS. As Eugene Volokh puts it: "Anti-BDS laws, which bar government contractors from boycotting Israel, are generally constitutional—for the same reason that anti-discrimination laws are generally constitutional: Refusals to deal are, outside some narrow situations, generally unprotected by the First Amendment."[63] Yet, regardless of whether anti-BDS laws are ultimately constitutional, they are still, clearly, government efforts to marginalize and deter a political movement that the government disfavors. They undermine the spirit, if not the letter, of the Constitution's protection of free political association.

Since the outbreak of war between Israel and Hamas in October 2023, states have more aggressively acted on examples set in DC. After Representative Elise Stefanik (R-NY) publicly condemned several college presidents for failing to suppress allegedly genocidal rhetoric on their campuses, California Senator Steven Glazer introduced a bill that would simply ban such rhetoric. As *The Forward* reported in March 2024, Glazer's bill "does not stipulate what would constitute a call for genocide, leaving open whether controversial slogans such as 'From the river to the sea, Palestine will be free' would be included. . . . In its current form, the bill would leave the determination of what language might qualify to school administrations in the state's University of California, California State University and community college systems."[64] Meanwhile, Republican legislators in New York proposed similar legislation, including the criminalization of vandalism of "pro-Israel materials" such as posters of Israeli hostages held by Hamas in Gaza.[65] States, the federal government, and universities have the right and the obligation to protect their students, faculty, and staff against all forms of discrimination, including anti-Semitism. However, under American constitutional traditions and elementary principles of free expression, political speech cannot be suppressed by state actors on the grounds that it is offensive, inherently harmful, or denigrating.

The ultimate consequences of these legislative proposals are unclear. Those that attempt to prohibit "genocidal" rhetoric are almost certainly doomed under the Supreme Court's existing First Amendment jurisprudence, which protects such rhetoric unless it is part of a plan of "imminent lawless action."[66] In this sense, some of this legislation resembles Congress's effort to criminalize flag burning in 1989 after the Supreme Court explicitly said that flag burning was protected by the First Amendment—obviously unconstitutional, but perhaps politically useful.[67] Yet this legislation, with its focus on policing speech in American universities and the way that its drafters have taken inspiration from the legislation and investigations of the federal Congress, recalls the memory of the federally inspired state-level McCarthyism described in this chapter, which enabled widespread assaults on freedom of expression.

The relationships between state and federal legislators may have evolved since the era of McCarthyism. National legislators may increasingly see the state legislative process as preferable to the slow and cumbersome legislative process in Washington, DC, encouraging them to transfer their ideas to state-level allies and to coordinate these allies through organizational networks such as the American Legislative Exchange Council. According to Grumbach, such networks have been used in recent years, particularly by Republicans, who are "innovating new ways to restrict the franchise, gerrymander districts, exploit campaign finance loopholes, and circumvent civil rights in the criminal justice system."[68] If these networks are, as Grumbach suggests, relatively sophisticated, they are not completely new. National legislators have long realized that the federal government may be either unwilling or unable to carry out a repressive agenda, so they have worked, with some success, to disperse repression across the states.

Subsidizing Repression

Congress has also enabled state-level restrictions on civil liberties through its control over the federal purse strings. Since 1968, Congress has subsidized the militarization of American police forces. The 1968 Safe Streets Act, passed by large bipartisan majorities and only reluctantly signed into law by President Lyndon Johnson, introduced the first federal program of investment in local police forces across the country. Advocates of this legislation framed it as part of the fight against the perceived domestic lawlessness that accompanied the Vietnam War. On its face, this investment in local police forces seemed mundane and harmless—and President Johnson's initial draft of the Safe Streets Act included some form of federal support for local police. However, legislators crafted the legislation in a way that would incentivize states to invest in riot control and the suppression of civil disorder. These measures endangered civil liberties over the long term by giving local police forces a greater capacity to curtail protest activity and to arrest, surveil, and incarcerate citizens.

After passage of the Safe Streets Act, the Law Enforcement Assistance Administration (LEAA)—the agency that distributed the grant money—received annual appropriations of $63 million for fiscal year 1969, $268 million for 1970, $529 million for 1971, and $699 million for 1972. By 1976, the LEAA's annual appropriations exceeded $1 billion.[69] Block grants to states were distributed on the basis of population. Thus, California received a generous $2.4 million in 1969 and earmarked it for a wide variety of purposes, including "a thorough examination of the entire court system," "narcotics, drugs, and alcohol abuse," "organized crime," and "special projects." California invested most heavily, however, in "civil disorders." Nationwide, nearly a quarter of LEAA grants were directed toward this purpose in 1969, more than the amount spent on "detection and apprehension" and the "prevention of crime" combined.[70]

The focus on riots and civil disorders was not part of President Johnson's original proposal for the Safe Streets Act, but legislators added section 307(b) to put "special emphasis" on civil disorders and to waive the requirement—spelled out elsewhere in the law—that "action grants" aimed at combating such "disorders" could be doled out only to states with an LEAA-approved law enforcement plan.[71] Forty states received section 307(b) grants in 1969. Itemized descriptions are imprecise in LEAA documents, but various states invested in "correctional institution riot control," "state patrol riot control," "local riot control," "riot control equipment," "specialized training for special units," a "riot control state plan," "riot control operations plan development," a "mobile riot control unit," "riot readiness," and a "mobile riot control supply unit."[72]

As LEAA's resources expanded, state planning agencies (SPAs) diversified their operations. In fiscal year 1971, police helicopters were purchased for Riverside and Richmond, California; the District of Columbia; Charlotte, North Carolina; Seattle, Washington; Huntsville,

Alabama; and "more than 30 police agencies" in Texas.[73] In February 1971 the Justice Department reported that twenty-two state and local police agencies had operational helicopter teams. Some of their functions were relatively mundane, including "ambulance escort," "search and rescue," "disaster warning," and "traffic control." However, twelve teams were engaged in "riot control," seven were used for "preventive night patrols with lights," and nineteen were engaged in "surveillance."[74] The deployment of helicopters for riot control had been foreshadowed as early as 1965, when the Los Angeles Police Department employed helicopters during the Watts uprising. There, helicopters provided aerial intelligence for officers on the ground, and residents of Watts futilely shot at the helicopters, in imitation of guerrillas in Vietnam.[75] A more dramatic and violent use of police helicopters occurred on May 13, 1985, when the Philadelphia police dropped two bombs from a helicopter onto a house full of members of the antigovernment MOVE group, killing eleven people and destroying sixty neighboring homes.[76] Although helicopter teams can assist the police in important search-and-rescue missions, they can also enable serious violations of civil liberties.

In addition to helicopters, LEAA money supported the creation or upgrade of narcotics squads in Tucson, Arizona; Atlanta, Georgia; Minneapolis, Minnesota; and Elizabeth, New Jersey.[77] Such squads would soon become notorious for violent dawn raids.[78] Everywhere, LEAA money was earmarked for patrol vehicles, prisons, juvenile delinquency, and drug enforcement. Proportionally, riot control received less emphasis in 1971 than it did in 1969, but almost every SPA allocated some portion of its funds to civil disorders, despite the decline of protests and uprisings. The logic described by Alabama SPA Director Robert Davis may have applied elsewhere. "Alabama has had very little trouble with civil disorders during the past year," he conceded. "This is no indication, however, that the state will not have trouble during the coming year." Thus 4.5 percent of the state's LEAA allocation was reserved for "four 50-man civil disorder units."[79]

The ongoing investment in riot control reflected a deeper logic: once the spigot of federal support for local policing was turned on, it was never shut off. Even when the post-Johnson conservative revival was interrupted by Nixon's resignation and the liberal triumph in the 1974 elections, there was no collective legislative effort to end—or regulate—federal funding of local police forces. Thus, by the end of the 1970s, the

United States had transformed from a country with no federal financial support for local policing into a country where the federal government was subsidizing everything from local prisons and jails to undercover sting operations, helicopters, surveillance programs, and narcotics squads.[80]

To be sure, LEAA funding accounted for only 4 percent of total criminal justice and police spending by state and local governments in 1979.[81] Congress was not thrusting money onto unwilling recipients, but its role in transforming American policing was decisive. The original Safe Streets Act directly and explicitly incentivized investment in riot-control equipment. States continued to purchase this equipment—and supplement it with the latest technological developments, such as the helicopter—even as the tumultuous protests and uprisings of the 1960s receded into history.

Although Richard Nixon is often identified as the architect of this War on Crime,[82] in truth, the war preceded him, and it originated in Congress. The Safe Streets Act was wartime legislation, but it was not emergency legislation. It was not a hurried grant of authority to the executive branch. Indeed, it was the product of a lengthy battle between Congress and the executive, and the president signed it with great reluctance. Studies of war and civil liberties tend to caution against delegations of authority to the executive branch that are sold as temporary but become permanent. In the Safe Streets Act, the danger stemmed, instead, from financial support to the states. This support was conceived in the context of urban uprisings and antiwar protests. It long outlasted both.

In 1997, section 1033 of the National Defense Authorization Act further increased the repressive capacity of local police forces. It gave the secretary of defense the authority to "transfer to Federal and State agencies personal property of the Department of Defense, including small arms and ammunition" that was "(A) suitable for use by the agencies in law enforcement activities, including counter-drug and counter-terrorism activities; and (B) excess to the needs of the Department of Defense."[83] As the House National Security Committee that conceived the 1033 program recounted, "Section 1208 of the National Defense Authorization Act for fiscal year 1990 and 1991 . . . established a one year program to provide excess personal property to law enforcement agencies for use in drug enforcement activities," and "this provision was extended until September 30, 1997 by section 1005 of the National

Defense Authorization Act for Fiscal Year 1991." Because "this program appears to be beneficial to many law enforcement agencies, the committee recommends that the program be made permanent and that it be expanded to include all law enforcement activities with a priority for drug enforcement activities." Along with drug enforcement, the House committee highlighted the need for greater local counterterrorism assistance following the 1995 Oklahoma City bombing and in response to the global proliferation of chemical and biological weapons after the fall of the Soviet Union.[84]

In the aftermath of the highly militarized police response to protests following the police shooting of Michael Brown in Ferguson, Missouri, in 2014, President Barack Obama created an interagency Law Enforcement Equipment Working Group to review the 1033 program. This working group proceeded quickly, and Obama implemented its recommendations in May 2015. Most impactfully, it recommended the "Establishment of Federal Government-wide Prohibited Equipment Lists" that would identify "categories of equipment that LEAs [law enforcement administrations] will not be able to acquire via transfer from Federal agencies or purchase using Federally-provided funds." These included "Tracked Armored Vehicles, Bayonets, Grenade Launchers, Large Caliber Weapons and Ammunition." The working group also recommended the "Establishment of Federal Government-wide Controlled Equipment Lists," which included categories of equipment that "LEAs . . . may acquire if they provide additional information, certifications, and assurances." These included "Wheeled Armored or Tactical Vehicles, Specialized Firearms and Ammunition, Explosives and Pyrotechnics, Riot Equipment."[85]

Obama's actions were a drop in the bucket. Under the 1033 program, between 2006 and 2014, "the Department of Defense transferred over $1.5 billion worth of equipment including over 600 mine-resistant ambush-protected vehicles, 79,288 assault rifles, 205 grenade launchers, 11,959 bayonets, 50 airplanes, 422 helicopters, and $3.6 million worth of camouflage and other 'deception equipment'" to state and local police forces.[86] "Eighty percent of US counties received transfers, and those transfers increased over time from 2006 to 2013 by 1414%."[87] Jurisdictions that received this equipment were more likely to experience police brutality than those that did not.[88]

Collectively, these federal programs turned American police forces into high-tech, high-powered machines with ample capacity to curtail civil liberties. While the 1968 Safe Streets Act enabled and incentivized investments in helicopters, narcotics squads, and riot gear, the 1033 program provided police forces with equipment designed for foreign wars. This long-term growth in the repressive capacity of American police forces cannot be attributed to the transfer of power from Congress to the executive or to the abuse of executive discretion. Only Congress can authorize federal government spending, and Congress began to create financial incentives for police militarization back in 1968, passing legislation that a president renowned for his legislative skills failed to shape to his liking. As the next chapter demonstrates, the so-called imperial presidency may have damaged civil liberties in many other ways during the Vietnam War, but Congress was the branch of government most responsible for the militarization of American policing that began during the Vietnam era.

6

The Vietnam Anomaly

The final years of the Vietnam War are widely regarded as a rare and perhaps unique period when the US Congress vigorously defended civil liberties. Unlike after the two world wars—when legislators doubled down on wartime violations of constitutional rights—legislators seemed to confront, expose, and rein in these violations as the Vietnam War dragged on and eventually ended. The Federal Bureau of Investigation (FBI), Central Intelligence Agency (CIA), National Security Agency (NSA), US Army Intelligence, Internal Revenue Service (IRS), Nixon White House, and former high-level national security officials such as Allen Dulles and John McCone were all investigated by Congress. Often on live television, Americans learned of numerous sinister-sounding operations, including "COINTELPRO," "Minaret," "Chaos," and "Shamrock." In 1975 Senator Frank Church (D-ID) became particularly renowned for his select committee's work on the activities of the intelligence agencies, which revealed not only far-reaching domestic surveillance programs but also assassination and coup plots against foreign leaders.[1]

Although a similar inquiry in the House, led by New York Democrat Otis Pike, became mired in controversy after its draft report was leaked to the press in February 1976,[2] the post-Vietnam Congress could claim real results. The 1978 Foreign Intelligence Surveillance Act (FISA) created a special court to review surveillance requests by the executive branch related to national security. Congress also required the intelligence agencies to regularly report on their activities to the newly created permanent, specialized intelligence committees in the House and Senate.[3]

This history has presented scholars with a plausible narrative of civil liberties being restored at the hands of an assertive postwar Congress. This narrative has become increasingly popular since September 11, 2001, as a wide variety of scholars and commentators have criticized the post-9/11 Congress for its habitual renewal of counterterrorism statutes, its apparent lack of enthusiasm for oversight of the executive, and its far-reaching delegations of power through the 2001 PATRIOT Act, the 2008 FISA Amendments Act, and other legislation. The contrast could not be clearer, they argue, with the courage and determination that defined the age of the Church Committee.

Senator Frank Church was, according to James Risen, the "last honest man" in American politics, a man who attempted to "save democracy" through his post-Vietnam investigations of the nation's intelligence agencies.[4] Kim Lane Scheppele argues that "following the intense political battles over Vietnam and Watergate in the 1970s, when the presidency itself came into disrepute, Congress reclaimed some of its powers in the perpetual state of emergency"—an "emergency" that involved near-limitless executive power and wartime violations of civil liberties.[5] Frederick Schwarz and Aziz Huq praise the Church Committee for confronting an "unchecked and unbalanced" executive.[6] For Samuel Walker, the post-Vietnam Congress was central to "the greatest upsurge of public concern about civil liberties and the abuse of government power in American history."[7] "Congress," according to Arthur Schlesinger, was "seized by a temporary passion to prevent future Vietnams and Watergates," and it "enacted laws designed to reclaim lost powers, to dismantle the executive secrecy system and to ensure future presidential accountability."[8]

These scholars do not necessarily argue that the post-Vietnam Congress was heroic. While Bruce Ackerman cautiously commends Congress for its post-Watergate, post-Vietnam assertiveness, he regrets that "it didn't go further to revise the disorganized, but massive grants of substantive authority to declare emergencies that the presidency had accumulated over the decades."[9] Similarly, while describing the Church Committee as "one of the most sweeping congressional investigations in U.S. history," uncovering "widespread abuses in the CIA and FBI," Amy Zegart argues that the committee "ultimately failed to obtain many of the oversight reforms it sought."[10] However, all these scholarly accounts share the view that the Church Committee epitomized a

Congress that was at least interested in questions of civil liberties and national security, before its goals were undermined by the executive branch.[11] In short, this literature frames the Church Committee, FISA, and the other achievements of the post-Vietnam Congress as rare acts of congressional defiance in a general story of executive domination since the Second World War.

However, this chapter argues that the documentary record tells a different story. I advance three core claims based on the Church Committee's own hearings and reports, internal executive branch communications, the legislative history of FISA, and the NSA's formerly secret history of the post-Vietnam period, among other sources. First, although the Church Committee produced priceless documentation, it focused on past abuses that had already been publicized. The committee's most controversial investigation—of the NSA—began by accident, when staffers stumbled upon Defense Department documents describing NSA surveillance programs.[12] Other surveillance programs were exposed by journalists, court cases, and daring acts of civil disobedience.

Second, to the extent that civil liberties were restored in the final years of the Vietnam War and in its aftermath, congressional pressure played a marginal role. The FBI immediately terminated its counterintelligence programs (COINTELPROs) after the "Citizens' Commission to Investigate the FBI"—eight antiwar activists led by physics professor William Davidon—ransacked a Bureau office in Media, Pennsylvania, on March 8, 1971. When the Media burglars sent their stolen documents to carefully selected members of Congress in the hope that an official investigation would begin, these Congress members responded by calling the FBI and offering to cooperate with its investigation of the burglary.[13] Similarly, several surveillance programs across the executive branch were preemptively terminated on the advice of President Nixon's attorney general, Elliot Richardson, after the Supreme Court's 1972 ruling in *United States v. U.S. District Court for Eastern District of Michigan*, better known as the Keith case.[14] Others were terminated because they were deemed ineffective and obsolete as antiwar protests diminished in the early 1970s. The documentary record provides sparse evidence of major surveillance programs ending because of direct or indirect congressional pressure.

Third, the legislative fruits of the Church Committee—FISA and the creation of permanent intelligence committees in the House and

Senate—were the product of cooperative rather than adversarial relations between the executive and legislative branches. The Ford and Carter administrations strongly supported legislative efforts to create an oversight framework for intelligence regulation in the aftermath of the Keith case and the Vietnam War. They felt this framework would allow the intelligence community to restore the legitimacy and confidence it had lost during the war.[15]

Civil Liberties During the Vietnam War

For scholars concerned with the impact of wartime executive power on American civil liberties, the Vietnam War is a compelling cautionary tale. The war in Vietnam was part of the larger Cold War, but it prompted its own problems for civil liberties, especially during the war's most turbulent years between 1965 and 1973.[16] At almost every juncture, these problems were caused by the executive branch, often without the knowledge of Congress, and they seemed to recede only when legislators finally confronted the "imperial presidency" in the final years of the war and after.

The most extensive violation of civil liberties came from the FBI's COINTELPROs, which began in the mid-1950s and grew in scope and number during the Vietnam War.[17] By 1971, there were seven different COINTELPROs focused on espionage, the New Left, disruption of white hate groups, the Communist Party USA, counterintelligence and special operations, black extremists, and the Socialist Workers Party.[18] The key words in COINTELPRO planning documents were "expose, disrupt, misdirect, discredit or otherwise neutralize."[19] In practice, this meant constant physical and electronic surveillance, blackmail, and infiltration and exploitation of organizational factions. As stated in one of the first COINTELPRO documents made public, these tactics were designed to "enhance the paranoia" and give the impression of "an FBI agent behind every mailbox."[20] Overall, the various COINTELPROs yielded around 500,000 intelligence files.[21]

Although the fruits of warrantless surveillance were potentially inadmissible in court under the Fourth Amendment to the US Constitution, long-serving FBI Director J. Edgar Hoover had convinced successive attorneys general and presidents that the surveillance itself was not necessarily illegal. They were often eager to encourage Hoover, recognizing the potential value of derogatory information about their political opponents.[22] There was no legal defense for another signature COINTELPRO tactic: "black-bag jobs," which involved break-ins or "surreptitious entries" for the purpose of planting surveillance devices. The full extent of this practice was clouded by Hoover's destruction of many relevant files, although the FBI did admit to the Church Committee in 1975 that it had "conducted over two hundred 'black bag jobs'" involving theft between 1948 and 1966 and "more than five hundred warrantless surreptitious microphone installations against intelligence and internal security targets" between 1960 and 1975.[23]

The FBI was not alone in conducting surveillance activities. The NSA had been shrouded in mystery since its establishment by President Truman in 1952. Its primary remit was signals intelligence, but its role was never fully defined by statute or executive order. Absent meaningful constraints or oversight, the NSA developed three major surveillance programs that targeted Americans during the Vietnam War.[24] The first was Project Minaret. NSA Director Lew Allen told the Church Committee that this operation began in October 1967 when the military asked the NSA to "obtain communications intelligence regarding foreign control or influence over certain U.S. individuals and groups." Allen added that, over the next six years, "about 1,900 reports were issued covering the three areas of terrorism, Executive protection and foreign influence over U.S. groups. This would average about two reports per day." Most of the reports involved "at least one foreign communicant."[25] An NSA internal history declassified in 2013 admitted that "the watch list eventually contained over 1,600 names and included such personages as columnist Art Buchwald, journalist Tom Wicker, civil rights leaders Martin Luther King [Jr.] and Whitney Young, the boxer Muhammed Ali, and even politicians such as Frank Church and Howard Baker."[26]

A longer-running NSA program was code-named Shamrock. According to Church, this was "a message-collection program in which the Government persuaded three international telegraph companies, RCA Global, ITT World Communications, and Western Union International to make available in various ways their international telegraph traffic to the U.S. Government." From 1945 to 1975, "copies of most international telegrams originating in or forwarded through the United States were turned over to the National Security Agency and its predecessor agencies."[27] "At the outset," Church continued, "the purpose apparently was only to extract international telegrams relating to certain foreign targets. Later, the Government began to extract the telegrams of certain U.S. citizens"—those on the Minaret watch lists. "Of all the messages made available to NSA each year," Church concluded, "it is estimated that NSA in recent years selected about 150,000 messages a month for NSA analysts to review."[28]

Finally, "from 1970 to 1973, at the request of the Bureau of Narcotics and Dangerous Drugs (BNDD), NSA monitored selected telephone circuits between the United States and certain countries in South America to obtain information relating to drug trafficking." This program involved something of an interagency merry-go-round: "BNDD submitted the names of 450 Americans to NSA for a 'drug' watch list. This list resulted in the dissemination of about 1,900 reports on drug traffickers to BNDD and CIA."[29]

Unlike the vaguely defined role of the NSA, the CIA was legally prohibited from spying on Americans.[30] Like the NSA, however, the CIA encroached on the domestic realm—as Seymour Hersh first reported in the *New York Times* in December 1974.[31] The CIA "conducted four mail opening programs in four cities within the United States for varying lengths of time between 1953 and 1973." The most egregious abuses occurred during the Vietnam War, when "numerous domestic dissidents, including peace and civil rights activists, were specifically targeted for mail opening." Over the twenty years of the New York mail-opening program alone, "a total of 28,322,796 letters were made available to CIA agents," 2,705,706 were photographed, and 215,820 were opened. "The height of the project in terms of volume was 1967, when a total of 23,617 letters were opened and analyzed."[32]

The CIA also compiled its own watch list, under the code name Operation Chaos. The CIA tracked American radicals abroad, hoping to catch a member of the Black Panthers or Students for a Democratic Society in a foreign plot. From 1967 to 1973, "300,000 individuals were indexed in a CIA computer system and separate files were created on approximately 7,200 Americans and over 100 domestic groups."[33] Operation Chaos was supplemented by Operation Merrimac, which involved "the infiltration by CIA agents of Washington-based peace groups and black activist groups," and Operation Resistance, "a broad effort to obtain general background information for predicting violence which might create threats to CIA installations, recruiters or contractors and for security evaluation of CIA applicants."[34]

The CIA program about which the least is known, even today, was MKULTRA. Drawing primarily on a 1963 report by the CIA inspector general, the Church Committee was able to conclude that MKULTRA, which lasted from 1953 to 1964, "originally included testing of drugs involving witting human subjects, and culminated in tests using unwitting, nonvolunteer human subjects. These tests were designed to determine the potential effects of chemical or biological agents when used operationally against individuals unaware that they had received a drug." MKULTRA resulted "in massive abridgements of the rights of American citizens, sometimes with tragic consequences," including "the deaths of two Americans."[35] In 1977 the director of central intelligence, Admiral Stansfield Turner, was able to testify—based on the discovery of previously unknown documents in response to a Freedom of Information Act request—that "44 colleges or universities, 15 research foundations or chemical or pharmaceutical companies and the like, 12 hospitals or clinics (in addition to those associated with universities), and 3 penal institutions" had participated in MKULTRA. Whether they participated in the "tests using unwitting, nonvolunteer human subjects" and how many of these tests were conducted remain unknown. Admiral Turner added, "We now have collaborating information that some of the unwitting drug testing was carried on in safehouses in San Francisco and New York City, and we have identified that three individuals were involved in this undertaking as opposed to the previously reported one person." He continued, "We also know now that some unwitting testing took place on criminal sexual psychopaths confined at a State hospital and that, additionally, research was done on a knock-out or 'K' drug in parallel with research to develop pain killers for cancer patients."[36]

The White House also initiated its own surveillance programs. Tom Charles Huston, a Nixon aide, attempted (unsuccessfully) to resurrect black-bag jobs in 1970, prompting an acrimonious turf war with J. Edgar Hoover.[37] The Huston Plan was matched in clumsiness only by the work of Nixon's "Plumbers," whose main achievements included the bungled Watergate burglary in June 1972 and the pilfering of files from the office of Daniel Ellsberg's psychiatrist—actions that succeeded in forcing Nixon out of office and getting Ellsberg acquitted in his Espionage Act trial arising from the leak of the Pentagon Papers.[38] With greater subtlety, the White House instructed the IRS to collect intelligence files "on more than 11,000 individuals" between 1969 and 1973 and to start "tax investigations . . . on the basis of political rather than tax criteria."[39] An IRS Special Service Staff ran this program, whose targets included "the American Civil Liberties Union, the American Library Association, the Conservative Book Club, the Ford Foundation, the Headstart program, the NAACP, the Lawyers Committee for Civil Rights Under Law, the University of North Carolina, and approximately 50 branches of the National Urban League."[40]

Finally, the US Army engaged in covert surveillance as well. "After the army was called upon to quell civil disorders in Detroit and to cope with an antiwar demonstration at the Pentagon in 1967," the Church Committee recounted, "the army Chief of Staff approved a recommendation for 'continuous counterintelligence investigations' to obtain information on 'subversive personalities, groups or organizations' and their 'influence on urban populations' in promoting civil disturbances." In the end, "an estimated 100,000 Americans were the subjects of United States Army intelligence files created between the mid-1960's and 1971."[41]

Explaining the Rollback

What brought these programs to an end? A resurgent Congress may be part of the answer. The Watergate investigation drove Nixon from office and exposed the machinations of the White House Plumbers, the NSA terminated Project Shamrock in the middle of the Church Committee hearings in 1975, and the US Army ended its surveillance programs after their exposure by the Senate Subcommittee on Constitutional Rights in 1971.[42]

However, legislators played no role in the termination of COINTELPRO. Although the Church Committee memorably exposed the FBI's infamous blackmail letter to Martin Luther King Jr., it did not expose COINTELPRO.[43] COINTELPRO was first revealed in 1971 when the Citizens' Commission to Investigate the FBI stole several thousand documents from a Bureau office in Media, Pennsylvania, that detailed FBI activities in that state and hinted at the scope of national operations. These files included broad strategy documents emphasizing the need to "enhance paranoia," as well as specific plans to recruit informants in black student organizations to counter "increased campus disorders involving black students" that "pose a definite threat to the Nation's stability and security." There was also a STAG (student agitation) file describing surveillance of a War Resisters International conference at Haverford College in August 1969 and the wide variety of FBI informants ("a campus security officer, a switchboard operator, the town's chief of police, and the postmaster") monitoring would-be radicals at Swarthmore College.[44] These stolen files only scratched the surface of COINTELPRO. Indeed, the acronym itself was not fully defined in the files, prompting NBC News journalist Carl Stern to sue the Justice Department for additional documents under the Freedom of Information Act. Stern prevailed in 1973, two years before the Church Committee began its probe of COINTELPRO.[45]

Why did Congress take four years to investigate COINTELPRO? In 1971 the Media burglars sent copies of the stolen documents to Senator George McGovern (D-SD) and Representative Parren Mitchell (D-MD), in the hope that these lawmakers would launch an official inquiry. Both of them immediately handed the documents to the FBI and condemned the burglary. As *Time* reported on April 5, "Although a harsh critic of FBI surveillance techniques, Senator McGovern quickly returned his copies [of the files] to the Justice Department, saying he refused to be linked with 'this illegal action by a private group' and adding that the burglary hampered 'reasonable and constructive efforts to secure appropriate public review' of bureau activities."[46] As Betty Medsger notes, referencing the files from the FBI's "MEDBURG" (Media burglary) investigation, this response apparently led J. Edgar Hoover to briefly consider "ask[ing] a select group of members of Congress to help the FBI solve this important crime."[47] Hoover's plan was never implemented, but the fact that he even considered it speaks to his confidence in congressional support. Under the "speech or debate" clause of the Constitution, which immunizes members of Congress from executive or legislative punishment for statements made in Congress, McGovern, Mitchell, or others could have read portions of the Media files into the *Congressional Record*, as Senator Mike Gravel (D-AK) would do in June 1971 with the Pentagon Papers.[48] The only thing stopping congressional dissemination of the Media files was self-censorship. In any event, all COINTELPROs had already been terminated immediately after the Media burglary—a panicked action documented in internal FBI memoranda.[49]

Other programs were also terminated by the executive branch before legislators started investigating them. The NSA's Minaret and drug surveillance programs, first revealed to the public by the Church Committee, whose staffers stumbled upon them when reading Defense Department documents, had been discontinued by NSA Director Lew Allen on the advice of the attorney general.[50] The IRS's Special Service Staff was abolished by new Commissioner of Internal Revenue Donald Alexander in August 1973. Alexander told the Church Committee that he abolished the Special Service Staff because it was involved in "activities which are antithetical to proper tax administration."[51] The Huston Plan was quashed by J. Edgar Hoover.[52] CIA documents suggest that Operation Chaos was scaled back in 1972 and ended in 1973 due to declining antiwar protest activity and legal concerns raised in an internal inspector general's report.[53] Likewise, MKULTRA was terminated in 1964 due to "the high risk of embarrassment" to the CIA and the obvious "moral problem" it raised.[54]

In the final National Security Council (NSC) meeting of the Ford administration in January 1977, the president and his advisers blamed the Justice Department for the rollback of surveillance programs. "We are dealing with an adversary in Justice," claimed CIA Director George Bush. "The Justice Department's role today is a threat to national security," claimed Secretary of State Henry Kissinger. "The Justice Department treats us like an adversary rather than a client," Deputy Defense Secretary William Clements added. Several complaints were overblown or inaccurate, such as Kissinger's notion that "classification no longer means anything or is accepted in law."[55] However, the general thrust contained some truth: the Justice Department—which had questioned the legality of COINTELPRO, Minaret, and Chaos—was engaged in a process of internal executive branch reform. These reformist impulses in turn stemmed from judicial pressure. In his letter to Lew Allen ordering the termination of Project Minaret in 1973, Attorney General Elliot Richardson cited "a case entitled United States v. Keith," which held "that the Federal Government could not conduct electronic surveillance on citizens of this country without a warrant in certain circumstances." Richardson feared that the Keith case "raises a number of serious legal questions which have yet to be resolved," potentially threatening "your current practice of disseminating to the FBI and Secret Service information acquired by you through the use of electronic devices." Thus, "it is requested that you immediately curtail the further dissemination of such information to these agencies."[56]

Keith was a district court judge in the Eastern District of Michigan, and in 1972 the Justice Department asked the Supreme Court to set aside his ruling in *United States v. Sinclair*, which held that the government had violated the Fourth Amendment when it wiretapped a cofounder of the White Panther Party without a warrant.[57] The Justice Department maintained that it did not need a warrant because the White Panthers were a threat to the nation's domestic security, but Keith found that this position had no basis in either the Constitution or Supreme Court precedent. The Supreme Court upheld the position of Judge Keith.[58] When he became attorney general in May 1973, Richardson accepted the implications of the court's decision and told the NSA that it would have to do the same and terminate Project Minaret.

The available documentary evidence indicates that Congress played no meaningful role in prompting the termination of Chaos, MKULTRA, Minaret, or COINTELPRO. All these programs were terminated by executive branch officials in response to various considerations and pressures, including legal concerns (in the case of Chaos and Minaret), unexpected exposure through an act of civil disobedience (in the case of COINTELPRO), and the general sense that the programs were either no longer useful or potentially embarrassing (in the case of Chaos and MKULTRA). The Church Committee revealed crucial details surrounding government surveillance programs, but several of the programs had already been disclosed by journalists (in the case of the CIA) or by the Citizens' Committee to Investigate the FBI. In short, the Church Committee merely continued the process of exposing and ending government abuses of civil liberties during the Vietnam War. At most, the committee was a partner in building a general political atmosphere conducive to reform—or what Richard Aldrich and Daniela Richterova call (in a different context) "ambient accountability."[59]

Evaluating the Fruits of the Church Committee

To be sure, it would be harsh to criticize the post-Vietnam Congress on its inability to dismantle the various surveillance programs of the executive branch, especially when most of the programs were secret. Scholars and commentators who have called for a "new Church Committee" in the twenty-first century see such a proposal as a starting point, rather than a silver bullet in their efforts to promote intelligence reform.[60] Yet proponents of a new Church Committee must reckon with the fact that the original Church Committee displayed a large amount of conservatism and caution in both its investigations and its recommendations, ultimately working with executive officials to modestly reform the national security state.

The Senate created the Church Committee on January 27, 1975. The primary sponsor of the resolution establishing the committee, Senator John Pastore (D-RI), framed it cautiously. "I wish to make it abundantly clear at the outset that the FBI, the CIA, and Military Intelligence are absolutely necessary to the security and the survival of this Republic," Pastore told his colleagues. Nevertheless, he conceded "that there have been some very serious abuses." The press was "replete with . . . charges and countercharges," some of which were "exaggerated," others that "minimized some of the wrongs." Now, "the important thing here is to restore public confidence so that these agencies, in the final analysis, will be responsive. That is what this is all about." By "creat[ing] a select committee consisting of 11 members—6 from the majority [Democrats], 5 from the minority [Republicans]," the intelligence agencies could be investigated in a bipartisan, measured, and sober way. The Pastore resolution passed with 82 yeas, 4 nays, and 11 abstentions.[61]

Pastore himself had no desire to join the committee, and its members—appointed by their respective party leaders—were Chairman Frank Church (D-ID), Vice Chairman John Tower (R-TX), Philip Hart (D-MI), Walter Mondale (D-MN), Walter Huddleston (D-KY), Robert Morgan (D-NC), Gary Hart (D-CO), Howard Baker (R-TN), Barry Goldwater (R-AZ), Charles Mathias (R-MD), and Richard Schweiker (R-PA). Church and Tower disagreed over how aggressively the committee should examine covert actions by the intelligence agencies abroad. Tower wanted to "make sure we do not hobble ourselves and render ourselves at such a disadvantage that we cannot maintain the kind of international posture we need," whereas Church was willing to pry more deeply into covert action.[62] "Tower was there to watch Frank Church," according to Bill Miller, staff director of the Church Committee. Tower described himself as the committee's "damage control officer."[63]

Yet Church and Tower agreed on the need to investigate the domestic activities of the intelligence agencies. They also agreed to investigate only past activities, to not hold anyone accountable for these activities, and to make only future recommendations for the better regulation of these activities. As Church told Gerald Ford and Henry Kissinger in March 1975, "If the work is well done it will clear the air and restore the agencies to the good position they should enjoy."[64] On the floor of the Senate, Goldwater struck a similar chord. "Because the attacks on the intelligence community persist," he said, "I am supporting Senate Resolution 21 [authorizing the Church Committee] as a way to clear the air and set the record [straight]."[65]

This was the spirit in which the Church Committee conducted its business over the next sixteen months. Unlike the Pike Committee in the House of Representatives—which was concerned primarily with covert action abroad—the Church Committee did not threaten a single executive official with a contempt citation.[66] The biggest dispute both within the Church Committee and in its relations with the executive branch concerned the public testimony of NSA Director Allen, which threatened to lift the lid on an agency that had long been almost completely secret. But Allen agreed to testify, and just like officials from the FBI, CIA, and others who appeared before the committee, he spoke honestly about his agency's past (not present) conduct. Everyone, it seemed, was happy to "clear the air."[67]

The two Church Committee recommendations taken up by the wider Congress were the creation of permanent intelligence committees in both chambers and the passage of FISA in 1978.[68] FISA aimed to regulate the surveillance of individuals identified as national security threats by the executive branch—people like the White Panther Party leader in the Keith case. Indeed, FISA was as much a response to the Keith case as it was to the recommendations of the Church Committee.[69]

Executive officials supported and cooperated in the drafting of FISA. As Church Committee member Walter Huddleston told the Senate Subcommittee on Intelligence and the Rights of Americans during hearings on FISA in 1977, "The Ford administration, particularly Attorney General Levy [*sic*], the Carter administration, particularly Attorney General Bell, have worked closely with the Congress" throughout the drafting process. Indiana Democrat Birch Bayh also thanked Attorney General Griffin Bell and his assistants "for their close cooperation with the committee during the development of this bill,"[70] just as Massachusetts

Democrat Edward Kennedy had commended the "cooperative and helpful" approach of the Ford administration in 1976.[71]

This amicable feeling was mutual. "Any lingering doubts as to the legality of proper intelligence activities will be laid to rest," Attorney General Bell commented on FISA in 1978. "The dedicated and patriotic men and women who serve this country in intelligence positions, often under substantial hardships and even danger, will have the affirmation of Congress that their activities are proper and necessary." Meanwhile, Bell added, both branches were "striking a balance between the need to collect foreign intelligence to secure the safety and well-being of this nation and the concurrent [need] to protect the civil liberties of all persons in the United States and the United States citizens abroad."[72]

To be sure, several contentious questions animated the congressional debates over FISA, especially the proper legal standard required to subject American citizens to electronic surveillance. However, FISA did not involve a major confrontation between Congress and the executive: from beginning to end, the Ford and Carter administrations and their attorneys general supported the core idea of creating a legal framework for national security surveillance. As Americo Cinquegrana concludes from an overview of FISA's legislative history, it was, ultimately, "the fruit of interbranch cooperation."[73]

The cooperative spirit of FISA's drafting was reflected in the law's content, particularly its creation of the Foreign Intelligence Surveillance Court (FISA Court), which would differ from regular federal courts in two major respects. First, its seven (later, eleven) judges would be appointed not by the president with the advice and consent of the Senate but by the chief justice of the Supreme Court. Second, its proceedings would not be adversarial; they would be secret and ex parte—involving only the government's legal team and the judge. Thus, prior judicial approval was now required where it previously had not been, but in a way that protected state secrets and limited outside scrutiny. Under FISA, the attorney general would also have to issue regular reports on surveillance activities to the House and Senate intelligence committees.[74]

The impact of the FISA Court on civil liberties is difficult to measure. It has hardly distinguished itself as a forceful check on surveillance. As Emily Berman notes, "Over its first two and a half decades, the FISA Court approved nearly every single [warrant] application without modification."[75] Defenders of FISA argue that this success rate is due to the care and diligence of the Justice Department when devising FISA warrant requests.[76] Yet, given the intense secrecy surrounding FISA Court procedures, it is almost impossible to cross-examine this claim. More generally, the FISA Court's secrecy impedes the ability of anyone who is subject to a FISA warrant to challenge it: their lawyers cannot introduce suppression motions in the FISA Court, and the government is under no obligation to give anyone notice that they are under FISA surveillance. All this amounts to a process that falls far short of the protections offered by the Fourth and Fifth Amendments in criminal proceedings.[77]

Civil libertarians arguing in support of FISA countered these objections by emphasizing that FISA warrants must have the "primary purpose" of national security surveillance, rather than regular law enforcement. This "wall" between intelligence activities and criminal prosecution supposedly ensured that FISA warrants—at least those issued between 1978 and 2001—were reserved for a narrow category of targets.[78] However, neither the "wall" nor the "primary purpose" doctrine were actually written into the statute. Indeed, as the FISA Court of Review underscored in 2002, both the text and the legislative history of the statute clearly indicate that "the FISA as passed by Congress in 1978 clearly did not preclude or limit the government's use or proposed use of foreign intelligence information, which included evidence of certain kinds of criminal activity, in a criminal prosecution."[79] Instead, the wall and the primary purpose doctrine emerged from a Fourth Circuit case in 1980, which the other circuit courts then followed, before the Justice Department incorporated the wall into its own internal guidelines in 1995.[80] Both the executive branch and the Government Accountability Office (which is independent of the executive) identified these guidelines, rather than FISA, as the principal source of the so-called wall prior to 9/11.[81] The 2001 PATRIOT Act amended FISA to explicitly encourage the integration of intelligence gathering and regular law enforcement after legislators and executive officials blamed the wall for the intelligence failures that led to 9/11. But the wall could have been broken down without changing FISA for the simple reason that it was never required by FISA.

The other output of the Church Committee was the creation of permanent congressional intelligence committees. As Amy Zegart writes, "These committees routinized intelligence oversight for the first time"—a process that was reinforced by FISA, which required regular executive consultation with the committees. "The days of ad hoc and informal relations between agencies and Congress were over." Moreover, in an attempt to re-create the bipartisanship of the Church Committee—or at least lessen partisan pressures in the future—"both chambers decided to make the intelligence committees select rather than standing committees, which meant that members were personally selected by party leaders in each chamber, not the party caucuses."[82] Yet, as chapter 3 demonstrated, these committees have not distinguished themselves as checks on the intelligence community, at least in the realm of civil liberties. Indeed, as their reactions to the Snowden revelations in 2013 (among other examples) demonstrate, members of these committees—especially their chairs—are usually either defenders of or "cheerleaders" for the agencies they are supposed to be monitoring.

In short, even though civil liberties were undoubtedly strengthened in the United States after the Vietnam War, neither FISA nor the congressional intelligence committees should be credited with this achievement. These reforms were, perhaps, part of the broader "ambient accountability" that both branches helped generate during this period under various external political pressures. What the Church Committee did achieve—in both its investigations and its legislative outputs—was achieved in a largely cooperative interbranch environment, not a bitter struggle between a newly assertive Congress and a stubborn executive.

The post-Vietnam Congress merits praise on many fronts. It did not preserve or expand wartime restrictions on civil liberties. It conducted unprecedented and far-reaching investigations of the national security state. It was a key partner in postwar reforms of the intelligence community. The Church Committee, in particular, was disciplined, professional, and bipartisan to a degree that appears shocking to observers of more recent Congresses. Its hearings and reports were and still are extremely valuable to anyone concerned with the history and development of American intelligence agencies. The endnotes in this chapter are testament to this fact.

However, the post-Vietnam Congress played, at most, a marginal role in restoring and strengthening civil liberties. Most of the executive programs examined by the Church Committee had already been terminated by the executive branch for various reasons, and the reforms of the intelligence community that followed the Vietnam War were more concerned with mending interbranch relations—and giving legislators and judges a formal seat at the table of the national security state—than with curbing government surveillance programs. This is, perhaps, an admirable legacy, especially when compared with the record of other postwar Congresses. But in the final analysis, it is much better described as a legacy of fighting for the separation of powers rather than for civil liberties.

Conclusion

The Vietnam era is a partial and qualified exception to what appears to be a historical rule: in the aftermath of war, legislators have endangered civil liberties. They have done so not only by passing repressive legislation but also by wielding a wide variety of powers—formal and informal, constitutional and political—over their own institution, the executive branch, the judiciary, and the states. The framers of the US Constitution were on to something. When they made Congress the strongest branch of government, they believed it would also be the most dangerous branch of government. They may not have had specific threats to civil liberties in mind—let alone the kinds of dangers documented in this book—but their general fear of legislative tyranny was far from unfounded.

Although the primary objective of this book was to develop this central argument, I have admittedly either avoided or only partially addressed several questions that may have crossed the reader's mind. In this concluding chapter, I reflect on four of these questions—to satisfy the reader's curiosity and to point toward further possibilities for future research and scholarship. First, why have legislators seemed so willing and able to curtail civil liberties in the aftermath of war? Second, how do we normatively or morally grapple with a case like Reconstruction—or with the larger question of when wartime restrictions on civil liberties should outlast their original purposes? Third, why have some postwar moments been different from others? Finally, what are the practical implications of my arguments for advocates of civil liberties and policymakers today?

Why Restrict Liberties?

The question of why legislators have restricted civil liberties in the aftermath of war can be answered in many ways. One explanation is that legislators have responded to public opinion. Opinion polls, election returns, and the energetic activities of private citizens' organizations seem to reflect some popular will for the Red Scares that followed the world wars. In eras with more sophisticated means of measuring public opinion—especially during the War on Terror—there is also evidence of public support for violations of civil liberties, especially of noncitizens.[1] Although the true motives of individual legislators are notoriously difficult to pin down, it seems likely that when Senator Joseph McCarthy cross-examined Owen Lattimore or when Representative Elise Stefanik cross-examined the presidents of Harvard, MIT, and the University of Pennsylvania, they perceived some kind of political or electoral benefit. There also seems to be no doubt that figures like McCarthy reaped these benefits—at least in the short term.

Yet, as John Mueller notes in a study of the War on Terror, it remains difficult to determine whether—or in what way—public opinion is manipulated by elites or drives elite behavior.[2] Moreover, especially when we are examining Congress after Reconstruction and before the 1965 Voting Rights Act, we are examining an institution that was far from majoritarian. The Southern Democrats who were powerful and persistent advocates of repressive legislation in Congress after both world wars represented not only a tiny proportion of the nation but also a tiny proportion of their grossly malapportioned or otherwise democratically deficient states and districts. Their influence in Congress was further inflated by the then-powerful congressional norm of assigning committee chairmanships on the basis of seniority—which they had no problem accruing in the absence of competitive elections.[3] Even since the passage of the Voting Rights Act, Congress has remained an institution in which political minorities and factions can thrive.[4] Many of the specific examples of legislative repression described in this book have been led by a relatively small number of legislators or, in the case of Reconstruction, a "rump" Congress. In short, although public opinion cannot possibly be irrelevant to congressional campaigns against civil liberties, I would hesitate to describe such campaigns as evidence of the tyranny of the majority—at least the majority of the US population—in action.

Partisanship is also, clearly, part of the picture. Congressional Republicans implemented military Reconstruction over the will of a president who officially left the Democratic Party for the National Union Party but reverted and became a de facto Democrat after the Civil War. Republicans (albeit different Republicans) also led the Red Scares while Democrats held the White House, and both Democrats and Republicans in Congress have recently shown the will and capacity to use their investigatory powers against partisan opponents. Even the post-Vietnam Congress—distinguished for its cautious efforts to reform the intelligence community—represented something of a liberal-Democratic rebellion against a Republican White House, and Frank Church, who led the Senate's investigations of the intelligence community, harbored presidential ambitions.[5]

If partisan allegiances and struggles are dampened during wartime (which may itself be a debatable proposition), they seem to reemerge in the aftermath of war and often generate negative consequences for civil liberties. Their reemergence could be explained, in part, by the fact that the United States has never broken its constitutionally prescribed regime of House elections every two years, presidential elections every four years, and Senate elections every six years. This regime allows for divided government and for regular referendums on the performance of incumbent presidents. When these referendums take the form of midterm elections, they rarely produce positive results for the president's party, even in the best of times. When the country is emerging from the bloodshed, sacrifice, and cost of war, the president's party has consistently fared poorly in midterm elections, from Andrew Johnson in 1866 (with the caveat that Johnson was essentially a Democrat in Union Party clothing) and Woodrow Wilson in 1918 to Harry Truman in 1946 and Gerald Ford in 1974. In these contexts (except for the Vietnam anomaly), newly elected legislators have used the powers of Congress to curtail the civil liberties of their political and partisan enemies.

In a more general sense, we could conclude that wartime restrictions on civil liberties have helped legislators achieve a variety of political objectives. Martial law in the former Confederacy was indispensable for Reconstruction after the Civil War. Harsh wartime immigration laws were valuable for conservative legislators who wanted to crush left-wing political movements after the First World War. The invasive wartime investigations conducted by the House Un-American Activities

Committee (HUAC) provided a perfect stick with which conservative legislators could beat labor unions, peace activists, and liberal government employees after the Second World War. In various ways, legislators have benefited from wartime restrictions on civil liberties, explaining why they have attempted to sustain them.

At the same time, a more charitable interpretation of legislative motivations would argue that wars tend to create social, economic, and national security problems that outlast hostilities. These problems necessitate—or at least provide strong grounds for—the continuation of wartime measures. After the Civil War, congressional Republicans had to grapple with the terms on which Southerners could be readmitted to Congress, political order and stability in the former Confederacy, the rights and liberties of liberated slaves, how to manage the collapse of the plantation economy, and many other enormous questions. After the First World War, legislators had to deal with widespread labor unrest and shocking instances of political violence, such as the bombing of Attorney General A. Mitchell Palmer's house in 1919 and Wall Street in 1920.[6] After the Second World War, legislators were confronted with the emerging Cold War and the related—and real—threat of Soviet espionage in the United States. Since the 9/11 attacks, legislators have faced various national security problems, including terrorism and cyberwarfare.

The subject of legislative motives has long preoccupied political scientists. Yet apart from studies of specific legislative campaigns like McCarthyism, little has been written about why and under what conditions legislators support restrictions on civil liberties—beyond the relatively obvious observation that they are more likely to do so in wartime or during other major crises. The core finding of this book—that legislators tend to restrict civil liberties in the aftermath of war—should encourage further research on the question of why this is true.

Normative Questions

It is almost impossible to investigate the motives behind legislative repression in the aftermath of war without discussing when, if ever, postwar restrictions on civil liberties are justified. Especially since the demise of the Dunning School of historiography, historians of Reconstruction have generally argued that the imposition of martial law in the former

Confederacy was justified by the necessity of overcoming the recalcitrance of those who had waged war against the United States to uphold the institution of slavery.[7] I am inclined to sympathize with this view. As W. E. B. Du Bois described the goals of martial law:

> To a few far-seeing leaders of democracy this experiment appeared in its truer light. It was a test of the whole theory of American government. It was a dictatorship backed by the military arm of the United States by which the governments of the Southern states were to be coerced into accepting a new form of administration, in which the freedmen and the poor whites were to hold the overwhelming balance of political power. As soon as political power was successfully delivered into the hands of these elements, the Federal government was to withdraw and full democracy ensue.[8]

If anything, the congressional architects of Reconstruction were too squeamish about curtailing the civil liberties of those opposed to "full democracy." Congress's "military dictatorship" was short-lived, cautiously enforced, and ultimately withdrawn after ratification of a constitutional amendment that the Southern states would soon be able to subvert. Despite the "radical" promises of Reconstruction and the "radical" ideas of many Republicans, a cautious and legalistic conservatism also ran through the postwar Republican Party and held back the revolutionary potential of Reconstruction.

Were other postwar restrictions on civil liberties justifiable? In the aftermath of the First World War, antiradical legislation and the "deportations delirium" were fueled by various strikes, riots, and bombings. In the aftermath of the Second World War—and into the early Cold War—McCarthyism (broadly defined) was fueled by the very real fact of Soviet espionage in the United States, as well as traumatic events such as the "fall" of China, the testing of a Soviet nuclear bomb in 1949, and the outbreak of the Korean War in 1950. The War on Terror, of course, is directed against the threat of "terrorism," and sweeping congressional investigations under the first Trump administration and the Biden administration have been justified by claims of presidential corruption, foreign interference in American elections, or the January 6, 2021, attack on Congress itself.

Defenses of Joseph McCarthy, his predecessors, his collaborators, or the Red Scare after the First World War are rare in scholarly literature.[9]

One reason for this apparent revulsion toward McCarthyism is the view that it was founded on threat inflation and that, to the extent threats like Soviet espionage existed, the cure administered to them was far worse than the disease, creating a stifling and suffocating culture of conformity and self-censorship in the United States that lasted until the end of the 1950s. McCarthyism, from this perspective, stands in stark contrast to military Reconstruction, which was rather reluctantly and only temporarily imposed on political actors who had recently, openly, and, arguably, continually engaged in armed insurrection and combat against the United States. To put it simplistically, when comparing Reconstruction with the Red Scares, one could argue that postwar restrictions on civil liberties may be justified, but only if serious threats to the country persist and if the countermeasures are—at least conceivably—proportionate to those threats.

These general principles related to threat and proportionality have been hotly debated in the aftermath of the January 6, 2021, attack on the US Capitol. Many scholars and commentators have argued that this attack was an "insurrection" and that its orchestrators—up to and including President Donald Trump—should be banned from running for political office under section 3 of the Fourteenth Amendment or criminally prosecuted.[10] Although I understand the desire to punish the perpetrators of the January 6 attack—and the broader desire to make American democracy more "militant" in order to withstand antidemocratic pressures[11]—there are serious implications for civil liberties associated with methods of European-style militant democracy in response to Trumpism.

As chapter 2 documents, the congressional committee investigating the January 6 attack on the Capitol created dangerous precedents involving the right to protest by asking third parties to provide the private communications records of anyone even remotely connected to the initial January 6 rally. In addition, federal prosecutors threatened to set an overly broad precedent for punishing the disruption of official government functions by enhancing the sentences of the January 6 rioters under the 2002 Sarbanes-Oxley Act for "interfering with the administration of justice." This law was originally passed by Congress in response to the Enron scandal and other financial corruption scandals. These sentencing enhancements were eventually invalidated by the Supreme Court.[12]

Likewise, state efforts to exclude Donald Trump from the 2024 ballot under section 3 of the Fourteenth Amendment were concerning enough to prompt all justices on the Supreme Court to rule that Trump was eligible to run and to reserve this exclusion power for Congress. The case of Victor L. Berger, who was excluded from Congress because of his opposition to American involvement in the First World War, suggests that such a power can be dangerous in congressional hands as well. Some readers may wish that Congress had used this power against Trump, but as Justice Douglas warned in *Powell v. McCormack*, it can also be used in the event "the electors choose a person who is repulsive to the Establishment in Congress," rendering those "electors . . . disenfranchised."[13]

More broadly, although many Americans see the Trump movement as a threat to democracy, militant anti-Trumpism is not without risk. We should not forget that McCarthyism was also about protecting the United States from an enemy that allegedly loathed democracy, specialized in a mixture of propaganda and misinformation, and sought to undermine Americans' trust in their form of government through subtle methods short of invasion or occupation of American soil. In the end, this incarnation of militant democracy seriously damaged American democracy while claiming to be its savior. Similar claims were made repeatedly in Congress during the first Trump administration, along with provocative, McCarthy-reminiscent claims about Russian "collusion" with then-candidate Trump during the 2016 campaign that were never substantiated.[14] Congressional efforts to suppress or bully social media companies into suppressing the online "misinformation" that supposedly brought Trump to power were also motivated by legitimate concerns about defending democracy and informed public discourse, but censorship justified by fears of misinformation can also pose serious threats to freedom of speech.[15]

During Trump's second administration, concerns about overly broad congressional investigations or restrictions on the civil liberties of Trump followers are unlikely to be widespread subjects of conversation in the scholarly literature or in the press. Instead, concerns about presidential power and abuse are becoming more acute as Trump promises to act more aggressively using the powers of his office and to demand greater loyalty and unity from executive branch employees. The second Trump administration may well pose serious threats to civil liberties. However, the historical record outlined in this book underlines the importance of keeping a close eye on Congress too—and not only when it is controlled by the president's party.

Explaining Variation

This book has presented a general picture of Congress curtailing civil liberties in the aftermath of war, but Congress has not always done so in the same way or for the same purposes. What explains these variations? One explanation may be the varying impact of different wars on American society. The Civil War began as a war to preserve the Union, but as enslaved people fled behind Union lines and Lincoln recognized the military value of emancipation, it became a war of liberation. This war was unavoidably radical; it destroyed the foundation of Southern plantation society and carried out the largest expropriation of private property in US and possibly world history. It is no wonder that such a titanic struggle led to the closest thing to a genuinely revolutionary legislature in American history—a legislature willing to curtail civil liberties to pursue a "new birth of freedom."

The world wars, in contrast, brought social unrest, racial conflict, and economic disruption to the United States, without setting in motion revolutionary processes anywhere near the scale of those engendered by emancipation. Therefore, the 1918 and 1946 elections were business as usual: Republicans and conservative Democrats ran against price controls, socialism, and unruly labor unions.[16] These forces of conservative backlash—who, to be sure, had some liberal allies[17]—then used their legislative powers to stifle and suppress political activity on the left. In short, the Civil War is by far the most destructive and destabilizing war examined in this book. It is no surprise that this was the only war to produce anything resembling a radical or revolutionary postwar moment.

What explains the Vietnam anomaly? Why did wartime restrictions on civil liberties largely end before the war was over? Why did Congress make some effort to expose wartime abuses of civil liberties by the executive branch in 1975? As chapter 6 documents, specific wartime restrictions on civil liberties ended for various reasons: COINTELPRO was terminated after the theft of FBI files in 1971, most NSA surveillance programs were terminated in the wake of the Keith case, MKULTRA and other CIA programs were terminated because of internal concerns about their legality and effectiveness. In a broader sense, the lengthy, expensive, and apparently futile war in Vietnam seemed to provoke widespread dissatisfaction with many symbols of authority in the United States, including the national security state. The new generation of legislators elected in the aftermath of Watergate sympathized with this feeling. Nevertheless, as my account of the Church Committee emphasizes, these legislators also aimed to rehabilitate the reputation and legitimacy of the intelligence community, arguably saving it from scandal by "clearing the air" about the past and providing a legal framework to regulate its conduct in the future.

It is difficult to say—perhaps too early to say—the extent to which the "post-9/11 wars" vary from the others discussed throughout this book. Nor is it clear exactly what should be counted as the "post-9/11 wars": Afghanistan and Iraq, surely, but what about the numerous other covert US military interventions in the Middle East and North and West Africa? What about various more recent events that have sparked serious debates about civil liberties and national security, including the alleged Russian interference in the 2016 presidential election, the COVID-19 pandemic, the January 6 "insurrection" at the Capitol, the "new cold war" with China, the 2022 Russian invasion of Ukraine, and the massive US-backed Israeli military campaign against Gaza beginning in October 2023?

At a minimum, legislators have been key players in many of these debates, and rarely have they acted to protect civil liberties: sabotaging President Obama's attempts to close the Guantanamo Bay detention facility, publicly castigating college presidents for upholding the First Amendment rights of pro-Palestinian students, banning social media companies that serve as communication platforms for millions of young Americans, and weaponizing investigative powers in ways that could yet pose major risks to freedom of association and due process. War in the twenty-first century may be more remote, more technologically advanced, and more nebulous than the wars examined in this book, yet this does not mean that outcomes for civil liberties—or Congress's role in driving these outcomes—will necessarily be different.

Future research could consider why different wars produce different postwar political environments and different outcomes for civil liberties. Isser Woloch's study of "progressive forces in Britain, France, and the United States after World War II" is a useful example of how we might study different postwar political environments. He argues that while the British Labour Party and the British labor movement became one and the same before the Second World War, the US Democratic Party and the US labor movement remained separate. This left American progressives open to attacks from the right in the aftermath of the war, whereas the Labour Party oversaw a postwar reconstruction program that built the foundation of the modern British welfare state. The French Left, meanwhile, suffered from its long-standing divisions in the "postwar moment," enabling the exclusion of communists from government and the triumph of the "Third Force" centrist alliance in May 1947.[18]

With respect to civil liberties, several studies of the COVID-19 pandemic reveal possible directions for future scholarship. In a widely cited 2021 article, Tom Ginsburg and Mila Versteeg argue—on the basis of "data from an original and global survey of over one hundred countries"—that "courts, legislatures and subnational governments have played important roles in constraining national executives" in their exercise of emergency pandemic response powers.[19] By contrast, a 2020 study by Erwin Chemerinsky and Michele Goodwin argues that "there is every reason to fear that the [COVID-19] pandemic could be used as a justification for a massive deprivation of rights and abuses" across the world. They describe several alarming actions: "in Hungary, the prime minister used COVID-19 as the basis for greatly increasing his powers"; "in the Philippines . . . President Rodrigo Duterte threatened to order the police and military to 'shoot them dead' when he referred to those who protested the lack of food, which violated coronavirus-related lockdowns"; "Bolivia cancelled its elections, and countries like Thailand and Jordan used their COVID-19 lockdowns to greatly restrict freedom of speech."[20]

To some extent, these studies revive the spirit of Clinton Rossiter's classic comparative study of "constitutional dictatorship" in ancient Rome, the United Kingdom, France, and the United States.[21] A comparative study building on my arguments here could examine the degree to which my conclusions travel, especially my primary conclusion about legislators' decisive role in curtailing civil liberties in the aftermath of war. This conclusion could well be a distinctive product of the US Constitution, which provides for a much stronger legislature and a much weaker executive than most presidential systems. The US president has no formal power to advance legislation through Congress or compel the legislature to consider it. The president cannot dissolve the legislature, although he can technically adjourn it if the House and Senate cannot agree on the timing of their own adjournment.[22] The president has no formal role in the constitutional amendment process, while Congress is central to it. "If we consider an index of executive lawmaking power from a set of seven legislating powers," Zachary Elkins writes, "the US president appears utterly powerless."[23] Although public officials are fond of referring to the three "coequal" branches of government, the US Constitution clearly seems to say that Congress is more equal than the others.

To be sure, the US presidency can compensate for its relatively modest constitutional powers through effective party leadership, expertise and control over information, unilateral executive orders, direct access to the media, and direct communication with citizens. In addition, it can squeeze the best leverage out of what the Constitution does provide, such as the veto, which is a bargaining chip as much as a roadblock.[24] But these extraconstitutional strategies often flail in the face of Congress, as the various difficulties of postwar presidents have demonstrated.

Legislators' capacity to curtail civil liberties in the aftermath of war may exist in other democracies with strong legislatures, such as the United Kingdom. Parliament's 1911 Official Secrets Act, 1914 Defense of the Realm Act, 1939 Emergency Powers (Defense) Act, 1974 Prevention of Terrorism Act (and its successors), and 2000 Terrorism Act have not been friendly to "ancient" British liberties, including freedom of the press, privacy, and due process.[25] Despite the creation of a UK Supreme Court in 2009, the devolution of power to the Scottish Parliament and the Northern Irish and Welsh Assemblies in 1998, and the incorporation of the European Convention on Human Rights into British law through the 1998 Human Rights Act, Parliament enjoys almost unchecked authority in the British constitutional system.[26] Unsurprisingly, it has often abused this authority.

In democracies with weaker legislatures, the executive branch may be the primary danger to civil liberties. The French Constitution, for instance, grants the president far-reaching emergency powers, as does the continually valid 1955 emergency law that predates the Fifth Republic. Such powers were deployed in the aftermath of violent Islamist attacks across Paris in November 2015, particularly "administrative control measures" that allowed the interior secretary to carry out searches and seizures and to close private residences without judicial approval. From November 2015 to November 2017, 4,469 homes were searched under this authority, and 19 mosques were forcibly closed.[27] President Jacques Chirac also invoked emergency powers in response to the November 2005 Paris riots, giving police the power to impose curfews, conduct warrantless searches, close public meeting places, and place residents under house arrest.[28]

Comparative scholars of democratic backsliding have assessed the relationship between the relative strength of legislatures and executives and the strength of democracy. In a comparative study of sixteen cases of backsliding (including the United States), Stephan Haggard and Robert Kaufmann conclude that "weaker legislatures" have resulted in "weaker democracies."[29] Other comparative democratization scholars agree with this assessment.[30]

However, comparative studies of the relationship between legislative strength and civil liberties might yield different results because civil liberties can be curtailed without democratic backsliding. Civil liberties can also be curtailed in ways that large comparative databases do not observe, so future quantitative studies in this area may encounter serious hurdles. The more qualitative historical approach applied in this book may be better equipped to capture varying outcomes for civil liberties in constitutional democracies. A key challenge here would be developing a viable sample of cases: identifying, for instance, democracies with legislatures of varying strength, varieties of presidential and parliamentary systems, and varying economic circumstances that experience similar outcomes for civil liberties in the aftermath of war or democracies that are similar in terms of these variables but experience differing outcomes.

Policy and Advocacy Implications

Finally, how, if at all, can the findings of this book provide guidance for policymakers and advocates of civil liberties? I am tempted to avoid this question altogether, given that this book has primarily sought to tell a story that has not been adequately told; it carries no particular agenda for reform. On the other hand, it is hard to think of any book on this subject that is not at least somewhat concerned with the future of civil liberties in the United States, and it would be dishonest to pretend that this concern—conscious or unconscious—does not exist here.

The most obvious—if overly generalized and frankly negative—recommendation that flows from this book is for advocates of civil liberties both inside and outside government to avoid putting too much faith in Congress. Congress has undoubtedly displayed a limited ability to protect civil liberties—such as in the aftermath of the Vietnam War—but its track record is generally poor. Scholars usually criticize Congress for inaction or excessive deference to the executive branch, but as this book demonstrates, this is only part of the picture: Congress possesses various independent powers, powers over the other branches of the federal government, and mechanisms of influence over the states that have allowed—and enabled—national legislators to launch their own campaigns against civil liberties throughout American history. Congress simply is not an institution that should have earned the trust or confidence of civil libertarians.

At least in the aftermath of war, unilateral executive abuses of civil liberties have been rare in US history. In fact, this book documents several examples of the executive branch displaying a capacity and a willingness to fight for civil liberties. Assistant Labor Secretary Louis Post contained the "deportations delirium" after the First World War, President Harry Truman obstructed the Red Scare that followed the Second World War, Attorney General Elliot Richardson terminated electronic surveillance programs in the latter years of the Vietnam War, and President Barack Obama substantially reduced the population of the Guantanamo Bay detention facility. President Andrew Johnson also fought hard for the civil liberties of ex-Confederates after the Civil War, albeit with the unpleasant parallel aim of perpetuating the subjugation of African Americans in the former Confederacy.

I cannot say with certainty what motivated these executive officials. Obama wanted to fulfill a campaign promise, Truman did not believe domestic communism was a serious threat—and he personally loathed the people who made it seem so—and Johnson was, by all accounts, deeply racist and believed that Reconstruction was unconstitutional. These three presidents seemed to act out of a combination of political, principled, and pragmatic motives. It is surely no coincidence that each sought to defend his political allies from a hostile Congress. Political considerations seemed less prominent in the thinking of Louis Post and the executive officials who wound down the repressive programs of the Vietnam era. Post, who was well into his twilight years and apparently happy with his far-from-glamorous title of assistant labor secretary, had no new ambitions to pursue or promises to fulfill. He simply could not see the utility or the justice of strictly adhering to the 1918 Immigration Act. In a similar vein, Elliot Richardson dutifully accepted the US Supreme Court's invalidation of warrantless surveillance practices and ordered his colleagues in the NSA to follow suit.

To put it bluntly, while this book carries a negative message about Congress, it carries a somewhat positive message about the executive branch. I have not argued or demonstrated that the executive branch has been harmless or angelic with respect to civil liberties in the aftermath of war, but there is a potential for positive executive action that is not widely acknowledged in existing scholarship.

Despite the focus on the role of Congress and the executive in shaping postwar restrictions on civil liberties, the judiciary has received significant attention in this book. As demonstrated in chapter 4, the Supreme Court has sometimes succumbed to legislative pressure, conceding to an attack on its jurisdiction during Reconstruction and backing down in the face of threats to its jurisdiction in the latter years of the second Red Scare. At other times, the Supreme Court has been cut out of the picture more subtly, such as through the retroactive immunity measures passed by Congress during the War on Terror or through the use of deportation as a form of punishment during the first Red Scare.

These examples might lead us to conclude—like many scholars studying courts in times of crisis—that the law falls silent when the state wants it to. Nevertheless, the preceding chapters also point to several cases of the Supreme Court indirectly protecting civil liberties. Consider the 1972 Keith case, described in chapter 6. "We do not attempt to detail the precise standards for domestic security warrants," the court cautiously concluded. "We do hold, however, that prior judicial approval is required for the type of domestic security surveillance involved in this case and that such approval may be made in accordance with such reasonable standards as the Congress may prescribe."[31] This was a diplomatic way of telling the federal government: right now, what you are doing is probably illegal, until you find a way to make it legal. For Attorney General Richardson, this judicial challenge was enough to require the termination of the NSA's Minaret surveillance program.

The ruling in the Keith case was directed at Congress as much as the executive, inviting Congress to clarify what the law really said about domestic national security surveillance. The eventual result was the Foreign Intelligence Surveillance Act (FISA), which legalized such surveillance as long as legislators (through the intelligence committees) and judges (through the FISA Court) had a role in authorizing it. The Supreme Court invited congressional intervention more explicitly in its Guantanamo cases, especially *Hamdan v. Rumsfeld* in 2006. *Hamdan* told the Bush administration that it could not run the Guantanamo legal regime unilaterally. Congress had to sanction it. The court thus put Guantanamo in jeopardy without explicitly invalidating indefinite military detention—a balancing act that recognized the court's inability to enforce its own decisions. However, after Congress was given this window of opportunity to either wind down or question the Guantanamo legal regime, it chose instead to entrench it through the 2006 Military Commissions Act.

In other cases, the Supreme Court made firmer statements in support of civil liberties, but only when the programs restricting those liberties were already fading away. Notably, the Warren Court clipped the wings of HUAC in the 1957 *Watkins* case. At that point, HUAC had been harassing accused communists for well over a decade as a standing committee of Congress and for nearly two decades if we include its existence as a special committee from 1938 to 1945. All the same—and despite a retreat from "communist" cases in response to congressional pressure—the court never overruled its decisions that belatedly questioned the Red Scare. Their core principles thus endured. Of particular importance was the court's clear statement in *Watkins*: "there is no congressional power to expose for the sake of exposure."[32] Since then, this statement has been cited in every major case involving the scope of Congress's subpoena and contempt powers.[33]

I did not analyze the Pentagon Papers case—when the nation's newspapers overcame the Nixon administration's attempts at censorship in 1971—but this was another example of the Supreme Court acting better late than never. Thanks in part to the Hollywood motion picture *The Post*, this case is often remembered as a triumph of judicial independence and press freedom. But the Supreme Court's decision to side with the press against Nixon was also simply a practical recognition that the Pentagon Papers were already public—and not just snippets in newspapers. As the court deliberated, Democratic Senator Mike Gravel of Alaska was reading the entire collection into the *Congressional Record*.[34] Justice

Hugo Black's famous concurrence in the Pentagon Papers case mattered more because of its ringing tribute to freedom of the press and the First Amendment than because of its immediate impact on the controversy at hand. Black wrote:

> In the First Amendment, the Founding Fathers gave the free press the protection it must have to fulfill its essential role in our democracy. The press was to serve the governed, not the governors. The Government's power to censor the press was abolished so that the press would remain forever free to censure the Government. The press was protected so that it could bare the secrets of government and inform the people. Only a free and unrestrained press can effectively expose deception in government. And paramount among the responsibilities of a free press is the duty to prevent any part of the government from deceiving the people and sending them off to distant lands to die of foreign fevers and foreign shot and shell. In my view, far from deserving condemnation for their courageous reporting, the *New York Times*, the *Washington Post*, and other newspapers should be commended for serving the purpose that the Founding Fathers saw so clearly. In revealing the workings of government that led to the Vietnam war, the newspapers nobly did precisely that which the Founders hoped and trusted they would do.[35]

Finally, the 1866 decision in *Ex parte Milligan*, prohibiting the imposition of martial law when the civilian courts are open, was functionally irrelevant at the time because Congress had determined that a legal state of war still existed in the former Confederacy. Yet *Milligan*'s overarching message—"The Constitution of the United States is a law for rulers and people, equally in war and in peace, and covers with the shield of its protection all classes of men, at all times, and under all circumstances"[36]—has (for better or worse) frequently been cited in modern cases concerning civil liberties during times of crisis, including, most recently, *Hamdi v. Rumsfeld*, *Hamdan v. Rumsfeld*, and *Boumediene v. Bush*.[37]

Even when the Supreme Court is slow to speak on controversies involving civil liberties, its voice can still have an impact on future generations—and future courts. At first glance, the slow, ponderous, and hesitant court may seem useless to advocates of civil liberties.[38] Yet, when we acknowledge the constraints the judiciary faces as the weakest branch of government, its record looks more promising. If civil libertarians expect judges to step in and save the day in real time, they are likely to be disappointed. If civil libertarians expect judges to create uncertainty for government policies that may violate the Constitution (as in the Keith case), open up opportunities for the elected branches to act (as in *Hamdan*), or emphatically denounce declining or extinct governmental abuses (as in *Watkins* and *Milligan*), they could yet find the courts useful.

Beyond the institutions of the federal government, chapter 6 strongly suggests that bold—and at times illegal—actions by whistleblowers, journalists, and activists can be catalysts for legal or executive measures to protect civil liberties. COINTELPRO was terminated not by a judge or by an act of Congress but by the audacious burglary of the FBI office in Media, Pennsylvania, in 1971. The intrepid reporting of Seymour Hersh and his sources within the CIA led to the exposure of the CIA's domestic spying activities and the Church Committee's investigations in 1975. More recently, Edward Snowden's leaks of classified information in 2013 eventually led to passage of the 2015 USA Freedom Act, which cautiously constrained the NSA's surveillance powers. Although the United States has a long tradition of attacks on civil liberties, it also has a long, rich, and courageous tradition of citizens who are willing to put their own lives and liberties in jeopardy to defend the liberties of the nation as a whole. The preservation of this tradition will be essential to the protection of rights and liberties in the future.

Epilogue
Civil Liberties in the Age of Trump

As you know if you have ever applied for a visa or a green card in the United States, you have to answer several questions that do not seem to comport with the country's constitutional commitment to freedom of speech. Consider, for example, question 46.d. of the green card application: "Do you intend to engage in any activity that could endanger the welfare, safety, or security of the United States?" Or question 47: "Are you engaged in, or, upon your entry into the United States, do you intend to engage in any activity that could have potentially serious adverse foreign policy consequences for the United States?" Or the classic, question 56: "Have you EVER been a member of, or in any way affiliated with, the Communist Party or any other totalitarian party (in the United States or abroad)?"

You have to answer these questions because Congress requires it. If the immigration authorities determine that you intend to endanger the welfare of the United States, to engage in any activity with potentially serious adverse foreign policy consequences for the United States, that you were a member of a "totalitarian" political party, or that you "endorse" or "support" (or encourage others to "endorse" or "support") "terrorist activity" or a "terrorist organization," this would constitute grounds for denial of entry (if you are abroad) or possibly deportation (if you are already in the United States).[1]

It seems to me that most constitutional commentators and scholars have been alarmed, during the first one hundred days of the second Trump administration, about Congress failing to do its job. Yet, in defining who can be excluded or deported from the country, Congress has, in fact, done its job. It has said, clearly, that noncitizens can and should be deported from this country for purely political reasons. As this book has documented, such deportations are nothing new in American history, nor is the willingness of Congress to authorize them: the 1918 Immigration Act explicitly sanctioned the 1919–20 Palmer Raids, and the 1952 McCarran-Walter Immigration Act sanctioned the deportation of alleged communist sympathizers. Indeed, many of the current "grounds for inadmissibility" in US immigration law originate in the 1952 McCarran-Walter Act.

This context is essential for understanding what could be the worst violation of civil liberties during the first one hundred days of the second Trump administration: efforts to deport campus activists who have apparently done little more than oppose US complicity in Israel's lengthy and brutal war against the people of Gaza. Advocates of free speech probably do not and should not care whether these deportations are authorized by 8 USC §1182 or 8 USC §1227. You do not need to be a constitutional law professor to be profoundly disturbed by images such as Tufts Ph.D. student Rümeysa Öztürk being bundled into the back of an SUV by plainclothes immigration agents in March 2025, ostensibly for the crime of publishing an article critical of Israel in a student newspaper.[2] Yet, if we recognize that politically motivated deportations may well be legal and that they are certainly not unprecedented, we might think twice about how we respond to such acts of repression under the Trump administration. In particular, we might question the wisdom of calls for Congress to "check" the executive. Congress, after all, wrote the repressive legislation in question and has never shown any appetite—under either party—to rewrite it with greater care for civil liberties.

To be sure, it is the Trump administration that has dusted off these sections of the federal code and used them to justify serious attacks on freedom of expression. Moreover, some of the deportations being carried out by the Trump administration do appear to be utterly lawless. The idea that the government can summarily deport foreign nationals by invoking the 1798 Alien Enemies Act and by adopting a definition of "invasion" that the federal courts have never accepted is legally preposterous. It certainly cannot be plausibly traced to any obscure corner of the US Code.[3]

I concluded in this book that truly unilateral executive violations of civil liberties are extremely rare. This is one of several statements written before 2025 that may now require revision. Others would include the claim that only Congress has the power to curtail civil liberties through the flow of federal funds to state and local jurisdictions. Although this claim remains technically correct, the first one hundred days of the Trump administration have demonstrated that the executive branch can gain significant leverage through its control of discretionary grant programs and contracts—especially with universities. Most notably, after the administration threatened Columbia University's access to $400 million worth of contracts and grants in March 2025, Columbia agreed to hire more campus security officers, to grant these officers more powers, and to appoint a new senior vice provost to "conduct a thorough review of the portfolio of programs in regional areas across the University, starting immediately with the Middle East." This review would include an examination of "educational programs to ensure the educational offerings are comprehensive and balanced" and efforts to "appoint new faculty members with joint positions in both the Institute for Israel and Jewish Studies and the departments of Economics, Political Science, and School for International and Public Affairs." It is hard to disagree with Professor Jonathan Zimmerman's statement that "the government is using the money as a cudgel to micromanage a university."[4]

More broadly, sixty universities—including my own, which I was happy to see labeled "elite"—have been identified by the Department of Education as potentially violating federal civil rights legislation due to their failure to deal with anti-Semitism on campus.[5] These serious allegations could lead to the loss of federal funds, with potentially crippling consequences for many universities. Given what the Trump administration demanded of Columbia University, it is hard to believe that civil rights investigations conducted by the Trump Justice Department will proceed with any deep respect for academic freedom. Everything the administration has said and done on this subject strongly suggests that the goal is to intimidate universities into suppressing activism the government disapproves of. If this does not violate the letter of the First Amendment, it certainly violates its spirit.

On the other hand, it would be inaccurate to describe these attacks on academic freedom as purely executive excesses. Indeed, they remind me of the so-called Palmer Raids, which were implemented by Attorney General A. Mitchell Palmer and "Radical Division" Chief J. Edgar Hoover, but under significant political pressure from Palmer's political opponents in Congress. Likewise, the Trump administration's multifront campaign against college activists was fueled and largely designed by the House of Representatives in 2024. Not only did House interrogations of college presidents lead to high-profile resignations, firings, and disciplinary actions against students but, on December 18, 2024, a multicommittee House report on anti-Semitism precisely outlined the larger program of repression the Trump administration has begun to implement.

The report included some dubious evidence to support its claims of pervasive anti-Semitism on college campuses. The Committee on Education and the Workforce noted, for example, that "Harvard administrators deliberately chose not to condemn Hamas in their widely criticized October 9th [2023] statement" that "Harvard's then-President Gay and then-Provost Garber asked Harvard Corporation Senior Fellow Penny Pritzker not to call the slogan 'From the river to the sea' antisemitic" and that "so-called university leaders expressed hostility to congressional oversight and treated campus antisemitism as a public relations issue, not a serious problem demanding action." Despite the tenuous foundation of some of its core claims, the Education and Workforce Committee went on to recommend that universities "reform admissions and hiring processes that have filled their student bodies, faculties, and staffs with pro-Hamas anti-Semites" and that "the executive branch should aggressively enforce Title VI and hold universities accountable for violating their obligations. . . . Universities that fail to fulfill the obligations upon which their federal funding is predicated or whose actions make clear they are unfit stewards of taxpayer dollars should be treated accordingly." The committee underlined that "while criticism of Israel is not inherently antisemitic, hatred against 'Zionists' is. Anti-Zionism has been recognized as a form of antisemitism by major Jewish organizations and a bipartisan vote of the U.S. House of Representatives."[6]

Meanwhile, the House Judiciary Committee argued that "certain conduct during the antisemitic protests may render aliens removable from the United States." It noted that "under the Immigration and Nationality Act, an alien is inadmissible to and removable from the United States if the alien 'endorses or espouses terrorist activity or persuades others to endorse or espouse terrorist activity or support a terrorist organization.'" Yet, "despite the clear statutory language, in October 2023, only three weeks after Hamas's attacks on Israel, U.S. Department of Homeland

Security (DHS) Secretary Alejandro Mayorkas declined to state whether foreign students should 'have their visas revoked' if they 'advocate for the elimination of Israel and attacks on Jewish individuals.'"[7]

The Judiciary Committee also noted that it had requested data from the State Department on "the total number of aliens, including those on student visas, for whom the State Department has revoked visas based on their actions related to anti-Israel protests disaggregated by visa category, country of nationality, and the specific action that precipitated the revocation." From DHS, the committee requested data on "the number of aliens, including those on student visas, who have endorsed or espoused terrorist activity or have persuaded others to endorse or espouse terrorist activity or support a terrorist organization during anti-Israel protests." Overall, the Judiciary Committee lamented what it described as the lack of a "substantive response from either Department."[8]

Congress clearly did not respond to the US-backed war in Gaza by abdicating its constitutional responsibilities. The House of Representatives, in particular, was active and assertive: collecting data, informing the public, and scrutinizing the activities of the executive branch. To a large degree, it was also bipartisan. As the House Committee on Education and the Workforce noted in the *Staff Report on Antisemitism*, the December 2023 House resolution equating anti-Zionism with anti-Semitism was passed by an overwhelming (311–14) majority.[9] Overall, the constitutional system worked just as it should: Congress took the lead, and the executive faithfully executed its wishes.

If there was something constitutionally wrong with this process, it was that Congress did not pass any legislation. In this sense, this latest wave of repression is not much different from the old McCarthyism, demonstrating the enduring capacity of members of Congress to use their independent powers—particularly the power to launch searching inquiries into the activities of both public and private persons—to create a national climate of intimidation and intolerance of dissent. Advocates of civil liberties should keep this in mind as they lament the alleged emergence of a superpowered "imperial presidency" under Donald Trump and J. D. Vance.

Of course, no one should ignore the potentially grave constitutional problems this new administration has already created. It is facing or has already faced numerous lawsuits related to its refusal to respect civil service protections for federal employees, its impoundment of congressionally appropriated funds, and its gutting of federal government agencies established or funded by Congress—to name just a few examples. If the executive not only consistently defies the law but also claims the right to so, the dangers to both civil liberties and the wider constitutional system are too obvious to state.

At the same time, it is far from certain that efforts to rein in the presidency and empower Congress will better secure civil liberties. It is possible, even, that such efforts will backfire. The question of the president's duty to "faithfully execute" the laws is instructive here. Several influential scholars and commentators have strongly condemned the Trump administration for its various efforts to manipulate, withhold, or impound funds appropriated by Congress, as well as its refusal to implement Congress's TikTok ban after the Supreme Court upheld its constitutionality. Professor Melissa Murray described the latter act as a presidential defiance of Congress amounting to a "constitutional crisis."[10] Yet, if refusing to enforce the TikTok ban is a "constitutional crisis," how should we describe the Obama administration's deferred action programs for undocumented immigrants, which not only deferred deportations but also offered benefits such as Social Security numbers and work authorization documents to thousands of noncitizens? The law is clear: if you enter the United States illegally, you must be removed from the country. However, the Obama administration justified deferred action based on the president's "prosecutorial discretion": his right—like that of local prosecutors throughout the country—to occasionally determine that strict enforcement of the law is either impractical or even inhumane. This prosecutorial discretion can insulate citizens and noncitizens from laws that might otherwise harm them or deprive them of their liberty, as when President Jefferson refused to enforce the 1798 Sedition Act or when Assistant Labor Secretary Louis Post refused to carry out mass deportations under the 1918 Immigration Act. Restricting or condemning such discretion could hamper the ability of future presidents or executive branch officials to curb the worst effects of repressive legislation.

In a similar sense, particularly during his first administration, President Trump was roundly criticized for his refusal to cooperate with congressional investigations of the executive branch and of his personal financial records. His obstinance, critics alleged, undermined Congress's unwritten but well-established right to compel testimony before its committees. Did we hear very much, at least outside conservative and Republican circles, about the dangers of congressional committees having practically unfettered power to pry into public and private documents, as long as they can assert a vague "legislative purpose" for doing so?[11] We do not have to look too far back in history to find evidence of these dangers, such as when President Truman unequivocally asserted his right to conceal information from Joseph McCarthy and the House Un-American Activities Committee to protect federal government employees from congressional show trials. Was Truman a tyrant? Should he have been forced to cooperate with Congress in order to preserve the sacred separation of powers?

Some readers might say yes. Others might seek to draw various distinctions between Truman and Trump and, certainly, between Obama and Trump. I probably would not argue with these distinctions. However, my core point is that if we care about civil liberties, we should be careful not to deprive the executive branch of powers that can be used—and have been used—to protect our rights just because we do not trust the current president to use these powers responsibly. This would leave us at the mercy of future lawmakers who might be eager to use the postwar moment—or some other crisis or postcrisis moment—to carry out a campaign of repression that our country and our Constitution would not normally tolerate. The historical record strongly suggests that this is not a fanciful scenario.

Perhaps, during the second Trump administration, these concerns will be overshadowed by threats to the constitutional system itself. Yet, if this book proves anything, it is that the central feature of the constitutional system—a separation of powers with the legislature as the strongest branch of government—seems to emerge from even the most serious wars and crises more or less intact. This, however, does not usually result in positive outcomes for civil liberties. We might, then, survive Trump but continue to betray our commitments to values such as freedom of expression, due process, and humane judicial punishment. My only hope is that public revulsion toward much of what is happening under the second Trump administration—especially the persecution of student activists and the summary deportation of foreign nationals—will endure even when, one way or another, Trump himself is finally gone.

NOTES

INTRODUCTION: THE MOST DANGEROUS BRANCH

1. Alexander Hamilton, "Federalist 70," in *The Federalist Papers*, ed. Alexander Hamilton, James Madison, and John Jay (Simon and Schuster, 2004), 502.
2. Kim Lane Scheppele, "Exceptions that Prove the Rule: Embedding Emergency Government in Everyday Constitutional Life," in *The Limits of Constitutional Democracy*, ed. Jeffrey K. Tulis and Stephen Macedo (Princeton University Press, 2010), 124–154. See also Kim Lane Scheppele, "Law in a Time of Emergency: States of Exception and the Temptations of 9/11," *University of Pennsylvania Journal of Constitutional Law* 6 (2003–4): 1001–1075. I elaborate on these arguments later.
3. US Constitution, Article II, Section 3.
4. Generally, see Josh Chafetz, *Congress's Constitution: Legislative Authority and the Separation of Powers* (Yale University Press, 2017). In the realm of foreign policy, see William G. Howell and Jon C. Pevehouse, *While Dangers Gather: Congressional Checks on Presidential War Powers* (Princeton University Press, 2007); Douglas L. Kriner, *After the Rubicon: Congress, Presidents, and the Politics of Waging War* (University of Chicago Press, 2010). Congressional authority over the federal bureaucracy has been investigated at length in Mathew D. McCubbins, Roger G. Noll, and Barry R. Weingast, "Administrative Procedures as Instruments of Political Control," *Journal of Law, Economics, & Organization* 3, no. 2 (1987): 243–277; Mathew D. McCubbins and Thomas Schwartz, "Congressional Oversight Overlooked: Police Patrols Versus Fire Alarms," *American Journal of Political Science* (1984): 165–179; Roderick D. Kiewiet and Mathew D. McCubbins, *The Logic of Delegation* (University of Chicago Press, 1991); Jason A. McDonald, "Limitation Riders and Congressional Influence over Bureaucratic Policy Decisions," *American Political Science Review* 104, no. 4 (2010): 766–782.
5. US Constitution, Article I, Section 5.
6. *Trump v. Anderson*, 601 U.S. ___ (2024).
7. The precedents in this area are well summarized in *Trump v. Mazars USA, LLP*, 591 U.S. ___ (2020). On the long history of the contempt power, see Josh Chafetz, "Executive Branch Contempt of Congress," *University of Chicago Law Review* 76 (2009): 1146.
8. See Harry Blain, "Israel and the New McCarthyism," *Foreign Policy in Focus*, December 15, 2023.
9. Diba Mohtasham, "Tom Cotton Grills Singaporean TikTok CEO: Are You a Chinese Communist?" NPR, February 1, 2024.
10. American Civil Liberties Union (ACLU), "ACLU Slams House for Latest Plan to Ban TikTok and Stifle Free Speech," March 5, 2024.
11. Harry Blain, "No Gestapo: J. Edgar Hoover's World-Wide Intelligence Service and the Limits of Bureaucratic Autonomy in the National Security State," *Studies in American Political Development* 35, no. 2 (2021): 214–222.

12. Loch K. Johnson, "Ostriches, Cheerleaders, Skeptics, and Guardians," *SAIS Review of International Affairs* 28, no. 1 (2008): 93–108.
13. Kenneth A. Shepsle, "Congress Is a 'They,' Not an 'It': Legislative Intent as Oxymoron," *International Review of Law and Economics* 12, no. 2 (1992): 239–256.
14. As discussed later, the detention or deportation of noncitizens is not always a violation of civil liberties, but I identify cases and conditions (including Guantanamo and the Red Scare) in which the rights noncitizens enjoy under the Constitution were violated.
15. W. E. B. Du Bois, *Black Reconstruction: An Essay Toward a History of the Part Which Black Folk Played in the Attempt to Reconstruct Democracy in America, 1860–1880* (Harcourt, Brace, 1935), 345.
16. Generally, see Robert J. Goldstein, *Political Repression in Modern America from 1870 to 1976* (University of Illinois Press, 1976); Alan Wolfe, *The Seamy Side of Democracy: Repression in America* (David McKay, 1973); David Cunningham, *There's Something Happening Here: The New Left, the Klan, and FBI Counterintelligence* (University of California Press, 2004); Ward Churchill and Jim Vander Wall, *The COINTELPRO Papers* (South End, 1990); Nelson Blackstock, *COINTELPRO: The FBI's Secret War on Political Freedom* (Pathfinder Press, 1975). On the state and local levels, see James L. Gibson, "Pluralism, Federalism and the Protection of Civil Liberties," *Western Political Quarterly* 43, no. 3 (1990): 511–533; Don E. Carleton, "McCarthyism Was More than McCarthy: Documenting the Red Scare at the State and Local Level," *Midwestern Archivist* (1987): 13–19; Frank Donner, *Protectors of Privilege: Red Squads and Police Repression in Urban America* (University of California Press, 1990); Elizabeth Hinton, *From the War on Poverty to the War on Crime: The Making of Mass Incarceration in America* (Harvard University Press, 2016); Elizabeth Hinton, *America on Fire: The Untold History of Police Violence and Black Rebellion Since the 1960s* (W. W. Norton, 2021). On mass and elite opinion, see James L. Gibson, "Political Intolerance and Political Repression During the McCarthy Red Scare," *American Political Science Review* 82, no. 2 (1988): 511–529; Samuel A. Stouffer, *Communism, Conformity, and Civil Liberties: A Cross-Section of the Nation Speaks Its Mind* (Doubleday, 1955); John Sides and Kimberly Gross, "Stereotypes of Muslims and Support for the War on Terror," *Journal of Politics* 75, no. 3 (2013): 583–598; Marc Hetherington and Elizabeth Suhay, "Authoritarianism, Threat, and Americans' Support for the War on Terror," *American Journal of Political Science* 55, no. 3 (2011): 546–560; Peter Liberman, "Retributive Support for International Punishment and Torture," *Journal of Conflict Resolution* 57, no. 2 (2013): 285–306.
17. Shepsle, "Congress Is a 'They'"; Eric Schickler, *Disjointed Pluralism: Institutional Innovation and the Development of the US Congress* (Princeton University Press, 2001), 189–248. On earlier debates surrounding the motivations of legislators, see David Mayhew, *Congress: The Electoral Connection* (Yale University Press, 1974); Richard Fenno, *Home Style: House Members in Their Districts* (Little, Brown, 1978). On how partisanship complicates the study of congressional motives—and the separation of powers more broadly—see Daryl J. Levinson and Richard H. Pildes, "Separation of Parties, Not

Powers," *Harvard Law Review* (2006): 2311–2386. On the application of these concepts outside the United States, see Steven S. Smith and Thomas F. Remington, *The Politics of Institutional Choice: The Formation of the Russian State Duma* (Princeton University Press, 2001), 15–22.

18. Chafetz, *Congress's Constitution*. I am grateful to the editors of the Constitutional Thinking series—especially Mariah Zeisberg—for suggesting that I alter my earlier chronological structure to one based on categories of congressional power and for suggesting that I engage more closely with Chafetz's work.
19. In the realm of foreign policy, see Howell and Pevehouse, *While Dangers Gather*; Kriner, *After the Rubicon*; Ralph G. Carter and James M. Scott, *Choosing to Lead: Understanding Congressional Foreign Policy Entrepreneurs* (Duke University Press, 2009); Robert David Johnson, *Congress and the Cold War* (Cambridge University Press, 2005); Robert David Johnson, "Congress and the Cold War," *Journal of Cold War Studies* 3, no. 2 (2001): 76–100. In the realm of control over the federal bureaucracy, see McCubbins, Noll, and Weingast, "Administrative Procedures as Instruments of Political Control"; McCubbins and Schwartz, "Congressional Oversight Overlooked"; Kiewiet and McCubbins, *Logic of Delegation*; McDonald, "Limitation Riders and Congressional Influence."
20. See Marc De Wilde, "Why Dictatorial Authority Did Good, and Not Harm, to the Roman Republic: Dictatorship and Constitutional Change in Machiavelli," *Ratio Juris* 31, no. 1 (2018): 86–99.
21. Clinton Rossiter, *Constitutional Dictatorship: Crisis Government in the Modern Democracies* (Transaction Publishers, 1948). See also Frederick Mundell Watkins, *The Failure of Constitutional Emergency Powers Under the German Republic* (Harvard University Press, 1939).
22. James Madison, "Helvidius IV," in *The Pacificus-Helvidius Debates of 1793–1794: Toward the Completion of the American Founding*, ed. Alexander Hamilton and James Madison (Liberty Fund, 2007), 87.
23. Rossiter, *Constitutional Dictatorship*, 314.
24. See, especially, Paddy Hillyard, *Suspect Community: People's Experience of the Prevention of Terrorism Acts in Britain* (Pluto Press in association with Liberty, 1993); Joe Sim and Philip A. Thomas, "The Prevention of Terrorism Act: Normalising the Politics of Repression," *Journal of Law and Society* 10, no. 1 (1983): 71–84; Clive Walker, *The Prevention of Terrorism in British Law* (Manchester University Press, 1992); Colin Warbrick, "The European Convention on Human Rights and the Prevention of Terrorism," *International & Comparative Law Quarterly* 32, no. 1 (1983): 82–119. On the permanent Terrorism Act, see Conor Gearty, "11 September 2001, Counter-Terrorism, and the Human Rights Act," *Journal of Law and Society* 32, no. 1 (2005): 18–33.
25. Kurt Groenewold, "The German Federal Republic's Response and Civil Liberties," *Terrorism and Political Violence* 4, no. 4 (1992): 136–150; Peter Chalk, "The Response to Terrorism as a Threat to Liberal Democracy," *Australian Journal of Politics & History* 44, no. 3 (1998): 373–388. See also Fernando Jimenez, "Spain: The Terrorist Challenge and the Government's Response," *Terrorism and Political Violence* 4, no. 4 (1992): 110–130.
26. Bruce A. Ackerman, *Before the Next Attack: Preserving Civil Liberties in an*

Age of Terrorism (Yale University Press, 2006); Ryan Alford, *Permanent State of Emergency: Unchecked Executive Power and the Demise of the Rule of Law* (McGill-Queen's Press–MQUP, 2017); Karen J. Greenberg, *Rogue Justice: The Making of the Security State* (Random House, 2016); Jane Mayer, *The Dark Side: The Inside Story of How the War on Terror Turned into a War on American Ideals* (Doubleday, 2008); Glenn Greenwald, *No Place to Hide: Edward Snowden, the NSA, and the U.S. Surveillance State* (Macmillan, 2014); Louis Fisher, *The Constitution and 9/11: Recurring Threats to America's Freedoms* (University Press of Kansas, 2008); Emily Berman, "The Paradox of Counterterrorism Sunset Provisions," *Fordham Law Review*, 81 (2012): 1777–1833; Susan N. Herman, *Taking Liberties: The War on Terror and the Erosion of American Democracy* (Oxford University Press, 2011); Christopher J. Coyne and Abigail R. Hall, *Tyranny Comes Home: The Domestic Fate of US Militarism* (Stanford University Press, 2018).

27. Giorgio Agamben, *State of Exception*, trans. Kevin Attell (University of Chicago Press, 2005). On Agamben's limited empirical contributions, see Stephen Humphreys, "Legalizing Lawlessness: On Giorgio Agamben's State of Exception," *European Journal of International Law* 17, no. 3 (2006): 677–687.
28. Scheppele, "Exceptions that Prove the Rule"; Scheppele, "Law in a Time of Emergency."
29. Scheppele, "Exceptions that Prove the Rule," 137; Sanford Levinson and Jack M. Balkin, "Constitutional Dictatorship: Its Dangers and Its Design," *Minnesota Law Review* 94 (2009): 1848. The specter of "contrived crises" is also investigated in Chris Edelson, *Emergency Presidential Power: From the Drafting of the Constitution to the War on Terror* (University of Wisconsin Press, 2013).
30. Tom Ginsburg and Aziz Z. Huq, *How to Save a Constitutional Democracy* (University of Chicago Press, 2018), 224.
31. Bob Bauer and Jack Goldsmith, *After Trump: Reconstructing the Presidency* (Lawfare Press, 2020); Caroline Fredrickson, Jamal Greene, and Melissa Murray, *The Progressive Constitution*; Robert P. George, Michael McConnell, Colleen A. Sheehan, and Ilan Wurman, *The Conservative Constitution*; Ilya Shapiro, Timothy Sandefur, and Christina Mulligan, *The Libertarian Constitution*, all available at https://constitutioncenter.org/debate/special-projects/constitution-drafting-project.
32. Frederick Schwarz Jr. and Aziz Z. Huq, *Unchecked and Unbalanced: Presidential Power in a Time of Terror* (New Press, 2008). See also Spencer Ackerman, *Reign of Terror: How the 9/11 Era Destabilized America and Produced Trump* (Viking Press, 2021); Karen J. Greenberg, *Subtle Tools: The Dismantling of American Democracy from the War on Terror to Donald Trump* (Princeton University Press, 2021). For a more general statement of this argument, see Linda L. Fowler, *Watchdogs on the Hill: The Decline of Congressional Oversight of US Foreign Relations* (Princeton University Press, 2015); James Goldgeier and Elizabeth N. Saunders, "The Unconstrained Presidency: Checks and Balances Eroded Long Before Trump," *Foreign Affairs* 97 (2018): 144–156.
33. Michael J. Glennon, *National Security and Double Government* (Oxford University Press, 2016), 106.
34. Fisher, *Constitution and 9/11*, 364, 366.

35. Laura Donohue, *The Cost of Counterterrorism: Power, Politics, and Liberty* (Cambridge University Press, 2008), 11.
36. See, for example, Andrew Polsky, *Elusive Victories: The American Presidency at War* (Oxford University Press, 2012); Howell and Pevehouse, *While Dangers Gather*; Kriner, *After the Rubicon*; William G. Howell, Saul P. Jackman, and Jon C. Rogowski, *The Wartime President: Executive Influence and the Nationalizing Politics of Threat* (University of Chicago Press, 2013); William G. Howell, "Presidential Power in War," *Annual Review of Political Science* 14 (2011): 89–105.
37. William G. Howell, *Power Without Persuasion: The Politics of Direct Presidential Action* (Princeton University Press, 2003); Howell, "Presidential Power in War."
38. Polsky, *Elusive Victories*, 202–273; Schickler, *Disjointed Pluralism*, 189–248. For a more critical view of the War Powers Resolution, see Harry Blain, "The Useless War Powers Resolution," *Foreign Policy in Focus*, January 9, 2020.
39. Benjamin Wittes, introduction to *Legislating the War on Terror: An Agenda for Reform*, ed. Benjamin Wittes (Brookings Institution Press, 2009), 1.
40. Eric A. Posner and Adrian Vermeule, *The Executive Unbound: After the Madisonian Republic* (Oxford University Press, 2011), 176. See also John Yoo, *The Powers of War and Peace: The Constitution and Foreign Affairs After 9/11* (University of Chicago Press, 2008); John Yoo, *Defender in Chief: Donald Trump's Fight for Presidential Power* (All Points Books, 2020). For an insider's account of these debates within the George W. Bush administration, see Jack Goldsmith, *The Terror Presidency: Law and Judgment Inside the Bush Administration* (W. W. Norton, 2007).
41. The unitary executive theory was expounded in *Morrison v. Olson*, 487 U.S. 654, 697 (1988) (Scalia, J., dissenting); Christopher S. Yoo, Steven G. Calabresi, and Anthony J. Colangelo, "The Unitary Executive in the Modern Era, 1945–2004," *Iowa Law Review* 90 (2004): 601. The theory (and its variants) is explained in Mark Tushnet, "A Political Perspective on the Theory of the Unitary Executive," *University of Pennsylvania Journal of Constitutional Law* 12 (2009): 313; Stephen Skowronek, "The Conservative Insurgency and Presidential Power: A Developmental Perspective on the Unitary Executive," *Harvard Law Review* 122 (2008): 2070. See also William G. Howell and Terry Moe, *Relic: How Our Constitution Undermines Effective Government—and Why We Need a More Powerful Presidency* (Basic Books, 2016); Stephen Skowronek, John A. Dearborn, and Desmond King, *Phantoms of a Beleaguered Republic: The Deep State and the Unitary Executive* (Oxford University Press, 2021).
42. Nancy Bermeo, "On Democratic Backsliding," *Journal of Democracy* 27, no. 1 (2016): 10–13; Catherine M. Conaghan, "Ecuador: Correa's Plebiscitary Presidency," *Journal of Democracy* 19, no. 2 (2008): 46–60; Tarunabh Khaitan, "Killing a Constitution with a Thousand Cuts: Executive Aggrandizement and Party-State Fusion in India," *Law & Ethics of Human Rights* 14, no. 1 (2020): 49–95; Tarunabh Khaitan, "Executive Aggrandizement in Established Democracies: A Crisis of Liberal Democratic Constitutionalism," *International Journal of Constitutional Law* 17, no. 1 (2019): 342–356; Will Freeman,

"Sidestepping the Constitution: Executive Aggrandizement in Latin America and East Central Europe," *Constitutional Studies* 6 (2020): 35; Aníbal Pérez-Liñán, Nicolás Schmidt, and Daniela Vairo, "Presidential Hegemony and Democratic Backsliding in Latin America, 1925–2016," *Democratization* 26, no. 4 (2019): 606–625; Stephan Haggard and Robert Kaufman, "The Anatomy of Democratic Backsliding," *Journal of Democracy* 32, no. 4 (2021): 27–41.

43. Juan J. Linz and Alfred C. Stepan, "Toward Consolidated Democracies," *Journal of Democracy* 7, no. 2 (1996): 19. More generally, see Juan J. Linz and Alfred C. Stepan, eds., *The Breakdown of Democratic Regimes* (Johns Hopkins University Press, 1979).
44. For an overview of democratic conceptualization and operationalization, see Michael Coppedge, John Gerring, David Altman, Michael Bernhard, Steven Fish, Allen Hicken, Matthew Kroenig, Staffan I. Lindberg, Kelly McMann, Pamela Paxton, Holli A. Semetko, Svend-Erik Skaaning, Jeffrey Staton, and Jan Teorell, "Conceptualizing and Measuring Democracy: A New Approach," *Perspectives on Politics* 9, no. 2 (2011): 247–267.
45. José Antonio Cheibub, *Presidentialism, Parliamentarism, and Democracy* (Cambridge University Press, 2007).
46. Steven Levitsky and Daniel Ziblatt, *How Democracies Die* (Random House, 2018), 92, 110.
47. Max Farrand, ed., *The Records of the Federal Convention of 1787*, rev. ed., vol. 2 (Yale University Press, 1937), 52. See also Daniel J. McCarthy, "James Wilson and the Creation of the Presidency," *Presidential Studies Quarterly* 17, no. 4 (1987): 689–696.
48. Judith A. Best, "Legislative Tyranny and the Liberation of the Executive: A View from the Founding," *Presidential Studies Quarterly* 17, no. 4 (1987): 697–709; Jack N. Rakove, *Original Meanings: Politics and Ideas in the Making of the Constitution* (Alfred A. Knopf, 1996), 244–288.
49. See Michael W. McConnell, *The President Who Would Not Be King: Executive Power Under the Constitution* (Princeton University Press, 2020).
50. See Pauline Maier, *Ratification: The People Debate the Constitution, 1787–1788* (Simon and Schuster, 2010).
51. Martin S. Flaherty, "The Most Dangerous Branch," *Yale Law Journal* 105 (1995): 1725–1839.
52. Larry Tye, *Demagogue: The Life and Long Shadow of Senator Joe McCarthy* (Houghton Mifflin Harcourt, 2020), 300–341. On the State Department, see E. J. Kahn, *The China Hands: America's Foreign Service Officers and What Befell Them* (Viking Press, 1972).
53. See, especially, Ellen Schrecker, *Many Are the Crimes: McCarthyism in America* (Princeton University Press, 1998).
54. Ackerman, *Before the Next Attack*, 124. See also Rachel Riegelhaupt, "Manufactured Emergencies: The Crisis at the Core of the National Emergencies Act," *NYU Journal of Legislation & Public Policy* 23 (2020): 277; Glennon, *National Security and Double Government*; Donohue, *Cost of Counterterrorism*. More generally, see Leonard C. Feldman, "The Banality of Emergency: On the Time and Space of 'Political Necessity,'" in *Sovereignty, Emergency, Legality*, ed. Austin Sarat (Cambridge University Press, 2010), 136–164.

55. For a summary of conservative critiques and liberal defenses of delegation, see *Gundy v. United States*, 588 U.S. ___ (2019). Emergency delegation is not explicitly spelled out in the US Constitution, but it is in most constitutions. See John Ferejohn and Pasquale Pasquino, "The Law of the Exception: A Typology of Emergency Powers," *International Journal of Constitutional Law* 2, no. 2 (2004): 210–239. Delegation is also heavily criticized in Glennon, *National Security and Double Government*; Scheppele, "Law in a Time of Emergency"; Fisher, *Constitution and 9/11*; Donohue, *Cost of Counterterrorism*.
56. Glennon, *National Security and Double Government*.
57. Loch K. Johnson, *Spy Watching: Intelligence Accountability in the United States* (Oxford University Press, 2017); Amy B. Zegart, *Eyes on Spies: Congress and the United States Intelligence Community* (Hoover Press, 2013).
58. Glennon, *National Security and Double Government.*
59. Scheppele, "Exceptions that Prove the Rule," 137.
60. See, especially, Ginsburg and Huq, *How to Save a Constitutional Democracy*; Levitsky and Ziblatt, *How Democracies Die*; Haggard and Kaufman, "Anatomy of Democratic Backsliding."
61. Generally, see Conor Gearty, *Civil Liberties* (Oxford University Press, 2007), 10–29.
62. The Second Amendment was first defined as an individual right to self-defense in the home (rather than a right attached to militia service) in *District of Columbia v. Heller*, 554 U.S. 570 (2008), incorporated against the states in *McDonald v. City of Chicago*, 561 U.S. 742 (2010), and extended outside the home in *New York State Rifle & Pistol Association, Inc. v. Bruen*, 597 U.S. ___ (2022). On "civil rights," see Christopher W. Schmidt, "The Civil Rights–Civil Liberties Divide," *Stanford Journal of Civil Rights & Civil Liberties* 12 (2016): 1.
63. See, notably, *Dobbs v. Jackson Women's Health Organization*, 597 U.S. ___ (2022).
64. See *Yick Wo v. Hopkins*, 118 U.S. 356 (1886); *Yamataya v. Fisher*, 189 U.S. 86 (1903). See also *Plyler v. Doe*, 457 U.S. 202 (1982).
65. See *Fong Yue Ting v. United States*, 149 U.S. 698 (1893).
66. See *Boumediene v. Bush*, 553 U.S. 723 (2008).
67. Gearty, *Civil Liberties*, 10–29.
68. Du Bois, *Black Reconstruction*, 185.
69. Mary Dudziak, *War Time: An Idea, Its History, Its Consequences* (Oxford University Press, 2012). On the global picture, see Tanisha M. Fazal, "Why States No Longer Declare War," *Security Studies* 21, no. 4 (2012): 557–593; Tanisha M. Fazal, "The Demise of Peace Treaties in Interstate War," *International Organization* 67, no. 4 (2013): 695–724. See also Samuel Moyn, *Humane: How the United States Abandoned Peace and Reinvented War* (Farrar, Straus, and Giroux, 2021).
70. These are roughly the same conflicts discussed, for example, in Geoffrey Stone, *Perilous Times: Free Speech in Wartime* (W. W. Norton, 2005).
71. See, especially, David Hackett Fischer, *Washington's Crossing* (Oxford University Press, 2004), which examines George Washington's tumultuous relationship with the Continental Congress in the early phase of the Revolutionary War.

72. See Mark A. Graber, "Counter-Stories: Maintaining and Expanding Civil Liberties in Wartime," in *The Constitution in Wartime: Beyond Alarmism and Complacency*, ed. Mark Tushnet (Duke University Press, 2005), 95–123; Mary L. Dudziak, *Cold War Civil Rights* (Princeton University Press, 2011); Mary L. Dudziak, "Brown as a Cold War Case," *Journal of American History* 91, no. 1 (2004): 32–42. See also Frances Fox Piven and Richard Cloward, *Poor People's Movements: Why They Succeed, How They Fail* (Vintage Books, 1979), 1–40. More broadly, see Margaret MacMillan, *War: How Conflict Shaped Us* (Random House, 2020); Sidney Tarrow, *War, States, and Contention: A Comparative Historical Study* (Cornell University Press, 2015). For the idea that "emergency" can be used creatively to advance rights and liberties within a constitutional framework, see Mariah Zeisberg, "Frederick Douglass and Constitutional Emergency: An Homage to the Political Creativity of Abolitionist Activism," in *States of Exception in American History*, ed. Gary Gerstle and Joel Isaac (University of Chicago Press, 2020), 257–288.
73. On this fraught practice, see Ian S. Lustick, "History, Historiography, and Political Science: Multiple Historical Records and the Problem of Selection Bias," *American Political Science Review* 90, no. 3 (1996): 605–618.
74. For the broader idea of "networked repression," see Thuy Anh Tran, "The Invisible Hand of Networked Repression" (doctoral dissertation, City University of New York, 2024). For an outline of the documentation on state-level McCarthyism, see Carleton, "McCarthyism Was More than McCarthy." See also Michael J. Heale, *McCarthy's Americans: Red Scare Politics in State and Nation* (University of Georgia Press, 1998); Walter Gellhorn, ed., *The States and Subversion* (Cornell University Press, 1952).

CHAPTER 1: REPRESSIVE LEGISLATION

1. Thomas Jefferson to Abigail Adams, July 22, 1804, https://founders.archives.gov/documents/Jefferson/01-44-02-0122.
2. New York Times Co. v. Sullivan, 376 U.S. 254, 276 (1964) (also quoting the text of the statute).
3. Geoffrey Stone, *Perilous Times: Free Speech in Wartime* (W. W. Norton, 2005), 63.
4. President Adams did not explicitly propose the Sedition Act or the Alien Act to Congress, but in his words, "Congress passed the measures. I knew there was need enough of both, and therefore I consented to them." He certainly enforced them. See Charles Slack, *Liberty's First Crisis: Adams, Jefferson, and the Misfits Who Saved Free Speech* (Open Road+ Grove/Atlantic, 2015), 74.
5. This is not to say that there were no restrictions on civil liberties during the War of 1812, for example, or that the War of 1812 should not be studied. As Benjamin Wittes and Ritika Singh note in "Executive Power, Civil Liberties, and the War of 1812," *Lawfare*, March 29, 2012: "The story of civil liberties during the War of 1812 is often ignored because it is a story of a dog that didn't bark—of repression that didn't happen, of strong executive actions not taken, and of risks incurred and tolerated, not preempted. But it actually raises a vexing question—kind of the mirror image question we generally confront in thinking

about presidential conduct during wartime: Was Madison's restraint a virtue or a vice?"

6. All these measures are described at length in James G. Randall, *Constitutional Problems Under Lincoln* (D. Appleton, 1926); Mark E. Neely, *The Fate of Liberty: Abraham Lincoln and Civil Liberties* (Oxford University Press, 1991); Daniel Farber, *Lincoln's Constitution* (University of Chicago Press, 2003). More recently, see Noah Feldman, *The Broken Constitution: Lincoln, Slavery, and the Refounding of America* (Farrar, Straus, and Giroux, 2021).
7. This is particularly prominent in Randall, *Constitutional Problems*, and Clinton Rossiter, *Constitutional Dictatorship: Crisis Government in the Modern Democracies* (Transaction Publishers, 1948), 223–240.
8. This is particularly prominent in Farber, *Lincoln's Constitution*, 196–201.
9. This is the core question in Neely, *Fate of Liberty*.
10. Randall, *Constitutional Problems*, 522, 47.
11. Benjamin Kleinerman, "Lincoln's Example: Executive Power and the Survival of Constitutionalism," *Perspectives on Politics* 3, no. 4 (2005): 801–816; Benjamin Kleinerman, "'In the Name of National Security': Executive Discretion and Congressional Legislation in the Civil War and World War I," in *The Limits of Constitutional Democracy*, ed. Jeffrey Tulis and Stephen Macedo (Princeton University Press, 2010), 91–111; Oren Gross, "Chaos and Rules: Should Responses to Violent Crises Always Be Constitutional?" *Yale Law Journal* 112 (2002): 1011–1134.
12. Some notable exceptions to this trend are Gregory P. Downs, *After Appomattox: Military Occupation and the Ends of War* (Harvard University Press, 2015), and John Fabian Witt, *Lincoln's Code: The Laws of War in American History* (Simon and Schuster, 2012), 283–324. See also Gregory P. Downs, "Powers of War in Times of Peace: Emergency Powers in the United States After the End of the Civil War," in *States of Exception in American History*, ed. Gary Gerstle and Joel Isaac (University of Chicago Press, 2020), 154–178; Andrew F. Lang, *In the Wake of War: Military Occupation, Emancipation, and Civil War America* (LSU Press, 2017).
13. I use the terms "Reconstruction Acts" for the legislation and "military Reconstruction" for the regime of martial law they created.
14. W. E. B. Du Bois, *Black Reconstruction: An Essay Toward a History of the Part Which Black Folk Played in the Attempt to Reconstruct Democracy in America, 1860–1880* (Harcourt, Brace, 1935), 336.
15. First Reconstruction Act, 14 Stat. 428–430, c. 153, March 2, 1867.
16. Second Reconstruction Act, 15 Stat. 2–5, c. 6, March 23, 1867.
17. Third Reconstruction Act, 15 Stat. 14–16, c. 30, July 19, 1867.
18. Third Reconstruction Act.
19. Fourth Reconstruction Act, 15 Stat. 41, c. 25, March 11, 1868.
20. On the importance of the republican guarantee clause in the Reconstruction debate, see Mark A. Graber, *Punish Treason, Reward Loyalty: The Forgotten Goals of Constitutional Reform After the Civil War* (University Press of Kansas, 2023), 37–38.
21. These events are described in Michael Les Benedict, *A Compromise of Principle:*

Congressional Republicans and Reconstruction, 1863–1869 (W. W. Norton, 1974), 141–156.

22. As Mark Graber notes, "Republicans were as committed to protecting white Unionists, civil war veterans, and Northern creditors as they were Southern Blacks. They were disturbed by all the pathologies of Southern constitutional politics in the wake of the Civil War." Graber, *Punish Treason, Reward Loyalty*, 162.
23. First Reconstruction Act.
24. Maxwell v. Dow, 176 U.S. 581, 611 (1900).
25. *The Trial of Hon. Clement L. Vallandigham: By a Military Commission; and the Proceedings Under His Application for a Writ of Habeas Corpus in the Circuit Court of the United States for the Southern District of Ohio* (Rickey and Carroll, 1863), 11.
26. *Trial of Vallandigham*, 271.
27. Ex parte Vallandigham, 68 U.S. 243 (1864). The court noted that Lincoln had mooted the case by commuting the sentence and exiling Vallandigham to Tennessee.
28. Ex parte Milligan, 71 U.S. (4 Wall.) 2 (1866). I discuss the *Milligan* case in greater depth in chapter 4.
29. On the history and legacy of the Wirz trial, see Benjamin G. Cloyd, *Haunted by Atrocity: Civil War Prisons in American Memory* (LSU Press, 2010), 31–56.
30. Abraham Lincoln to the US Senate, "Message on Minnesota Indians," December 11, 1862, in *Abraham Lincoln: Speeches and Writings 1859–1865*, ed. Roy P. Basler (Library of America, 1989), 416–417 (emphasis in original). On the trials, see Carol Chomsky, "The United States–Dakota War Trials: A Study in Military Injustice," *Stanford Law Review* (1990): 13–98.
31. United States Congress, *Trial of Henry Wirz: Letter from the Secretary of War Ad Interim, in Answer to a Resolution of the House of April 16, 1866, Transmitting a Summary of the Trial of Henry Wirz* (GPO, 1868), 4.
32. However, the last Confederate general, Stand Watie, did not surrender until June 23, 1865, in Oklahoma Territory.
33. United States Army Military Commission, *The Assassination of President Lincoln: And the Trial of the Conspirators David E. Herold, Mary E. Surratt, Lewis Payne, George A. Atzerodt, Edward Spangler, Samuel A. Mudd, Samuel Arnold, Michael O'Laughlin* (Moore, Wilstach & Boldwin, 1865), 18.
34. Detlev F. Vagts, "Military Commissions: A Concise History," *American Journal of International Law* 101, no. 1 (2007): 38.
35. Neely, *Fate of Liberty*, 168.
36. Neely, *Fate of Liberty*, 176–177; Detlev F. Vagts, "Military Commissions: The Forgotten Reconstruction Chapter," *American University International Law Review* 23, no. 2 (2007): 258–259.
37. Downs, *After Appomattox*, 37.
38. First Reconstruction Act.
39. Ulysses S. Grant (hereafter, USG) to Elihu B. Washburne, March 4, 1867, in *The Papers of Ulysses S. Grant*, vol. 17, *January 1–September 30, 1867*, ed. John Simon (Southern Illinois University Press, 1991), 76; USG to Philip Sheridan, April 5, 1867, in *Papers of Grant*, 17:95; USG to John Pope, June 28, 1867,

in *Papers of Grant*, 17:204; USG to Edward Ord, June 23, 1867, in *Papers of Grant*, 17:192.

40. Daniel Sickles to USG, June 17, 1867, in *Papers of Grant*, 17:167; Sheridan to USG, April 19, 1867, in *Papers of Grant*, 17:96; Pope to USG, April 24, 1867, in *Papers of Grant*, 17:118.
41. On registration boards, see USG to Ord, June 23, 1867, in *Papers of Grant*, 17:192.
42. William W. Van Alstyne, "A Critical Guide to Ex Parte McCardle," *Arizona Law Review* 15 (1973): 236. See also Ord to USG, n.d. (likely December 1867), in *Papers of Grant*, 17:6. I say more about McCardle's case in chapter 4.
43. On the governor of Louisiana, see Sheridan to USG, June 4, 1867, in *Papers of Grant*, 17:186–187; on the governor of Texas, see Sheridan to USG, May 22 or 23, 1867, in *Papers of Grant*, 17:170; on the streetcars, see Sheridan to USG, May 10, 1867, in *Papers of Grant*, 17:126; on early removals in the Carolinas, see Sickles to USG, June 17, 1867, in *Papers of Grant*, 17:167.
44. Sheridan to USG, April 26, 1867, in *Papers of Grant*, 17:124; Pope to USG, May 16, 1867, in *Papers of Grant*, 17:120; Pope to USG, April 24, 1867, in *Papers of Grant*, 17:118 (emphasis in original).
45. Pope to USG, July 24, 1867, in *Papers of Grant*, 17:258.
46. United States Senate, 40th Congress, Second Session, Executive Document 53, *Letter of the General of the Army of the United States: Communicating in Compliance with a Resolution of the Senate of December 5, 1867, a Statement of the Number of White and Colored Voters Registered in Each of the States Subject to the Reconstruction Acts of Congress, with Other Statistics Relative to the Same Subject*, Mississippi State University Libraries.
47. Du Bois, for example, says: "Many leading whites, small in total number but large in influence and in former wealth and power, were disfranchised, perhaps 200,000 in all." Du Bois, *Black Reconstruction*, 372.
48. Forrest G. Wood, "On Revising Reconstruction History: Negro Suffrage, White Disfranchisement, and Common Sense," *Journal of Negro History* 51, no. 2 (1966): 107.
49. George W. Paschal, *Letter to the President Asking for the Pardon of Ludovic P. Alford and Other Citizens Imprisoned by Military Commissions Under the Reconstruction Laws* (M'Gill and Witherow, 1870), 1.
50. See Allen W. Trelease, *White Terror: The Ku Klux Klan Conspiracy and Southern Reconstruction* (LSU Press, 1971); Nicholas Lemann, *Redemption: The Last Battle of the Civil War* (Macmillan, 2007); Douglas R. Egerton, *The Wars of Reconstruction: The Brief, Violent History of America's Most Progressive Era* (Bloomsbury Press, 2014).
51. An Act to Enforce the Provisions of the Fourteenth Amendment to the Constitution of the United States, and for Other Purposes, 17 Stat. 13 (1871).
52. Lou Falkner Williams, *The Great South Carolina Ku Klux Klan Trials, 1871–1872* (University of Georgia Press, 1996), 122–123.
53. Sheridan to USG, September 15, 1867, in *Papers of Grant*, 17:317.
54. Some low-level local offices were held by black men in antebellum New England. As Van Gosse writes: "Black Yankees, if they displayed the requisite

Puritan virtues, could earn social standing as men of business, learning, or piety; a few participated in politics and held office." Van Gosse, *The First Reconstruction: Black Politics in America from the Revolution to the Civil War* (University of North Carolina Press, 2021), 149. Individual portraits of black officeholders can be found in Eric Foner, *Freedom's Lawmakers: A Directory of Black Officeholders During Reconstruction* (LSU Press, 1993).

55. C. Vann Woodward, *The Strange Career of Jim Crow*, 3rd ed. (Oxford University Press, 2002).
56. On HBCUs, see William McFeely, *Yankee Stepfather: General O. O. Howard and the Freedmen* (W. W. Norton, 1994).
57. An Act to Punish Acts of Interference with the Foreign Relations, and the Foreign Commerce of the United States, to Punish Espionage, and Better to Enforce the Criminal Laws of the United States, and for Other Purposes, 40 Stat. 217, 230 (1917).
58. Internal memo, May 8, 1918, Albert Sidney Burleson Papers, box 19, Library of Congress, Washington, DC.
59. See Charles Warren, "War Notes," April 2, 1918, Charles Warren Papers, box 6, folder 2, and "War Notes," box 6, folder 3, 612–613, Library of Congress; Stone, *Perilous Times*, 151, summarizing the "grueling debate"; William H. Manz, *Civil Liberties in Wartime: Legislative Histories of the Espionage Act of 1917 and the Sedition Act of 1918* (W. S. Hein, 2007).
60. Charles Warren to Thomas Watt Gregory, April 3, 1918; Gregory to Warren, April 4, 1918, Warren Papers, box 6.
61. Walter Nelles, *Espionage Act Cases* (National Civil Liberties Bureau, 1918); Zachariah Chaffee, *Free Speech in the United States* [1941] (Harvard University Press, 1964) (including an updated version of his original *Freedom of Speech in Wartime*).
62. Schenck v. United States, 249 U.S. 47 (1919); Debs v. United States, 249 U.S. 211 (1919); Abrams v. United States, 250 U.S. 616 (1919).
63. The ACLU's "amnesty" campaigns for political prisoners are documented at length in American Civil Liberties Union Records, Subgroup 1, The Roger Baldwin Years, 1917–1950, vols. 83, 98, and 195, Mudd Library, Princeton University (hereafter, ACLU Papers).
64. On the repeal of the sedition amendment and retention of the Espionage Act, see Albert de Silver to William Borah, May 13, 1921, ACLU Papers, vol. 167. See also Borah to de Silver, May 14, 1921, and de Silver to Borah, July 20, 1921, ACLU Papers, vol. 167. On Senator France's efforts, see American Union Against Militarism, *Republicans Give Burleson a Longer Lease of Life*, n.d. (likely December 1919), ACLU Papers, vol. 106.
65. Sam Lebovic, *State of Silence: The Espionage Act and the Rise of America's Secrecy Regime* (Basic Books, 2023); Harry Blain, "The Sun Never Sets on the Espionage Act," *Foreign Policy in Focus*, April 4, 2019.
66. For the two veto messages, see Woodrow Wilson, "Message to the House of Representatives, January 28, 1915," in *The New Democracy: Presidential Messages, Addresses, and Other Papers (1913–1917)*, vol. 1, ed. Ray Stannard Baker and William E. Dodd (Harper, 1926), 252; Woodrow Wilson, "Message to the House of Representatives, January 29, 1917," in Baker and Dodd, *New*

Democracy, 420. I quote from the first veto message—the objections and the bills were virtually the same.

67. United States Congress, Senate Committee on the Judiciary, *Charges of Illegal Practices of the Department of Justice* (GPO, 1921), 31.
68. *Congressional Record*, 65th Congress, 2nd Session (GPO, 1919), 8109–8110. The last quote is from Congressman Albert Johnson (D-WA), 8111.
69. See the speech of Congressman Jacob Meeker (R-MO) in *Congressional Record*, 65th Congress, 2nd Session (1919), 8116.
70. *Congressional Record*, 65th Congress, 2nd Session, 8109–8127.
71. An Act to Exclude and Expel from the United States Aliens Who Are Members of the Anarchistic and Similar Classes, 40 Stat. 1012 (1918).
72. See US Congress, Senate Committee on the Judiciary, *Charges of Illegal Practices*, 31. For more on the Palmer Raids, see chapter 4.
73. R. G. Brown, Zachariah Chafee, Felix Frankfurter, Ernst Freund, Swinburne Hale, Francis Fisher Kane, Alfred S. Niles, Dean Roscoe Pound, Jackson H. Ralston, David Wallerstein, Frank P. Walsh, and Tyrrell Williams, *To the American People: Report Upon the Illegal Practices of the Department of Justice* (National Popular Government League, 1920).
74. Emma Goldman, *Living My Life* (Alfred A. Knopf, 1931), 614. Arrest and deportation statistics are provided in United States Congress, House Committee on Rules, *Investigation of Administration of Louis F. Post, Assistant Secretary of Labor, in the Matter of Deportation of Aliens: Hearings Before the Committee on Rules, House of Representatives, Sixty-Sixth Congress, Second Session, on H. Res. 522, April 27* (GPO, 1920), 53.
75. Louis F. Post, *The Deportations Delirium of Nineteen-Twenty: A Personal Narrative of an Historic Official Experience* (CH Kerr, 1923), 149.
76. US Congress, House Committee on Rules, *Investigation of Administration of Louis F. Post*, 5 (Johnson), 53 (statistics).
77. US Congress, House Committee on Rules, *Investigation of Administration of Louis F. Post*, 6 (Hoch), 22 (Tincher), 5 (Johnson).
78. US Congress, House Committee on Rules, *Investigation of Administration of Louis F. Post*, 61.
79. Post quoted in Brown et al., *To the American People*, 62–63.
80. Post, *Deportations Delirium*, 309.
81. See United States Congress, *Hearing Before the Committee on the Judiciary, House of Representatives Sixty-Sixth Congress Second Session on* S. *3317, H.R. 10650 and 12041 Serial 16* (GPO, 1920) 5–131.
82. See Ellen Schrecker, *Many Are the Crimes: McCarthyism in America* (Princeton University Press, 1998), 359–417.
83. Richard W. Steele, *Free Speech in the Good War* (St. Martin's Press, 1999), 81.
84. An Act to Prohibit Certain Subversive Activities; to Amend Certain Provisions of Law with Respect to the Admission and Deportation of Aliens; to Require the Fingerprinting and Registration of Aliens; and for Other Purposes, 54 Stat. 670 (1940).
85. See Zachariah Chafee to Robert H. Jackson, April 22, 1941, Robert H. Jackson Papers, box 90, folder 1, Library of Congress; Jackson to Chafee, April 25, 1941, Jackson Papers, box 90, folder 1.

86. ACLU Publications—War-Time Prosecutions for Speech, ACLU Papers, box addendum 2–3, folder 13.
87. United States Congress, House Un-American Activities Committee, *Hearings on Proposed Legislation to Curb and Control the Communist Party* (GPO, 1948), 16–38.
88. Michal R. Belknap, *Cold War Political Justice: The Smith Act, the Communist Party, and American Civil Liberties* (Greenwood Press, 1977), 35–58.
89. Schrecker, *Many Are the Crimes,* 191.
90. Dennis v. United States, 341 U.S. 494, 515, 580, 590 (1951) (Black, J., dissenting; Douglas, J., dissenting). *Dennis* was repudiated, but not explicitly overruled, in *Brandenburg v. Ohio*, 395 U.S. 444 (1969).
91. Irving Richter, *Labor's Struggles, 1945–1950: A Participant's View* (Cambridge University Press, 1994), 48; Barton J. Bernstein "The Truman Administration and the Steel Strike of 1946," *Journal of American History* 52, no. 4 (1966): 791–803.
92. United States Congress, House of Representatives, *Hearings Before the Committee on Education and Labor: Amendments to the National Labor Relations Act* (GPO, 1947), 84.
93. American Communications Assn. v. Douds, 339 U.S. 382, 388 (1950).
94. *American Communications Assn.*, 339 U.S. at 386.
95. Harry Truman, Veto of the Taft-Hartley Labor Bill, June 20, 1947, Public Papers of Harry Truman, Online Collection, https://www.trumanlibrary.gov/library/public-papers/120/veto-taft-hartley-labor-bill. The internal deliberations of the Truman administration indicated greater concerns over other aspects of the Taft-Hartley bill. See Dennis Merrill, ed., *A Documentary History of the Truman Presidency*, vol. 9, *The Debate over Labor Policy* (University Publications of America, 1995).
96. *American Communications Assn.*, 339 U.S. at 447 (Black, J., dissenting).
97. On the broader impact of Taft-Hartley, see Steven E. Abraham, "How the Taft-Hartley Act Hindered Unions," *Hofstra Labor Law Journal* 12 (1994): 1–37; Jane McAlevey, *A Collective Bargain: Unions, Organizing, and the Fight for Democracy* (HarperCollins, 2020), 58–64; Jane McAlevey, "Blowout in Bessemer: A Postmortem on the Amazon Campaign," *Nation*, April 9, 2021; Philip Taft, "Internal Affairs of Unions and the Taft-Hartley Act," *ILR Review* 11, no. 3 (April 1958): 352–359.
98. William S. White, "Marchers Picket the White House, Swarm in Capital," *New York Times*, June 3, 1948.
99. President's News Conference, May 13, 1948, Harry S. Truman Papers, Truman Library and Museum, Independence, MO.
100. See Subversive Activities Control Bills (Mundt-Nixon), ACLU Papers.
101. See *Albertson v. Subversive Activities Control Board*, 382 U.S. 70 (1965); Masumi Izumi, "Prohibiting 'American Concentration Camps,'" *Pacific Historical Review* 74, no. 2 (2005): 165–194.
102. Harry Truman, Veto of the Internal Security Bill, September 22, 1950, Public Papers of Harry Truman, Truman Library, Online Collection, https://www.trumanlibrary.gov/library/public-papers/254/veto-internal-security-bill.
103. On the overall political context in 1950, see Walter Goodman, *The Committee:*

The Extraordinary Career of the House Committee on Un-American Activities (Farrar, Straus, and Giroux, 1968), 291. There were 48 votes to sustain Truman's veto in the House; 10 in the Senate.

104. Izumi, "Prohibiting 'American Concentration Camps.'"
105. Justice Hugo Black summarized the consequences of registration in *Communist Party v. Subversive Activities Control Board*, 367 U.S. 1, 142 (1961) (Black, J., dissenting).
106. Francis H. Thompson, *The Frustration of Politics: Truman, Congress, and the Loyalty Issue, 1945–1953* (Associated University Presses, 1979), 153.
107. When the Supreme Court ruled in favor of the party, Tom Clark, now an as-sociate justice, reminded his colleagues of the prediction he had made as at-torney general back in 1948. See *Albertson v. Subversive Activities Control Board*, 382 U.S. 70, 85 (1965) (Clark, J., concurring).
108. United States Congress, Senate Committee on the Judiciary, *History of the Immigration and Naturalization Service: A Report Prepared at the Request of Senator Edward M. Kennedy, Chairman, Committee on the Judiciary, United States Senate, for the Use of the Select Commission on Immigration and Refugee Policy, Prepared by the Congressional Research Service* (GPO, 1980), 61.
109. United States Congress, House and Senate Committees on the Judiciary, *Revision of Immigration, Naturalization, and Nationality Laws: Hearings Before the United States Senate Committee on the Judiciary, Subcommittee on S. 716* (GPO, 1951), 2–3 (McCarran), 5 (Walter).
110. An Act to Revise the Laws Relating to Immigration, Naturalization, and Na-tionality; and for Other Purposes, 66 Stat. 163, 204–206 (1952).
111. Harry S. Truman, Veto of Bill to Revise the Laws Relating to Immigration, Naturalization, and Nationality, June 25, 1952, Truman Papers.
112. In the House, 113 representatives voted to sustain his veto, as did 26 senators. "Immigration and Nationality Act," *CQ Almanac, 1952* (Congressional Quar-terly, 1953), 154–160.
113. Ellen Schrecker, "Immigration and Internal Security: Political Deportations During the McCarthy Era," *Science & Society* (1996): 416.
114. United States Department of Justice, *Statement by Tom C. Clark, Attorney General of the United States Before Committee on Un-American Activities, House of Representatives, Washington, D.C.*, February 5, 1948, https://www .justice.gov/ag/speeches-attorney-general-thomas-campbell-clark.
115. Schrecker, "Immigration and Internal Security," 400.
116. Although, in *Bridges v. Wixon*, 326 U.S. 135 (1945), the court invalidated the deportation of Harry Bridges on due process grounds, it affirmed, in *Harisiades v. Shaughnessy*, 342 U.S. 580 (1952), that the Smith Act authorized the deportation of Communist Party members past and present. Only in 1957 did the Supreme Court decide—by a narrow 5–4 majority—that an individual had to have a "meaningful relationship" with the Communist Party in order to be deported. See *Rowoldt v. Perfetto*, 355 U.S. 115 (1957).
117. Schrecker, "Immigration and Internal Security," 402.
118. Albertson v. Subversive Activities Control Board, 382 U.S. 70 (1965).
119. Yates v. United States, 354 U.S. 298 (1957).
120. Scales v. United States, 367 U.S. 203 (1961).

121. Brandenburg v. Ohio, 395 U.S. 444 (1969).
122. Rowoldt v. Perfetto, 355 U.S. 115 (1957).
123. David Cole, "The New McCarthyism: Repeating History in the War on Terrorism," *Harvard Civil Rights and Civil Liberties Review* 38 (2003): 1.
124. Quoted in *Holder v. Humanitarian Law Project*, 561 U.S. 1, 2–3 (2010).
125. Uniting and Strengthening America by Providing Appropriate Tools Required to Intercept and Obstruct Terrorism Act of 2001, 115 Stat. 272 (2001).
126. *Holder v. Humanitarian Law Project*, 561 U.S. 1 (2010).
127. See David Cole, "The First Amendment's Borders: The Place of Holder v. Humanitarian Law Project in First Amendment Doctrine," *Harvard Law & Policy Review* 6 (2012): 147; Wadie E. Said, "Humanitarian Law Project and the Supreme Court's Construction of Terrorism," *Brigham Young University Law Review* (2011): 1455.
128. *The Intercept*, Trial and Terror database, https://trial-and-terror.theintercept.com/.
129. United States v. El-Mezain, 664 F.3d 467 (5th Cir. 2011).
130. See Charles Glass, "The Unjust Prosecution of the Holy Land Foundation Five," *Intercept*, August 5, 2018; Miko Peled, *Injustice: The Story of the Holy Land Foundation Five* (Just World Books, 2018).
131. National Association for the Advancement of Colored People v. Alabama, 357 U.S. 449 (1958); Bates v. City of Little Rock, 361 U.S. 516 (1960); Americans for Prosperity Foundation v. Bonta, 141 S.Ct. 2373 (2021); Buckley v. Valeo, 424 U.S. 1 (1976); Citizens United v. Federal Election Commission, 558 U.S. 310 (2010).

CHAPTER 2: INDEPENDENT TOOLS

1. Josh Chafetz, "Executive Branch Contempt of Congress," *University of Chicago Law Review* 76 (2009): 1146.
2. Trump v. Anderson, 601 U.S. ___ (2024).
3. For the strongest statement of this view, see William Baude and Michael Stokes Paulsen, "The Sweep and Force of Section Three," *University of Pennsylvania Law Review* 172 (2024): 605. For a critique, see Josh Blackman and Seth Barrett Tillman, "Sweeping and Forcing the President into Section 3," *Texas Review of Law & Policy* 28 (2023): 350.
4. Farnoush Amiri, "House Votes to Censure Rep. Rashida Tlaib over Her Israel-Hamas Rhetoric in a Stunning Rebuke," Associated Press, November 8, 2023.
5. See Harry Blain, "Israel and the New McCarthyism," *Foreign Policy in Focus*, December 15, 2023.
6. This problem is explained in United States Congress, *Report of the Joint Committee on Reconstruction* (GPO, 1866), xiii. I elaborate on the joint committee later.
7. Proclamation by the President of the United States, May 29, 1865, in United States Congress, *Senate Executive Documents for the First Session of the Thirty-Ninth Congress of the United States of America, 1865–66* (GPO, 1866), 12.
8. Ulysses S. Grant to Andrew Johnson, December 18, 1865, in *The Papers of*

Ulysses S. Grant, vol. 15, *May 1–December 31, 1865*, ed. John Simon (Southern Illinois University Press, 1988), 435.

9. Peter J. Osterhaus to John A. Rawlins, November 11, 1865, in *The Papers of Ulysses S. Grant*, vol. 16, *1866*, ed. John Simon (Southern Illinois University Press, 1988), 53.
10. Carl Schurz to Andrew Johnson, July 28, 1865, in *Advice After Appomattox: Letters to Andrew Johnson, 1865–1866, Special Volume No. 1 of the Papers of Andrew Johnson*, ed. Brooks D. Simpson, Leroy P. Graf, and John Muldowny (University of Tennessee Press, 1988), 81.
11. *Congressional Globe*, 39th Congress, 1st Session (GPO, 1866), 3.
12. *Congressional Globe*, 39th Congress, 1st Session, 4.
13. *Congressional Globe*, 39th Congress, 1st Session, 6.
14. US Congress, *Report of the Joint Committee on Reconstruction*, vii. Other than the final report, the only other major primary source on the committee's activities is United States Congress, *Journal of the Joint Committee on Reconstruction* (GPO, 1915).
15. Mark A. Graber, *Punish Treason, Reward Loyalty: The Forgotten Goals of Constitutional Reform After the Civil War* (University Press of Kansas, 2023), 38.
16. Graber, *Punish Treason, Reward Loyalty*, xix. The Democrats on the committee regarded its entire project as illegitimate, and they said so in a minority report.
17. Graber, *Punish Treason, Reward Loyalty*, ix.
18. US Constitution, Article IV, Section 4: "The United States shall guarantee to every State in this Union a Republican Form of Government, and shall protect each of them against Invasion; and on Application of the Legislature, or of the Executive (when the Legislature cannot be convened) against domestic Violence."
19. Congressional control over territories also comes from Article IV (Section 3, clause 2): "The Congress shall have Power to dispose of and make all needful Rules and Regulations respecting the Territory or other Property belonging to the United States; and nothing in this Constitution shall be so construed as to Prejudice any Claims of the United States, or of any particular State."
20. US Congress, *Report of the Joint Committee on Reconstruction*, xi.
21. Dana is quoted in John Fabian Witt, *Lincoln's Code: The Laws of War in American History* (Simon and Schuster, 2012), 307, and US Congress, *Report of the Joint Committee on Reconstruction*, xi.
22. Powell v. McCormack, 395 U.S. 486, 548 (1969).
23. The *Powell* court came close to saying this, although it mentioned only the later exclusions of ex-Confederates, rather than the initial exclusions at the first session of the Thirty-Ninth Congress. *Powell*, 395 U.S. at 544.
24. *Powell*, 395 U.S. at 548 (Warren), 553 (Douglas, J., concurring).
25. *Powell*, 395 U.S. 486.
26. Russell Duncan, *Freedom's Shore: Tunis Campbell and the Georgia Freedmen* (University of Georgia Press, 1986), 69–70, 82.
27. US Constitution, Article I, Section 5.
28. On the declining commitment of Republicans, see W. E. B. Du Bois, *Black*

Reconstruction: An Essay Toward a History of the Part Which Black Folk Played in the Attempt to Reconstruct Democracy in America, 1860–1880 (Harcourt, Brace, 1935), 670–710.

29. Edward J. Muzik, "Victor L. Berger: Congress and the Red Scare," *Wisconsin Magazine of History* (1964): 311.
30. *Congressional Record*, 66th Congress, 1st Session, November 10, 1919 (GPO, 1920), 8222–8223.
31. *Congressional Record*, 66th Congress, 1st Session, 8230, 8232–8233.
32. *Congressional Record*, 66th Congress, 1st Session, January 10, 1920 (GPO, 1921), 1339 (Dallinger), 1340 (Eagle), 1343 (vote). Eagle's comment also hints that Berger's Austrian origins made his loyalty suspect.
33. Berger v. United States, 255 U.S. 22 (1921).
34. *Powell*, 395 U.S. at 545, fn. 83.
35. United States Congress, Senate Committee on the Judiciary, *Brewing and Liquor Interests and German Propaganda: Hearings Before a Subcommittee of the Committee on the Judiciary, United States Senate, Sixty-Fifth Congress, Second and Third Sessions, Pursuant to S. Res. 307*, 2 vols. (GPO, 1919).
36. United States Congress, Senate Committee on the Judiciary, *Bolshevik Propaganda: Hearings Before a Subcommittee of the Committee on the Judiciary, United States Senate, Sixty-Fifth Congress, Third Session and Thereafter, Pursuant to S. Res. 439 and 469, February 11, 1919, to March 10, 1919* (GPO, 1919), 6.
37. Robert K. Murray puts the number at twenty-four. See Robert K. Murray, *Red Scare: A Study in National Hysteria, 1919–1920* (University of Minnesota Press, 1955), 95. However, Murray appears to exclude the one witness who testified in executive session. See US Congress, Senate Committee on the Judiciary, *Bolshevik Propaganda*, 235–242.
38. US Congress, Senate Committee on the Judiciary, *Brewing and Liquor Interests*, 2690, 2729–2744. An excerpt of Stevenson's testimony was reproduced in US Congress, Senate Committee on the Judiciary, *Bolshevik Propaganda*, 11–36.
39. See, for example, US Congress, Senate Committee on the Judiciary, *Bolshevik Propaganda*, 466–649. As chapter 5 explores in more depth, the Overman Subcommittee's largest impact on civil liberties was probably the example it set for state legislatures, especially New York's, which created a similar committee with similar targets; Archibald Stevenson was its chief investigator.
40. On Poindexter's background, see Regin Schmidt, *Red Scare: The FBI and the Origins of Anticommunism in the United States, 1919–1943* (Museum Tusculanum Press, 2000), 238–239.
41. *Congressional Record*, 66th Congress, 1st Session (GPO, 1920), 6865.
42. *Congressional Record*, 66th Congress, 1st Session, 6869 (quoting Duncan Fletcher [D-FL]). The vote is on p. 7063.
43. Quoted in Stanley Coben, *A. Mitchell Palmer: Politician* (Columbia University Press, 1963), 215.
44. United States Congress, *Investigation Activities of the Department of Justice: Letter from the Attorney General Transmitting in Response to a Senate Resolution of October 17, 1919, a Report on the Activities of the Bureau of Investigation of the Department of Justice Against Persons Advising Anarchy, Sedition,*

and the Forcible Overthrow of the Government, Senate Document No. 153 (GPO, 1919), 5–13.

45. Beverly Gage, *G-Man: J. Edgar Hoover and the Making of the American Century* (Viking Press, 2022), 68.
46. Gage, *G-Man*, 70–71.
47. Shortly after the January 1920 raids, Palmer communicated his desire to seek the presidency to Woodrow Wilson's close confidant Colonel House. See "From the Diary of Colonel House," January 31, 1920, in *The Papers of Woodrow Wilson*, ed. Arthur S. Link (Princeton University Press, 1991), 347.
48. Quoted in Thomas Knock, *To End All Wars: Woodrow Wilson and the Quest for a New World Order* (Oxford University Press, 1992), 168–169. See also Schmidt, *Red Scare*, 237–240.
49. Schmidt, *Red Scare*, 241.
50. See, for example, Christopher M. Finan, *From the Palmer Raids to the Patriot Act: A History of the Fight for Free Speech in America* (Beacon Press, 2007); Harlan Grant Cohen, "The (Un)favorable Judgment of History: Deportation Hearings, the Palmer Raids, and the Meaning of History," *NYU Law Review* 78 (2003): 1431–1474; Rachel Meeropol, "Muslim Until Proven Innocent: The Post-9/11 Ashcroft Raids," *Security Journal* 28, no. 2 (2015): 184–197.
51. Walter Goodman, *The Committee: The Extraordinary Career of the House Committee on Un-American Activities* (Farrar, Straus, and Giroux, 1968).
52. *Congressional Record*, 75th Congress, 3rd Session (GPO, 1939), 7568.
53. *Congressional Record*, 75th Congress, 3rd Session, 7569.
54. *Congressional Record*, 75th Congress, 3rd Session, 7579 (Rep. John M. Coffee [D-WA]), 7586.
55. Goodman, *The Committee*, 26.
56. Goodman, *The Committee*, 28, 42, 46–47.
57. Goodman, *The Committee*, 59–88.
58. "Help Stop the Dies Committee," February 1941, ACLU pamphlet, ACLU Papers, Correspondence—Vol. 2450.
59. The events described here and below are well summarized in Goodman, *The Committee*, 167–189.
60. *Congressional Record*, 79th Congress, 1st Session (GPO, 1946), 10.
61. *Congressional Record*, 79th Congress, 1st Session, 11 (Sabath), 13 (McCormack), 15 (the vote).
62. Goodman, *The Committee,* 169.
63. Roger H. Davidson, "The Advent of the Modern Congress: The Legislative Reorganization Act of 1946," *Legislative Studies Quarterly* (1990): 357–373.
64. Goodman, *The Committee*, 167.
65. United States Congress, House Un-American Activities Committee (HUAC), *Investigation of Un-American Propaganda Activities in the United States: Executive Board, Joint Anti-Fascist Refugee Committee* (GPO, 1946), 2.
66. US Congress, HUAC, *Investigation of Un-American Propaganda Activities*, 103, 104–105.
67. Phillip Deery, "'A Blot Upon Liberty': McCarthyism, Dr. Barsky and the Joint Anti-Fascist Refugee Committee," *American Communist History* 8, no. 2 (2009): 167.

68. Compiled from United States Congress, HUAC, *Annual Reports* (GPO, 1946–65).
69. United States Congress, House Committee on Un-American Activities, *Hearings Regarding the Communist Infiltration of the Motion Picture Industry: Hearings Before the Committee on Un-American Activities, House of Representatives, Eightieth Congress, First Session* (GPO, 1947).
70. "The SIMPP President Presents the Waldorf Agreement to the Independents," *Society of Independent Motion Producers Archive*, December 1, 1947; Arthur Eckstein, "The Hollywood Ten in History and Memory," *Film History*, 16, no. 4 (2004): 424.
71. Robert P. Newman, *Owen Lattimore and the Loss of China* (University of California Press, 1992).
72. United States Congress, Senate Committee on Foreign Relations, *State Department Employee Loyalty Investigation: Hearings Before the United States Senate Committee on Foreign Relations, Subcommittee on S. Res. 231, Eighty-First Congress, Second Session* (GPO, 1950), 104.
73. William L. Holland, "Source Materials on the Institute of Pacific Relations," *Pacific Affairs* 58, no. 1 (1985): 91.
74. See Ellen Schrecker, "McCarthyism: Political Repression and the Fear of Communism," *Social Research* (2004): 1041–1086.
75. Variations of this claim have been made in Jack Goldsmith and Cass R. Sunstein, "Military Tribunals and Legal Culture: What a Difference Sixty Years Makes," *Constitutional Commentary* 19 (2002): 261–289; Mark Tushnet, "Defending Korematsu? Reflections on Civil Liberties in Wartime," *Wisconsin Law Review* (2003): 273.
76. Watkins v. United States, 354 U.S. 178, 197–198, 200 (1957).
77. *Watkins*, 354 U.S. at 215.
78. Barenblatt v. United States, 360 U.S. 109, 160 (1959) (Black, J., dissenting).
79. Quoted in Khatya Chorr, "After Winning House, Democrats' Real Power May Lie in Investigating Trump," *France 24*, November 13, 2018.
80. Trump v. Mazars USA, LLP, 591 U.S. ___, 1 (slip opinion) (2020).
81. *Trump v. Mazars USA*, 3 (Finance Committee), 4 (Intelligence Committee), 5 (Oversight and Reform Committee).
82. *Trump v. Mazars USA*. See also *Quinn v. United States*, 349 U.S. 155 (1955); *McGrain v. Daugherty*, 273 U.S. 135 (1927); *Kilbourn v. Thompson*, 103 U.S. 168 (1881).
83. Elizabeth Goitein, "Congress' Access to Individuals' Private Communications: The Jan. 6 Committee's Troubling Precedent," *Just Security*, September 22, 2021.
84. Li Zhou, "The House GOP's Many, Many Investigations, Explained," *Vox*, February 11, 2023.
85. Dara Kerr, "Lawmakers Grilled TikTok CEO Chew for 5 Hours in a High-Stakes Hearing About the App," NPR, March 23, 2023.
86. Sapna Maheshwari and Amanda Holpuch, "Why the U.S. Is Forcing TikTok to Be Sold or Banned," *New York Times*, April 26, 2024.
87. See Blain, "Israel and the New McCarthyism."
88. See Kiara Alfonseca, "The Forces Behind Harvard President Claudine Gay's

Resignation," *ABC News*, January 5, 2024; Reeves Wiedeman, "Raging Bill: Bill Ackman's Fight Against Harvard Has Made Him the Public Face of a Billionaire Class Anxious It No Longer Rules the World," *New Yorker*, February 12, 2024.

89. Generally, see Ellen W. Schrecker, *No Ivory Tower: McCarthyism and the Universities* (Oxford University Press, 1986).
90. Blain, "Israel and the New McCarthyism"; Al Jazeera Staff, "Columbia University Leaders Face Scrutiny over Anti-Semitism on Campus," *Al Jazeera*, April 17, 2024.
91. Al Jazeera Staff, "Columbia University Leaders Face Scrutiny."
92. Abdallah Fayyad, "The Lessons from Colleges that Didn't Call the Police," *Vox*, May 3, 2024.

CHAPTER 3: CONGRESS AND THE EXECUTIVE

1. Kenneth A. Shepsle, "Congress Is a 'They,' Not an 'It': Legislative Intent as Oxymoron," *International Review of Law and Economics* 12, no. 2 (1992): 239–256; William G. Howell, *Power Without Persuasion: The Politics of Direct Presidential Action* (Princeton University Press, 2003); William Howell and Terry Moe, *Relic: How Our Constitution Undermines Effective Government—and Why We Need a More Powerful Presidency* (Basic Books, 2016); Christopher S. Yoo, Steven G. Calabresi, and Anthony J. Colangelo, "The Unitary Executive in the Modern Era, 1945–2004," *Iowa Law Review* 90 (2004): 601; Mark Tushnet, "A Political Perspective on the Theory of the Unitary Executive," *University of Pennsylvania Journal of Constitutional Law* 12 (2009): 313; Stephen Skowronek, "The Conservative Insurgency and Presidential Power: A Developmental Perspective on the Unitary Executive," *Harvard Law Review* 122 (2008): 2070.
2. See, for example, Curt Gentry, *J. Edgar Hoover: The Man and the Secrets* (W. W. Norton, 1991); Anthony Summers, *Official and Confidential: The Secret Life of J. Edgar Hoover* (G. P. Putnam's Sons, 1993). For a more recent biography of Hoover that (persuasively) casts him as a less shadowy figure, see Beverly Gage, *G-Man: J. Edgar Hoover and the Making of the American Century* (Viking Press, 2022).
3. Josh Chafetz, *Congress's Constitution: Legislative Authority and the Separation of Powers* (Yale University Press, 2017), 45–152.
4. Tennessee had already been reconstructed in 1866. The House of Representatives agreed to readmit seven other states in 1868: Alabama (July 13), Arkansas (June 22), Florida (June 25), Georgia (July 21), Louisiana (July 9), North Carolina (July 4), and South Carolina (July 9). Georgia was reexpelled in September 1868, and its final representative was not seated until February 1871. See Gregory P. Downs, "Powers of War in Times of Peace: Emergency Powers in the United States After the End of the Civil War," in *States of Exception in American History*, ed. Gary Gerstle and Joel Isaac (University of Chicago Press, 2020), 154–178.
5. Andrew Johnson, *Declaring the Insurrection at an End in Certain States of the Union*, April 2, 1866, Printed Ephemera Collection, portfolio 236, folder 1, Library of Congress, Washington, DC.

6. Alfred Terry to Ulysses S. Grant (hereafter, USG), April 3, 1866, in *The Papers of Ulysses S. Grant*, vol. 16, *1866*, ed. John Simon (Southern Illinois University Press, 1988), 149–150.
7. John W. Turner to John A. Rawlins, April 7, 1866, in *Papers of Grant*, 16:150; George Thomas to USG, April 9, 1866, in *Papers of Grant*, 16:150.
8. USG to Turner, April 9, 1866, in *Papers of Grant*, 16:150; USG to Thomas, April 10, 1866, in *Papers of Grant*, 16:150; USG to Terry, April 3, 1866, in *Papers of Grant*, 16:149.
9. An Act Regulating the Tenure of Certain Civil Offices, 14 Stat. 430 (1867).
10. Andrew Johnson, "Message Accompanying the Approval of the Army Appropriation Bill, March 2, 1867," in *The Political History of the United States of America During the Period of Reconstruction*, ed. Edward McPherson (James J. Chapman, 1880), 178.
11. US Constitution, Article I, Section 8, clause 18.
12. Myers v. United States, 272 U.S. 52 (1926). On the wider debate surrounding Congress's ability to create "quasi-independent" executive agencies, see *Humphrey's Executor v. United States*, 295 U.S. 602 (1935); *Bowsher v. Synar*, 478 U.S. 714 (1986); *Seila Law LLC v. Consumer Financial Protection Bureau*, 591 U.S. ____ (2020).
13. US Constitution, Article I, Section 9, clause 7.
14. Johnson to USG, August 19, 1867, in *The Papers of Ulysses S. Grant*, vol. 17, *January 1–September 30, 1867*, ed. John Simon (Southern Illinois University Press, 1991), 280.
15. Johnson to USG, August 26, 1867, in *Papers of Grant*, 17:296.
16. See USG to Johnson, August 1, 1867, in *Papers of Grant*, 17:250–252; USG to Johnson, August 17, 1867, in *Papers of Grant*, 17:277–278.
17. Edward McPherson to USG, November 26, 1867, in *The Papers of Ulysses S. Grant*, vol. 18, *October 1, 1867–June 30, 1868*, ed. John Simon (Southern Illinois University Press, 1991), 58.
18. Johnson to the Cabinet, November 30, 1867, in *Papers of Grant*, 18:58–59.
19. USG to Johnson, February 3, 1868, in *Papers of Grant*, 18:126.
20. For an overview of the historiography criticizing the impeachment, see Brenda Wineapple, *The Impeachers: The Trial of Andrew Johnson and the Dream of a Just Nation* (Random House, 2019), xvii–xxix. See also Keith Whittington, "Bill Clinton Was No Andrew Johnson: Comparing Two Impeachments," *University of Pennsylvania Journal of Constitutional Law* 2, no. 2 (2000): 422–465.
21. Harold M. Hyman, *A More Perfect Union: The Impact of the Civil War and Reconstruction on the Constitution* (Alfred A. Knopf, 1973), 510.
22. Louis F. Post, *The Deportations Delirium of Nineteen-Twenty: A Personal Narrative of an Historic Official Experience* (CH Kerr, 1923).
23. United States v. Lovett, 328 U.S. 303 (1946).
24. United States Congress, House Un-American Activities Committee (HUAC), *Legislative Recommendations by House Committee on Un-American Activities: Subsequent Action Taken by Congress or Executive Agencies. A Research Study by Legislative Reference Service of the Library of Congress* (GPO, 1960), 5, 7, 9, 8.
25. On the 1946 elections, see William E. Leuchtenburg, "New Faces of 1946: An

Unpopular President, a War-Weary People," *Smithsonian* 37, no. 8 (2006): 48–55.

26. Humphrey's Executor v. United States, 295 U.S. 602 (1935).
27. Clifford J. Durr, Allen Tullos, and Candace Waid, Oral History Interview with Clifford Durr, December 29, 1974, Interview B-0017, Southern Oral History Program Collection (#4007), University Library, University of North Carolina–Chapel Hill. In *Yes, Prime Minister*, fictional Whitehall bureaucrat Sir Humphrey Appleby channeled Truman, telling the prime minister, "The whole object of internal security inquiries is to find no evidence."
28. "Supporting Arguments of Northern California Branch," addressed "To the Members of the Corporation," April 14, 1948; "Supporting Arguments of the Southern California Branch," addressed "To the Members of the Corporation," January 2, 1948; Ernest Besig to Roger Nash Baldwin, December 14, 1948, ACLU Papers, The Roger Baldwin Years, Correspondence–Volume 84, Mudd Library, Princeton University.
29. Philip Murray to Harry Truman, April 14, 1947; Abram Flaxer to Truman, November 24, 1948; Walter White to Truman, November 26, 1948, Harry S. Truman Papers, Truman Presidential Library, Independence, MO.
30. "Groups Called Disloyal," *New York Times*, December 4, 1947; Tom Clark to Seth Richardson, May 27, 1948, ACLU Papers, Correspondence–Volume 84; Robert J. Goldstein, "The Grapes of McGrath: The Supreme Court and the Attorney General's List of Subversive Organizations in Joint Anti-Fascist Refugee Committee v. McGrath (1951)," *Journal of Supreme Court History* 33, no. 1 (2008): 68–88.
31. Landon R. Y. Storrs, "Revisiting Truman's Federal Employee Loyalty Program," in *Civil Liberties and the Legacy of Harry S. Truman*, ed. Richard S. Kirkendall (Truman State University Press, 2012), 70.
32. Robert J. Goldstein, *American Blacklist: The Attorney General's List of Subversive Organizations* (University Press of Kansas, 2008).
33. Clifford Forster to Alfred Baker Lewis, November 11, 1948, ACLU Papers, Correspondence–Volume 84.
34. Joint Anti-Fascist Refugee Committee v. McGrath, 341 U.S. 123, 144 (1952) (Black, J., concurring).
35. J. Parnell Thomas to Harry Truman, April 23, 1947, Truman Papers.
36. The classic statement of the view that Truman trapped himself with his foreign policy is Richard M. Freeland, *The Truman Doctrine and the Origins of McCarthyism: Foreign Policy, Domestic Politics, and Internal Security, 1946–1948* (Alfred A. Knopf, 1972).
37. Cameron McWhirter, *Red Summer: The Summer of 1919 and the Awakening of Black America* (Henry Holt, 2011), 163.
38. On Byrnes's comments, see *Congressional Record*, 66th Congress, 1st Session, August 25, 1919 (GPO, 1919), 4303, 4304. On the Bureau's investigations of black leaders, see Theodore Kornweibel, ed., *Federal Surveillance of Afro-Americans (1917–1925): The First World War, the Red Scare, and the Garvey Movement*, microform, reel 1, Schomburg Center for Research in Black Culture. The surveillance is also recounted in Regin Schmidt, *Red Scare: The FBI and the Origins of Anticommunism in the United States, 1919–1943* (Museum

Tusculanum Press, 2000), 195–203. Specific targets included pan-Africanists Marcus Garvey and Cyril Briggs, as well as A. Philip Randolph and Claude McKay. The Bureau was particularly interested in divisions among these leaders. See, for example, "800" to George F. Ruch, October 6, 1921 (on Garvey); "800" to Ruch, October 18, 1921 (claiming credit for encouraging Briggs to sue Garvey for libel); Joseph G. Tucker, "Special Report," November 26, 1921 (Briggs "practically charges that MARCUS GARVEY had to leave England for having raped a little white girl"); "Special Report," August 19, 1922 (Randolph said the Garveyites "had neither the brains nor the capital to run a steamship line, much less build an empire"), all in Kornweibel, *Federal Surveillance of Afro-Americans*. On Claude McKay, see "W. Hurley" to William J. Burns, March 17, 1923; Boylston A. Beal to Norman Armour, March 11, 1924, in Kornweibel, *Federal Surveillance of Afro-Americans.*

39. Roger Nash Baldwin to Harlan Fiske Stone, May 21, 1924, ACLU Papers, Correspondence–Volume 272.
40. Baldwin to Stone, May 21, 1924; Alpheus Thomas Mason, "Harlan Fiske Stone: In Defense of Individual Freedom, 1918–20," *Columbia Law Review* 51 (1951): 147.
41. See Douglas M. Charles, "Informing FDR: FBI Political Surveillance and the Isolationist-Interventionist Foreign Policy Debate, 1939–1945," *Diplomatic History* 24, no. 2 (2000): 211–232.
42. All these quotes and statements are documented and discussed in Harry Blain, "No Gestapo: J. Edgar Hoover's World-Wide Intelligence Service and the Limits of Bureaucratic Autonomy in the National Security State," *Studies in American Political Development* 35, no. 2 (2021): 214–222.
43. Harry S. Truman, Directive on the Need for Maintaining the Confidential Status of Employee Loyalty Records, March 13, 1948, Truman Papers.
44. Clark M. Clifford, Memorandum for the President: Congressional Requests for Personnel Files, August 4, 1948, Truman Papers.
45. McCarthy to Truman, March 22, 1950, Truman Papers.
46. Thomas to Truman, September 29, 1948; E. H. Foley to William P. Rogers (chief counsel of the Investigations Subcommittee), August 5, 1948, Truman Papers.
47. Robert H. Ferrell, ed., *Off the Record: The Private Papers of Harry S. Truman* (Harper and Row, 1980), 172, 176, 201.
48. Hoover to McCarthy, May 11, 1949; Hoover to McCarthy, August 6, 1952; Hoover to Anonymous, November 24, 1967; Hoover to Lou Nichols, March 18, 1953, all in Federal Bureau of Investigation (FBI), The Vault—Senator McCarthy, https://vault.fbi.gov/.
49. Statement of J. Edgar Hoover, director, FBI, before Subcommittee of the Senate Committee on Foreign Relations, 3:30 p.m., Monday, March 27, 1950; D. M. Ladd to Hoover, March 29, 1950; McCarthy to Hoover, July 30, 1952; Hoover to O L'Allier, April 3, 1953, all in FBI, The Vault—Senator McCarthy.
50. On Hoover's support for the Red Scare, see Gage, *G-Man*, 384–397.
51. On the Tydings Committee, see Memorandum for the Attorney General, March 10, 1950, FBI, The Vault—Senator McCarthy. A rare glimpse into Bureau files

revealed illegal searches and seizures in *United States v. Coplon*, 185 F.2d 629 (2d Cir. 1950).

52. Athan G. Theoharis, *Chasing Spies: How the FBI Failed in Counter-Intelligence but Promoted the Politics of McCarthyism in the Cold War Years* (Ivan R. Dee, 2002), 161, 203; Athan G. Theoharis, "A Lawless Agency: The FBI and the 'Hollywood Ten,'" *Rhetoric & Public Affairs* 2, no. 3 (1999): 415–430.
53. Walter Goodman, *The Committee: The Extraordinary Career of the House Committee on Un-American Activities* (Farrar, Straus, and Giroux, 1968), 282.
54. Gage, *G-Man*, 339.
55. Kenneth O'Reilly, "The FBI and the Origins of McCarthyism," *Historian* 45, no. 3 (1983): 375.
56. Jerry N. Hess, Oral History Interview with Tom C. Clark, Washington, DC, October 17, 1972, 210–211, Truman Papers.
57. O'Reilly, "FBI and Origins of McCarthyism," 377.
58. United State Congress, HUAC, *Hearings Regarding Communist Espionage in the United States Government* (GPO, 1948), 561. Parts of this exchange are quoted in O'Reilly, "FBI and Origins of McCarthyism," 379.
59. Quoted in *Report of the Seditious Activities Investigation Commission: Submitted Pursuant to the Provisions of an Act of the 65th General Assembly* (1949), 227.
60. See Theoharis, *Chasing Spies*, 91.
61. Frank Wilkinson, "FBI Crackdown on Opposition to HUAC," in *It Did Happen Here: Recollections of Political Repression in America*, ed. Bud Schultz and Ruth Schultz (University of California Press, 1989), 265.
62. O'Reilly, "FBI and Origins of McCarthyism," 382.
63. Memorandum for the Attorney General, March 10, 1950, FBI, The Vault—Senator McCarthy.
64. See General Memoranda—Department of Justice, FBI, February 24, 1950, ACLU Papers.
65. J. Edgar Hoover to Harry Hawkins Vaughan, November 8, 1945; Hoover to Vaughan, February 1, 1946; Hoover to Fred M. Vinson, February 6, 1946, all in Truman Papers.
66. *Report of the President's Temporary Commission on Employee Loyalty*, 13–14, 25, Truman Papers.
67. Michal R. Belknap, *Cold War Political Justice: The Smith Act, the Communist Party, and American Civil Liberties* (Greenwood Press, 1977), 35–58.
68. I discuss the origins of these intelligence reforms in more detail in chapter 6.
69. See Loch K. Johnson, "Ostriches, Cheerleaders, Skeptics, and Guardians," *SAIS Review of International Affairs* 28, no. 1 (2008): 93–108.
70. United States Congress, Senate Select Committee on Intelligence, *Committee Study of the Central Intelligence Agency's Detention and Interrogation Program* (GPO, 2014); Spencer Ackerman, "'A Constitutional Crisis': The CIA Turns on the Senate," *Guardian*, September 10, 2016.
71. Spencer Ackerman, "Senate Torture Report to Be Kept from Public for 12 Years After Obama Decision," *Guardian*, December 12, 2016.
72. Intelligence committee knowledge of the Terrorist Surveillance Program is

documented in James Risen and Eric Lichtblau, "Bush Lets U.S. Spy on Callers Without Courts," *New York Times*, December 16, 2005; United States Department of Justice, *Legal Authorities Supporting the Activities of the National Security Agency Described by the President* (2006), http://www.usdoj.gov/opa/whitepaperonnsalegalauthorities.pdf; Offices of the Inspectors General of the Department of Defense, Department of Justice, Central Intelligence Agency, and Office of the Director of National Intelligence, *Unclassified Report on the President's Surveillance Program*, July 10, 2009, 16. Senator Ron Wyden (D-OR) discusses intelligence committee knowledge of the programs revealed by Snowden in Janet Reitman, "Q&A: Senator Ron Wyden on NSA Surveillance and Government Transparency," *Rolling Stone*, August 15, 2013. See also Brendan Sasso, "Wyden Considered Disclosing National Security Agency Secrets on Senate Floor," *Hill*, August 15, 2013.

73. Memorandum of Conversation, October 13, 1975, National Security Adviser, Memoranda of Conversations, box 16, Gerald Ford Presidential Library, Ann Arbor, MI.
74. "In Speech, Wyden Says Official Interpretations of Patriot Act Must Be Made Public," May 26, 2011, https://www.wyden.senate.gov/news/press-releases/in-speech-wyden-says-official-interpretations-of-patriot-act-must-be-made-public.
75. Reitman, "Q&A: Senator Ron Wyden."
76. Dianne Feinstein, "Continue NSA Call-Records Program," *USA Today*, October 20, 2013.
77. Glenn Greenwald, *No Place to Hide: Edward Snowden, the NSA, and the U.S. Surveillance State* (Macmillan, 2014), 171–172.
78. United States Congress, House Permanent Select Committee on Intelligence, *How Disclosed NSA Programs Protect Americans, and Why Disclosure Aids Our Adversaries: Hearing Before the United States House of Representatives, Permanent Select Committee on Intelligence, One Hundred Thirteenth Congress, First Session,* June 18, 2013, https://intelligence.house.gov/calendar/eventsingle.aspx?EventID=598.
79. Jonathan Weisman and Jennifer Steinhauer, "Surveillance Bill Awaits Verdicts on Amendments from Hawks in Senate," *New York Times*, June 1, 2015.
80. Eric Holder to Patrick Leahy, Office of the Attorney General, May 22, 2013, https://www.justice.gov/slideshow/AG-letter-5-22-13.pdf.
81. See, for example, Glenn Greenwald, "Chilling Legal Memo from Obama DOJ Justifies Assassination of US Citizens," *Guardian*, February 5, 2013.
82. New York Times Co. v. US Dept. of Justice, 756 F.3d 100 (2d Cir. 2014). See also Charlie Savage, *Power Wars: Inside Obama's Post-9/11 Presidency* (Little, Brown, 2015), 224–293.
83. Quoted in Holder to Leahy, May 22, 2013.
84. Brandenburg v. Ohio, 395 U.S. 444 (1969).
85. Holder to Leahy, May 22, 2013.
86. United States Department of Justice, *Lawfulness of a Lethal Operation Directed Against a U.S. Citizen Who Is a Senior Operational Leader of Al-Qa'ida or an Associate Force*, November 8, 2011, 7, https://irp.fas.org/eprint/doj-lethal.pdf.

87. Michael Stokes Paulsen, "Drone On: The Commander in Chief Power to Target and Kill Americans," *Harvard Journal of Law & Public Policy* 38 (2015): 43.
88. Kate Crockford, "Obama Must Reveal Legal Memos on His Administration's Drone Killing Program," *Guardian*, March 7, 2013; United States Congress, House Committee on the Judiciary, to President Barack Obama, February 8, 2013, http://big.assets.huffingtonpost.com/dojmemo.pdf.
89. Adam Serwer, "Senators Will Get to Know When Obama Can Kill Americans—but You Won't," *Mother Jones*, March 5, 2013. The Wyden-Paul effort is also described in Chafetz, *Congress's Constitution*, 78–152.
90. See Savage, *Power Wars*, 224–293.
91. Adam Serwer, "Senators Defend Killing of Anwar al-Awlaki as Legal," MSBNC, November 26, 2013.
92. Mark Mazetti and Matt Apuzzo, "Deep Support in Washington for C.I.A.'s Drone Missions," *New York Times,* April 15, 2015.
93. "The Guantanamo Docket," *New York Times*, https://www.nytimes.com/interactive/2021/us/guantanamo-bay-detainees.html.
94. "JTF-GITMO Threat Index," May 29 2008, Wikileaks: The Guantanamo Files, https://wikileaks.org/gitmo/pdf/notes/JTF-GTMO_THREAT_MATRIX.pdf.
95. Guantanamo Review Task Force, *Final Report*, January 22, 2010, ii, https://www.justice.gov/sites/default/files/ag/legacy/2010/06/02/guantanamo-review-final-report.pdf. See also Andy Worthington, *The Guantanamo Files: The Stories of the 759 Detainees in America's Illegal Prison* (Pluto Press, 2007).
96. Most of the Guantanamo detainees were not American citizens. A notable exception was dual US-Saudi citizen Yasser Hamdi. See *Hamdi v. Rumsfeld*, 542 U.S. 507 (2004).
97. See *Boumediene v. Bush*, 553 U.S. 723 (2008).
98. See, especially, US Congress, Senate Select Committee on Intelligence, *Committee Study of Central Intelligence Agency's Detention and Interrogation Program.*
99. Hamdan v. Rumsfeld, 548 U.S. 557 (2006). Chief Justice Roberts recused himself because he had participated in the case at the circuit level (see *Hamdan v. Rumsfeld*, 415 F.3d 33 [D.C. Cir. 2005]). Roberts's ruling at the circuit level suggests that he would have voted with the three dissenters.
100. An Act Making Appropriations for the Department of Defense for the Fiscal Year Ending September 30, 2010, and for Other Purposes, 123 Stat. 3409, 3466–3467 (2009).
101. An Act Making Appropriations for the Department of Defense. See also David Manners-Weber, "Certification as Sabotage: Lessons from Guantanamo Bay," *Yale Law Journal* 127 (2017): 1416.
102. Savage, *Power Wars*, 126–130.
103. Eric Schmitt and Charlie Savage, "Bowe Bergdahl, American Soldier, Freed by Taliban in Prisoner Trade," *New York Times*, May 14, 2014.
104. Statement by the President on H.R. 3304, White House, December 16, 2013, https://obamawhitehouse.archives.gov/the-press-office/2013/12/26/statement-president-hr-3304.
105. President Bush was criticized for using signing statements in this way. See

Louis Fisher, "Signing Statements: Constitutional and Practical Limits," *William & Mary Bill of Rights Journal* 16 (2007): 183.

106. US Constitution, Article I, Section 9, clause 7.
107. Chafetz, *Congress's Constitution*, 45–78.
108. See, especially, Benjamin Wittes, ed., *Legislating the War on Terror: An Agenda for Reform* (Brookings Institution Press, 2009).

CHAPTER 4: CONGRESS AND THE JUDICIARY

1. See, especially, Clinton Rossiter, *The Supreme Court and the Commander-in-Chief* (Cornell University Press, 1951); William H. Rehnquist, *All the Laws but One: Civil Liberties in Wartime* (Random House, 2000); John Ip, "The Supreme Court and House of Lords in the War on Terror: Inter Arma Silent Leges," *Michigan State University Journal of International Law* 19 (2010): 1. For a more nuanced perspective, see Lee Epstein, Daniel E. Ho, Gary King, and Jeffrey A. Segal, "The Supreme Court During Crisis: How War Affects Only Non-War Cases," *NYU Law Review* 80 (2005): 1–116.
2. Earl Warren, *The Memoirs of Earl Warren* (Doubleday, 1977), 313.
3. For classic statements of this argument in general terms, see Robert A. Dahl, "Decision-Making in a Democracy: The Supreme Court as a National Policy-Maker," *Journal of Public Law* 6 (1957): 279; Alexander Bickel, *The Least Dangerous Branch: The Supreme Court at the Bar of Politics* (Bobbs-Merrill, 1962); Gerald N. Rosenberg, *The Hollow Hope: Can Courts Bring About Social Change?* 2nd ed. (University of Chicago Press, 2008); Lucas A. Powe, *The Supreme Court and the American Elite, 1789–2008* (Harvard University Press, 2009).
4. W. E. B. Du Bois, *Black Reconstruction: An Essay Toward a History of the Part Which Black Folk Played in the Attempt to Reconstruct Democracy in America, 1860–1880* (Harcourt, Brace, 1935), 375.
5. Ex parte Milligan, 71 U.S. (4 Wall.) 2, 127 (1866).
6. For an extended discussion of civil libertarian celebrations of *Milligan*—and their flaws—see Stewart L. Winger and Jonathan W. White, eds., *Ex Parte Milligan Reconsidered: Race and Civil Liberties from the Lincoln Administration to the War on Terror* (University Press of Kansas, 2020).
7. Thaddeus Stevens, "Reconstruction," January 3, 1867, in *The Selected Papers of Thaddeus Stevens*, vol. 2, *April 1865–August 1868*, ed. Beverly Palmer and Holly Ochoa (University of Pittsburgh Press, 1998), 211–212.
8. The Supreme Court has never settled this question; however, it has said that "the cessation of hostilities does not necessarily end the war power," which "includes the power to remedy the evils which have arisen from [the war's] rise and progress." Baker v. Carr, 369 U.S. 186, 213 (1962), quoting earlier cases.
9. Mark E. Neely, *The Fate of Liberty: Abraham Lincoln and Civil Liberties* (Oxford University Press, 1991), 162–184.
10. Mississippi v. Johnson, 71 U.S. 475, 497 (1867). See also *Georgia v. Stanton*, 73 U.S. 50 (1868).
11. Quoted in William W. Van Alstyne, "A Critical Guide to Ex Parte McCardle," *Arizona Law Review* 15 (1973): 236, fn. 42.
12. Stanbery to Ulysses S. Grant (hereafter, USG), December 31, 1867, in *The*

Papers of Ulysses S. Grant, vol. 17, *January 1–September 30, 1867*, ed. John Simon (Southern Illinois University Press, 1991), 99; USG to Lyman Trumbull, January 8, 1688, in *Papers of Grant*, 17:99.

13. See Neal Devins and Saikrishna Prakash, "The Indefensible Duty to Defend," *Columbia Law Review* (2012): 507–577. A notable example was the Obama administration's refusal to defend the Defense of Marriage Act in court. The Supreme Court later effectively nullified the act in *Obergefell v. Hodges*, 576 U.S. 644 (2015).
14. Meade to USG, February 14, 1868, in *Papers of Grant*, 17:153.
15. Quoted in Stanley I. Kutler "Ex Parte McCardle: Judicial Impotency? The Supreme Court and Reconstruction Reconsidered," *American Historical Review* 72, no. 3 (1967): 842–843.
16. Ex parte McCardle, 74 U.S. 506, 515 (1869).
17. Kutler, "Ex parte McCardle," 849; Ex parte Yerger, 75 U.S. 85 (1869).
18. Kutler, "Ex parte McCardle," 842.
19. Kutler, "Ex parte McCardle," 848–849.
20. Dred Scott v. Sandford, 60 U.S. 393 (1857); Mark A. Graber, *Dred Scott and the Problem of Constitutional Evil* (Cambridge University Press, 2006).
21. Abraham Lincoln, First Inaugural Address: Final Version, March 4, 1861, Abraham Lincoln Papers, series 1, General Correspondence, 1833–1916, Library of Congress, Washington, DC.
22. Ex parte Merryman, 17 F. Cas. 144 (1861). As Seth Barrett Tillman points out, contrary to what many scholars and judges have claimed, *Merryman* did not involve the issuance of a judicial order by Taney that Lincoln either defied or ignored. See Seth Barrett Tillman, "*Ex parte Merryman*: Myth, History, and Scholarship," *Military Law Review* 224 (2016): 481.
23. Prize Cases, 67 U.S. 635 (1863).
24. David Mayer Silver, *Lincoln's Supreme Court* (University of Illinois Press, 1998).
25. For an overview and strong critique of the widespread idea that the Supreme Court cut Reconstruction short, see Pamela Brandwein, *Rethinking the Judicial Settlement of Reconstruction* (Cambridge University Press, 2011).
26. See *Arver v. United States*, 245 U.S. 366 (1918) (upholding the Selective Service Act); *Frohwerk v. United States*, 249 U.S. 204 (1919) (upholding the prosecution of a newspaperman under the Espionage Act); *Schenck v. United States*, 249 U.S. 47 (1919) (upholding the prosecution of Philadelphia socialist leaders under the Espionage Act); *Debs v. United States*, 249 U.S. 211 (1919) (upholding the prosecution of Socialist Party leader Eugene Debs); *Abrams v. United States*, 250 U.S. 616 (1919) (upholding the 1918 Sedition Act).
27. *Congressional Record*, 65th Congress, Second Session (GPO, 1919), 8109.
28. Colyer v. Skeffington, 265 F. 17 (1920).
29. United States Department of Justice, *Annual Report of the Attorney General for the Year 1920* (GPO, 1921), 177.
30. United States v. Bryan, 339 U.S. 323 (1950) (contempt); United States v. Fleischman, 339 U.S. 349 (1950) (contempt); Dennis v. United States, 341 U.S. 494 (1951) (Smith Act).
31. Bailey v. Richardson, 182 F.2d 46 (1950), affirmed by an equally divided court,

341 U.S. 918 (1951); Joint Anti-Fascist Refugee Committee v. McGrath, 341 U.S. 123 (1951).

32. Communist Party of the United States v. Subversive Activities Control Board, 351 U.S. 115 (1956).
33. *Congressional Record*, 84th Congress, 2nd Session (GPO, 1957), 7341; also quoted in Robert M. Lichtman, *The Supreme Court and McCarthy-Era Repression: One Hundred Decisions* (University of Illinois Press, 2012), 83.
34. Brown v. Board of Education, 347 U.S. 483 (1954). On "massive resistance," see Michael J. Klarman, "How Brown Changed Race Relations: The Backlash Thesis," *Journal of American History* 81, no. 1 (1994): 81–118.
35. Pennsylvania v. Nelson, 350 U.S. 497 (1956).
36. Cole v. Young, 351 U.S. 536 (1956).
37. Lichtman, *Supreme Court and McCarthy-Era Repression*, 89.
38. Watkins v. United States, 354 U.S. 178, 200 (1957). Among the other controversial cases were *Yates v. United States*, 354 U.S. 298 (1957); *Jencks v. United States*, 353 U.S. 657 (1957); and *Sweezy v. New Hampshire*, 354 U.S. 234 (1957). See also Lichtman, *Supreme Court and McCarthy-Era Repression*, 90.
39. Quoted in Lichtman, *Supreme Court and McCarthy-Era Repression*, 107.
40. United States Congress, Senate Committee on the Judiciary, Subcommittee to Investigate the Administration of the Internal Security Act and Other Internal Security Laws, *Limitation of Appellate Jurisdiction of the U.S. Supreme Court: Hearings* (GPO, 1957), 38.
41. Lichtman, *Supreme Court and McCarthy-Era Repression*, 107. See also Lucas A. Powe, *The Warren Court and American Politics* (Harvard University Press, 2000), 135–156.
42. Powe, *Warren Court*, 135–156. Earlier, Eisenhower had allegedly called the appointment of Warren as chief justice "the biggest damn-fool mistake" he ever made. Powe, *Warren Court*, 74.
43. Powe, *Warren Court*, 135–156. See also Robert A. Caro, *The Years of Lyndon Johnson: Master of the Senate* (Knopf, 2002), 1030–1033.
44. Barenblatt v. United States, 360 U.S. 109 (1959).
45. United States Congress, HUAC, *Annual Report for the Year 1959* (GPO, 1960), 123 (praising *Barenblatt*); United States Congress, HUAC, *Communist Activities Among Puerto Ricans in New York City and Puerto Rico: Hearings* (GPO, 1960).
46. HUAC, *Annual Report for the Year 1960* (GPO, 1961), 117.
47. HUAC, *Annual Report for the Year 1964* (GPO, 1965), 66.
48. Warren, *Memoirs*, 313.
49. See *Helvering v. Davis*, 301 U.S. 619 (1937) (upholding Social Security); *West Coast Hotel Co. v. Parrish*, 300 U.S. 379 (1937) (upholding state minimum wage legislation); *Wickard v. Filburn*, 317 U.S. 111 (1942) (upholding far-reaching federal agricultural regulations). The comparison between 1937 and 1958 is also made in Powe, *Warren Court*, 135. On the broader struggle between Roosevelt and the Supreme Court (which was not nearly as simple as suggested in my brief summary), see Jeff Shesol, *Supreme Power: Franklin Roosevelt vs. the Supreme Court* (W. W. Norton, 2011).

50. It may even be debatable whether Article III's mandate that federal judges "shall hold their Offices during good Behavior" provides for life tenure. See Michael J. Mazza, "A New Look at the Old Debate: Life Tenure and the Article III Judge," *Gonzaga Law Review* 39 (2003): 131.
51. Watkins v. United States, 354 U.S. 178 (1957). The durability of this principle is evident by its recent citation in *Trump v. Mazars USA, LLP*, 591 U.S. ___ 12 (slip opinion) (2020).
52. I refer to the Supreme Court's criminal procedure "revolution" in quotation marks because the revolutionary nature of these decisions is debatable. An old but enduringly relevant discussion of the decisions and their context can be found in Kenneth A. Pye, "The Warren Court and Criminal Procedure," *Michigan Law Review* 67, no. 2 (1968): 249–268. I have argued elsewhere—and, I must admit, briefly—that the decisions were not quite as revolutionary as some scholars and commentators have suggested. See Harry Blain, "Why Americans Are Losing Faith in the Supreme Court and Why That's a Good Thing," *American Constitution Society*, September 21, 2022.
53. The best account of these events is Powe, *Warren Court.* However, the Fortas nomination is examined in greater depth in Robert David Johnson, "Lyndon B. Johnson and the Fortas Nomination," *Journal of Supreme Court History* 41, no. 1 (2016): 103–122. Johnson's carefully sourced article is the main source for the discussion of Fortas.
54. Mapp v. Ohio, 367 U.S. 643 (1961); Gideon v. Wainwright, 372 U.S. 335 (1963); Miranda v. Arizona, 384 U.S. 436 (1966); United States v. Wade, 388 U.S. 218 (1967); Katz v. United States, 389 U.S. 347 (1967).
55. Mallory v. United States, 354 US 449 (1957).
56. "Memorandum of Disapproval of the District of Columbia Crime Bill," November 13, 1966, in *Public Papers of the President of the United States: Lyndon B. Johnson, 1966, Book II—July 1 to December 31* (GPO, 1967), 1381–1382. See also "D.C. Crime Bill," in *CQ Almanac 1965*, 21st ed. (Congressional Quarterly, 1966), 662–663.
57. Ramsey Clark, interview 5, June 3, 1969, by T. H. Baker, oral history transcript, LBJ Library Oral Histories, LBJ Presidential Library, Austin, TX, https://discoverlbj.org/item/oh-clarkr-19690603-5-79-37.
58. Clark interview.
59. "Memorandum of Disapproval of the District of Columbia Crime Bill," 1381–1382, https://www.presidency.ucsb.edu/documents/memorandum-disapproval-the-district-columbia-crime-bill.
60. See, especially, *The Challenge of Crime in a Free Society: A Report by the President's Commission on Law Enforcement and Administration of Justice* (GPO, 1967); "Statement by President upon Signing the Departments of State, Justice, and Commerce, the Judiciary and Related Agencies Appropriation Act, 1968," in *Public Papers of the Presidents of the United States: Lyndon B. Johnson, 1967, July 1–December 31* (GPO, 1968), 1005–1007.
61. Telephone conversation 11905, sound recording, LBJ and Ramsey Clark, June 13, 1967, 7:59 a.m., Recordings and Transcripts of Telephone Conversations and Meetings, LBJ Presidential Library; telephone conversation 12303 ("slap

the Supreme Court" comment), sound recording, LBJ and Ramsey Clark, October 11, 1967, 9:59 a.m., Recordings and Transcripts of Telephone Conversations and Meetings, LBJ Presidential Library.

62. Yale Kamisar, "Can (Did) Congress Overrule Miranda," *Cornell Law Review* 85 (1999): 887. Kamisar borrowed the words "a much broader piece of legislation" from Adam Carlyle Breckenridge, *Congress Against the Court* (University of Nebraska Press, 1970), 3
63. Kamisar, "Can (Did) Congress Overrule Miranda." The commentator was Fred P. Graham, "Congress Still Battling the Court," *New York Times*, May 26, 1968. I focus on Title II here and say more about Title III in chapter 6.
64. "Congress Passes Extensive Anticrime Legislation," in *CQ Almanac 1968*, 24th ed. (Congressional Quarterly, 1969).
65. Dickerson v. United States, 530 U.S. 428, 436 (2000).
66. Quoted in Powe, *Warren Court*, 399.
67. *Dickerson*, 530 U.S. 428 (2000).
68. Terry v. Ohio, 392 U.S. 1 (1968).
69. *Terry*, 392 U.S. at 39 (Douglas, J., dissenting).
70. Johnson, "Johnson and the Fortas Nomination," 104–105.
71. Quoted in Johnson, "Johnson and the Fortas Nomination," 117.
72. Johnson, "Johnson and the Fortas Nomination," 115.
73. For an overview of the successes and failures of Burger's "counterrevolution," see Carol S. Steiker, "Counter-Revolution in Constitutional Criminal Procedure: Two Audiences, Two Answers," *Michigan Law Review* 94 (1995): 2466. See also Erwin Chemerinsky, *Presumed Guilty: How the Supreme Court Empowered the Police and Subverted Civil Rights* (Liveright Publishing, 2021). Burger was helped when Fortas was forced to resign as associate justice in 1969 over ethics controversies. See "Justice's Resignation First Under Impeachment Threat," in *CQ Almanac 1969*, 25th ed. (Congressional Quarterly, 1970), 136–137.
74. Although the famous LBJ "treatment" helped cajole legislators to take his side, it could not succeed without substantial legislative majorities. See Julian E. Zelizer, *The Fierce Urgency of Now: Lyndon Johnson, Congress, and the Battle for the Great Society* (Penguin, 2015).
75. Generally, see Elizabeth Hinton, *From the War on Poverty to the War on Crime: The Making of Mass Incarceration in America* (Harvard University Press, 2016); Gerard Horne, *The Fire This Time: The Watts Uprising and the 1960s* (University Press of Virginia, 1995).
76. For the view that the criminal procedure "revolution" was rolled back, see Chemerinsky, *Presumed Guilty.* For the view that Burger Court could not reverse the core gains of the Warren Court, see Steiker, "Counter-Revolution."
77. Hamdan v. Rumsfeld, 548 U.S. 557, 636 (2006).
78. An Act to Authorize Trial by Military Commission for Violations of the Law of War, and for Other Purposes, 120 Stat. 2600 (2006). For a broader history and critique of the MCA, see Paul A. Diller, "When Congress Passes an Intentionally Unconstitutional Law: The Military Commissions Act of 2006," *Southern Methodist University Law Review* 61 (2008): 281.

79. See Michael J. Matheson, "The Amendment of the War Crimes Act," *American Journal of International Law* 101 (2007): 48.
80. *Fact Sheet: The Military Commissions Act of 2006*, White House, October 17, 2006.
81. Daniel Farber, *Lincoln's Constitution* (University of Chicago Press, 2003).
82. US Constitution, Article I, Section 8, clauses 11, 14, and 10.
83. US Constitution, Article III, Section 2, clause 2.
84. Calder v. Bull, 3 U.S. (3 Dall.) 386 (1798).
85. Boumediene v. Bush, 553 U.S. 723 (2008). Guantanamo's status as de facto US territory distinguished *Boumediene* from past cases that rejected habeas petitions from noncitizens held in US military custody, especially *Johnson v. Eisentrager*, 339 U.S. 763 (1950). In *Boumediene*, the court more awkwardly avoided the possible implications of *Ex parte Quirin*, 317 U.S. 1 (1942), which involved noncitizen Nazi saboteurs caught on US soil. *Boumediene*, 553 U.S. at 786.
86. *Boumediene,* 553 U.S. at 798, 795. Congress revised the MCA under the Obama administration. See American Civil Liberties Union (ACLU), *President Obama Signs Military Commissions Changes into Law*, October 28, 2009.
87. Congressional Research Service, *Due Process Rights for Guantanamo Detainees*, November 2, 2021. See also Shayana Kadidal, "Cutting Edge Issues in Year 20 of the Guantánamo Habeas Litigation," *Just Security*, January 11, 2022.
88. ACLU v. National Security Agency, 493 F.3d 644, 648 (6th Cir. 2007).
89. See *Hepting v. AT&T Corp.*, 439 F. Supp. 2d 974 (N.D. Cal. 2006).
90. An Act to Amend the Foreign Intelligence Surveillance Act of 1978 to Establish a Procedure for Authorizing Certain Acquisitions of Foreign Intelligence, and for Other Purposes, 122 Stat. 2436 (2008).
91. *Congressional Record*, 110th Congress, 2nd Session, July 9, 2008 (Senate), S6454.
92. "Senators Block Consideration of Wiretap Bill," CNN, June 26, 2008.
93. "Surveillance Bill Filibuster Falls Short in Senate," CNN, June 26, 2008.
94. Indeed, *Hepting v. AT&T* was pending when the FISA Amendments Act was passed. It was subsequently dismissed because AT&T was now immune. See *Hepting, et al. v. AT&T Corp., et al.* (9th Cir. 2011).
95. See Presidential Commission on the Supreme Court, *Final Report*, December 8, 2021.
96. Keith E. Whittington, *Political Foundations of Judicial Supremacy: The Presidency, the Supreme Court, and Constitutional Leadership in U.S. History* (Princeton University Press, 2009).
97. The much-quoted "political thicket" expression originates from Justice Felix Frankfurter, writing for a plurality in *Colegrove v. Green*, 328 U.S. 549, 556 (1946).

CHAPTER 5: CONGRESS AND THE STATES

1. James Madison, Federalist 45, https://avalon.law.yale.edu/18th_century/fed45.asp. Relatedly, Congress cannot "commandeer" state officials to carry out federal regulations. See *Printz v. United States*, 521 U.S. 898 (1997).
2. For the broader idea of "networked repression," see Thuy Anh Tran, "The

Invisible Hand of Networked Repression" (doctoral dissertation, City University of New York, 2024).

3. Jacob Grumbach, *Laboratories Against Democracy: How National Parties Transformed State Politics* (Princeton University Press, 2022).
4. See, especially, *South Dakota v. Dole*, 483 U.S. 203 (1987). However, the Supreme Court denied Congress the power to "coerce" the states with funding conditions in *National Federation of Independent Business v. Sebelius*, 567 U.S. 519 (2012), without properly defining the difference between "coercion" and "persuasion."
5. Pope to Ulysses S. Grant, in *The Papers of Ulysses S. Grant*, vol. 17, *January 1–September 30, 1867*, ed. John Simon (Southern Illinois University Press, 1991), 259.
6. Brandenburg v. Ohio, 395 U.S. 444, 447 (1969).
7. *Brandenburg*, 395 U.S. 444.
8. A. S. Coodey to Albert deSilver, August 7, 1920, ACLU Papers, Correspondence–Volume 131.
9. Gitlow v. New York, 268 U.S. 652 (1925).
10. Archibald E. Stevenson, ed., *Revolutionary Radicalism: Its History, Purpose and Tactics with an Exposition and Discussion of the Steps Being Taken and Required to Curb It: Filed April 24, 1920, in the Senate of the State of New York* (Lyon, 1920), 1.
11. McAlister Coleman, ed., *The Truth About the Lusk Committee: A Report by the Legislative Committee of the People's Freedom Union* (Nation Press, 1920), 4, 5.
12. Stevenson, *Revolutionary Radicalism*, 644.
13. See David R. Colburn, "Governor Alfred E. Smith and the Red Scare, 1919–20," *Political Science Quarterly* 88, no. 3 (1973): 423–444.
14. See Julian Jaffe, *Crusade Against Radicalism: New York During the Red Scare, 1914–1924* (Kennikat Press, 1972).
15. *Journal of the Assembly of the State of New York at Their One Hundred and Forty-Third Session*, vol. 1 (JB Lyon, 1920), 1–2, 20–21, 24.
16. "Assembly Again Expels Socialists," *New York Times*, September 21, 1920.
17. Thomas E. Vadney, "The Politics of Repression: A Case Study of the Red Scare in New York," *New York History* 49, no. 1 (1968): 56–75.
18. American Civil Liberties Union, *The States and Subversion* (ACLU, 1953), 5.
19. Jack Tenney, *The Tenney Committee . . . The American Record* (Standard Publications, 1952), i.
20. Joint Fact-Finding Committee of the California Legislature, *Un-American Activities in California: Report of the Joint Fact-Finding Committee to the California Legislature* (California State Printing Office, 1943), 25, 86, 104, 213.
21. Joint Fact-Finding Committee of the California Legislature, *Un-American Activities in California: Report of the Joint Fact-Finding Committee to the California Legislature* (California State Printing Office, 1945), 147–148.
22. Joint Fact-Finding Committee of the California Legislature, *Un-American Activities in California: Report of the Joint Fact-Finding Committee to the California Legislature* (California State Printing Office, 1947), 81–83, 313.

23. Michael J. Heale, "Red Scare Politics: California's Campaign Against Un-American Activities, 1940–1970," *Journal of American Studies* 20, no. 1 (1986): 22.
24. Heale, "Red Scare Politics," 19.
25. Joint Fact-Finding Committee of the California Legislature, *Un-American Activities in California: Report of the Joint Fact-Finding Committee to the California Legislature* (California State Printing Office, 1948), 98, 104.
26. Joint Fact-Finding Committee, *Un-American Activities in California* (1948), 129.
27. Heale, "Red Scare Politics," 19.
28. Joint Fact-Finding Committee of the California Legislature, *Un-American Activities in California: Report of the Joint Fact-Finding Committee to the California Legislature* (California State Printing Office, 1953), 146, 143.
29. Joint Fact-Finding Committee, *Un-American Activities in California* (1953), 133–134
30. Joint Fact-Finding Committee, *Un-American Activities in California* (1953), 133.
31. Generally, see Heale, "Red Scare Politics." Crucial Supreme Court decisions constraining state investigating committees include *Sweezy v. New Hampshire*, 354 U.S. 234 (1957), and *Gibson v. Florida Legislative Investigation Committee*, 372 U.S. 539 (1963).
32. Albert F. Canwell and Timothy Frederick, *Albert F. Canwell: An Oral History* (Washington State Oral History Program, Office of the Secretary of State, 1997), 136, 150.
33. Canwell and Frederick, *Albert F. Canwell*, 164–166.
34. Canwell and Frederick, *Albert F. Canwell*, 185.
35. Joint Legislative Fact-Finding Committee on Un-American Activities, *Report of Joint Fact-Finding Committee of Un-American Activities*, 2 vols. (1948), 1:28–29, 31. For Kornfeder's testimony, see 450–460.
36. Eleven of the witnesses were professors.
37. Joint Legislative Fact-Finding Committee, *Report of Un-American Activities*, 2:50.
38. Nancy Wick, "Anti-Communist Firings Linger on UW's Conscience 50 Years Later," *University of Washington Magazine*, December 1997. See also Jane A. Sanders "Clio Confronts Conformity: The University of Washington History Department During the Cold War Era," *Pacific Northwest Quarterly* 88, no. 4 (1997): 185–194.
39. Canwell and Frederick, *Albert F. Canwell*, 172
40. *Report of the [Illinois] Seditious Activities Investigation Commission: Submitted Pursuant to the Provisions of an Act of the 65th General Assembly* (1949), 208.
41. *Report of the Seditious Activities Investigation Commission*, 209, 211, 216.
42. *Report of the Seditious Activities Investigation Commission*, 217, 221–223.
43. *Report of the Seditious Activities Investigation Commission*, 225.
44. *Report of the Seditious Activities Investigation Commission*, 225–226, 228–229.
45. See American Civil Liberties Union, *"To Take a Copy from the Nazis": Statement of the ACLU on the Report of the Illinois State Seditious Activities Investigation Commission* (ACLU, 1951).

46. Seditious Activities Investigation Commission [Illinois], *Investigation of the University of Chicago and Roosevelt College, 1949, Special Report; Public Hearings Held in House of Representatives Chamber, State Capitol Building, April 21, 22, 23, 1949, May 19, 1949* (1949), 2.
47. ACLU, *"To Take a Copy from the Nazis,"* 21–22.
48. Manly W. Mumford, "Changes in the Illinois Law of Civil Rights," *DePaul Law Review* 10 (1960): 271.
49. "Loyalty Oath Upheld: Illinois High Court Rejects Appeal of 3 Teachers," *New York Times*, November 27, 1956.
50. The heading of this section comes from Jeff R. Woods, *Black Struggle, Red Scare: Segregation and Anti-Communism in the South, 1948–1968* (LSU Press, 2003).
51. J. B. Matthews, *Communism and the NAACP* (Georgia Commission on Education, 1958), 5.
52. FBI HQ file 62-103863, https://archive.org/details/louisianajointlegislativecommitteeonsegregationhq62103863.
53. FBI HQ file 62-103863.
54. Arkansas Legislative Council, *Hearing Before the Special Education Committee of the Arkansas Legislative Council* (1958), 20–21.
55. Arkansas Legislative Council, *Hearing*, 24–26.
56. SAC Little Rock to J. Edgar Hoover, regarding Arkansas Legislative Council Committee, FBI-HQ 62-105198, serial 8.
57. Arkansas Legislative Council, *Hearing*, 31.
58. National Association for the Advancement of Colored People v. Alabama, 357 U.S. 449 (1958); Gibson v. Florida Legislative Investigation Committee, 372 U.S. 539 (1963).
59. Grumbach, *Laboratories Against Democracy*. On the other side of this conversation, see Heather K. Gerken, "Distinguished Scholar in Residence Lecture: A User's Guide to Progressive Federalism," *Hofstra Law Review* 45 (2016): 1087. See also Nelson Lund, "Federalism and Civil Liberties," *University of Kansas Law Review* 45 (1996): 1045.
60. Human Rights Watch, *US: States Use Anti-Boycott Laws to Punish Responsible Businesses*, April 13, 2019.
61. See, for example, Ali Harb, "Top US Court Refuses to Review Anti-BDS Law. Here's What It Means," *Al Jazeera*, February 21, 2023.
62. National Association for the Advancement of Colored People v. Claiborne Hardware Co., 458 U.S. 886 (1982).
63. Eugene Volokh, "The First Amendment and Refusals to Deal," *University of the Pacific Law Review* 54 (2023): 732.
64. Louis Keene, "'Schools Are Not Doing Enough': California Proposal Would Ban Calling for Genocide on Campus," *Forward*, March 26, 2024. I would like to acknowledge a former student, Marcus Joe, for bringing this bill to my attention.
65. Jacob Kornbluh, "New York Republican Lawmakers Unveil Plan to Combat Antisemitism Ahead of Budget Vote," *Forward*, March 27, 2024.
66. Brandenburg v. Ohio, 395 U.S. 444 (1969); Hess v. Indiana, 414 U.S. 105 (1973) (applying the *Brandenburg* test).

67. Texas v. Johnson, 491 U.S. 397 (1989) (protecting flag burning); United States v. Eichman, 496 U.S. 310 (1990) (invalidating Congress's efforts to ban flag burning under the Flag Protection Act after *Texas v. Johnson*).
68. Grumbach, *Laboratories Against Democracy*, loc. 311, Kindle.
69. See Law Enforcement Assistance Administration (LEAA), *Annual Reports* (Department of Justice, 1969, 1971, 1976, 1979).
70. LEAA, *1969 Annual Report*, 9.
71. "Congress Passes Extensive Anticrime Legislation," in *CQ Almanac 1968*, 24th ed. (Congressional Quarterly, 1969).
72. LEAA, *1969 Annual Report*, 10–16.
73. LEAA, *1971 Annual Report*, 105–164.
74. National Institute of Law Enforcement and Criminal Justice, *The Utilization of Police Helicopters for Police Air Mobility* (LEAA, 1971), 3.
75. See Gerald Horne, *The Fire This Time: The Watts Uprising and the 1960s* (University Press of Virginia, 1995), 76,
76. Michael Levensen, "Decades After Police Bombing, Philadelphians 'Sickened' by Handling of Victim's Bones," *New York Times*, May 15, 2021.
77. LEAA, *1971 Annual Report*, 105–164.
78. American Civil Liberties Union, *War Comes Home: The Excessive Militarization of American Policing* (ACLU, 2014), 26. More generally, see Radley Balko, *Rise of the Warrior Cop: The Militarization of America's Police Forces* (Public Affairs, 2013).
79. Quoted in LEAA, *1971 Annual Report*, 110.
80. Sting operations are emphasized in LEAA, *1976 Annual Report.*
81. LEAA, *1979 Annual Report*, 4.
82. See especially Michelle Alexander, *The New Jim Crow: Mass Incarceration in the Age of Colorblindness* (New Press, 2012).
83. National Defense Authorization Act for Fiscal Year 1997, 110, *U.S. Statutes at Large*, 2422, 2640 (1996).
84. United States Congress, House Committee on National Security, *Report on H.R. 3230, Together with Additional, Supplemental, and Dissenting Views* (GPO, 1996), 280 (drug enforcement), 122–123 (Oklahoma City). Support for local counterterrorism measures was provided, despite the absence of any law defining domestic terrorist organizations.
85. Law Enforcement Equipment Working Group, *Recommendations Pursuant to Executive Order 13688: Federal Support for Local Law Enforcement Equipment Acquisition* (GPO, 2015), 4.
86. Arezou Rezvani, Jessica Pupovac, David Eads, and Tyler Fisher, "MRAPs and Bayonets: What We Know About the Pentagon's 1033 Program," NPR, September 2, 2014.
87. Casey Delehanty, Jack Mewhirter, Ryan Welch, and Jason Wilks, "Militarization and Police Violence: The Case of the 1033 Program," *Research & Politics* 4, no. 2 (2017): 2. Delehanty et al. try to control for endogeneity by "us[ing] two dependent variables in two separate models: (1) the number of civilians killed by LEAs in a given county for a given year; and (2) the observed change in killings in a county between a given year and the previous year" (3).
88. Delehanty et al., "Militarization and Police Violence," 5: "Holding all else

constant, police that received the highest 1033 transfers kill dogs at an order of magnitude higher rate than those with no transfers (0.161 [expected killings] compared with 0.009)." See also the Puppycide Database, documenting the sharp increase in police killings of pets: https://puppycidedb.com/landing.html (accessed November 2020).

CHAPTER 6: THE VIETNAM ANOMALY

1. United States Congress, Senate Select Committee to Study Governmental Operations with Respect to Intelligence Activities (hereafter, Church Committee), *Final Report, Book I: Foreign and Military Intelligence* (GPO, 1976); Loch K. Johnson, *A Season of Inquiry: The Senate Intelligence Investigation* (University Press of Kentucky, 1985).
2. See United States Congress, House Committee on Standards of Official Conduct, *Investigation of Publication of Select Committee on Intelligence Report* (GPO, 1976). On the findings of the Pike Committee, see United States Congress, House Committee on Intelligence, *Hearings Before the Select Committee on Intelligence U.S. House of Representatives* (GPO, 1976).
3. An Act to Authorize Electronic Surveillance to Obtain Foreign Intelligence Information, 92 Stat. 1783 (1978), known as the Foreign Intelligence Surveillance Act (FISA).
4. James Risen, *The Last Honest Man: The CIA, the FBI, the Mafia, and the Kennedys—and One Senator's Fight to Save Democracy* (Little, Brown, 2023).
5. Kim Lane Scheppele, "Law in a Time of Emergency: States of Exception and the Temptations of 9/11," *University of Pennsylvania Journal of Constitutional Law* 6 (2003–4): 1019.
6. Frederick Schwarz Jr. and Aziz Z. Huq, *Unchecked and Unbalanced: Presidential Power in a Time of Terror* (New Press, 2008), especially 50–65.
7. Samuel Walker, *Presidents and Civil Liberties from Wilson to Obama: A Story of Poor Custodians* (Cambridge University Press, 2012), 349.
8. Arthur M. Schlesinger, *The Cycles of American History* (Houghton Mifflin, 1999), 282. See also James L. Sundquist, *The Decline and Resurgence of Congress* (Brookings Institution Press, 1981).
9. Bruce Ackerman, *Before the Next Attack: Preserving Civil Liberties in an Age of Terrorism* (Yale University Press, 2006), 124.
10. Amy B. Zegart, *Eyes on Spies: Congress and the United States Intelligence Community* (Hoover Press, 2013), 23, 27.
11. See also Michael J. Glennon, "National Security and Double Government," *Harvard National Security Journal* 5 (2014): 76–77 (discussing the executive branch's undermining of FISA).
12. Thomas R. Johnson, *American Cryptology During the Cold War, 1945–1989. Book III: Retrenchment and Reform, 1972–1980*, vol. 5 of *United States Cryptologic History*, series VI, *The NSA Period, 1952–Present* (National Security Agency, 1998), 92–93.
13. Betty Medsger, *The Burglary: The Discovery of J. Edgar Hoover's Secret FBI* (Vintage Books, 2014).
14. United States v. U.S. District Court for Eastern District of Michigan, 407 U.S. 297 (1972).

15. Much of the analysis, argument, and narrative in this chapter can be found in Harry Blain, "A Partner, Not a Combatant: The U.S. Congress, Intelligence Reform, and Civil Liberties After Vietnam," *Journal of Intelligence History* (2024): 1–17.
16. The war could conceivably have a longer chronology. See Marilyn B. Young, *The Vietnam Wars, 1945–1990* (Harper Perennial, 1991).
17. See David Cunningham, *There's Something Happening Here: The New Left, the Klan, and FBI Counterintelligence* (University of California Press, 2004); Ward Churchill and Jim Vander Wall, *The COINTELPRO Papers* (South End, 1990); Nelson Blackstock, *COINTELPRO: The FBI's Secret War on Political Freedom* (Pathfinder Press, 1975). Although "COINTELPRO" is usually referred to in singular form, this chapter uses the plural when describing the separate counterintelligence programs.
18. C. D. Brennan to W. C. Sullivan, June 27, 1971, quoted in Blackstock, *COINTELPRO*, 32.
19. See the near-identical language in J. Edgar Hoover, internal memorandum, August 25, 1967, COINTELPRO Black Extremist Part 01 of 23; J. Edgar Hoover, internal memorandum, September 2, 1964, COINTELPRO White Hate Groups Part 01 of 14; Federal Bureau of Investigation (FBI), The Vault—COINTELPRO, https://vault.fbi.gov/cointel-pro.
20. Quoted in Medsger, *Burglary*, 108.
21. Church Committee, *Final Report of the Select Committee to Study Governmental Operations with Respect to Intelligence Activities, United States Senate: Together with Additional, Supplemental, and Separate Views, Book II: Intelligence Activities and the Rights of Americans* (GPO, 1976); FBI, The Vault—COINTELPRO.
22. See *Nardone v. United States*, 308 U.S. 338 (1939); Athan Theoharis, "FBI Wiretapping: A Case Study of Bureaucratic Autonomy," *Political Science Quarterly* 107, no. 1 (1992): 116.
23. See "Surreptitious Entries (Black Bag Jobs)," in FBI, The Vault; Athan G. Theoharis, "FBI Surveillance Past and Present," *Cornell Law Review* 69 (1983): 883–894; Church Committee, *Supplementary Detailed Staff Reports on Intelligence Activities and the Rights of Americans, Book III* (GPO, 1976), 355.
24. The history of the NSA is described at length in Church Committee, *Final Reports: Book III, National Security Agency Surveillance Affecting Americans*, 733–777. See also Church Committee, *Hearings: Volume 5, The National Security Agency and Fourth Amendment Rights (October 29 and November 6, 1975)* (GPO, 1976).
25. Church Committee, *Hearings: Volume 5*, 12, 15.
26. Johnson, *American Cryptology During the Cold War*, 85.
27. The primary predecessor agency was the Armed Forces Security Agency, established in 1949. During World War II, it was known as the Signal Intelligence Service. In 1952 President Truman broadened the agency's remit and gave it its own director. It then became the National Security Agency.
28. Church Committee, *Hearings: Volume 5*, 57–58, 60.
29. Church Committee, *Final Reports: Book III*, 741.
30. This prohibition was deliberately aimed at preventing the possibility of an

"American Gestapo." See Harry Blain, "No Gestapo: J. Edgar Hoover's World-Wide Intelligence Service and the Limits of Bureaucratic Autonomy in the National Security State," *Studies in American Political Development* 35, no. 2 (2021): 214–222.

31. Seymour Hersh, "Huge C.I.A. Operation Reported in U.S. Against Antiwar Forces, Other Dissidents in Nixon Years," *New York Times*, December 22, 1974.
32. Church Committee, *Final Reports: Book III*, 565, 571.
33. Church Committee, *Final Reports: Book III*, 6. See also Commission on CIA Activities Within the United States, *Report to the President*, June 1975, 130–151, box 7, Richard B. Cheney Files, Ford Presidential Library, Ann Arbor, MI.
34. Church Committee, *Final Reports: Book III*, 682.
35. Church Committee, *Final Report, Book I*, 385–386.
36. United States Congress, *Joint Hearing Before the Senate Select Committee on Intelligence and the Subcommittee on Health and Scientific Research of the Committee on Human Resources, United States Senate, Ninety-Fifth Congress, First Session, August 3, 1977* (GPO, 1977), 7.
37. Church Committee, *Hearings: Volume 2, Huston Plan, September 23, 24, and 25, 1975* (GPO, 1976).
38. United States Congress, Senate Select Committee on Presidential Campaign Activities, *The Final Report of the Select Committee on Presidential Campaign Activities* (GPO, 1974); United States v. Russo & Ellsberg, Crim. No. 9373 (C.D.Cal. dismissed May 11, 1973).
39. Church Committee, *Final Reports: Book III*, 6–7.
40. Church Committee, *Hearings: Volume 3, Internal Revenue Service, October 2, 1975* (GPO, 1976), 2.
41. Church Committee, *Final Reports: Book III*, 77, 6.
42. Johnson, *American Cryptology During the Cold War*, 93; United States Congress, Senate Committee on the Judiciary, Subcommittee on Constitutional Rights, *Federal Data Banks, Computers, and the Bill of Rights: Hearings . . . Ninety-Second Congress, First Session, Pt. 2: Relating to Departments of Army, Defense, and Justice Hearings Held Feb. 23–Mar. 17, 1971* (GPO, 1971). See also Lawrence M. Baskir, "Reflections on the Senate Investigation of Army Surveillance," *Indiana Law Journal* 49 (1973): 618–653.
43. See Johnson, *Season of Inquiry*, 124–128.
44. Medsger, *Burglary*, 226–231, 235.
45. Stern v. Richardson, 367 F. Supp. 1316, 1318, 1321 (D.C. 1973).
46. "Radicals: Ripping off the FBI," *Time*, April 5, 1971.
47. Medsger, *Burglary*, 165–166.
48. Gravel feared the FBI would raid his home for the Pentagon Papers, and he faced legal trouble because his dyslexia required his aides to do much of the reading, raising questions over the application of the speech or debate clause to congressional staff. Gravel v. United States, 408 U.S. 606 (1972).
49. Brennan to Sullivan, June 27, 1971.
50. Elliot Richardson to Lew Allen, October 1, 1973; Allen to Richardson, October 4, 1973, cited in Church Committee, *Hearings: Volume 5*, 160–163.
51. Church Committee, *Hearings: Volume 3*, 8.

52. Church Committee, *Final Reports: Book III*, 921–987 ("Report on the Huston Plan").
53. See Church Committee, *Final Reports: Book III*, 705–708.
54. Church Committee, *Final Report*, *Book I*, 402.
55. Minutes, NSC meeting, January 13, 1977, National Security Adviser's NSC Meeting File, box 2, Ford Presidential Library.
56. Richardson to Allen, October 1, 1973.
57. United States v. Sinclair, 321 F. Supp. 1074 (E.D. Mich. 1971).
58. The Supreme Court case was *United States v. U.S. District Court for the Eastern District of Michigan*, 407 U.S. 297 (1972).
59. Richard J. Aldrich and Daniela Richterova, "Ambient Accountability: Intelligence Services in Europe and the Decline of State Secrecy," *West European Politics* 41, no. 4 (2018): 1003–1024.
60. See, for example, Frederick Schwarz Jr., "Why We Need a New Church Committee to Fix Our Broken Intelligence System," Brennan Center, March 12, 2014, https://www.brennancenter.org/our-work/analysis-opinion/why-we-need-new-church-committee-fix-our-broken-intelligence-system.
61. *Congressional Record*, 94th Congress, 1st Session (GPO, 1976), 1416–1417; the vote is at 1431–1432.
62. *Congressional Record*, 94th Congress, 1st Session, 1419.
63. Quoted in Risen, *Last Honest Man*, 173–174. Tower's self-assessment (quoted by Risen) comes from John G. Tower, *Consequences: A Personal and Political Memoir* (Little, Brown, 1991), 132.
64. "Ford, Kissinger, Senators Church and Tower," March 5, 1975, National Security Adviser's Memoranda of Conversation Collection, box 9, Ford Presidential Library.
65. *Congressional Record*, 94th Congress, 1st Session, 1430.
66. For comparisons between the Church Committee and the Pike Committee, see Kathryn Olmsted, *Challenging the Secret Government: The Post-Watergate Investigations of the CIA and FBI* (UNC Press, 1996). See also Johnson, *Season of Inquiry*.
67. See Olmsted, *Challenging the Secret Government*, 1–11. The most in-depth accounts of the Church Committee's internal debates come from political scientist Loch K. Johnson, who conducted fieldwork on the committee staff. See Johnson, *Season of Inquiry*; Loch K. Johnson, "Congressional Supervision of America's Secret Agencies: The Experience and Legacy of the Church Committee," *Public Administration Review* 64, no. 1 (2004): 3–14. See also Risen, *Last Honest Man*.
68. The full domestic-focused recommendations are in Church Committee, *Final Reports: Book II*, 289–339.
69. See United States Congress, Senate Subcommittee on Intelligence and the Rights of Americans, *Hearings Before the Subcommittee on Intelligence and the Rights of Americans of the Select Committee on Intelligence of the United States Senate, Ninety-Fourth Congress, Second Session, on S. 3197, the Foreign Intelligence Surveillance Act, June 29, July 1, August 6, 10, and 24, 1976* (GPO, 1976); hereafter, 1976 FISA hearings.
70. United States Congress, Senate Subcommittee on Intelligence and the Rights

of Americans of the Select Committee on Intelligence, *Hearings on S. 1566, Foreign Intelligence Surveillance Act July 19, 21, 1977 and February 8, 24, 27, 1978* (GPO, 1978), 3–4; hereafter, 1978 FISA hearings.

71. 1976 FISA hearings, 5.
72. 1978 FISA hearings, 12–13.
73. Americo R. Cinquegrana, "Walls (and Wires) Have Ears: The Background and First Ten Years of the Foreign Intelligence Surveillance Act of 1978," *University of Pennsylvania Law Review* 137 (1988): 811.
74. The structure and history of the FISA Court are thoroughly assessed in Emily Berman, "The Two Faces of the Foreign Intelligence Surveillance Court," *Indiana Law Journal* 91 (2015): 1191–1250. See also United States Congress, *Foreign Intelligence Surveillance Act of 1978: Conference Report to Accompany S. 1566* (GPO, 1978).
75. Berman, "Two Faces," 1206, fn. 81.
76. For a summary of these arguments, see Cinquegrana, "Walls (and Wires) Have Ears," 815.
77. These criticisms were made forcefully in *United States v. Duggan*, 743 F.2d 59 (2d Cir. 1984).
78. See Elizabeth Goitein and Faiza Patel, *What Went Wrong with the FISA Court* (Brennan Center for Justice, New York University School of Law, 2015).
79. In re sealed Case, 310 F.3d 717 (2002), 18.
80. *In re sealed Case*, 14–15. The Fourth Circuit case was *United States v. Truong Dinh Hung*, 629 F.2d 908 (4th Cir. 1980). See also Cedric Logan, "The FISA Wall and Federal Investigations," *NYU Journal of Law & Liberty* 4 (2009): 223, which debates whether *Troung Dinh Hung* or the 1995 Justice Department regulations were the origin of the wall. Logan nonetheless observes, "It is (almost) universally acknowledged that the original FISA statute did not contain The Wall, at least not to its fullest extent."
81. United States Department of Justice, *Final Report of the Attorney General's Review Team on the Handling of the Los Alamos National Laboratory Investigation* (Department of Justice, 2000), 721–734; Government Accountability Office, *FBI Intelligence Investigations: Coordination Within Justice on Counterintelligence Criminal Matters Is Limited* (GPO, 2001). Both these reports were cited in *In re sealed Case*.
82. Zegart, *Eyes on Spies*, 24.

CONCLUSION

1. Generally, see John Sides and Kimberly Gross, "Stereotypes of Muslims and Support for the War on Terror," *Journal of Politics* 75, no. 3 (2013): 583–598; Marc Hetherington and Elizabeth Suhay, "Authoritarianism, Threat, and Americans' Support for the War on Terror," *American Journal of Political Science* 55, no. 3 (2011): 546–560; Peter Liberman, "Retributive Support for International Punishment and Torture," *Journal of Conflict Resolution* 57, no. 2 (2013): 285–306.
2. John Mueller, *Public Opinion and the War on Terror: Manipulated or Manipulating?* (Cato Institute, 2021).
3. Generally, see Ira Katznelson, *When Affirmative Action Was White: An Untold History of Racial Inequality in Twentieth-Century America* (W. W. Norton, 2005).

4. For a recent statement of this view (not just in Congress but in the country more broadly), see Steven Levitsky and Daniel Ziblatt, *Tyranny of the Minority: Why American Democracy Reached the Breaking Point* (Crown, 2023). On factions, see Daniel DiSalvo, *Engines of Change: Party Factions in American Politics, 1868–2010* (Oxford University Press, 2012); Matthew Green, *Legislative Hardball: The House Freedom Caucus and the Power of Threat-Making in Congress* (Cambridge University Press, 2019).
5. Dafydd Townley, "Too Responsible to Run for President: Frank Church and the 1976 Presidential Nomination," *Journal of Intelligence History* 21, no. 2 (2022): 213–231.
6. See Beverly Gage, *The Day Wall Street Exploded: A Story of America in Its First Age of Terror* (Oxford University Press, 2009).
7. George C. Rable, *But There Was No Peace: The Role of Violence in the Politics of Reconstruction* (University of Georgia Press, 1984); William A. Blair, *The Record of Murders and Outrages: Racial Violence and the Fight over Truth at the Dawn of Reconstruction* (University of North Carolina Press, 2021); Eric Foner, *Reconstruction: America's Unfinished Revolution, 1863–1877* (Harper Perennial, 1988); W. E. B. Du Bois, *Black Reconstruction: An Essay Toward a History of the Part Which Black Folk Played in the Attempt to Reconstruct Democracy in America, 1860–1880* (Harcourt, Brace, 1935); John Hope Franklin, *Reconstruction After the Civil War* (University of Chicago Press, 1961).
8. Du Bois, *Black Reconstruction*, 345.
9. A qualified defense of McCarthy's claims (based on evidence of actual Soviet espionage in the United States) can be found in John E. Haynes and Harvey Klehr, *Venona: Decoding Soviet Espionage in America* (Yale University Press, 2000). More robust defenses of McCarthy include Stanton M. Evans, *Blacklisted by History: The Untold Story of Senator Joe McCarthy and His Fight Against America's Enemies* (Three Rivers Press, 2007); Arthur Herman, *Joseph McCarthy: Re-Examining the Life and Legacy of America's Most Hated Senator* (Free Press, 2000).
10. On section 3, see William Baude and Michael Stokes Paulsen, "The Sweep and Force of Section Three," *University of Pennsylvania Law Review* 172 (2024): 605–745, and briefs and arguments on either side in *Trump v. Anderson*, 601 U.S. ___ (2024). On criminal prosecution (although not a prosecution for insurrection), see Grand Jury Indictment in the United States District Court for the District of Columbia, *United States of America v. Donald J. Trump*, filed August 8, 2023.
11. Giovanni Capoccia, "Militant Democracy: The Institutional Bases of Democratic Self-Preservation," *Annual Review of Law and Social Science* 9 (2013): 207–226.
12. The District of Columbia US Court of Appeals ruled in March 2024 that Larry Brock's two-year prison term, which included an enhancement for "interfering with the administration of justice," was improperly lengthened because certification of the Electoral College vote is not "the administration of justice" and was never considered as such by the drafters of the Sarbanes-Oxley Act. See *United States v. Brock*, D.C. Cir. (2024). The Supreme Court eventually sided with this view in *Fischer v. United States*, 603 U.S. ___ (2024).

13. Powell v. McCormack, 395 U.S. 486, 553 (1969) (Douglas, J., concurring).
14. See Richard Sakwa, *Deception: Russiagate and the New Cold War* (Lexington Books, 2021).
15. On the risks of "misinformation" or "disinformation" censorship, see Jacob Siegel, "A Guide to Understanding the Hoax of the Century: Thirteen Ways of Looking at Disinformation," *Tablet Magazine*, March 28, 2023.
16. On these elections, see Thomas Knock, *To End All Wars: Woodrow Wilson and the Quest for a New World Order* (Oxford University Press, 1992); Walter Goodman, *The Committee: The Extraordinary Career of the House Committee on Un-American Activities* (Farrar, Straus, and Giroux, 1968), 190–226.
17. With respect to liberals and the second Red Scare, see Samuel Moyn, *Liberalism Against Itself: Cold War Intellectuals and the Making of Our Times* (Yale University Press, 2023).
18. Isser Woloch, *The Postwar Moment: Progressive Forces in Britain, France, and the United States After World War II* (Yale University Press, 2019).
19. Tom Ginbsurg and Mila Versteeg, "The Bound Executive: Emergency Powers During the Pandemic," *International Journal of Constitutional Law* 19, no. 5 (2021): 1498–1535.
20. Erwin Chemerinsky and Michele Goodwin, "Civil Liberties in a Pandemic: The Lessons of History," *Cornell Law Review* 106 (2020): 818.
21. Clinton Rossiter, *Constitutional Dictatorship: Crisis Government in the Modern Democracies* (Transaction Publishers, 1948).
22. US Constitution, Article II, Section 3, gives the president the power "on extraordinary Occasions," to "convene both Houses, or either of them, and in Case of Disagreement between them, with Respect to the Time of Adjournment, he may adjourn them to such Time as he shall think proper." Although presidents have convened special sessions of Congress, they have never adjourned Congress.
23. Zachary Elkins, "Is the Sky Falling? Constitutional Crises in Historical Perspective," in *Constitutional Democracy in Crisis*, ed. Mark A. Graber, Sanford Levinson, and Mark Tushnet (Oxford University Press, 2018), 64. The seven powers are to initiate bills, issue decrees, declare emergencies, propose amendments, propose referenda, challenge the constitutionality of a law, and dissolve the legislature.
24. Justice Robert Jackson pithily described the various powers the president has accrued outside the Constitution: "No appraisal of his necessities is realistic which overlooks that he heads a political system as well as a legal system. Party loyalties and interests, sometimes more binding than law, extend his effective control into branches of government other than his own and he often may win, as a political leader, what he cannot command under the Constitution." Youngstown Sheet & Tube Co. v. Sawyer, 343 U.S. 579, 654 (1952) (Jackson, J, concurring). In the scholarly literature, see, for instance, Stephen Skowronek, *The Politics Presidents Make: Leadership from John Adams to Bill Clinton* (Harvard University Press, 1997); Samuel Kernell, *Going Public: New Strategies of Presidential Leadership* (CQ Press, 2006); Charles M. Cameron, *Veto Bargaining: Presidents and the Politics of Negative Power* (Cambridge University Press,

2000); William G. Howell, *Power Without Persuasion: The Politics of Direct Presidential Action* (Princeton University Press, 2003). Some of these factors, especially control over information, are central to foreign policy. See Helen V. Milner and Dustin Tingley, *Sailing the Water's Edge: The Domestic Politics of American Foreign Policy* (Princeton University Press, 2015).

25. Keith D. Ewing and Conor A. Gearty, *The Struggle for Civil Liberties: Political Freedom and the Rule of Law in Britain, 1914–1945* (Oxford University Press, 2001); Neil Stammers, *Civil Liberties in Britain During the Second World War: A Political Study* (St. Martin's Press, 1983); David Miller and Rizwaan Sabir, "Counter-Terrorism as Counterinsurgency in the UK 'War on Terror,'" in *Counter-Terrorism and State Political Violence*, ed. Scott Poynting and David Whyte (Routledge, 2012), 12–32.
26. Vernon Bogdanor, *The New British Constitution* (Bloomsbury Publishing, 2009).
27. Amnesty International, *Punished Without Trial—The Use of Administrative Control Measures in the Context of Counter-terrorism in France* (Amnesty International, 2018), 7.
28. Amnesty International, "Breaches of the Law Cannot Be Solved by Breaking the Law," November 22, 2005.
29. Stephan Haggard and Robert Kaufman, "The Anatomy of Democratic Backsliding," *Journal of Democracy* 32, no. 4 (2021): 32.
30. See, especially, Steven M. Fish, "Stronger Legislatures, Stronger Democracies," *Journal of Democracy* 17, no. 1 (2006): 5–20.
31. United States v. U.S. District Court, 407 U.S. 297, 323–324 (1972).
32. Watkins v. United States, 354 U.S. 178, 200 (1957).
33. See, most recently, *Trump v. Mazars USA, LLP*, 591 U.S. ___ (2020).
34. John Nichols, "Mike Gravel Told Americans What Was Being Done in Their Name but Without Their Consent," *Nation*, June 28, 2021.
35. New York Times Co. v. United States, 403 U.S. 713, 717 (1971) (Black, J., concurring).
36. Ex parte Milligan, 71 U.S. (4 Wall.) 2, 120–121 (1866).
37. Hamdi v. Rumsfeld, 542 U.S. 507 (2004); Hamdan v. Rumsfeld, 548 U.S. 557 (2006); Boumediene v. Bush, 553 U.S. 723 (2008).
38. The classic statement of this view is Gerald N. Rosenberg, *The Hollow Hope: Can Courts Bring About Social Change?* 2nd ed. (University of Chicago Press, 2008).

EPILOGUE

1. 8 USC §1182.
2. Associated Press, "Rümeysa Öztürk, Tufts Student Held by ICE, Vows to Continue Legal Action After Jail Release," *Guardian*, May 11, 2025.
3. For a discussion of these deportations, see National Constitution Center, "Deportations and the Law," March 20, 2025, https://constitutioncenter.org/media/files/Deportations-and-the-Law-WTP-transcript.pdf.
4. Reuters, "Columbia University Caves to Demands to Restore $400m from Trump Administration," *Guardian*, March 21, 2025.

5. US Department of Education, "U.S. Department of Education's Office for Civil Rights Sends Letters to 60 Universities Under Investigation for Antisemitic Discrimination and Harassment," March 10, 2025.
6. United States Congress, House of Representatives, *Staff Report on Antisemitism*, December 18, 2024, 10–15, 16–17.
7. US Congress, House of Representatives, *Staff Report on Antisemitism*, 30.
8. US Congress, House of Representatives, *Staff Report on Antisemitism*, 31.
9. Karoun Demirjian, "House Declares Anti-Zionism Is Antisemitism, Dividing Democrats," *New York Times*, December 5, 2023.
10. Melissa Murray, remarks made during a National Constitution Center event, "The Supreme Court and the Trump Administration," February 27, 2025, https://constitutioncenter.org/media/files/The-Supreme-Court-and-the-Trump-Administration-WTP-transcript.pdf.
11. To be fair, the "liberals" on the Supreme Court recognized these potential dangers in *Trump v. Mazars USA, LLP*, 591 U.S. ___ (2020).

BIBLIOGRAPHY

Archival Sources

American Civil Liberties Union Papers. Mudd Library, Princeton University.

Burleson, Albert Sidney. Papers. Library of Congress, Washington, DC.

Federal Bureau of Investigation. Records on the Louisiana and Arkansas Legislative Investigating Committees. https://archive.org/details/louisianajointlegislativecommitteeonsegregationhq62103863.

Ford, Gerald R. Papers. Ford Presidential Library, Ann Arbor, MI.

Gregory, Thomas Watt. Papers. Library of Congress, Washington, DC.

Jackson, Robert H. Papers. Library of Congress, Washington, DC.

Johnson, Lyndon B. Papers. LBJ Presidential Library, Austin, TX.

Lincoln, Abraham. Papers. Library of Congress, Washington, DC.

Printed Ephemera Collection. Library of Congress, Washington, DC.

Southern Oral History Program Collection (#4007). University Library, University of North Carolina–Chapel Hill.

Truman, Harry S. Papers. Truman Presidential Library, Independence, MO.

Warren, Charles. Papers. Library of Congress, Washington, DC.

Books, Articles, and Government Documents

Abraham, Steven E. "How the Taft-Hartley Act Hindered Unions." *Hofstra Labor Law Journal* 12 (1994): 1–37.

Ackerman, Bruce. *Before the Next Attack: Preserving Civil Liberties in an Age of Terrorism*. Yale University Press, 2006.

Ackerman, Spencer. "'A Constitutional Crisis': The CIA Turns on the Senate." *Guardian*, September 10, 2016.

Ackerman, Spencer. *Reign of Terror: How the 9/11 Era Destabilized America and Produced Trump*. Viking Press, 2021.

Ackerman, Spencer. "Senate Torture Report to Be Kept from Public for 12 Years After Obama Decision." *Guardian*, December 12, 2016.

Agamben, Giorgio. *State of Exception*. Translated by Kevin Attell. University of Chicago Press, 2005.

Al Jazeera Staff. "Columbia University Leaders Face Scrutiny over Anti-Semitism on Campus." Al Jazeera, April 17, 2024.

Aldrich, Richard J., and Daniela Richterova. "Ambient Accountability: Intelligence Services in Europe and the Decline of State Secrecy." *West European Politics* 41, no. 4 (2018): 1003–1024.

Alexander, Michelle. *The New Jim Crow: Mass Incarceration in the Age of Colorblindness*. New Press, 2012.

Alfonseca, Kiara. "The Forces Behind Harvard President Claudine Gay's Resignation." *ABC News*, January 5, 2024.

Alford, Ryan. *Permanent State of Emergency: Unchecked Executive Power and the Demise of the Rule of Law*. McGill-Queen's Press–MQUP, 2017.

American Civil Liberties Union. *President Obama Signs Military Commissions Changes into Law.* October 28, 2009.

American Civil Liberties Union. *The States and Subversion.* ACLU, 1953.

American Civil Liberties Union. *"To Take a Copy from the Nazis": Statement of the ACLU on the Report of the Illinois State Seditious Activities Investigation Commission.* ACLU, 1951.

American Civil Liberties Union. *War Comes Home: The Excessive Militarization of American Policing.* ACLU, 2014.

Amiri, Farnoush. "House Votes to Censure Rep. Rashida Tlaib over Her Israel-Hamas Rhetoric in a Stunning Rebuke." Associated Press, November 8, 2023.

Amnesty International. "Breaches of the Law Cannot Be Solved by Breaking the Law." November 22, 2005.

Amnesty International. *Punished Without Trial—The Use of Administrative Control Measures in the Context of Counter-Terrorism in France.* Amnesty International, 2018.

Arkansas Legislative Council. *Hearing Before the Special Education Committee of the Arkansas Legislative Council.* 1958.

"Assembly Again Expels Socialists." *New York Times*, September 21, 1920.

Associated Press. "Rümeysa Öztürk, Tufts Student Held by ICE, Vows to Continue Legal Action After Jail Release." *Guardian*, May 11, 2025.

Baker, Ray Stannard, and William E. Dodd, eds. *The New Democracy: Presidential Messages, Addresses, and Other Papers (1913–1917).* Vol. 1. Harper, 1926.

Balko, Radley. *Rise of the Warrior Cop: The Militarization of America's Police Forces.* Public Affairs, 2013.

Baskir, Lawrence M. "Reflections on the Senate Investigation of Army Surveillance." *Indiana Law Journal* 49 (1973): 618–653.

Basler, Roy P., ed. *Abraham Lincoln: Speeches and Writings 1859–1865.* Library of America, 1989.

Baude, William, and Michael Stokes Paulsen. "The Sweep and Force of Section Three." *University of Pennsylvania Law Review* 172 (2024): 605–745.

Bauer, Bob, and Jack Goldsmith. *After Trump: Reconstructing the Presidency.* Lawfare Press, 2020.

Belknap, Michal R. *Cold War Political Justice: The Smith Act, the Communist Party, and American Civil Liberties.* Greenwood Press, 1977.

Bergeron, Paul H., ed. *The Papers of Andrew Johnson.* Vol. 8, *May–August 1865.* University of Tennessee Press, 1989.

Berman, Emily. "The Paradox of Counterterrorism Sunset Provisions." *Fordham Law Review* 81 (2012): 1777–1833.

Berman, Emily. "The Two Faces of the Foreign Intelligence Surveillance Court." *Indiana Law Journal* 91 (2015): 1191–1250.

Bermeo, Nancy. "On Democratic Backsliding." *Journal of Democracy* 27, no. 1 (2016): 10–13.

Bernstein, Barton J. "The Truman Administration and the Steel Strike of 1946." *Journal of American History* 52, no. 4 (1966): 791–803.

Best, Judith A. "Legislative Tyranny and the Liberation of the Executive: A View from the Founding." *Presidential Studies Quarterly* 17, no. 4 (1987): 697–709.

Bickel, Alexander. *The Least Dangerous Branch: The Supreme Court at the Bar of Politics*. Bobbs-Merrill, 1962.

Blackman, Josh, and Seth Barrett Tillman. "Sweeping and Forcing the President into Section 3." *Texas Review of Law & Policy* 28 (2023): 350–587.

Blackstock, Nelson. *COINTELPRO: The FBI's Secret War on Political Freedom.* Pathfinder Press, 1975.

Blain, Harry. "Israel and the New McCarthyism." *Foreign Policy in Focus*, December 15, 2023.

Blain, Harry. "No Gestapo: J. Edgar Hoover's World-Wide Intelligence Service and the Limits of Bureaucratic Autonomy in the National Security State." *Studies in American Political Development* 35, no. 2 (2021): 214–222.

Blain, Harry. "A Partner, Not a Combatant: The U.S. Congress, Intelligence Reform, and Civil Liberties After Vietnam." *Journal of Intelligence History* (2024): 1–17.

Blain, Harry. "The Sun Never Sets on the Espionage Act." *Foreign Policy in Focus*, April 4, 2019.

Blain, Harry. "The Useless War Powers Resolution." *Foreign Policy in Focus*, January 9, 2020.

Blain, Harry. "Why Americans Are Losing Faith in the Supreme Court and Why That's a Good Thing." *American Constitution Society*, September 21, 2022.

Blair, William A. *The Record of Murders and Outrages: Racial Violence and the Fight over Truth at the Dawn of Reconstruction*. University of North Carolina Press, 2021.

Bogdanor, Vernon. *The New British Constitution*. Bloomsbury Publishing, 2009.

Brandwein, Pamela. *Rethinking the Judicial Settlement of Reconstruction.* Cambridge University Press, 2011.

Breckenridge, Adam Carlyle. *Congress Against the Court.* University of Nebraska Press, 1970.

Brown, R. G., Zachariah Chafee, Felix Frankfurter, Ernst Freund, Swinburne Hale, Francis Fisher Kane, Alfred S. Niles, Dean Roscoe Pound, Jackson H. Ralston, David Wallerstein, Frank P. Walsh, and Tyrrell Williams. *To the American People: Report upon the Illegal Practices of the Department of Justice.* National Popular Government League, 1920.

Cameron, Charles M. *Veto Bargaining: Presidents and the Politics of Negative Power.* Cambridge University Press, 2000.

Canwell, Albert F., and Timothy Frederick. *Albert F. Canwell: An Oral History.* Washington State Oral History Program, Office of the Secretary of State, 1997.

Capoccia, Giovanni. "Militant Democracy: The Institutional Bases of Democratic Self-Preservation." *Annual Review of Law and Social Science* 9 (2013): 207–226.

Carleton, Don E. "McCarthyism Was More than McCarthy: Documenting the Red Scare at the State and Local Level." *Midwestern Archivist* (1987): 13–19.

Caro, Robert A. *The Years of Lyndon Johnson: Master of the Senate*. Knopf, 2002.

Carter, Ralph G., and James M. Scott. *Choosing to Lead: Understanding Congressional Foreign Policy Entrepreneurs*. Duke University Press, 2009.

Chafee, Zachariah. *Free Speech in the United States* [1941]. Harvard University Press, 1964.

Chafetz, Josh. *Congress's Constitution: Legislative Authority and the Separation of Powers*. Yale University Press, 2017.
Chafetz, Josh. "Executive Branch Contempt of Congress." *University of Chicago Law Review* 76 (2009): 1083–1156.
Chalk, Peter. "The Response to Terrorism as a Threat to Liberal Democracy." *Australian Journal of Politics & History* 44, no. 3 (1998): 373–388.
The Challenge of Crime in a Free Society: A Report by the President's Commission on Law Enforcement and Administration of Justice. GPO, 1967.
Charles, Douglas M. "Informing FDR: FBI Political Surveillance and the Isolationist-Interventionist Foreign Policy Debate, 1939–1945." *Diplomatic History* 24, no. 2 (2000): 211–232.
Cheibub, José Antonio. *Presidentialism, Parliamentarism, and Democracy*. Cambridge University Press, 2007.
Chemerinsky, Erwin. *Presumed Guilty: How the Supreme Court Empowered the Police and Subverted Civil Rights*. Liveright Publishing, 2021.
Chemerinsky, Erwin, and Michele Goodwin. "Civil Liberties in a Pandemic: The Lessons of History." *Cornell Law Review* 106 (2020): 815–850.
Chomsky, Carol. "The United States–Dakota War Trials: A Study in Military Injustice." *Stanford Law Review* (1990): 13–98.
Chorr, Khatya. "After Winning House, Democrats' Real Power May Lie in Investigating Trump." *France 24*, November 13, 2018.
Churchill, Ward, and Jim Vander Wall. *The COINTELPRO Papers*. South End, 1990.
Cinquegrana, Americo R. "Walls (and Wires) Have Ears: The Background and First Ten Years of the Foreign Intelligence Surveillance Act of 1978." *University of Pennsylvania Law Review* 137 (1988): 793–828.
Cloyd, Benjamin G. *Haunted by Atrocity: Civil War Prisons in American Memory*. LSU Press, 2010.
Coben, Stanley. *A. Mitchell Palmer: Politician*. Columbia University Press, 1963.
Cohen, Harlan Grant. "The (Un)favorable Judgment of History: Deportation Hearings, the Palmer Raids, and the Meaning of History." *NYU Law Review* 78 (2003): 1431–1474.
Colburn, David R. "Governor Alfred E. Smith and the Red Scare, 1919–20." *Political Science Quarterly* 88, no. 3 (1973): 423–444.
Cole, David. *Enemy Aliens: Double Standards and Constitutional Freedoms in the War on Terrorism*. New Press, 2003.
Cole, David. "The First Amendment's Borders: The Place of Holder v. Humanitarian Law Project in First Amendment Doctrine." *Harvard Law & Policy Review* 6 (2012): 147–177.
Cole, David. "The New McCarthyism: Repeating History in the War on Terrorism." *Harvard Civil Rights and Civil Liberties Review* 38 (2003): 1–30.
Coleman, McAlister, ed. *The Truth About the Lusk Committee: A Report by the Legislative Committee of the People's Freedom Union*. Nation Press, 1920.
Conaghan, Catherine M. "Ecuador: Correa's Plebiscitary Presidency." *Journal of Democracy* 19, no. 2 (2008): 46–60.
"Congress Passes Extensive Anticrime Legislation." *CQ Almanac 1968*. 24th ed. Congressional Quarterly, 1969.

Congressional Research Service. *Due Process Rights for Guantanamo Detainees*. November 2, 2021.

Coppedge, Michael, John Gerring, David Altman, Michael Bernhard, Steven Fish, Allen Hicken, Matthew Kroenig, Staffan I. Lindberg, Kelly McMann, Pamela Paxton, Holli A. Semetko, Svend-Erik Skaaning, Jeffrey Staton, and Jan Teorell. "Conceptualizing and Measuring Democracy: A New Approach." *Perspectives on Politics* 9, no. 2 (2011): 247–267.

Coyne, Christopher J., and Abigail R. Hall. *Tyranny Comes Home: The Domestic Fate of US Militarism*. Stanford University Press, 2018.

Crockford, Kate. "Obama Must Reveal Legal Memos on His Administration's Drone Killing Program." *Guardian*, March 7, 2013.

Cunningham, David. *There's Something Happening Here: The New Left, the Klan, and FBI Counterintelligence*. University of California Press, 2004.

Dahl, Robert A. "Decision-Making in a Democracy: The Supreme Court as a National Policy-Maker." *Journal of Public Law* 6 (1957): 279–295.

Davidson, Roger H. "The Advent of the Modern Congress: The Legislative Reorganization Act of 1946." *Legislative Studies Quarterly* (1990): 357–373.

"D.C. Crime Bill." *CQ Almanac 1965*. 21st ed. Congressional Quarterly, 1966.

De Wilde, Marc. "Why Dictatorial Authority Did Good, and Not Harm, to the Roman Republic: Dictatorship and Constitutional Change in Machiavelli." *Ratio Juris* 31, no. 1 (2018): 86–99.

Deery, Phillip. "'A Blot upon Liberty': McCarthyism, Dr. Barsky and the Joint Anti-Fascist Refugee Committee." *American Communist History* 8, no. 2 (2009): 167–196.

Delehanty, Casey, Jack Mewhirter, Ryan Welch, and Jason Wilks. "Militarization and Police Violence: The Case of the 1033 Program." *Research & Politics* 4, no. 2 (2017): 1–6.

Devins, Neal, and Saikrishna Prakash. "The Indefensible Duty to Defend." *Columbia Law Review* (2012): 507–577.

Diller, Paul A. "When Congress Passes an Intentionally Unconstitutional Law: The Military Commissions Act of 2006." *Southern Methodist University Law Review* 61 (2008): 281–336.

DiSalvo, Daniel. *Engines of Change: Party Factions in American Politics, 1868–2010*. Oxford University Press, 2012.

Donner, Frank. *Protectors of Privilege: Red Squads and Police Repression in Urban America*. University of California Press, 1990.

Donohue, Laura. *The Cost of Counterterrorism: Power, Politics, and Liberty*. Cambridge University Press, 2008.

Downs, Gregory P. *After Appomattox: Military Occupation and the Ends of War*. Harvard University Press, 2015.

Downs, Gregory P. "Powers of War in Times of Peace: Emergency Powers in the United States After the End of the Civil War." In *States of Exception in American History*, edited by Gary Gerstle and Joel Isaac. University of Chicago Press, 2020.

Du Bois, W. E. B. *Black Reconstruction: An Essay Toward a History of the Part Which Black Folk Played in the Attempt to Reconstruct Democracy in America, 1860–1880*. Harcourt, Brace, 1935.

Dudziak, Mary L. "Brown as a Cold War Case." *Journal of American History* 91, no. 1 (2004): 32–42.
Dudziak, Mary L. *Cold War Civil Rights*. Princeton University Press, 2011.
Dudziak, Mary L. *War Time: An Idea, Its History, Its Consequences*. Oxford University Press, 2012.
Duncan, Russell. *Freedom's Shore: Tunis Campbell and the Georgia Freedmen*. University of Georgia Press, 1986.
Eckstein, Arthur. "The Hollywood Ten in History and Memory." *Film History* 16, no. 4 (2004): 424–436.
Edelson, Chris. *Emergency Presidential Power: From the Drafting of the Constitution to the War on Terror.* University of Wisconsin Press, 2013.
Egerton, Douglas R. *The Wars of Reconstruction: The Brief, Violent History of America's Most Progressive Era*. Bloomsbury Press, 2014.
Elkins, Zachary. "Is the Sky Falling? Constitutional Crises in Historical Perspective." In *Constitutional Democracy in Crisis*, edited by Mark A. Graber, Sanford Levinson, and Mark Tushnet. Oxford University Press, 2018.
Epstein, Lee, Daniel E. Ho, Gary King, and Jeffrey A. Segal. "The Supreme Court During Crisis: How War Affects Only Non-War Cases." *NYU Law Review* 80 (2005): 1–116.
Evans, Stanton M. *Blacklisted by History: The Untold Story of Senator Joe McCarthy and His Fight Against America's Enemies.* Three Rivers Press, 2007.
Ewing, Keith D., and Conor A. Gearty. *The Struggle for Civil Liberties: Political Freedom and the Rule of Law in Britain, 1914–1945.* Oxford University Press, 2001.
Fact Sheet: The Military Commissions Act of 2006. White House, October 17, 2006.
Farber, Daniel. *Lincoln's Constitution.* University of Chicago Press, 2003.
Farrand, Max, ed. *The Records of the Federal Convention of 1787.* Rev. ed. Vol. 2. Yale University Press, 1937.
Fayyad, Abdallah. "The Lessons from Colleges that Didn't Call the Police." *Vox*, May 3, 2024.
Fazal, Tanisha M. "The Demise of Peace Treaties in Interstate War." *International Organization* 67, no. 4 (2013): 695–724.
Fazal, Tanisha M. "Why States No Longer Declare War." *Security Studies* 21, no. 4 (2012): 557–593.
Federal Bureau of Investigation. The Vault. https://vault.fbi.gov/.
Feinstein, Dianne. "Continue NSA Call-Records Program." *USA Today*, October 20, 2013.
Feldman, Leonard C. "The Banality of Emergency: On the Time and Space of 'Political Necessity.'" In *Sovereignty, Emergency, Legality*, edited by Austin Sarat. Cambridge University Press, 2010.
Feldman, Noah. *The Broken Constitution: Lincoln, Slavery, and the Refounding of America.* Farrar, Straus, and Giroux, 2021.
Fenno, Richard. *Home Style: House Members in Their Districts.* Little, Brown, 1978.
Ferejohn, John, and Pasquale Pasquino. "The Law of the Exception: A Typology of Emergency Powers." *International Journal of Constitutional Law* 2, no. 2 (2004): 210–239.

Ferrell, Robert H., ed. *Off the Record: The Private Papers of Harry S. Truman.* Harper and Row, 1980.

Finan, Christopher M. *From the Palmer Raids to the Patriot Act: A History of the Fight for Free Speech in America*. Beacon Press, 2007.

Fischer, David Hackett. *Washington's Crossing*. Oxford University Press, 2004.

Fish, Steven M. "Stronger Legislatures, Stronger Democracies." *Journal of Democracy* 17, no. 1 (2006): 5–20.

Fisher, Louis. *The Constitution and 9/11: Recurring Threats to America's Freedoms.* University Press of Kansas, 2008.

Fisher, Louis. "Signing Statements: Constitutional and Practical Limits." *William & Mary Bill of Rights Journal* 16 (2007): 183–210.

Flaherty, Martin S. "The Most Dangerous Branch." *Yale Law Journal* 105 (1995): 1725–1839.

Foner, Eric. *Freedom's Lawmakers: A Directory of Black Officeholders During Reconstruction.* LSU Press, 1993.

Foner, Eric. *Reconstruction: America's Unfinished Revolution, 1863–1877.* Harper Perennial, 1988.

Fowler, Linda L. *Watchdogs on the Hill: The Decline of Congressional Oversight of US Foreign Relations*. Princeton University Press, 2015.

Franklin, John Hope. *Reconstruction After the Civil War.* University of Chicago Press, 1961.

Fredrickson, Caroline, Jamal Greene, and Melissa Murray. *The Progressive Constitution*. https://constitutioncenter.org/debate/special-projects/constitution-drafting-project.

Freeland, Richard M. *The Truman Doctrine and the Origins of McCarthyism: Foreign Policy, Domestic Politics, and Internal Security, 1946–1948*. Alfred A. Knopf, 1972.

Freeman, Will. "Sidestepping the Constitution: Executive Aggrandizement in Latin America and East Central Europe." *Constitutional Studies* 6 (2020): 35–58.

Gage, Beverly. *The Day Wall Street Exploded: A Story of America in Its First Age of Terror*. Oxford University Press, 2009.

Gage, Beverly. *G-Man: J. Edgar Hoover and the Making of the American Century.* Viking Press, 2022.

Gearty, Conor. *Civil Liberties*. Oxford University Press, 2007.

Gearty, Conor. "11 September 2001, Counter-Terrorism, and the Human Rights Act." *Journal of Law and Society* 32, no. 1 (2005): 18–33.

Gellhorn, Walter, ed. *The States and Subversion.* Cornell University Press, 1952.

Gentry, Curt. *J. Edgar Hoover: The Man and the Secrets*. W. W. Norton, 1991.

George, Robert P., Michael McConnell, Colleen A. Sheehan, and Ilan Wurman. *The Conservative Constitution*. https://constitutioncenter.org/debate/special-projects/constitution-drafting-project.

Gerken, Heather K. "Distinguished Scholar in Residence Lecture: A User's Guide to Progressive Federalism." *Hofstra Law Review* 45 (2016): 1087–1096.

Gibson, James L. "Pluralism, Federalism and the Protection of Civil Liberties." *Western Political Quarterly* 43, no. 3 (1990): 511–533.

Gibson, James L. "Political Intolerance and Political Repression During the

McCarthy Red Scare." *American Political Science Review* 82, no. 2 (1988): 511–529.

Ginsburg, Tom, and Aziz Z. Huq. *How to Save a Constitutional Democracy.* University of Chicago Press, 2018.

Ginsburg, Tom, and Mila Versteeg. "The Bound Executive: Emergency Powers During the Pandemic." *International Journal of Constitutional Law* 19, no. 5 (2021): 1498–1535.

Glass, Charles. "The Unjust Prosecution of the Holy Land Foundation Five." *Intercept*, August 5, 2018.

Glennon, Michael J. "National Security and Double Government." *Harvard National Security Journal* 5 (2014): 1–114.

Glennon, Michael J. *National Security and Double Government*. Oxford University Press, 2016.

Goitein, Elizabeth. "Congress' Access to Individuals' Private Communications: The Jan. 6 Committee's Troubling Precedent." *Just Security*, September 22, 2021.

Goitein, Elizabeth, and Faiza Patel. *What Went Wrong with the FISA Court*. Brennan Center for Justice, New York University School of Law, 2015.

Goldgeier, James, and Elizabeth N. Saunders. "The Unconstrained Presidency: Checks and Balances Eroded Long Before Trump." *Foreign Affairs* 97 (2018): 144–156.

Goldman, Emma. *Living My Life*. Alfred A. Knopf, 1931.

Goldsmith, Jack. *The Terror Presidency: Law and Judgment Inside the Bush Administration*. W. W. Norton, 2007.

Goldsmith, Jack, and Cass R. Sunstein. "Military Tribunals and Legal Culture: What a Difference Sixty Years Makes." *Constitutional Commentary* 19 (2002): 261–289.

Goldstein, Robert J. *American Blacklist: The Attorney General's List of Subversive Organizations.* University Press of Kansas, 2008.

Goldstein, Robert J. "The Grapes of McGrath: The Supreme Court and the Attorney General's List of Subversive Organizations in Joint Anti-Fascist Refugee Committee v. McGrath (1951)." *Journal of Supreme Court History* 33, no. 1 (2008): 68–88.

Goldstein, Robert J. *Political Repression in Modern America from 1870 to 1976.* University of Illinois Press, 1976.

Goodman, Walter. *The Committee: The Extraordinary Career of the House Committee on Un-American Activities*. Farrar, Straus, and Giroux, 1968.

Gosse, Van. *The First Reconstruction: Black Politics in America from the Revolution to the Civil War.* University of North Carolina Press, 2021.

Government Accountability Office. *FBI Intelligence Investigations: Coordination Within Justice on Counterintelligence Criminal Matters Is Limited.* GPO, 2001.

Graber, Mark A. "Counter-Stories: Maintaining and Expanding Civil Liberties in Wartime." In *The Constitution in Wartime: Beyond Alarmism and Complacency*, edited by Mark Tushnet. Duke University Press, 2005.

Graber, Mark A. *Dred Scott and the Problem of Constitutional Evil.* Cambridge University Press, 2006.

Graber, Mark A. *Punish Treason, Reward Loyalty: The Forgotten Goals of Constitutional Reform After the Civil War.* University Press of Kansas, 2023.

Graham, Fred P. "Congress Still Battling the Court." *New York Times*, May 26, 1968.

Green, Matthew. *Legislative Hardball: The House Freedom Caucus and the Power of Threat-Making in Congress.* Cambridge University Press, 2019.

Greenberg, Karen J. *Rogue Justice: The Making of the Security State.* Random House, 2016.

Greenberg, Karen J. *Subtle Tools: The Dismantling of American Democracy from the War on Terror to Donald Trump*. Princeton University Press, 2021.

Greenwald, Glenn. "Chilling Legal Memo from Obama DOJ Justifies Assassination of US Citizens." *Guardian*, February 5, 2013.

Greenwald, Glenn. *No Place to Hide: Edward Snowden, the NSA, and the U.S. Surveillance State*. Macmillan, 2014.

Groenewold, Kurt. "The German Federal Republic's Response and Civil Liberties." *Terrorism and Political Violence* 4, no. 4 (1992): 136–150.

Gross, Oren. "Chaos and Rules: Should Responses to Violent Crises Always Be Constitutional?" *Yale Law Journal* 112 (2002): 1011–1134.

"Groups Called Disloyal." *New York Times*, December 4, 1947.

Grumbach, Jacob. *Laboratories Against Democracy: How National Parties Transformed State Politics*. Princeton University Press, 2022.

"The Guantanamo Docket." *New York Times.* https://www.nytimes.com/interactive/2021/us/guantanamo-bay-detainees.html.

Guantanamo Review Task Force. *Final Report.* January 22, 2010. https://www.justice.gov/sites/default/files/ag/legacy/2010/06/02/guantanamo-review-final-report.pdf.

Haggard, Stephan, and Robert Kaufman. "The Anatomy of Democratic Backsliding." *Journal of Democracy* 32, no. 4 (2021): 27–41.

Hamilton, Alexander. "Federalist 70." In *The Federalist Papers*, edited by Alexander Hamilton, James Madison, and John Jay. Simon and Schuster, 2004.

Harb, Ali. "Top US Court Refuses to Review Anti-BDS Law: Here's What It Means." Al Jazeera, February 21, 2023.

Haynes, John E., and Harvey Klehr. *Venona: Decoding Soviet Espionage in America.* Yale University Press, 2000.

Heale, Michael J. *McCarthy's Americans: Red Scare Politics in State and Nation.* University of Georgia Press, 1998.

Heale, Michael J. "Red Scare Politics: California's Campaign Against Un-American Activities, 1940–1970." *Journal of American Studies* 20, no. 1 (1986): 5–32.

Herman, Arthur. *Joseph McCarthy: Re-Examining the Life and Legacy of America's Most Hated Senator.* Free Press, 2000.

Herman, Susan N. *Taking Liberties: The War on Terror and the Erosion of American Democracy*. Oxford University Press, 2011.

Hersh, Seymour. "Huge C.I.A. Operation Reported in U.S. Against Antiwar Forces, Other Dissidents in Nixon Years." *New York Times*, December 22, 1974.

Hetherington, Marc, and Elizabeth Suhay. "Authoritarianism, Threat, and Americans' Support for the War on Terror." *American Journal of Political Science* 55, no. 3 (2011): 546–560.

Hillyard, Paddy. *Suspect Community: People's Experience of the Prevention of Terrorism Acts in Britain*. Pluto Press in association with Liberty, 1993.

Hinton, Elizabeth. *America on Fire: The Untold History of Police Violence and Black Rebellion Since the 1960s.* W. W. Norton, 2021.

Hinton, Elizabeth. *From the War on Poverty to the War on Crime: The Making of Mass Incarceration in America*. Harvard University Press, 2016.

Holland, William L. "Source Materials on the Institute of Pacific Relations." *Pacific Affairs* 58, no. 1 (1985): 91–97.

Horne, Gerald. *The Fire This Time: The Watts Uprising and the 1960s*. University Press of Virginia, 1995.

Howell, William G. *Power Without Persuasion: The Politics of Direct Presidential Action*. Princeton University Press, 2003.

Howell, William G. "Presidential Power in War." *Annual Review of Political Science* 14 (2011): 89–105.

Howell, William G., Saul P. Jackman, and Jon C. Rogowski. *The Wartime President: Executive Influence and the Nationalizing Politics of Threat*. University of Chicago Press, 2013.

Howell, William G., and Terry Moe. *Relic: How Our Constitution Undermines Effective Government—and Why We Need a More Powerful Presidency*. Basic Books, 2016.

Howell, William G., and Jon C. Pevehouse. *While Dangers Gather: Congressional Checks on Presidential War Powers*. Princeton University Press, 2007.

Human Rights Watch. *US: States Use Anti-Boycott Laws to Punish Responsible Businesses*. April 13, 2019.

Humphreys, Stephen. "Legalizing Lawlessness: On Giorgio Agamben's State of Exception." *European Journal of International Law* 17, no. 3 (2006): 677–687.

Hyman, Harold M. *A More Perfect Union: The Impact of the Civil War and Reconstruction on the Constitution*. Alfred A. Knopf, 1973.

"Immigration and Nationality Act." *CQ Almanac 1952*. Congressional Quarterly, 1953.

Ip, John. "The Supreme Court and House of Lords in the War on Terror: Inter Arma Silent Leges." *Michigan State University Journal of International Law* 19 (2010): 1–61.

Izumi, Masumi. "Prohibiting 'American Concentration Camps.'" *Pacific Historical Review* 74, no. 2 (2005): 165–194.

Jaffe, Julian. *Crusade Against Radicalism: New York During the Red Scare, 1914–1924*. Kennikat Press, 1972.

Jimenez, Fernando. "Spain: The Terrorist Challenge and the Government's Response." *Terrorism and Political Violence* 4, no. 4 (1992): 110–130.

Johnson, Loch K. "Congressional Supervision of America's Secret Agencies: The Experience and Legacy of the Church Committee." *Public Administration Review* 64, no. 1 (2004): 3–14.

Johnson, Loch K. "Ostriches, Cheerleaders, Skeptics, and Guardians." *SAIS Review of International Affairs* 28, no. 1 (2008): 93–108.

Johnson, Loch K. *A Season of Inquiry: The Senate Intelligence Investigation*. University Press of Kentucky, 1985.

Johnson, Loch K. *Spy Watching: Intelligence Accountability in the United States*. Oxford University Press, 2017.

Johnson, Robert David. "Congress and the Cold War." *Journal of Cold War Studies* 3, no. 2 (2001): 76–100.

Johnson, Robert David. *Congress and the Cold War*. Cambridge University Press, 2005.

Johnson, Robert David. "Lyndon B. Johnson and the Fortas Nomination." *Journal of Supreme Court History* 41, no. 1 (2016): 103–122.

Johnson, Thomas R. *American Cryptology During the Cold War, 1945–1989. Book III: Retrenchment and Reform, 1972–1980.* Vol. 5 of *United States Cryptologic History*, series VI, *The NSA Period, 1952–Present*. National Security Agency, 1998.

Joint Fact-Finding Committee of the California Legislature. *Un-American Activities in California: Report of the Joint Fact-Finding Committee to the California Legislature.* California State Printing Office, 1943, 1945, 1947, 1948, 1953.

Joint Legislative Fact-Finding Committee on Un-American Activities. *Report of Joint Fact-Finding Committee of Un-American Activities*. 2 vols. 1948.

Journal of the Assembly of the State of New York at Their One Hundred and Forty-Third Session. Vol. 1. JB Lyon, 1920.

"Justice's Resignation First Under Impeachment Threat." *CQ Almanac 1969*, 25th ed. Congressional Quarterly, 1970.

Kadidal, Shayana. "Cutting Edge Issues in Year 20 of the Guantánamo Habeas Litigation." *Just Security*, January 11, 2022.

Kahn, E. J. *The China Hands: America's Foreign Service Officers and What Befell Them.* Viking Press, 1972.

Kamisar, Yale. "Can (Did) Congress Overrule Miranda." *Cornell Law Review* 85 (1999): 883–955.

Katznelson, Ira. *When Affirmative Action Was White: An Untold History of Racial Inequality in Twentieth-Century America.* W. W. Norton, 2005.

Keene, Louis. "'Schools Are Not Doing Enough': California Proposal Would Ban Calling for Genocide on Campus." *Forward*, March 26, 2024.

Kernell, Samuel. *Going Public: New Strategies of Presidential Leadership.* CQ Press, 2006.

Kerr, Dara. "Lawmakers Grilled TikTok CEO Chew for 5 Hours in a High-Stakes Hearing About the App." NPR, March 23, 2023.

Khaitan, Tarunabh. "Executive Aggrandizement in Established Democracies: A Crisis of Liberal Democratic Constitutionalism." *International Journal of Constitutional Law* 17, no. 1 (2019): 342–356.

Khaitan, Tarunabh. "Killing a Constitution with a Thousand Cuts: Executive Aggrandizement and Party-State Fusion in India." *Law & Ethics of Human Rights* 14, no. 1 (2020): 49–95.

Kiewiet, Roderick D., and Mathew D. McCubbins. *The Logic of Delegation*. University of Chicago Press, 1991.

Klarman, Michael J. "How Brown Changed Race Relations: The Backlash Thesis." *Journal of American History* 81, no. 1 (1994): 81–118.

Kleinerman, Benjamin. "'In the Name of National Security': Executive Discretion and Congressional Legislation in the Civil War and World War I." In *The Limits of Constitutional Democracy*, edited by Jeffrey Tulis and Stephen Macedo. Princeton University Press, 2010.

Kleinerman, Benjamin. "Lincoln's Example: Executive Power and the Survival of Constitutionalism." *Perspectives on Politics* 3, no. 4 (2005): 801–816.

Knock, Thomas. *To End All Wars: Woodrow Wilson and the Quest for a New World Order.* Oxford University Press, 1992.

Kornbluh, Jacob. "New York Republican Lawmakers Unveil Plan to Combat Antisemitism Ahead of Budget Vote." *Forward*, March 27, 2024.

Kornweibel, Theodore, ed. *Federal Surveillance of Afro-Americans (1917–1925): The First World War, the Red Scare, and the Garvey Movement*. Microform. Schomburg Center for Research in Black Culture.

Kriner, Douglas L. *After the Rubicon: Congress, Presidents, and the Politics of Waging War*. University of Chicago Press, 2010.

Kutler, Stanley I. "Ex Parte McCardle: Judicial Impotency? The Supreme Court and Reconstruction Reconsidered." *American Historical Review* 72, no. 3 (1967): 835–851.

Lang, Andrew F. *In the Wake of War: Military Occupation, Emancipation, and Civil War America*. LSU Press, 2017.

Law Enforcement Assistance Administration. *Annual Reports*. Department of Justice, 1969, 1971, 1976, 1979.

Law Enforcement Equipment Working Group. *Recommendations Pursuant to Executive Order 13688: Federal Support for Local Law Enforcement Equipment Acquisition*. GPO, 2015.

Lebovic, Sam. *State of Silence: The Espionage Act and the Rise of America's Secrecy Regime*. Basic Books, 2023.

Lemann, Nicholas. *Redemption: The Last Battle of the Civil War*. Macmillan, 2007.

Les Benedict, Michael. *A Compromise of Principle: Congressional Republicans and Reconstruction, 1863–1869*. W. W. Norton, 1974.

Leuchtenburg, William E. "New Faces of 1946: An Unpopular President, a War-Weary People." *Smithsonian* 37, no. 8 (2006): 48–55.

Levensen, Michael. "Decades After Police Bombing, Philadelphians 'Sickened' by Handling of Victim's Bones." *New York Times*, May 15, 2021.

Levine, Bruce. *Thaddeus Stevens: Civil War Revolutionary, Fighter for Racial Justice*. Simon and Schuster, 2021.

Levinson, Daryl J., and Richard H. Pildes. "Separation of Parties, Not Powers." *Harvard Law Review* (2006): 2311–2386.

Levinson, Sanford, and Jack M. Balkin. "Constitutional Dictatorship: Its Dangers and Its Design." *Minnesota Law Review* 94 (2009): 1848–1866.

Levitsky, Steven, and Daniel Ziblatt. *How Democracies Die*. Random House, 2018.

Levitsky, Steven, and Daniel Ziblatt. *Tyranny of the Minority: Why American Democracy Reached the Breaking Point*. Crown, 2023.

Liberman, Peter. "Retributive Support for International Punishment and Torture." *Journal of Conflict Resolution* 57, no. 2 (2013): 285–306.

Lichtman, Robert M. *The Supreme Court and McCarthy-Era Repression: One Hundred Decisions*. University of Illinois Press, 2012.

Link, Arthur S., ed. *The Papers of Woodrow Wilson*. Princeton University Press, 1991.

Linz, Juan J., and Alfred C. Stepan, eds. *The Breakdown of Democratic Regimes*. Johns Hopkins University Press, 1979.

Linz, Juan J., and Alfred C. Stepan. "Toward Consolidated Democracies." *Journal of Democracy* 7, no. 2 (1996): 14–33.

Logan, Cedric. "The FISA Wall and Federal Investigations." *NYU Journal of Law & Liberty* 4 (2009): 210–251.

"Loyalty Oath Upheld: Illinois High Court Rejects Appeal of 3 Teachers." *New York Times*, November 27, 1956.
Lund, Nelson. "Federalism and Civil Liberties." *University of Kansas Law Review* 45 (1996): 1045–1073.
Lustick, Ian S. "History, Historiography, and Political Science: Multiple Historical Records and the Problem of Selection Bias." *American Political Science Review* 90, no. 3 (1996): 605–618.
MacMillan, Margaret. *War: How Conflict Shaped Us*. Random House, 2020.
Madison, James. "Helvidius IV." In *The Pacificus-Helvidius Debates of 1793–1794: Toward the Completion of the American Founding*, edited by Alexander Hamilton and James Madison. Liberty Fund, 2007.
Maheshwari Sapna, and Amanda Holpuch. "Why the U.S. Is Forcing TikTok to Be Sold or Banned." *New York Times*, April 26, 2024.
Maier, Pauline. *Ratification: The People Debate the Constitution, 1787–1788*. Simon and Schuster, 2010.
Manners-Weber, David. "Certification as Sabotage: Lessons from Guantanamo Bay." *Yale Law Journal* 127 (2017): 1416–1446.
Manz, William H. *Civil Liberties in Wartime: Legislative Histories of the Espionage Act of 1917 and the Sedition Act of 1918*. W. S. Hein, 2007.
Mason, Alpheus Thomas. "Harlan Fiske Stone: In Defense of Individual Freedom, 1918–20." *Columbia Law Review* 51 (1951): 147–169.
Matheson, Michael J. "The Amendment of the War Crimes Act." *American Journal of International Law* 101 (2007): 48–55.
Matthews, J. B. *Communism and the NAACP.* Georgia Commission on Education, 1958.
Mayer, Jane. *The Dark Side: The Inside Story of How the War on Terror Turned into a War on American Ideals*. Doubleday, 2008.
Mayhew, David. *Congress: The Electoral Connection.* Yale University Press, 1974.
Mazetti, Mark, and Matt Apuzzo. "Deep Support in Washington for C.I.A.'s Drone Missions." *New York Times*, April 15, 2015.
Mazza, Michael J. "A New Look at the Old Debate: Life Tenure and the Article III Judge." *Gonzaga Law Review* 39 (2003): 131–162.
McAlevey, Jane. "Blowout in Bessemer: A Postmortem on the Amazon Campaign." *Nation*, April 9, 2021.
McAlevey, Jane. *A Collective Bargain: Unions, Organizing, and the Fight for Democracy.* HarperCollins, 2020.
McCarthy, Daniel J. "James Wilson and the Creation of the Presidency." *Presidential Studies Quarterly* 17, no. 4 (1987): 689–696.
McConnell, Michael W. *The President Who Would Not Be King: Executive Power Under the Constitution*. Princeton University Press, 2020.
McCubbins, Mathew D., Roger G. Noll, and Barry R. Weingast. "Administrative Procedures as Instruments of Political Control." *Journal of Law, Economics, & Organization* 3, no. 2 (1987): 243–277.
McCubbins, Mathew D., and Thomas Schwartz. "Congressional Oversight Overlooked: Police Patrols Versus Fire Alarms." *American Journal of Political Science* (1984): 165–179.
McDonald, Jason A. "Limitation Riders and Congressional Influence over

Bureaucratic Policy Decisions." *American Political Science Review* 104, no. 4 (2010): 766–782.

McFeely, William. *Yankee Stepfather: General O. O. Howard and the Freedmen.* W. W. Norton, 1994.

McPherson, Edward, ed. *The Political History of the United States of America During the Period of Reconstruction.* James J. Chapman, 1880.

McWhirter, Cameron. *Red Summer: The Summer of 1919 and the Awakening of Black America.* Henry Holt, 2011.

Medsger, Betty. *The Burglary: The Discovery of J. Edgar Hoover's Secret FBI.* Vintage Books, 2014.

Meeropol, Rachel. "Muslim Until Proven Innocent: The Post-9/11 Ashcroft Raids." *Security Journal* 28, no. 2 (2015): 184–197.

Merrill, Dennis, ed. *A Documentary History of the Truman Presidency.* Vol. 9, *The Debate over Labor Policy.* University Publications of America, 1995.

Miller, David, and Rizwaan Sabir. "Counter-Terrorism as Counterinsurgency in the UK 'War on Terror.'" In *Counter-Terrorism and State Political Violence*, edited by Scott Poynting and David Whyte. Routledge, 2012.

Milner, Helen V., and Dustin Tingley. *Sailing the Water's Edge: The Domestic Politics of American Foreign Policy.* Princeton University Press, 2015.

Mohtasham, Diba. "Tom Cotton Grills Singaporean TikTok CEO: Are You a Chinese Communist?" NPR, February 1, 2024.

Moyn, Samuel. *Humane: How the United States Abandoned Peace and Reinvented War.* Farrar, Straus, and Giroux, 2021.

Moyn, Samuel. *Liberalism Against Itself: Cold War Intellectuals and the Making of Our Times.* Yale University Press, 2023.

Mueller, John. *Public Opinion and the War on Terror: Manipulated or Manipulating?* Cato Institute, 2021.

Mumford, Manly W. "Changes in the Illinois Law of Civil Rights." *DePaul Law Review* 10 (1960): 267–273.

Murray, Robert K. *Red Scare: A Study in National Hysteria, 1919–1920.* University of Minnesota Press, 1955.

Muzik, Edward J. "Victor L. Berger: Congress and the Red Scare." *Wisconsin Magazine of History* (1964): 311.

National Constitution Center. "Deportations and the Law." March 20, 2025. https://constitutioncenter.org/media/files/Deportations-and-the-Law-WTP-transcript.pdf.

National Institute of Law Enforcement and Criminal Justice. *The Utilization of Police Helicopters for Police Air Mobility.* Law Enforcement Assistance Administration, 1971.

Neely, Mark E. *The Fate of Liberty: Abraham Lincoln and Civil Liberties.* Oxford University Press, 1991.

Nelles, Walter. *Espionage Act Cases.* National Civil Liberties Bureau, 1918.

Newman, Robert P. *Owen Lattimore and the Loss of China.* University of California Press, 1992.

Nichols, John. "Mike Gravel Told Americans What Was Being Done in Their Name but Without Their Consent." *Nation*, June 28, 2021.

Offices of the Inspectors General of the Department of Defense, Department of

Justice, Central Intelligence Agency, and Office of the Director of National Intelligence. *Unclassified Report on the President's Surveillance Program.* July 10, 2009.
Olmsted, Kathryn. *Challenging the Secret Government: The Post-Watergate Investigations of the CIA and FBI.* UNC Press, 1996.
O'Reilly, Kenneth. "The FBI and the Origins of McCarthyism." *Historian* 45, no. 3 (1983): 375.
Palmer, Beverly, and Holly Ochoa, eds. *The Selected Papers of Thaddeus Stevens.* Vol. 2, *April 1865–August 1868.* University of Pittsburgh Press, 1998.
Paschal, George W. *Letter to the President Asking for the Pardon of Ludovic P. Alford and Other Citizens Imprisoned by Military Commissions Under the Reconstruction Laws.* M'Gill and Witherow, 1870.
Paulsen, Michael Stokes. "Drone On: The Commander in Chief Power to Target and Kill Americans." *Harvard Journal of Law & Public Policy* 38 (2015): 43–61.
Peled, Miko. *Injustice: The Story of the Holy Land Foundation Five.* Just World Books, 2018.
Pérez-Liñán, Aníbal, Nicolás Schmidt, and Daniela Vairo. "Presidential Hegemony and Democratic Backsliding in Latin America, 1925–2016." *Democratization* 26, no. 4 (2019): 606–625.
Piven, Frances Fox, and Richard Cloward. *Poor People's Movements: Why They Succeed, How They Fail.* Vintage Books, 1979.
Polsky, Andrew. *Elusive Victories: The American Presidency at War.* Oxford University Press, 2012.
Posner, Eric A., and Adrian Vermeule. *The Executive Unbound: After the Madisonian Republic.* Oxford University Press, 2011.
Posner, Eric A., and Adrian Vermeule. *Terror in the Balance: Security, Liberty, and the Courts.* Oxford University Press, 2007.
Post, Louis F. *The Deportations Delirium of Nineteen-Twenty: A Personal Narrative of an Historic Official Experience.* CH Kerr, 1923.
Powe, Lucas A. *The Supreme Court and the American Elite, 1789–2008.* Harvard University Press, 2009.
Powe, Lucas A. *The Warren Court and American Politics.* Harvard University Press, 2000.
Presidential Commission on the Supreme Court. *Final Report*, December 8, 2021.
Public Papers of the President of the United States: Lyndon B. Johnson, 1966. Book II—July 1 to December 31. GPO, 1967.
Public Papers of the Presidents of the United States: Lyndon B. Johnson, 1967, July 1–December 31. GPO, 1968.
Pye, Kenneth A. "The Warren Court and Criminal Procedure." *Michigan Law Review* 67, no. 2 (1968): 249–268.
Rable, George C. *But There Was No Peace: The Role of Violence in the Politics of Reconstruction.* University of Georgia Press, 1984.
"Radicals: Ripping Off the FBI." *Time*, April 5, 1971.
Rakove, Jack N. *Original Meanings: Politics and Ideas in the Making of the Constitution.* Alfred A. Knopf, 1996.
Randall, James G. *Constitutional Problems Under Lincoln.* D. Appleton, 1926.
Rehnquist, William H. *All the Laws but One: Civil Liberties in Wartime.* Random House, 2000.

Reitman, Janet. "Q&A: Senator Ron Wyden on NSA Surveillance and Government Transparency." *Rolling Stone*, August 15, 2013.

Report of the [Illinois] Seditious Activities Investigation Commission: Submitted Pursuant to the Provisions of an Act of the 65th General Assembly. 1949.

"The Report on the CIA that President Ford Doesn't Want You to Read." *Village Voice*, February 16, 1976.

Reuters. "Columbia University Caves to Demands to Restore $400m from Trump Administration." *Guardian*, March 21, 2025.

Rezvani, Arezou, Jessica Pupovac, David Eads, and Tyler Fisher. "MRAPs and Bayonets: What We Know About the Pentagon's 1033 Program." NPR, September 2, 2014.

Richter, Irving. *Labor's Struggles, 1945–1950: A Participant's View.* Cambridge University Press, 1994.

Riegelhaupt, Rachel. "Manufactured Emergencies: The Crisis at the Core of the National Emergencies Act." *NYU Journal of Legislation & Public Policy* 23 (2020): 277–319.

Risen, James. *The Last Honest Man: The CIA, the FBI, the Mafia, and the Kennedys—and One Senator's Fight to Save Democracy.* Little, Brown, 2023.

Risen, James, and Eric Lichtblau. "Bush Lets U.S. Spy on Callers Without Courts." *New York Times*, December 16, 2005.

Rosenberg, Gerald N. *The Hollow Hope: Can Courts Bring About Social Change?* 2nd ed. University of Chicago Press, 2008.

Rossiter, Clinton. *Constitutional Dictatorship: Crisis Government in the Modern Democracies.* Transaction Publishers, 1948.

Rossiter, Clinton. *The Supreme Court and the Commander-in-Chief.* Cornell University Press, 1951.

Said, Wadie E. "Humanitarian Law Project and the Supreme Court's Construction of Terrorism." *Brigham Young University Law Review* (2011): 1455–1508.

Sakwa, Richard. *Deception: Russiagate and the New Cold War.* Lexington Books, 2021.

Sanders, Jane A. "Clio Confronts Conformity: The University of Washington History Department During the Cold War Era." *Pacific Northwest Quarterly* 88, no. 4 (1997): 185–194.

Sasso, Brendan. "Wyden Considered Disclosing National Security Agency Secrets on Senate Floor." *Hill*, August 15, 2013.

Savage, Charlie. *Power Wars: Inside Obama's Post-9/11 Presidency.* Little, Brown, 2015.

Scheppele, Kim Lane. "Exceptions that Prove the Rule: Embedding Emergency Government in Everyday Constitutional Life." In *The Limits of Constitutional Democracy*, edited by Jeffrey K. Tulis and Stephen Macedo. Princeton University Press, 2010.

Scheppele, Kim Lane. "Law in a Time of Emergency: States of Exception and the Temptations of 9/11." *University of Pennsylvania Journal of Constitutional Law* 6 (2003–4): 1001–1075.

Schickler, Eric. *Disjointed Pluralism: Institutional Innovation and the Development of the US Congress.* Princeton University Press, 2001.

Schlesinger, Arthur M. *The Cycles of American History.* Houghton Mifflin, 1999.

Schmidt, Christopher W. "The Civil Rights–Civil Liberties Divide." *Stanford Journal of Civil Rights & Civil Liberties* 12 (2016): 1–28.

Schmidt, Regin. *Red Scare: The FBI and the Origins of Anticommunism in the United States, 1919–1943*. Museum Tusculanum Press, 2000.

Schmitt, Eric, and Charlie Savage. "Bowe Bergdahl, American Soldier, Freed by Taliban in Prisoner Trade." *New York Times*, May 14, 2014.

Schrecker, Ellen. "Immigration and Internal Security: Political Deportations During the McCarthy Era." *Science & Society* (1996): 393–426.

Schrecker, Ellen. *Many Are the Crimes: McCarthyism in America*. Princeton University Press, 1998.

Schrecker, Ellen. "McCarthyism: Political Repression and the Fear of Communism." *Social Research* (2004): 1041–1086.

Schrecker, Ellen. *No Ivory Tower: McCarthyism and the Universities.* Oxford University Press, 1986.

Schwarz, Frederick, Jr. "Why We Need a New Church Committee to Fix Our Broken Intelligence System." Brennan Center, March 12, 2014. https://www.brennancenter.org/our-work/analysis-opinion/why-we-need-new-church-committee-fix-our-broken-intelligence-system.

Schwarz, Frederick, Jr., and Aziz Z. Huq. *Unchecked and Unbalanced: Presidential Power in a Time of Terror*. New Press, 2008.

Seditious Activities Investigation Commission [Illinois]. *Investigation of the University of Chicago and Roosevelt College, 1949, Special Report; Public Hearings Held in House of Representatives Chamber, State Capitol Building, April 21, 22, 23, 1949, May 19, 1949*. 1949.

"Senators Block Consideration of Wiretap Bill." CNN, June 26, 2008.

Serwer, Adam. "Senators Defend Killing of Anwar al-Awlaki as Legal." MSBNC, November 26, 2013.

Serwer, Adam. "Senators Will Get to Know When Obama Can Kill Americans—but You Won't." *Mother Jones*, March 5, 2013.

Shapiro, Ilya, Timothy Sandefur, and Christina Mulligan. *The Libertarian Constitution*. https://constitutioncenter.org/debate/special-projects/constitution-drafting-project.

Shepsle, Kenneth A. "Congress Is a 'They,' Not an 'It': Legislative Intent as Oxymoron." *International Review of Law and Economics* 12, no. 2 (1992): 239–256.

Shesol, Jeff. *Supreme Power: Franklin Roosevelt vs. the Supreme Court*. W. W. Norton, 2011.

Sides, John, and Kimberly Gross. "Stereotypes of Muslims and Support for the War on Terror." *Journal of Politics* 75, no. 3 (2013): 583–598.

Siegel, Jacob. "A Guide to Understanding the Hoax of the Century: Thirteen Ways of Looking at Disinformation." *Tablet Magazine*, March 28, 2023.

Silver, David Mayer. *Lincoln's Supreme Court.* University of Illinois Press, 1998.

Sim, Joe, and Philip A. Thomas. "The Prevention of Terrorism Act: Normalising the Politics of Repression." *Journal of Law and Society* 10, no. 1 (1983): 71–84.

Simon, John, ed. *The Papers of Ulysses S. Grant*. Vols. 15–18. Southern Illinois University Press, 1988, 1991.

"The SIMPP President Presents the Waldorf Agreement to the Independents." *Society of Independent Motion Producers Archive*, December 1, 1947.

Simpson, Brooks D., Leroy P. Graf, and John Muldowny, eds. *Advice After Appomattox: Letters to Andrew Johnson, 1865–1866, Special Volume No.1 of the Papers of Andrew Johnson.* University of Tennessee Press, 1988.

Skowronek, Stephen. "The Conservative Insurgency and Presidential Power: A Developmental Perspective on the Unitary Executive." *Harvard Law Review* 122 (2008): 2070–2103.

Skowronek, Stephen. *The Politics Presidents Make: Leadership from John Adams to Bill Clinton*. Harvard University Press, 1997.

Skowronek, Stephen, John A. Dearborn, and Desmond King. *Phantoms of a Beleaguered Republic: The Deep State and the Unitary Executive*. Oxford University Press, 2021.

Slack, Charles. *Liberty's First Crisis: Adams, Jefferson, and the Misfits Who Saved Free Speech*. New York: Open Road+ Grove/Atlantic, 2015.

Smith, Steven S., and Thomas F. Remington. *The Politics of Institutional Choice: The Formation of the Russian State Duma.* Princeton University Press, 2001.

Stammers, Neil. *Civil Liberties in Britain During the Second World War: A Political Study*. St. Martin's Press, 1983.

Steele, Richard W. *Free Speech in the Good War.* St. Martin's Press, 1999.

Steiker, Carol S. "Counter-Revolution in Constitutional Criminal Procedure: Two Audiences, Two Answers." *Michigan Law Review* 94 (1995): 2466–2551.

Stevenson, Archibald E., ed. *Revolutionary Radicalism: Its History, Purpose and Tactics with an Exposition and Discussion of the Steps Being Taken and Required to Curb It: Filed April 24, 1920, in the Senate of the State of New York.* Lyon, 1920.

Stone, Geoffrey. *Perilous Times: Free Speech in Wartime.* W. W. Norton, 2005.

Storrs, Landon R. Y. "Revisiting Truman's Federal Employee Loyalty Program." In *Civil Liberties and the Legacy of Harry S. Truman*, edited by Richard S. Kirkendall. Truman State University Press, 2012.

Stouffer, Samuel A. *Communism, Conformity, and Civil Liberties: A Cross-Section of the Nation Speaks Its Mind.* Doubleday, 1955.

Summers, Anthony. *Official and Confidential: The Secret Life of J. Edgar Hoover*. G. P. Putnam's Sons, 1993.

Sundquist, James L. *The Decline and Resurgence of Congress.* Brookings Institution Press, 1981.

"Surveillance Bill Filibuster Falls Short in Senate." CNN, June 26, 2008.

Taft, Philip. "Internal Affairs of Unions and the Taft-Hartley Act." *ILR Review* 11, no. 3 (April 1958): 352–359.

Tarrow, Sidney. *War, States, and Contention: A Comparative Historical Study*. Cornell University Press, 2015.

Tenney, Jack. *The Tenney Committee . . . The American Record.* Standard Publications, 1952.

Theoharis, Athan G. *Chasing Spies: How the FBI Failed in Counter-Intelligence but Promoted the Politics of McCarthyism in the Cold War Years.* Ivan R. Dee, 2002.

Theoharis, Athan G. "FBI Surveillance Past and Present." *Cornell Law Review* 69 (1983): 883–894.

Theoharis, Athan G. "FBI Wiretapping: A Case Study of Bureaucratic Autonomy." *Political Science Quarterly* 107, no. 1 (1992): 101–122.

Theoharis, Athan G. "The FBI's Stretching of Presidential Directives, 1936–1953." *Political Science Quarterly* 91, no. 4 (1976): 649–672.

Theoharis, Athan G. "A Lawless Agency: The FBI and the 'Hollywood Ten.'" *Rhetoric & Public Affairs* 2, no. 3 (1999): 415–430.

Thompson, Francis H. *The Frustration of Politics: Truman, Congress, and the Loyalty Issue, 1945–1953.* Associated University Presses, 1979.

Tillman, Seth Barrett. "*Ex parte Merryman*: Myth, History, and Scholarship." *Military Law Review* 224 (2016): 481–540.

Tower, John G. *Consequences: A Personal and Political Memoir.* Little, Brown, 1991.

Townley, Dafydd. "Too Responsible to Run for President: Frank Church and the 1976 Presidential Nomination." *Journal of Intelligence History* 21, no. 2 (2022): 213–231.

Tran, Thuy Anh. "The Invisible Hand of Networked Repression." Doctoral dissertation, City University of New York, 2024.

Trelease, Allen W. *White Terror: The Ku Klux Klan Conspiracy and Southern Reconstruction.* LSU Press, 1971.

The Trial of Hon. Clement L. Vallandigham: By a Military Commission; and the Proceedings Under His Application for a Writ of Habeas Corpus in the Circuit Court of the United States for the Southern District of Ohio. Rickey and Carroll, 1863.

Tushnet, Mark. "Defending Korematsu? Reflections on Civil Liberties in Wartime." *Wisconsin Law Review* (2003): 273–307.

Tushnet, Mark. "A Political Perspective on the Theory of the Unitary Executive." *University of Pennsylvania Journal of Constitutional Law* 12 (2009): 313–329.

Tye, Larry. *Demagogue: The Life and Long Shadow of Senator Joe McCarthy.* Houghton Mifflin Harcourt, 2020.

United States Army Military Commission. *The Assassination of President Lincoln: And the Trial of the Conspirators David E. Herold, Mary E. Surratt, Lewis Payne, George A. Atzerodt, Edward Spangler, Samuel A. Mudd, Samuel Arnold, Michael O'Laughlin*. Moore, Wilstach & Boldwin, 1865.

United States Congress. *Foreign Intelligence Surveillance Act of 1978: Conference Report to Accompany S. 1566*. GPO, 1978.

United States Congress. *Hearing Before the Committee on the Judiciary, House of Representatives Sixty-Sixth Congress Second Session on S. 3317, H.R. 10650 and 12041 Serial 16*. GPO, 1920.

United States Congress. *Investigation Activities of the Department of Justice: Letter from the Attorney General Transmitting in Response to a Senate Resolution of October 17, 1919, a Report on the Activities of the Bureau of Investigation of the Department of Justice Against Persons Advising Anarchy, Sedition, and the Forcible Overthrow of the Government.* Senate Document No. 153. GPO, 1919.

United States Congress. *Joint Hearing Before the Senate Select Committee on Intelligence and the Subcommittee on Health and Scientific Research of the Committee on Human Resources, United States Senate, Ninety-Fifth Congress, First Session, August 3, 1977.* GPO, 1977.

United States Congress. *Journal of the Joint Committee on Reconstruction.* GPO, 1915.

United States Congress. *Journal of the Senate of the United States of America, First Session, 39th Congress.* GPO, 1866.

United States Congress. *Report of the Joint Committee on Reconstruction.* GPO, 1866.

United States Congress. *Senate Executive Documents for the First Session of the Thirty-Ninth Congress of the United States of America, 1865–66.* GPO, 1866.

United States Congress. *Trial of Henry Wirz: Letter from the Secretary of War Ad Interim, in Answer to a Resolution of the House of April 16, 1866, Transmitting a Summary of the Trial of Henry Wirz.* GPO, 1868.

United States Congress, House and Senate Committees on the Judiciary. *Revision of Immigration, Naturalization, and Nationality Laws: Hearings Before the United States Senate Committee on the Judiciary, Subcommittee on S. 716.* GPO, 1951.

United States Congress, House Committee on Education and Labor. *Hearings Before the Committee on Education and Labor: Amendments to the National Labor Relations Act.* GPO, 1947.

United States Congress, House Committee on Intelligence. *Hearings Before the Select Committee on Intelligence U.S. House of Representatives.* GPO, 1976.

United States Congress, House Committee on the Judiciary. *Foreign Intelligence Surveillance Act: Hearings Before the Subcommittee on Courts, Civil Liberties, and the Administration of Justice of the Committee on the Judiciary, House of Representatives, Ninety-Fifth Congress, Second Session on H.R. 7308 . . . June 22, 28, and 29, 1978.* GPO, 1978.

United States Congress, House Committee on National Security. *Report on H.R. 3230, Together with Additional, Supplemental, and Dissenting Views.* GPO, 1996.

United States Congress, House Committee on Rules. *Attorney General A. Mitchell Palmer on Charges Made Against Department of Justice by Louis F. Post and Others.* GPO, 1920.

United States Congress, House Committee on Rules. *Investigation of Administration of Louis F. Post, Assistant Secretary of Labor, in the Matter of Deportation of Aliens: Hearings Before the Committee on Rules, House of Representatives, Sixty-Sixth Congress, Second Session, on H. Res. 522, April 27.* GPO, 1920.

United States Congress, House Committee on Standards of Official Conduct. *Investigation of Publication of Select Committee on Intelligence Report.* GPO, 1976.

United States Congress, House Committee on Un-American Activities. *Hearings Regarding the Communist Infiltration of the Motion Picture Industry: Hearings Before the Committee on Un-American Activities, House of Representatives, Eightieth Congress, First Session.* GPO, 1947.

United States Congress, House of Representatives. *Hearings Before the Committee on Education and Labor: Amendments to the National Labor Relations Act.* GPO, 1947.

United States Congress, House of Representatives. *Hearings Before the Special Committee Appointed Under the Authority of House Resolution No. 6 Concerning the Right of Victor L. Berger to Be Sworn in as a Member of the Sixty-Sixth Congress, Wednesday June 11, 1919.* GPO, 1919.

United States Congress, House Permanent Select Committee on Intelligence. *How Disclosed NSA Programs Protect Americans, and Why Disclosure Aids Our Adversaries: Hearing Before the United States House of Representatives, Permanent

Select Committee on Intelligence, One Hundred Thirteenth Congress, First Session. June 18, 2013. https://intelligence.house.gov/calendar/eventsingle.aspx?EventID=598.

United States Congress, House Un-American Activities Committee. *Annual Reports.* GPO, 1946–1965.

United States Congress, House Un-American Activities Committee. *Communist Activities Among Puerto Ricans in New York City and Puerto Rico: Hearings.* GPO, 1960.

United States Congress, House Un-American Activities Committee. *Hearings on Proposed Legislation to Curb and Control the Communist Party.* GPO, 1948.

United States Congress, House Un-American Activities Committee. *Hearings Regarding Communist Espionage in the United States Government.* GPO, 1948.

United States Congress, House Un-American Activities Committee. *Investigation of Un-American Propaganda Activities in the United States: Executive Board, Joint Anti-Fascist Refugee Committee.* GPO, 1946.

United States Congress, House Un-American Activities Committee. *Investigation of Un-American Propaganda Activities in the United States: Hearings Before the Committee on Un-American Activities on H.R. 1884 and H.R. 2122.* GPO, 1947.

United States Congress, House Un-American Activities Committee. *Legislative Recommendations by House Committee on Un-American Activities: Subsequent Action Taken by Congress or Executive Agencies. A Research Study by Legislative Reference Service of the Library of Congress.* GPO, 1960.

United States Congress, Senate Committee on Foreign Relations. *State Department Employee Loyalty Investigation: Hearings Before the United States Senate Committee on Foreign Relations, Subcommittee on S. Res. 231, Eighty-First Congress, Second Session.* GPO, 1950.

United States Congress, Senate Committee on the Judiciary. *Bolshevik Propaganda: Hearings Before a Subcommittee of the Committee on the Judiciary, United States Senate, Sixty-Fifth Congress, Third Session and Thereafter, Pursuant to S. Res. 439 and 469, February 11, 1919, to March 10, 1919.* GPO, 1919.

United States Congress, Senate Committee on the Judiciary. *Brewing and Liquor Interests and German Propaganda: Hearings Before a Subcommittee of the Committee on the Judiciary, United States Senate, Sixty-Fifth Congress, Second and Third Sessions, Pursuant to S. Res. 307.* 2 vols. GPO, 1919.

United States Congress, Senate Committee on the Judiciary. *Charges of Illegal Practices of the Department of Justice.* GPO, 1921.

United States Congress, Senate Committee on the Judiciary. *Foreign Intelligence Surveillance Act of 1976: Report Together with Additional and Minority Views to Accompany S. 3197.* GPO, 1976.

United States Congress, Senate Committee on the Judiciary. *History of the Immigration and Naturalization Service: A Report Prepared at the Request of Senator Edward M. Kennedy, Chairman, Committee on the Judiciary, United States Senate, for the Use of the Select Commission on Immigration and Refugee Policy, Prepared by the Congressional Research Service.* GPO, 1980.

United States Congress, Senate Committee on the Judiciary, Subcommittee on Constitutional Rights. *Federal Data Banks, Computers, and the Bill of Rights: Hearings . . . Ninety-Second Congress, First Session, Pt. 2: Relating to Departments of Army, Defense, and Justice Hearings Held Feb. 23–Mar. 17, 1971*. GPO, 1971.

United States Congress, Senate Committee on the Judiciary, Subcommittee to Investigate the Administration of the Internal Security Act and Other Internal Security Laws. *Limitation of Appellate Jurisdiction of the U.S. Supreme Court: Hearings.* GPO, 1957.

United States Congress, Senate Select Committee on Intelligence. *Committee Study of the Central Intelligence Agency's Detention and Interrogation Program.* GPO, 2014.

United States Congress, Senate Select Committee on Intelligence. *Hearings Before the Committee on Intelligence and the Rights of Americans, Ninety-Fifth Congress, Second Session, on S. 1566, Foreign Intelligence Surveillance Act of 1978, July 19, 21, 1977 and February 8, 24, 27, 1978.* GPO, 1978.

United States Congress, Senate Select Committee on Presidential Campaign Activities. *The Final Report of the Select Committee on Presidential Campaign Activities.* GPO, 1974.

United States Congress, Senate Select Committee to Study Governmental Operations with Respect to Intelligence Activities. *Final Report, Book I: Foreign and Military Intelligence.* GPO, 1976.

United States Congress, Senate Select Committee to Study Governmental Operations with Respect to Intelligence Activities. *Final Report of the Select Committee to Study Governmental Operations with Respect to Intelligence Activities, United States Senate: Together with Additional, Supplemental, and Separate Views. Book II: Intelligence Activities and the Rights of Americans.* GPO, 1976.

United States Congress, Senate Select Committee to Study Governmental Operations with Respect to Intelligence Activities. *Final Reports: Book III, Supplementary Detailed Staff Reports on Intelligence Activities and the Rights of Americans.* GPO, 1976.

United States Congress, Senate Select Committee to Study Governmental Operations with Respect to Intelligence Activities. *Hearings: Volume 2, Huston Plan, September 23, 24, and 25, 1975; Volume 3, Internal Revenue Service, October 2, 1975; Volume 5, The National Security Agency and Fourth Amendment Rights (October 29 and November 6, 1975).* GPO, 1976.

United States Congress, Senate Subcommittee on Intelligence and the Rights of Americans. *Hearings Before the Subcommittee on Intelligence and the Rights of Americans of the Select Committee on Intelligence of the United States Senate, Ninety-Fourth Congress, Second Session, on S. 3197, the Foreign Intelligence Surveillance Act of June 29, July 1, August 6, 10, and 24, 1976.* GPO, 1976.

United States Congress, Senate Subcommittee on Intelligence and the Rights of Americans of the Select Committee on Intelligence. *Hearings on S. 1566, Foreign Intelligence Surveillance Act July 19, 21, 1977 and February 8, 24, 27, 1978.* GPO, 1978.

United States Department of Justice. *Annual Report of the Attorney General for the Year 1920.* GPO, 1921.

United States Department of Justice. *Final Report of the Attorney General's Review Team on the Handling of the Los Alamos National Laboratory Investigation.* Department of Justice, 2000.

United States Department of Justice. *Lawfulness of a Lethal Operation Directed*

Against a U.S. Citizen Who Is a Senior Operational Leader of Al-Qa'ida or an Associate Force. November 8, 2011. https://irp.fas.org/eprint/doj-lethal.pdf.

United States Department of Justice. *Legal Authorities Supporting the Activities of the National Security Agency Described by the President* (2006). http://www.usdoj.gov/opa/whitepaperonnsalegalauthorities.pdf.

United States Department of Justice. *Statement by Tom C. Clark, Attorney General of the United States Before Committee on Un-American Activities, House of Representatives, Washington, D.C.* February 5, 1948. https://www.justice.gov/ag/speeches-attorney-general-thomas-campbell-clark.

United States Senate, 40th Congress, 2nd Session. *Letter of the General of the Army of the United States: Communicating in Compliance with a Resolution of the Senate of December 5, 1867, a Statement of the Number of White and Colored Voters Registered in Each of the States Subject to the Reconstruction Acts of Congress, with Other Statistics Relative to the Same Subject.* Executive Document 53. Mississippi State University Libraries.

Vadney, Thomas E. "The Politics of Repression: A Case Study of the Red Scare in New York." *New York History* 49, no. 1 (1968): 56–75.

Vagts, Detlev F. "Military Commissions: A Concise History." *American Journal of International Law* 101, no. 1 (2007): 35–48.

Vagts, Detlev F. "Military Commissions: The Forgotten Reconstruction Chapter." *American University International Law Review* 23, no. 2 (2007): 258–259.

Van Alstyne, William W. "A Critical Guide to Ex Parte McCardle." *Arizona Law Review* 15 (1973): 229–269.

Volokh, Eugene. "The First Amendment and Refusals to Deal." *University of the Pacific Law Review* 54 (2023): 732–745.

Walker, Clive. *The Prevention of Terrorism in British Law.* Manchester University Press, 1992.

Walker, Samuel. *Presidents and Civil Liberties from Wilson to Obama: A Story of Poor Custodians.* Cambridge University Press, 2012.

Warbrick, Colin. "The European Convention on Human Rights and the Prevention of Terrorism." *International & Comparative Law Quarterly* 32, no. 1 (1983): 82–119.

Warren, Earl. *The Memoirs of Earl Warren.* Doubleday, 1977.

Watkins, Frederick Mundell. *The Failure of Constitutional Emergency Powers Under the German Republic.* Harvard University Press, 1939.

Weisman, Jonathan, and Jennifer Steinhauer. "Surveillance Bill Awaits Verdicts on Amendments from Hawks in Senate." *New York Times*, June 1, 2015.

Wheildon, L. B. "Contempt of Congress: Editorial Research Reports 1947 (Vol. I)." *Congressional Quarterly* (1947).

White, William S. "Marchers Picket the White House, Swarm in Capital." *New York Times*, June 3, 1948.

Whittington, Keith E. "Bill Clinton Was No Andrew Johnson: Comparing Two Impeachments." *University of Pennsylvania Journal of Constitutional Law* 2, no. 2 (2000): 422–465.

Whittington, Keith E. *Political Foundations of Judicial Supremacy: The Presidency, the Supreme Court, and Constitutional Leadership in U.S. History.* Princeton University Press, 2009.

Wick, Nancy. "Anti-Communist Firings Linger on UW's Conscience 50 Years Later." *University of Washington Magazine*, December 1997.

Wiedeman, Reeves. "Raging Bill: Bill Ackman's Fight Against Harvard Has Made Him the Public Face of a Billionaire Class Anxious It No Longer Rules the World." *New Yorker*, February 12, 2024.

Wilkinson, Frank. "FBI Crackdown on Opposition to HUAC." In *It Did Happen Here: Recollections of Political Repression in America*, edited by Bud Schultz and Ruth Schultz. University of California Press, 1989.

Williams, Lou Falkner. *The Great South Carolina Ku Klux Klan Trials, 1871–1872.* University of Georgia Press, 1996.

Wineapple, Brenda. *The Impeachers: The Trial of Andrew Johnson and the Dream of a Just Nation.* Random House, 2019.

Winger, Stewart L., and Jonathan W. White, eds. *Ex Parte Milligan Reconsidered: Race and Civil Liberties from the Lincoln Administration to the War on Terror.* University Press of Kansas, 2020.

Witt, John Fabian. *Lincoln's Code: The Laws of War in American History.* Simon and Schuster, 2012.

Wittes, Benjamin, ed. *Legislating the War on Terror: An Agenda for Reform.* Brookings Institution Press, 2009.

Wittes, Benjamin, and Ritika Singh. "Executive Power, Civil Liberties, and the War of 1812." *Lawfare*, March 29, 2012.

Wolfe, Alan. *The Seamy Side of Democracy: Repression in America.* David McKay, 1973.

Woloch, Isser. *The Postwar Moment: Progressive Forces in Britain, France, and the United States After World War II*. Yale University Press, 2019.

Wood, Forrest G. "On Revising Reconstruction History: Negro Suffrage, White Disfranchisement, and Common Sense." *Journal of Negro History* 51, no. 2 (1966): 98–113.

Woods, Jeff R. *Black Struggle, Red Scare: Segregation and Anti-Communism in the South, 1948–1968*. LSU Press, 2003.

Woodward, C. Vann. *The Strange Career of Jim Crow.* 3rd ed. Oxford University Press, 2002.

Worthington, Andy. *The Guantanamo Files: The Stories of the 759 Detainees in America's Illegal Prison.* Pluto Press, 2007.

Yoo, Christopher S., Steven G. Calabresi, and Anthony J. Colangelo. "The Unitary Executive in the Modern Era, 1945–2004." *Iowa Law Review* 90 (2004): 601–731.

Yoo, John. *Defender in Chief: Donald Trump's Fight for Presidential Power.* All Points Books, 2020.

Yoo, John. *The Powers of War and Peace: The Constitution and Foreign Affairs After 9/11*. University of Chicago Press, 2008.

Young, Marilyn B. *The Vietnam Wars, 1945–1990*. New York: Harper Perennial, 1991.

Zegart, Amy B. *Eyes on Spies: Congress and the United States Intelligence Community*. Hoover Press, 2013.

Zeisberg, Mariah. "Frederick Douglass and Constitutional Emergency: An Homage to the Political Creativity of Abolitionist Activism." In *States of Exception in*

American History, edited by Gary Gerstle and Joel Isaac. University of Chicago Press, 2020.
Zelizer, Julian E. *The Fierce Urgency of Now: Lyndon Johnson, Congress, and the Battle for the Great Society*. Penguin, 2015.
Zhou, Li. "The House GOP's Many, Many Investigations, Explained." *Vox*, February 11, 2023.

Cases

Abrams v. United States, 250 U.S. 616 (1919).
ACLU v. National Security Agency, 493 F.3d 644 (6th Cir. 2007).
Albertson v. Subversive Activities Control Board, 382 U.S. 70 (1965).
American Communications Association v. Douds, 339 U.S. 382 (1950).
Arver v. United States, 245 U.S. 366 (1918).
Bailey v. Richardson, 182 F.2d 46 (1950).
Bailey v. Richardson, 341 U.S. 918 (1951).
Baker v. Carr, 369 U.S. 186 (1962).
Barenblatt v. United States, 360 U.S. 109 (1959).
Berger v. United States, 255 U.S. 22 (1921).
Boumediene v. Bush, 553 U.S. 723 (2008).
Bowsher v. Synar, 478 U.S. 714 (1986).
Brandenburg v. Ohio, 395 U.S. 444 (1969).
Bridges v. Wixon, 326 U.S. 135 (1945).
Brown v. Board of Education, 347 U.S. 483 (1954).
Calder v. Bull, 3 U.S. (3 Dall.) 386 (1798).
Cole v. Young, 351 U.S. 536 (1956).
Colegrove v. Green, 328 U.S. 549 (1946).
Colyer v. Skeffington, 265 F. 17 (1920).
Communist Party v. Subversive Activities Control Board, 367 U.S. 1 (1961).
Debs v. United States, 249 U.S. 211 (1919).
Dennis v. United States, 341 U.S. 494 (1951).
Dickerson v. United States, 530 U.S. 428 (2000).
District of Columbia v. Heller, 554 U.S. 570 (2008).
Dobbs v. Jackson Women's Health Organization, 597 U.S. ___ (2022).
Dred Scott v. Sandford, 60 U.S. 393 (1857).
Ex parte McCardle, 74 U.S. 506 (1869).
Ex parte Merryman, 17 F. Cas. 144 (1861).
Ex parte Milligan, 71 U.S. (4 Wall.) 2 (1866).
Ex parte Quirin, 317 U.S. 1 (1942).
Ex parte Vallandigham, 68 U.S. 243 (1864).
Ex parte Yerger, 75 U.S. 85 (1869).
Fischer v. United States, 603 U.S. ___ (2024).
Fong Yue Ting v. United States, 149 U.S. 698 (1893).
Frohwerk v. United States, 249 U.S. 204 (1919).
Georgia v. Stanton, 73 U.S. 50 (1868).
Gibson v. Florida Legislative Investigation Committee, 372 U.S. 539 (1963).
Gideon v. Wainwright, 372 U.S. 335 (1963).

Gitlow v. New York, 268 U.S. 652 (1925).
Gravel v. United States, 408 U.S. 606 (1972).
Gundy v. United States, 588 U.S. ___ (2019).
Hamdan v. Rumsfeld, 415 F.3d 33 (D.C. Cir. 2005).
Hamdan v. Rumsfeld, 548 U.S. 557 (2006).
Hamdi v. Rumsfeld, 542 U.S. 507 (2004).
Harisiades v. Shaughnessy, 342 U.S. 580 (1952).
Helvering v. Davis, 301 U.S. 619 (1937).
Hepting v. AT&T Corp., 439 F. Supp. 2d 974 (N.D. Cal. 2006).
Hepting, et al. v. AT&T Corp., et al. (9th Cir. 2011).
Hess v. Indiana, 414 U.S. 105 (1973).
Holder v. Humanitarian Law Project, 561 U.S. 1 (2010).
Humphrey's Executor v. United States, 295 U.S. 602 (1935);
In re Sealed Case, 310 F.3d 717 (D.C. Circ. 2002).
Jencks v. United States, 353 U.S. 657 (1957).
Johnson v. Eisentrager, 339 U.S. 763 (1950).
Joint Anti-Fascist Refugee Committee v. McGrath, 341 U.S. 123 (1951).
Katz v. United States, 389 U.S. 347 (1967).
Kilbourn v. Thompson, 103 U.S. 168 (1881).
Mallory v. United States, 354 U.S. 449 (1957).
Mapp v. Ohio, 367 U.S. 643 (1961).
Maxwell v. Dow, 176 U.S. 581 (1900).
McDonald v. City of Chicago, 561 U.S. 742 (2010).
McGrain v. Daugherty, 273 U.S. 135 (1927).
Miranda v. Arizona, 384 U.S. 436 (1966).
Mississippi v. Johnson, 71 U.S. 475 (1867).
Morrison v. Olson, 487 U.S. 654 (1988).
Myers v. United States, 272 U.S. 52 (1926).
National Association for the Advancement of Colored People v. Alabama, 357 U.S. 449 (1958).
National Association for the Advancement of Colored People v. Claiborne Hardware Co., 458 U.S. 886 (1982).
Nardone v. United States, 308 U.S. 338 (1939).
National Federation of Independent Business v. Sebelius, 567 U.S. 519 (2012).
New York State Rifle & Pistol Association, Inc. v. Bruen, 597 U.S. ___ (2022).
New York Times Co. v. Sullivan, 376 U.S. 254 (1964).
New York Times Co. v. United States, 403 U.S. 713 (1971).
New York Times Co. v. US Dept. of Justice, 756 F.3d 100 (2d Cir. 2014).
Obergefell v. Hodges, 576 U.S. 644 (2015).
Pennsylvania v. Nelson, 350 U.S. 497 (1956).
Plyler v. Doe, 457 U.S. 202 (1982).
Powell v. McCormack, 395 U.S. 486 (1969).
Printz v. United States, 521 U.S. 898 (1997).
Prize Cases, 67 U.S. 635 (1863).
Quinn v. United States, 349 U.S. 155 (1955).
Rowoldt v. Perfetto, 355 U.S. 115 (1957).
Scales v. United States, 367 U.S. 203 (1961).

Schenck v. United States, 249 U.S. 47 (1919).
Seila Law LLC v. Consumer Financial Protection Bureau, 591 U.S. ____ (2020).
South Dakota v. Dole, 483 U.S. 203 (1987).
Stern v. Richardson, 367 F. Supp. 1316 (D.C. 1973).
Sweezy v. New Hampshire, 354 U.S. 234 (1957).
Terry v. Ohio, 392 U.S. 1 (1968).
Texas v. Johnson, 491 U.S. 397 (1989).
Trump v. Anderson, 601 U.S. ___ (2024).
Trump v. Mazars USA, LLP, 591 U.S. ___ (2020).
United States v. Brock, D.C. Cir. (2024).
United States v. Bryan, 339 U.S. 323 (1950).
United States v. Coplon, 185 F.2d 629 (2d Cir. 1950).
United States v. Duggan, 743 F.2d 59 (2d Cir. 1984).
United States v. Eichman, 496 U.S. 310 (1990).
United States v. Fleischman, 339 U.S. 349 (1950).
United States v. Lovett, 328 U.S. 303 (1946).
United States v. Russo & Ellsberg, Crim. No. 9373 (C.D.Cal. dismissed May 11, 1973).
Yamataya v. Fisher, 189 U.S. 86 (1903).
Yates v. United States, 354 U.S. 298 (1957).
Yick Wo v. Hopkins, 118 U.S. 356 (1886).
Youngstown Sheet & Tube Co. v. Sawyer, 343 U.S. 579 (1952).

INDEX

Note: page numbers followed by n refer to notes, with note number.

www.ingramcontent.com/pod-product-compliance
Ingram Content Group UK Ltd.
Pitfield, Milton Keynes, MK11 3LW, UK
UKHW041854031026
15587UKWH00006B/1227/J

9 780700 641055